The PENDER ISLANDS handbook

By Richard Fox

Printed simultaneously in Canada and the United States by:

Printorium Bookworks, Inc.,   Booksurge, LLC; A Division of Amazon.com
A Division of Island Blue Print Co., Ltd..   South Carolina, USA
Victoria, British Columbia   www.booksurge.com
www.printoriumbookworks.com.   1.866.308.6235

ISBN: 1-4196-3885-8

Extra care was taken to ensure the accuracy of the information contained in this book. However, the author, printer, publishers and contributors can assume no liability from damage or loss as the result of use of this book. Read the full Disclaimer in Chapter 1.

Book Design and Layout: Richard Fox and Susan Petty
Cover Design: Richard Fox and Susan Petty
Photographs:
Front Cover: *Thieves Bay Breakwater* by Alan Lowe
Back Cover: All by Richard Fox except as otherwise credited:

Oaks Bluff	*Gulf Islands*	*Nicole in*	*Steve Biking*
Park Vista	*National Park-*	*Kayak (TF)*	*Spalding Road*
	Beaumont		
Roy & Caroline	*Poets Cove*	*Orcas in Swanson*	*Victoria Harbour*
at Golf Island	*Resort*	*Channel (TF)*	*Whale Boats*

All black & white photos in this book are by Richard Fox, except as otherwise credited: Tara Folk (TF), Alan Lowe (AL), John Mackenzie (JM) and others as noted.
Maps: Richard Fox. Basemaps referenced from CRD Natural Areas Atlas (2005).
Text Editor: Richard Fox and various parties listed in *Acknowledgements* in Chapter 1.

About the Author

Richard Fox has been thrilled to spend half of every year since 2002 on Pender Island with his partner. They have enjoyed hiking, boating, biking, golf, disc golf, and watching the orcas and eagles, collecting data all the while. What began as a compilation of information for their summer visitors kept growing into a project that could benefit all Pender residents and vacationers. As an environmental project manager for 25 years, Richard has written hundreds of technical reports. This guidebook represents his first foray into the travel writing arena.

To the Southern Resident Pods

LOCATION MAP

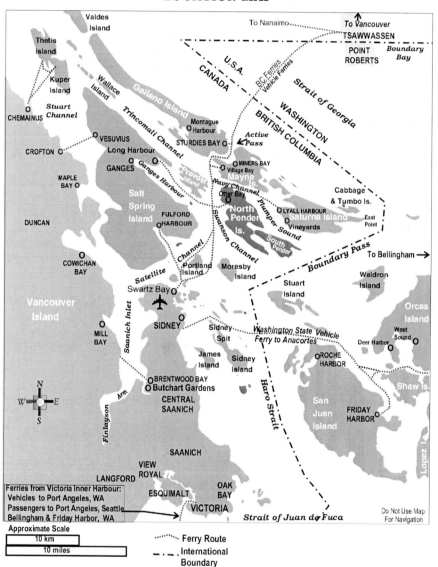

Ferries from Victoria Inner Harbour:
Vehicles to Port Angeles, WA
Passengers to Port Angeles, Seattle
Bellingham & Friday Harbor, WA

Approximate Scale

10 km

10 miles

·········· Ferry Route

_ . _ . International
Boundary

TABLE OF CONTENTS

1 HOW TO USE THIS BOOK

THE INFORMATION AND ITS LAYOUT

This handbook is a compilation of information about the Pender Islands in southern British Columbia that is relevant to its visitors as well as existing and prospective resi dents. Carry this book with you in your house, your car, or your boat, and chances are you will use it as a resource on many occasions. Over three years in the making, information previously available scattered throughout numerous sources has been brought together into one convenient volume. The depth of information is most extensive for the Pender Islands themselves. However, since most Penderites travel to the Victoria area when they leave the island, guides highlighting shopping, dining, entertainment and points of interest in that area are covered. Adjacent islands are visited mostly by private boat, and nearby points of interest to boaters in the Gulf Islands, San Juan Islands, and Saanich Peninsula are described. Although many weekenders and island visitors arrive from Vancouver, only the Vancouver transportation portals are described in detail in reference to getting to the Pender Islands. The detailed Table of Contents is organized to help you find the information you need quickly. For visitors, the section *Finding Your Favourite Pender Islands Activities* in this chapter provides a summary of the most popular Pender Island activities, and where to find detailed descriptions of those activities in this book. For other information relating to life on Pender in general, consult the Index and Table of Contents. Organizations are described in their most appropriate chapters, such as the *Let's Go Walking* Club in the *Coastal Access and Hiking Guide*, or *Pender Island Yacht Club* in the *Boating Guide*.

The information contained in this book was compiled from February 2003 through May 2006, with much of the original data updated just before publication. The Pender Islands continue to change, and certain information in the book will become outdated as time goes on. To the best of my knowledge, several establishments are for sale as the book goes to print, and are the most likely candidates for change in the near future if their sales go through.

The *Pender Islands Map Atlas* found at the end of this book contains detailed street and trail maps complete with topography, covering the portions of the islands of interest to the general public. All known public trails and ocean accesses are numbered and cross-referenced between the *Atlas*, the *Table of Contents*, and the text. Note that all distances and plotting of hiking trails are approximate. The *Atlas* also depicts other points of interest such as dining, accommodations and public facilities. For general navigation around Pender roadways, the free map available on the ferries works great. The maps in the *Map Atlas* provide more detail. Boaters must use appropriate nautical charts and other navigational aids to supplement the descriptive information in the *Boating Guide*. For information on *Hazards, Pests and Emergencies*, see that heading in Chapter 18 - *Living on Pender* before setting out on your Pender exploration.

FINDING YOUR FAVOURITE ACTIVITIES

Following is a summary of popular Pender Islands activities, and where to find information on those activities in this book. If you are here for the day in your car and want to follow a touring route, you can loosely follow the *Tour de Pender* in the *Bicycling Guide*, which covers most points of interest.

See the Coastal Access and Hiking Guide (Chapters 11-13)

TAKE A HIKE OR STROLL   The Penders are resplendent in public parks that occupy large portions of both islands. Trails of all levels are available, with rewards such as spectacular viewpoints or shorefront strolls. Gulf Islands National Park Reserve, Canada's 40th National Park, has a major presence here.

VISIT A BEACH   Spend some time exploring the intertidal zones at the many public ocean accesses found all over the islands, or lie out on some of the long, sand and pebble beaches of the Port Browning and Bedwell Harbour shores.

GO SWIMMING   The water here is COLD, but ocean water at some of the shallower beaches warms up enough for a chilly dip by the end of summer, and lake swimming is also available. Otherwise, jump in the pool at one of three public marinas.

See the Golfing Guide (Chapter 10)

PLAY GOLF   Pender's beautiful 9-hole course is popular and fun. No tee times are required, and you can 9-and-dine at Chippers licensed cafe.

PLAY DISC GOLF   Golf Island is an internationally renowned disc golf course in the woods of Magic Lake Estates that is free and fun for all skill levels.

See the Boating Guide (Chapter 15)

PADDLE A KAYAK   Take a guided kayak tour of Pender's scenic coves and become one with the aquatic environment. Kayaking has become one of the most popular activities in the Gulf Islands.

LAUNCH YOUR BOAT   Small trailered vessels can be launched from several locations, which are also close to marinas where they can be tied up, space permitting.

GO FISHING   Catch salmon as they swim past the Pender Bluffs. Licenses are sold locally and a couple of fishing charters operate on the Pender Islands.

GO DIVING   The waters of coastal British Columbia are teeming with life and Pender Island has a dive shop with charters available.

See the Bicycling Guide (Chapter 14)

CYCLE THE PENDER BYWAYS   Hilly, scenic riding awaits on the island roads, with some shorter rides suitable for most abilities. Rentals are available.

See the Recreation Guide (Chapter 9)

PLAY TENNIS   Courts open to the public (for a fee) are available at Magic Lake Estates, Poets Cove Resort and Port Browning Resort.

GO HORSEBACK RIDING   A riding concession can satisfy your equestrian pursuits.

See the Dining Guide (Chapter 5)

VISIT THE FARMERS MARKET at the Community Hall 9:30 am to 1:00 pm Saturdays from mid-spring to mid-fall. Check out the crafts, foods and people. **Map 3**.

BUY FRESH ORGANIC FOODS   Cruise the island for seasonal roadside stands, which sell eggs, fruit, vegetables, and more. Pick your own trailside blackberries in late summer.

VISIT A WINERY   Morning Bay Vineyard is open for tastings. Bring a picnic or combine your visit with a hike into the adjacent National Park. **Map 5**.

EAT!   The selection of Pender restaurants is better than ever.

DRINK!   Have a cold one at the Port Browning Pub, Syrens at Poets Cove Resort or Chippers Café at the golf course. *The RCMP reminds: Do not drink and drive.*

See The Arts and Annual Events Chapter (16)

BE MERRY!   Attend festivals, special events, concerts and plays held throughout the year. Highlights are late August's Fall Fair and New Years Eve's Lantern Festival.

VISIT A GALLERY OR ART SHOW   Pick up the free *Artists and Art Shows* brochure for the most current list of galleries and shows. Some are described in this book.

Pender organizations enjoy participating in the Fall Fair parade.

See The Living on Pender Chapter - Historical Guide (Chapter 18)

VISIT THE NEW OLD MUSEUM   The Pender Islands Museum opened in July 2005 and is open weekends; **Map 3**. Use their guide to do a historic Pender driving tour.

See The Shopping Guide (Chapter 6)

SHOP, NOT QUITE 'TIL YOU DROP   You can find many delightful surprises in Pender Islands' handful of gift shops. Pender also has a good pharmacy, grocery and hardware stores that carry gift items.

VISIT THE LEGENDARY NU-TO-YU THRIFT SHOP that raises buckets of money for local charities. Open Friday and Saturday. **Map 1.**

See The Nearby Attractions Off Island Chapter (8)

TAKE A BOAT EXCURSION   Local fishing charters also take groups to nearby islands to visit the Ganges Marketplace, Saturna Vineyards, or other locales.

VISIT VICTORIA   Highlights from Butchart Gardens to dining out and the arts are described.

See the Natural Environment Chapter (17)

WHALE WATCH Look for the magical orcas making their way along Swanson channel, as well as other exciting marine life.

BIRD WATCH   Look for year round, seasonal or transient birds around the islands.

CORRECTIONS, COMMENTS, UPDATES AND ERRATA

The information in this book was reviewed many times. However, as is inherent in all guidebooks, there will still be typos, errors and omissions, as well as outdated data, especially as time lapses from the time of writing. If the reader notes any errors or omissions in this volume, or becomes aware of any significant changes or updates, please send an email to penderhandbook@yahoo.ca with *Corrections* in the subject line. Updates to the book will either be posted at a web site to be established at a later date, or can be provided via email. If you wish to receive updates, send an email to penderhandbook@yahoo.ca with *Request Updates* in the subject line. For a period of time you will be provided either with periodic updates, or a web address that contains the updates.

DISCLAIMER

Read Before Using This Book

Use the information contained within the pages of this book ONLY if you are willing to do so at your own risk. The information in this book is of a descriptive nature only, and is not intended to be relied upon as the sole source of information for any endeavors, including but not restricted to navigation by land, sea, or air. Neither the author, contributors, nor the publisher shall be liable for any personal, financial, or emotional damages, whether direct, incidental or consequential, that persons using the information contained in this book incur. The author and publisher have used their best efforts in preparing this book, but make no representations or warranties with regard to the completeness or accuracy of the information provided. Although most known hazards associated with the activities described in the book have been identified, additional hazards may exist as well. Use your own judgment and common sense when undertaking the activities described herein, and obtain the proper training and certifications before proceeding. This book was compiled in one particular period of time, and things will change after date of publication, or may have already changed. Some commercial establishments may close, others may open, and prices will differ. Call the respective establishments to verify any vital information before traveling. Transportation companies, their polices, and routes may change. Hiking trails may become unsafe without warning, and some will be re-routed by their managing agency. Government regulations may change. Websites or telephone numbers may change or be discontinued. The *Boating Guide* is to be used for descriptive information only and not for navigation at sea. Boaters should use appropriate navigational aids, and possess all necessary certifications and equipment before setting out. Information in this book should not be used to form the sole basis for any decision making, including but not restricted to any legal or financial decisions or decisions regarding real estate transactions.

ACKNOWLEDGEMENTS

My sincere thanks to the Penderites that provided review of and inspiration for various sections of the book, including: *Boating:* John Cowan, Brian Elliott, Sue Kronen, Tony Merry, Roger Pilkington; *Climate:* Malcolm Armstrong; *Birding:* Mary Roddick and Marti Tilley; *Crime and the RCMP:* Cst. Nicole Grandmont; *Schools:* David Nickoli; *Emergencies:* Pat Haugh; and *Miscellany:* Vince Connors, Susan DeGryp, Andrew Higgs, John Mackenzie, Michel Pelletier, Greg Rowland, and others. Many thanks to Pender Parks Commissioner Newell Smith for park updates and various Pender factoids, and Meredith Reeve of Parks Canada for information and reviews. In addition, various parties and organizations have given kind permission to reference their information, and those are noted in the appropriate sections. A very special thanks to Steve Fisher for doing so much of the Pender Island exploring with me, Tara Folk and daughters Stacy and Nicole for being such a great help while I was off-island, and my hero, Susan Petty for being such a fabulous desktop publishing coach. Last but not least, thanks to those that allowed me to use their photographs to supplement my collection, as credited in the title pages.

CONVERSION FACTORS

Canada uses the metric system, while the U.S. uses the English system of measurement, so cross-border travel in either direction will require some calculations. This book uses the metric system, with some English conversions added for convenience.

DRIVING BIKING AND BOATING

On Land: Miles (mi) and Kilometres (km)
1 U.S. statute mi = 5,280 feet = 1.609 km
* Multiply km x 0.6 (which is 1/1.609) to approximate statute miles
* Conversely, multiply miles x 1.6 to approximate kilometers
Pender Islands' speed limit is 50 km/hour:
* 50 x 0.6 = 30 miles/hour
At sea: International nautical mile (NM):
* 1 NM = 6,076 feet = 1.852 km
* 1 NM = 1.15 Statute Mile
* Statute Mile = 0.868 NM.
Depth at sea: 1 fathom = 6 ft = 1.83 metres
Speed: knots x 1.15 = miles per hour (MPH)
* MPH x 0.868 = knots
Fuel
Gasoline and diesel are sold in Canada in litres, and in the U.S. in gallons.
* To convert litres to gallons = litres/3.785.
* In Canada, to get cost in U.S.$ per gallon, take cost/litre (assume $1.20 CDN), multiply x 3.785 (=$4.52CDN) and multiply by exchange rate (i.e. 0.90)= $4.09 U.S./gal.
* In the U.S., take cost per gallon (assume $3.20 US), divide by 3.785 (= $0.845 US) and multiply by exchange rate (assume 1.11) = $0.94/ litre CDN.

THE WEATHER

Precipitation: Measured in millimeters (mm) in Canada; vs. inches in the U.S.
* 1 mm ~ 0.04 inch; 1 inch ~ 25 mm.
Pender Island's average annual precipitation of 798 mm ~ (798 x 0.04=) 32 inches.
Temperature: Canada uses Celsius (C°), while the U.S. uses Fahrenheit (F°):
C° to F°: (C° x 1.8) + 32 = F°
So, 34.5°C, the record high Pender Island temperature = (34.5 x 1.8) + 32 = 94.1°F.

WEATHER continued
F° to C°: (F°-32) x 0.555 = C°
In the U.S. if the temperature is 72°F:
* (72 -32) x 0.555 = 22.2°C.
* 0°C = 32°F; 4°C = 40F; 10°C = 50°F;
* 21°C = 70°F; 27°C=80°F

IN THE MARKET
Food in Canada is sold by grams, (g), 100 grams (g), kilogram (kg) or pound (lb).
* 1 lb=0.4545 kg = 454.5g
* 100g approximates a *quarter-pound*.
* 1 kg = 2.2. lbs; 1 gram = 0.035 oz.
Beverages are usually sold in litres (l), which is equivalent to a quart (qt).
* 1 litre = 1.0567 qt = 33.8 ounces
* 1 quart = 0.9467 l = 947 millilitres (ml)

AROUND THE HOUSE
Property is measured in acres or hectares.
* 1 hectare=2.47 acres
* 1 acre=0.4047 hectares
* 1 inch = 2.54 centimetres
* 1 foot = 0.3048 metres
* 1 metre = 3.28 feet

CURRENCY
To convert currencies between all nations, check out **www.xe.com/ucc/**
The unit of currency in both the U.S. and Canada is the dollar, and each uses the coins pennies, nickels, dimes and quarters. Canada also uses coins for $1, known as a *loonie* (because of the loon on it), and $2, known as a *toonie* (because of its denomination). The exchange rate fluctuates frequently. At time of writing:
* 1 U.S. dollar (USD) = 1.11 Canadian Dollar (CAD).
* 1 CAD = 0.90 USD.

2   INTRODUCTION

THE PENDER ISLANDS

Welcome to the Pender Islands, British Columbia, a magical island community with forested hills and scenic rocky coves. The Pender Islands consist of two separate islands, North Pender and South Pender, which were split by a canal excavated in 1902 and connected by a bridge built in 1955. The islands are situated within an archipelago known as the Gulf Islands, located halfway between the cities of Vancouver and Victoria just north of the Washington/United States border. Known mostly as a summer playground for kayakers and hikers, the islands offer a unique way of life for their residents. Sharing the islands with their human inhabitants are eagles, seals and orcas fishing off shore, numerous birds, and countless deer peacefully grazing. The climate is among the mildest in Canada, with warm dry summers, and cool, moist winters.

Active people will find plenty to do on a vacation to the Pender Islands. Recreational opportunities abound, including hiking, road bicycling, kayaking, fishing, SCUBA diving, swimming, golf, disc golf, tennis, and horseback riding. Residents participate in soccer, roller hockey, curling, badminton, softball, and basketball. Shopping experiences consist of more subtle delights rather than overwhelming selection, with several small gallery-type shops scattered around the islands. Art lovers can browse several galleries open during regular hours, and others open by appointment. Art shows are common in the summer months. Quality live entertainment occurs throughout the year at several venues. Accommodations range from campgrounds to an upscale resort.

The greatest asset of the Pender Islands is its people. A strong sense of island pride prevails and local organizations such as the Lions Club work hard to improve the quality of life for its residents. While the small full-time population of about 2,200 creates a challenge to maintain institutions and facilities, the school, medical clinic and library are much more sophisticated than what one would expect in such a small community. The influx of visitors and weekenders helps support several top quality restaurants and a well-stocked supermarket. Improved infrastructure provides for increasingly dependable hydro (electric), phone, high-speed cable Internet, and digital television.

When the Coast Salish people first discovered Pender Island thousands of years ago, they found thick old-growth forested land surrounded by cold waters with bountiful shellfish and salmon. Europeans began taming the land in the late 1800's, removing forests to create agricultural fields. Local industry flourished in the early 20th century, including a brickyard, a fish reduction plant and a fish cannery. Commercial loggers and real estate developers followed, and by the 1970's not only had most of the old-growth forests been harvested at one time or another, but the largest planned development in Canada's history was well underway on North Pender Island at Magic Lake Estates. That development inspired the creation of the Islands Trust, a local governing body, to help establish a more moderate rate of development for the Gulf Islands. Growth continued through the end of the 20th century, with many new homes built and facilities created on the islands to serve their residents. The early 21st Century finds continued interest in the Gulf Islands, creating demands for growth and heated debates on sustainable development. Key issues include water supply and maintaining the unique rural character of the islands. Thankfully, a good portion of the islands, now containing lush second growth forest, has been set aside as parkland. An active local parks department maintains a plethora of hiking trails and ocean accesses, a conservancy has established several nature preserves, and Parks Canada has incorporated large areas of both North and South Pender Island into Canada's 40th National Park, the Gulf Islands National Park Reserve (GINPR). Since the majority of the island is still privately held, challenges remain to convince landowners to be good stewards of their land, especially where sensitive habitats exist.

Pender Islands Facts and Figures

The Name Game

The Pender Islands are divided into North Pender Island and South Pender Island by a one-lane wooden highway bridge that traverses the narrow man-made Pender Canal. *The Pender Islands* is BC Ferries' name for the islands, although the postal address is *Pender Island,* and most business names begin with *Pender Island.* Very few people when asked where they live, reply *The Pender Islands.* The most common reply is *Pender Island,* or *Pender.* Assuming that one is already aware that the topic is Pender, subsequent mentions, such is in this book, can be either *The Island* or *The Islands* depending on the context. In southern BC, *The Island* typically refers to Vancouver Island. However, in this Pender-centric book, both *The Island* and *The Islands* refer to Pender Island. Various databases and information listings may have the islands listed under *P* for Pender Island or Pender Islands, under *N* for North Pender or *S* for South Pender. People from the Pender Islands frequently refer to themselves as *Penderites.*

Pender Harbour is a community near Desolation Sound that is popular with yachters. It is located on the mainland north of Vancouver in an area known as the Sunshine Coast that is accessible only by ferry from Horseshoe Bay or Powell River. Any reference to *Pender* or *Penderite* in this book refers to the Pender Islands, and not to Pender Harbour.

Location Location Location

Refer to the *Location Map* in the *Map Atlas* for locations described in this section. The Pender Islands are located within a group of islands referred to as the Southern Gulf Islands. The principal Southern Gulf Islands are within the Capital Regional District (CRD) and are serviced by BC Ferries.
In order of full time populations they are:
* Salt Spring Island (to the west of North Pender Island);
* The Pender Islands;
* Galiano Island (to the northwest);
* Mayne Island (to the north); and
* Saturna Island (to the east).

All but Salt Spring Island are referred to as the Outer Gulf Islands within the Southern Gulf Islands. Other much more sparsely populated Outer Gulf Islands are:
* Prevost Island (to the northwest, between North Pender and Salt Spring Islands);
* Wallace and the Secretary Islands (between Salt Spring and Galiano Islands);
* Samuel Island (to the northeast, between Mayne and Saturna Islands); and
* Cabbage and Tumbo Islands (off the east coast of Saturna Island).
  Wallace Island is mainly a Provincial Park, and Cabbage and Tumbo Islands are in the Gulf Islands National Park Reserve (GINPR).

The Inner Gulf Islands are closest to Vancouver Island near Sidney. They consist of:
* Close-in James, Coal, and Piers Islands with private docks but no ferry service;
* Private Moresby Island, southwest of North Pender;
* Portland and D'Arcy Islands (part of GINPR);
* Sidney Island (whose northern portion, Sidney Spit, is part of the GINPR); and
* Numerous smaller islands, some of which are private and others are GINPR lands.

The other populated Southern Gulf Islands are located north of Salt Spring Island, and are not within the CRD:
* Thetis and Kuper Islands are serviced by BC Ferries from Chemainus.
* The long, narrow Valdes Island, separated from Galiano Island by the narrow Porlier Pass, is not serviced by BC Ferries, and is considered the northern extent of the Southern Gulf Islands.
* Gabriola Island, just to the north of Valdes Island across the narrow Gabriola Passage, is referred to by different parties as either a Northern or a Southern Gulf Island. A short BC Ferry route from Nanaimo services it.

The Pender Islands are located along the BC Ferries route between the Vancouver and Victoria metropolitan areas. The Penders are located approximately:
* 32 km (20 miles) southwest of the Vancouver ferry terminal at Tsawwassen;
* 48 km (30 miles) south of downtown Vancouver;
* 14 km (9 miles) northeast of Victoria's ferry terminal at Swartz Bay; and
* 42 km (26 miles) north of Victoria.
  See the *Boating Guide* for distances from the Pender Islands to nearby places of interest.

Victoria lies on the southeastern tip of Vancouver Island, and is the Capital of the Province of British Columbia. No *Victoria Island* exists in the area, although there is one that belongs to Canada in the Arctic Ocean. The City of Vancouver is on the *Lower Mainland* of British Columbia, just north of the U.S. border with Blaine, Washington.

Located just north of the U.S. border, the Pender Islands are the main summer customs check-in point for recreational boaters coming from the U.S. Just south of the U.S. border are Washington State's San Juan Islands, the largest of which, confusingly is San Juan Island. Friday Harbor on San Juan Island is the principal settlement. The other main San Juan Islands, which are serviced by Washington State Ferries from Anacortes, Washington (with a seasonal connection to Sidney, BC) are Orcas, Shaw, and Lopez Islands. Stuart and Waldron Islands, located closest to the Pender Islands, are private except for Stuart Island State Park. Many Washington State Parks, some of which cover entire small islands, are scattered throughout the region.

Vancouver Island (aka Van Isle) of BC is the largest island on the west coast of North America. It extends from the same latitude as Mt. Vernon (just south of Anacortes), Washington at the south end to about 440 km (270 miles) to the northwest, across from a wild sparsely populated Coast Mountain area of British Columbia. Hope Island is off the northeast tip of Vancouver Island (some boat insurance policies limit boat travel to Hope Island or south). The waterways separating Vancouver Island from the mainland are, from south to north, The Strait of Georgia to about Campbell River, Johnstone Strait to about Alert Bay and Queen Charlotte Strait north of there. The Queen Charlotte Islands are another 300 km (190 miles) northwest of the northern tip of Vancouver Island, across Queen Charlotte Sound from the mainland. The southern end of Vancouver Island is separated from Washington State's Olympic Peninsula by the Strait of Juan de Fuca.

The Pender Islands are within the Capital Regional District (CRD) political jurisdiction that includes Victoria, the capital of British Columbia, the Saanich Peninsula and Sooke, but not Nanaimo. Pender is more closely associated geographically and politically with the city of Victoria than it is with the city of Vancouver. Ferry schedules and fares are such that they provide easy access for Pender residents to Victoria, which is on Vancouver Island, and some Pender residents commute to work on Vancouver Island. Conversely, most services to the Pender Islands that come from off-island are provided by Victoria area businesses and organizations.

Geography

North Pender Island is approximately 11 km (7 miles) in length, and about 4.7 km (3 mi) wide at its widest point near the center of the island. It contains approximately 2,730 hectares (27.3 sq km, 6,746 acres, 10.5 sq miles). At the north end of the island are the original Pender communities of Port Washington and Hope Bay, both with government docks and stores. The Stanley Point community occupies the northern tip of the island. Port Washington is the commercial float plane landing spot for North Pender Island. Further south is the Otter Bay terminal for BC Ferries. Toward the center of the island is the Driftwood Centre, the main shopping complex on the Pender Islands. The Harbour Hill and Razor Point communities are to the east of Driftwood Centre, along Port Browning. The Pender Islands have no waterfront village, such as Salt Spring Island's Ganges. Magic Lake Estates, where most Penderites reside, is further south from the Driftwood Centre. At the southern tip of North Pender Island is the Trincomali community. **South Pender Island** is approximately 6.1 km (3.8 mi) in length, and 2.1 km (1.3 mi) wide at its midpoint, and contains approximately 930 hectares (9.3 sq km, 2,298 acres, 3.6 sq miles). Poets Cove Resort, with a marina, float plane dock and seasonal customs station is about halfway down the island from the canal bridge. In total, North and South Pender Island contain 3,660 hectares (36.6 sq km, 9,044 acres, 14.1 sq miles).

The Pender Islands' terrain is mostly hilly and wooded, with some flat interior agricultural valleys. The highest point is Mount Norman on South Pender Island at 244 metres. The highest point on North Pender Island is Cramer Hill (219 m), topped by a telecommunications tower (266 m). The coastline consists mainly of rocky coves and headlands, with beaches composed of shells, sand and gravel. Most of the shoreline (above the high tide line) is privately owned with public ocean access points available at many locations. Several public parks provide larger beach access area and shoreline.

No rivers flow on the Pender Islands. Intermittent streams flow at several locations during wet periods. Flooding is typically not a problem.

Four lakes are found on the islands. On North Pender, Roe Lake (Pender's only natural lake) is located south of Otter Bay in the GINPR. Magic Lake (formerly Pender Lake) lies at the entrance to Magic Lake Estates. Buck Lake, also in Magic Lake Estates, is a water supply reservoir and is not accessible to the general public. Greenburn Lake on South Pender Island is part of GINPR and is also used as a water supply.

Roads and Parking

Use common sense when parking on the Pender Islands. At trailheads where there are no parking lots, park only on safe shoulders and park completely off the pavement along any main roadway, but watch for ditches. There is no designated overnight parking, except for those users of parks and recreational facilities and resorts. The RCMP may tow vehicles that obstruct roadways.

Roads tend to be narrow and motorists, cyclists and pedestrians need to share the road. Road conditions vary from good to poor, and street names can change in confusing manners. Helmets are mandatory for all cyclists. Bicycles and motorized vehicles are prohibitied from all park trails on the Pender Islands. Pender Island is a designated 50km/h (30 mph) speed zone everywhere, except for secondary warnings and the three school zones which are 30km/h (18mph) zones. In addition, a large deer population roams freely on the island and motorists need to be vigilant.

The Population

The Pender Islands comprise the second most populated island in the Southern Gulf Islands after Salt Spring Island. Capital Regional District statistics are as follows:

Gulf Islands	2001 Census	Selected CRD Areas	2004 Estimate	2026 Projected
Pender	1,935	Salt Spring Island	10,229	n/a
Galiano	1,071	Total Southern Gulf Islands	15,190	19,900
Mayne	880	Peninsula:Sidney-N Saanich	41,893	46,300
Saturna	319	Western:Langford,Sooke etc	67,764	112,300
Salt Spring	9,381	Core: Victoria -Esquimalt etc	224,791	244,200
		Total Capital Regional Dist	349,638	422,700

The largest group of full-time Pender Islands' residents consists of retirees, many of whom work part-time. Residents also include artisans, tradespersons, farmers, and professionals of all ages. The major employers are Poets Cove Resort, BC Ferries, and the school. Most other working Penderites are self-employed and work out of their homes. The advent of high speed Internet has enabled people to telecommute from the islands. Others commute via ferry to other locations, while some commute to Vancouver via float plane. Many of the homes on the islands are weekend and summer retreats for Canadians, mostly from Vancouver, as well as Victoria, inland British Columbia and Alberta. A 2004 Times Colonist article stated that Americans comprise 20 percent of recent home sales on the Gulf Islands, though separate statistics for the Pender Islands were not available. Salt Spring is the island best known to Americans.

The following socioeconomic statistics on the full time residents of North and South Pender Island are from the 2001 Census, taken from B.C. Statistics, 2003:

Income	N Pender	S Pender	Education	N Pender	S Pender
Population	1776	159	Less Than Grade 9	2.6%	0.0%
Experienced Labour	685	60	9-13 No Graduation	20.4%	16.1%
Have Employment $	765	n/a	Secondary Graduate	8.2%	9.7%
- Full Time	37%	n/a	Trades Certificate	12.8%	6.5%
- Part Time	58%	n/a	College-Grad or Not	26.0%	16.1%
Total Income Is From:			University,NoDegree	8.2%	22.6%
Employment	44.4%	n/a	Bachelor's or Higher	21.7%	35.5%
Government Transfer	21.1%	n/a	Population Age15-24	55	10
Other	34.6%	n/a	Population Age 20+	1520	155

PENDER ISLANDS INFORMATION SOURCES

The Pender Post is published monthly with a cover price of $1.50. Annual subscriptions are available for the period of January to December for $15 for delivery on the Pender Islands. Off-island subscriptions cost more. It contains summaries and descriptions of events for the upcoming month, reports and information from various clubs and organizations, miscellaneous columns and articles, and advertisements, including most of the Pender Islands real estate listings. It is sold at most Pender retail establishments. If you are here just for a few days, you may want to at least look at the list of events that are printed on the front cover. You can also read the Pender Post at the Pender Island Public Library, which keeps many back issues.

The Pender Island Public Library contains materials of local interest including government reports and back issues of the Pender Post. (See *Shopping Guide - Books* for information on the library). **Map 1.**

Pender Islands Telephone and Email List is published annually by the Lions Club and delivered free to Pender Island residences with a request for donation, or sold for $6 in stores. Inclusion is not automatic; Forms sent out to residents must be filled out, and paid advertising is accepted for the yellow pages.

Island Tides is a free monthly newspaper covering articles of local interest to the Gulf Islands, as well as tide data. It also contains descriptions of some upcoming events, advertising, and classifieds. It is delivered free to Pender Island mailboxes, and can be found around the Gulf Islands, at BC Ferries terminals, or it can be downloaded at **www.islandtides.com**.

Message Boards are located at the Driftwood Centre next to the CRD office, Magic Lake Market, and outside the Port Browning Pub. Look here to find or to post various items for sale, services or lodgings offered, as well as island events. Check *sandwich boards*, mostly in front of the Driftwood Centre, for announcements from retail establishments.

The Times Colonist is the main Victoria newspaper, and offers daily subscriptions to residents of the Pender Islands. Papers are delivered reasonably early. Home subscribers can view on-line content: **www.timescolonist.com**; 250.382.2255.

Monday Magazine is a good source for Victoria arts and entertainment. Available free around the Victoria area, or check online at **www.mondaymag.com**.

Pender Island Cable Channel 3 runs display ads for businesses and upcoming events on the Gulf Islands. It may also carry information regarding disasters, power permitting.

WEB SITES

The following web sites contain information specific to the Pender Islands. Dozens of additional web sites are also mentioned in the appropriate chapters throughout this book. *See the Shopping and Services* Chapter for information on Internet access on the Pender Islands.

Typical rocky cove of the Pender Islands.

www.penderislandchamber.com: Pender Island Chamber of Commerce web site contains member listings of accommodations, restaurants, arts, services, marinas, and recreation.

www.penderislands.org: Website of the Pender Island Community Hall posts information about the facility (including bookings) and the Pender Islands in general.

www.penderisland.info: Contains information on transportation, weather, history, arts, parks, recreation, photographs, postcards, screensavers, slide shows, maps and links.

www.gulfislandsguide.com: Comprehensive site with such features as current photographs, free postcards, information on arts, recreation, services, real estate, history, parks, activities, maps, weather, transportation and links.

www.islands.bc.ca: Extensive information on Vancouver Island and the Gulf Islands, including general information, transportation, activities, recreation, marinas, weather, accommodations, tours, ski areas, and golf courses,

www.shim.bc.ca/gulfislands: The Gulf Islands Atlas is a web-based mapping tool that brings together a variety of information about the natural and cultural attributes and resources of the southern Gulf Islands region. Sponsored by Parks Canada and CPAWS.

www.travel-photos.info: Contains beautiful local photographs and screensavers from Pender Island and around the world from Pender photographer Kevin Oke.

www.pender-island.bc.ca: Greg Rowland of Newport Realty has posted interesting *Pender Virtual Tours*, 360-degree tours of some of Pender's most scenic vistas.

3 TRAVEL GUIDE

TRANSPORTATION OPTIONS

Options for travel to the Pender Islands from the Pacific Northwest include public ferry, floatplane or private boat. The main gateways, in order of convenience, are Victoria, Vancouver, and Seattle. Following is a brief summary of travel options. Each option is explained in detail later in this chapter. Refer to the **Location Map** in the *Map Atlas* that depicts the general layout of the region including location of ferry terminals.

From Vancouver, BC: Airport, Downtown or Cruise Ship Terminal
• Take a car, taxi, or bus south to BC Ferries' Tsawwassen Ferry Terminal to catch a sailing to the Pender Islands Otter Bay Terminal. Reservations are recommended. Either take the Gulf Islands Ferry, or catch a ferry to Swartz Bay then transfer to a ferry to Pender Island.

• Take a floatplane from the airport or downtown and land at the Port Washington Dock on North Pender Island, or the dock at Poets Cove Resort on South Pender Island.

From Victoria: Downtown or Airport
• Take a car, taxi, or bus to Swartz Bay Ferry Terminal and catch a non-stop BC Ferries sailing to the Pender Islands. No reservations are accepted on this route.

• Take a chartered boat trip, as available, from Sidney or Victoria Inner Harbour to Poets Cove/Bedwell Harbour on South Pender Island.

• Bicyclists can follow the Galloping Goose/Lochside Trail system, that connects the Victoria, Sidney and Swartz Bay ferry terminals, to cycle to the Pender Islands.

From Seattle and Washington State
• Drive north across the Canadian border to Vancouver/Tsawwassen Ferry Terminal to catch a BC Ferries sailing to the Pender Islands (reservations recommended).

• From Seattle, drive north to Anacortes and take a Washington State Ferry to Sidney on Vancouver Island (seasonal, reservations recommended), and then drive a few minutes north to Swartz Bay to catch the ferry to the Pender Islands (no reservations on this route). Return the same way or take BC Ferries from the Pender Islands to Vancouver/Tsawwassen, then drive south to Seattle.

• Take an Amtrak train or bus to Vancouver, and then take a taxi or bus to Tsawwassen Ferry Terminal to catch a BC Ferries sailing to the Pender Islands.

• Take a floatplane from Seattle/Lake Union to Poets Cove/Bedwell Harbour, South Pender Island, where there is a customs dock open May through September.

• Take the seasonal Victoria Clipper passenger ferry from Seattle to Victoria Harbour, then take a bus, taxi, or rental car to Swartz Bay to catch the ferry to Pender.

• Bicycle the San Juan Islands, catch the Washington State Ferry to Sidney, and take the Lochside Trail 5 km (3 mi) to Swartz Bay to catch the ferry to the Pender Islands.

• By car, take a scenic tour: Drive to and tour Olympic National Park. From Port Angeles take the M.V. Coho, a privately run ferry, to Victoria Inner Harbour. Clear customs in Victoria, take advantage of the location to tour Victoria, and then drive north to Swartz Bay Ferry Terminal with an option of stopping at Butchart Gardens along the way. Catch a BC Ferries sailing from Swartz Bay to the Pender Islands (no reservations). Return via the Gulf Islands Ferry to Vancouver/Tsawwassen. Drive north to tour Vancouver and Whistler, and then drive south to Seattle. *Note:* For those coming from Tacoma or south: Driving to Port Angeles enables you to miss the traffic of the Seattle and Vancouver areas. US 101 from Olympia is more scenic along the Hood Canal but slower going as compared to Routes 16, 3, and 104 from Tacoma via the Hood Canal Bridge.

Holiday Travel
Holidays in both Canada and the U.S. should be considered when planning a journey on a ferry or floatplane within BC or to Washington. Multi-ferry waits on the Vancouver to Victoria BC Ferries runs are common, and the Gulf Islands Ferry can be sold out well in advance. The Coho ferry from Victoria to Port Angeles and Washington State Ferry from Sidney to Anacortes may also be full to capacity. Summer holidays and weekends are the most crowded, when ferries may reach their quota of foot passengers on occasion.

MAJOR HOLIDAYS
New Years Day January 1 (Canada & U.S.)
Easter Good Friday through Easter Monday (Canada)
Victoria Day Third Monday in May (Canada)
Memorial Day Fourth Monday in May (U.S.)
Canada Day July 1 (Canada)
Independence Day July 4 (U.S.)
BC Day First Monday in August (Canada)
Labour Day First Monday in September (Canada & U.S.)
Thanksgiving Second Monday in October (Canada)
Thanksgiving Fourth Thursday in November (U.S.)
Christmas December 25 (Canada & U.S)
Boxing Day December 26 (Canada)

New Years Eve Lantern Festival

Driving Directions and Road Conditions

DRIVING DIRECTIONS

Web sites that include Canada and the U.S:
www.mapquest.com/directions/
www.TravelGIS.com/directions/
www.freetrip.com
www.ITools.com/maps
www.cnn.com/TRAVEL/DRIVING.DIRECTIONS

ROAD CONDITIONS

British Columbia
See **www.drivebc.ca** for BC Road Conditions, including links to border wait times, ferry conditions, weather, etc. While en route, call the toll numbers 1.800.550.4997, 1.900.565.4997 or cell *4997.
Talking Superpages is a pre-recorded telephone information service that provides updated critical road information. Phone one of the following numbers and enter code 7623 (ROAD) on a touch-tone phone:
Victoria: 250.953.9000 Vancouver: 604.299.9000 Nanaimo: 250.741.9000

Pender Islands road conditions or repair info: 629.3431.

For Canada Customs border wait times in both directions, check the website: **www.cbsa-asfc.gc.ca/general/times/menu-e.html**.
BC crossings are at the end of the list.

U.S. Customs border wait times near Vancouver: **http://apps.cbp.gov/bwt**
Includes Blaine/Peace Arch, Blaine/Pacific Highway and Sumas.

Washington
www.wsdot.wa.gov/traffic/
Phone: 1.800.695.ROAD

Oregon
www.tripcheck.com/Road/Cond/roadcondindex.htm
Phone: 1.800.977.6368

Alberta
www.ama.ab.ca (click on *Everything Automotive*, then *Road Reports*)
Phone: 403.246.5853.

General
www.highwayconditions.com provides links to Canadian and U.S. websites.

GETTING TO THE PENDER ISLANDS

Travel to the Pender Islands typically requires two phases. The first phase involves getting to a regional transportation gateway such as Vancouver, Victoria, or Seattle. The second phase consists of finding local transportation to the islands. This chapter describes both phases of travel in detail.

The Ferries

Ferry routes connecting locations solely within British Columbia are handled by BC Ferries, which services the Pender Islands. Several other companies operate ferries between Vancouver Island, British Columbia and Washington State in the U.S. If one travels to the Pender Islands from Victoria or Vancouver via ferry, it will be on BC Ferries. A trip from Washington via Vancouver Island will include one of the U.S. ferry companies, connecting to a BC Ferry to get to the Pender Islands.

Orcas are frequently spotted from the deck of the ferry vessels. A conglomeration of whale-watching boats is usually the tipoff. Bring your binoculars!

Part One: BC Ferries

Overview, Reservations and Service

BC Ferries services the Pender Islands. BC Ferries operates one of the largest fleets of vehicle-carrying vessels in the world, with 34 vessels ranging from small 16-vehicle ferries to the 470-vehicle capacity Spirit vessels. For complete information, consult their web site, **www.bcferries.com**, which continues to add features. In April 2003, operation of BC Ferries changed from Provincial control to a private transportation authority, BC Ferries Corporation, with promises of improved service and quality of concessions. Moderate rate increases will take effect each year, but the current routes are expected to remain in place until at least April 2008. Changes to rates and services are monitored closely by Gulf Islands residents who have a large stake in the outcome. The Southern Gulf Islands Ferry Advisory Committee serves as liaison between BC Ferries and island residents. Minutes of their meetings can be found on the BC Ferries website, and they typically submit an article to the Pender Post.

BC FERRIES INFORMATION AND RESERVATIONS
1.888.BCFERRY from BC
250.381.5452 from outside BC
www.bcferries.com

On the BC Ferries web site click on *schedules* or *fares* from the home page, then select *Southern Gulf Islands*. For travel to the Pender Islands, select *Victoria* or *Vancouver Departures* as appropriate, and *Pender Islands Departures* for the return. Schedules are now available for download in a format compatible with wireless handheld devices (click on that option).

Different schedules and fares are in effect throughout the year, with an expanded schedule on certain routes extending from late June through Labour Day. Make a note of this if you are planning a trip in a period where the current schedule will not be valid. On the web site, you can click on *Upcoming Schedules* for this purpose, or you can ask the telephone contact. Unless you don't mind an extra overnight stay in Vancouver or Victoria, consult ferry schedules and availability prior to making your air, rail, or other travel plans to the Pender Islands. In July 2005, fuel surcharges were implemented, amounting to 4% for the Vancouver-Victoria route and 6% for the Gulf Islands routes. At time of writing additional surcharges have been requested. Fares quoted in this book may not include all fuel surcharges or fare increases. Also, check the BC Ferries web site for occasional fare sales and discounts, including Auto Club (BCAA, CAA, AAA) discounts on selected sailings.

FERRY TERMINALS OFFERING SAILINGS TO THE PENDER ISLANDS

The most frequent and direct ferries are from Swartz Bay, north of Victoria on Vancouver Island (near Sidney).
* The last ferry to Pender Island varies from about 6:30 to 8:00 pm depending on the season and day of the week.

Access from the mainland is from Tsawwassen, south of Vancouver.
* The ferry that sails directly to the Gulf Islands is referred to as the Gulf Islands Ferry.

Access to other Southern Gulf Islands is available on the ferries sailing to or from Swartz Bay or Tsawwassen that stop at Pender:
* Village Bay, Mayne Island
* Sturdies Bay, Galiano Island
* Lyall Harbour, Saturna Island (limited)
* Long Harbour, Salt Spring Island (limited)

Notifications of Service Changes and Ferry Status

BC Ferries can notify you via email if ferry service changes on a route that impacts you. This is a must for frequent ferry travelers, as notices tend to occur fairly regularly. To subscribe to BC Ferries' email update system for changes in ferry service, go to **www.bcferries.com/subscribe/** and fill out the form, or if that does not work, send an email to **webmaster@bcferries.com** with your full name, email address, and any routes that you wish to be kept updated on (i.e. Pender Island Departures, Swartz Bay to Gulf Islands, etc.). The information provided in this email service can also be viewed on the BC Ferries website. Click on *Current Conditions* and then *Service Notices.* The website also displays up to the minute conditions and actual sailing times for the major terminals, so it will show the sailing times to the Pender Islands from Vancouver and Victoria, but not the reverse at time of writing. Click on *Actual Departures* under *Current Conditions.* Note that ferries can make up time. For example, if the Queen of Cumberland is running an hour late in the morning, it may only be a half hour late in the afternoon. Or, it can be 2 hours late. You can also call 1.888.BCFerry or the ferry terminal for status. Swartz Bay is 250.656.5571.

M.V. Queen of Cumberland

Reservations

Reservations for the Vancouver (Tsawwassen) to Pender Island ferry (the *Gulf Island Ferry*), as well as the Tsawwassen-Swartz Bay (Victoria) ferries can be made at the website **www.bcferries.com**, or by calling 1.888.BCFERRY (1.888.223.3779) from within BC, or 250.386.3431 from outside BC. Commercial (over 5,500 kg GVW) reservations can be made via the 1.888.BCFERRY phone number, or on line using the RBI-CV option. *No reservations are taken for the Swartz Bay to Pender Islands sailings.*

For the Gulf Islands Ferry, there is no extra charge to reserve a spot, but the fare must be paid for in advance with a credit card. Payment is fully refundable up to 8 days prior to sailing. If you change or cancel the reservation 7 days or less of the scheduled departure time, a $25 service fee *for each direction reserved* is charged against the fare you paid. You must check in at the ticket booth at least 30 minutes prior to sailing time to claim a reservation. If you arrive after this time you revert to stand-by status.

If a particular Gulf Islands Ferry sailing is sold out, you can call the reservations line and ask to be placed on a waiting list.

For the Tsawwassen – Swartz Bay ferry, a non-refundable/non-changeable reservation fee of $15 ($17.50 if less than 7 days out) is collected at the time you make the reservation. You must arrive between 30 to 60 minutes prior to your reserved sailing time to claim your reservation. The actual ferry tariff is collected at the ticket booth.

BC FERRIES' GULF ISLANDS ROUTES FACTS AND FIGURES
Ferries in service from Swartz Bay/Victoria to the Outer Gulf Islands (including the Pender Islands) are the M.V. Queen of Cumberland with a capacity of 127 vehicles and 450 passengers, and the M.V. Mayne Queen, with a capacity of 70 vehicles and 393 passengers. Peak travel months are by far July and August, followed by June, September, and May. In spring, 43% of ferry traffic is visitors, compared to 73% in summer. In spring, 57% of travelers reside in the Gulf Islands, versus 28% in summer. Conversely, Vancouver Island residents comprise 28% of spring traffic and 42% of summer travelers. Other summer travelers reside in the Lower Mainland (14%), other areas of BC (2%), or outside of BC (14%).

BC Ferries service from Tsawwassen/Vancouver to the Gulf Islands is provided by the M.V. Queen of Nanaimo with a capacity of 192 vehicles and 1183 passengers, and to a lesser extent, the M.V. Bowen Queen, with a capacity of 70 vehicles and 393 passengers. The journey frequently requires a transfer at Mayne Island to either the Queen of Cumberland or the Mayne Queen. In the winter, 60% of ferry traffic on this route is visitors, versus 86% in the summer. Gulf Islands residents comprise 49% of ferry travelers in winter, and 20% in summer. Residents of the lower mainland (Vancouver area) account for 47% of winter travelers and 59% of summer travelers. Other summer travelers reside on Vancouver Island (2%), other areas of BC (2%), or outside of BC (17%) (Data from **www.islandstrust.bc.ca**).

STRANDED! WHEN THE BC FERRIES DON'T RUN
For the most part, the BC Ferries system is dependable and interruptions in service infrequent. However, there are occasions when ferry service is interrupted. During major storms or gale force winds, sailings can be cancelled. Ferries also break down or have impaired operation. The Otter Bay dock was closed for ten days in October 2002 when the wing walls were replaced. During that time BC Ferries provided a free passenger-only water taxi service between Otter Bay Marina and Swartz Bay. Several months warning was provided by BC Ferries. Ferry worker strikes can wreak havoc with ferry travelers. A strike in Autumn 2003 reduced but did not stop ferry sailings. Other strikes have been threatened periodically. Locals remember the 1977 strike as being especially disruptive. For information on BC ferries, including a history of accidents, see **www.wikipedia.org/wiki/bcferries**.

BC Ferries Terminals

Detailed information on ferry travel is presented in this section, which describes the main ferry terminals relevant to travel to the Pender Islands. See the *Location Map* in the *Map Atlas* that depicts the BC Ferries terminals in Southern BC. A summary of the information contained in this section is as follows:

Otter Bay (The Pender Islands)
Directions, terminal amenities, destination options, fares to other Southern Gulf Islands, and locals' tips.

Tsawwassen (South of Vancouver); and
Swartz Bay/Sidney (North of Victoria)
How to get to the terminals, fares and service to Otter Bay, terminal and vessel amenities, and nearby gas, food and lodging.

Horseshoe Bay (Northwest of Vancouver)
Vancouver's scenic northwestern terminal is mentioned, although service is not available to the Pender Islands or Victoria/Swartz Bay.

OTTER BAY TERMINAL ON THE PENDER ISLANDS

Location
The Otter Bay ferry terminal is located in the northwest section of North Pender Island along Swanson Channel. Look for signs throughout the Pender Islands that direct motorists to *Ferries*. Follow Otter Bay Road from either direction to MacKinnon Road to the terminal. *See the Pender Islands Map Atlas,* **Maps 1** and **1A.**

Getting to the Terminal
One can make arrangements to stay at an accommodation that offers rides to the ferry terminal. Taxi services have come and gone on the Pender Islands. At time of writing the most recent service, **Pender Island Taxi and Tours** can be reached at 629.3555. They charge about $20 from Magic Lake Estates. See the section *Getting Around The Pender Islands*.

Parking
Free parking for ferry foot passengers is located along the north side of MacKinnon Road, where a row of cars is always parked. Do not park beyond the *No Parking* signs. A free parking lot with a 48-hour limit is located adjacent to the ticket kiosk.

Foot Passengers and Bicyclists
Those traveling without a vehicle must check in at the entry kiosk, even if traveling to Swartz Bay where there is no charge for travel in this direction. All other destinations require payment, which must be done at the kiosk. Passengers can be dropped off at the parking lot, after which they will have to walk for about 5-minutes down a moderate hill, or they can be driven to the bottom of the hill near the ferry landing. The BC Ferries attendant at the entry kiosk will direct the driver to an appropriate lane for the drop-off. Passengers can be picked up in a similar fashion.

Drop-Off by Private Boat
The terminal has no float available to drop someone off by private boat, but if the Otter Bay Marina outer float is not full (more likely in the off-season), you can probably get permission to drop off a passenger there and they can walk up and then down a steep hill to get to the ferry in about 10 to 15 minutes.

Amenities and Food
The single-berth terminal has an enclosed waiting room with washrooms and a pay phone. **The Stand** is a privately run eatery located adjacent to the ferry dock. Hours are limited in the off-season. Allow plenty of time for grilled items if ferry sailing time is approaching, or call in advance for pick-up: 629.3292. Other options for to-go food include the **Pender Island Bakery**, **Hope Bay Café** or other Pender restaurants. See the *Dining Guide* for further information.

Ferry Destinations
Ferries from the Pender Islands depart, in approximate order of frequency, to Victoria/Swartz Bay, Mayne Island, Galiano Island, Vancouver/Tsawwassen, Saturna Island, and Salt Spring Island/Long Harbour. Daily round trips are possible to most of these destinations, except there are very limited times/schedules to Saturna and Salt Spring Islands. Additional opportunity to tour Salt Spring Island by car is available if you travel to Swartz Bay and utilize the ferry between Swartz Bay and Fulford Harbour on Salt Spring Island. However, a throughfare discount is not available.

To get to the Nanaimo area (or other points north on Vancouver Island) from the Pender Islands, a few options are available. You can take the ferry from Otter Bay to Swartz Bay and drive to Nanaimo via Highway 17 and Canada 1 to Nanaimo, perhaps taking the shortcut ferry from Mill Bay to Brentwood Bay. Or, you can take the infrequent 45-minute ferry from Otter Bay to Long Harbour on Salt Spring Island, drive across the island to Vesuvius, then take the frequent 20-minute Vesuvius - Comox run.

Fares
For information on fares from the Pender Islands to Victoria/Swartz Bay and Vancouver/Tsawwassen, see the sections on those terminals. Fares are charged each way between the Pender Islands and Vancouver/Tsawwassen, though the fares are different in either direction. Fares are only charged one way between the Pender Islands and Swartz Bay, and that is on the Swartz Bay departures. Fares (2006) between Otter Bay and the other Southern Gulf Islands are $3.95/person in summer and $3.15 the rest of the year. Undersize vehicles cost $8.10 summer and $7.05 at non-peak times, so

that a roundtrip with two persons in peak season costs approximately $32.00 (plus $1.40 in fuel surcharges). No discount books are available for sailings between the Gulf Islands.

Reservations are available, and are recommended, on the sailings to Vancouver/ Tsawwassen, which are 100% reservable. If the ferries are booked you can travel to Vancouver via Swartz Bay. Ask for a throughfare pass at the Otter Bay ticket kiosk or on board the ferry to Swartz Bay, and then catch the next available ferry at Swartz Bay to Tsawwassen. That route is partially reservable. See the *Overview, Reservations and Service* section for details on making reservations.

LOCALS TIPS

If your sailing is aboard the M.V. Queen of Cumberland and you are placed on the movable ramp, you are not allowed to stay in your vehicle while the ramp is being raised and lowered. When you arrive, you can either exit to the passenger deck, or stand outside of your vehicle in the portion of the ramp that remains stationary. When you return to your vehicle upon arrival at either terminal, you must stand in the non-moving portion until the ramp is lowered, and then you will be told to return to your vehicle.

Find out from BC Ferries which vessel handles each particular sailing out of Otter Bay (or Swartz Bay), and where it is coming from. For example, if the Queen of Cumberland, which has the greatest capacity of the Pender – Swartz Bay vessels, is handling your sailing from Otter Bay, and is coming directly from Swartz Bay, it will let off its entire load, and will probably be able to take on three or four rows of vehicles lined up at Otter Bay. Therefore, it is probably not necessary to arrive early for this sailing, except on summer Sundays and holidays, or if an unusually large number of trucks are traveling (in which case a notification may be sent to email subscribers). If a smaller vessel, such as the Mayne Queen, is coming from two other islands on the way to Swartz Bay, there may only be room for one lane or less from Otter Bay. If it is vital that you catch this particular ferry, it is wise to line up a half hour or more before the sailing time. The local BC Ferries personnel publish a Local Schedule for the Pender Islands that is sometimes available at the ticket kiosk upon request. It shows the vessels assigned to each sailing and which ones are most likely to overload. Note that sometimes BC Ferries swaps vessels mid-schedule. The phone number for the ferry kiosk is 629.3344, but BC Ferries personnel ask that you please refrain from calling this number unless it is important, as they are deluged with phone calls. In other words, make an effort to find your schedule, call 1.888.BCFERRY or look up information on-line before you bug them. Do not call the RCMP for ferry schedule or status information.

MORE LOCALS TIPS
Discount Travel: BC Seniors Travel free Monday through Thursday except on holidays. This applies only to the passenger fare and not the vehicle. You must show your BC Gold Care Card to confirm age (65 years or older) and full-time residency in British Columbia. On school-sponsored events, BC students (18 years and under) travel at a special reduced rate when a letter from a school official confirming the nature of the event is presented. Consult the BC Ferries website for further information. Persons sent off island for medical treatment may also be eligible for free ferry travel. See the *Health Services Guide* for details.

Pender Boaters: If you need to take your untrailerable boat in for service on Vancouver Island, you can have someone drive a vehicle and leave it at the Otter Bay terminal or along MacKinnon Road in the designated area. They can then walk down to the Otter Bay Marina outer float to be picked up, with permission (in peak periods the marina may be full). Drop off the boat at one of the repair shops in the Sidney or Swartz Bay area, then make your way back to the ferry terminal by walking from Canoe Cove or Westport Marinas or by taking or connecting to the #70 bus northbound from other marinas.

TSAWWASSEN TERMINAL SOUTH OF VANCOUVER

The terminal that services the Pender Islands from Vancouver on the BC Lower Mainland is at Tsawwassen (pronounced *Twassen*), which is about a 20-30 minute drive north from the U.S. border (after clearing customs) and about a 30-minute drive south from Vancouver Airport, traffic-depending. Ferries from Tsawwassen service Swartz Bay (north of Victoria on Vancouver Island), Nanaimo (Duke Point Terminal) on Vancouver Island (90 km/54 miles north of Victoria) and the Southern Gulf Islands including the Pender Islands.

Getting to and From the Tsawwassen Terminal

CAR

From Seattle/US Border Follow I-5 north to the Canadian border, which becomes Highway 99 in British Columbia. Take 99 northbound to Highway 10 westbound to its terminus at Highway 17. Make a left, and follow Highway 17 southwest to the Tsawwassen ferry terminal. The approximate driving time is 30 minutes, not including traffic delays and border crossing wait times.

From Downtown Vancouver and Cruise Ship Terminal Follow signs southbound to the Tsawwassen ferries (not northbound to Horseshoe Bay ferries). Take Oak Street south to Highway 99 south. Follow it south to Highway 17 West. The terminal is 38 km (24 miles) south of Vancouver and takes an average of 40 minutes.

From Vancouver Airport Exit the terminal to Highway 99 South. Follow Highway 99 southbound through the George Massey Tunnel to Highway 17 westbound. The trip takes about 30 minutes, not including traffic delays.

From Whistler/North of Vancouver Follow Highway 99 southbound past Horseshoe Bay. Connect to Highway 1 East. Take Taylor Way Exit and cross Lions Gate Bridge. Continue through Stanley Park and onto Georgia Street. Turn right at Howe Street, cross the Granville Street Bridge. Turn left at 70th Ave, then right at Oak Street to Highway 99 South. Continue through the George Massey Tunnel, and then exit onto Highway 17 to the Tsawwassen Ferry Terminal. Expect an average of 2 hours 30 minutes driving time from Whistler.

From Canada, Points East on Highway 1/Chilliwak Take Highway 1 westbound to Fort Langley. Take Exit 66/Highway 10 westbound. Highway 10 ends at Highway 17. Turn left for the Tsawwassen ferry terminal. From Chilliwack expect 1 hour 15 minutes.

Upon Leaving the Tsawwassen Terminal Follow Highway 17 northeast. To go to Vancouver (downtown or airport) or Whistler, head north on Highway 99. For points east and south, turn right at Highway 10 (Ladner Trunk), which intersects with Highway 99 further south. To go south to the U.S. border, head south on Highway 99. For points east in British Columbia, continue east on Highway 10, which continues to Surrey and Abbotsford, connecting to Canada Highway 1. Highway 10 is not a freeway and it can be very slow and congested as it passes through those cities. This route also leads to alternative border crossings to the U.S. The main crossing at Highway 99/I-5 (Peace Arch/Blaine) can sometimes be very congested. The next crossing to the east is at the end of Highway 15 (Cloverdale Bypass-Pacific Highway/Blaine), followed by Aldergrove BC/Lynden WA at the south end of Highway 13. Further east down Canada 1 is the Highway 11 Abbottsford BC/Sumas WA crossing.

Parking
The Tsawwassen terminal parking lot has 1,200 parking spaces. Follow signs for parking, which is to the left as you near the terminal. Call, or check BC Ferries' website www.bcferries.com for parking availability. Short-term parking rates are $1 for 30 minutes, $9 for five hours, and $12 for the day, ending at midnight. Pay at the machines provided and place your receipt on your dashboard. Long-term parking rates are $8 for 6 hours or $12 for 24 hours. An economy parking area charges $5 for 6 hours or $9 for 24 hours. Payment is space-specific and is made at machines in the parking area or by calling toll free 1.866.277.5446 with a credit card (AE, MC, VI). Machines accept credit cards and cash. After parking, remember your space number and pay for the estimated time needed with either method. Keep your receipt in the event you need to extend your time, which can be done by phone. You do not need to display your receipt in the vehicle (assuming this method of payment is in effect). A private parking lot is also available north of the causeway, run by Park & Go 604.681.3233.

Passenger Drop-Off

As you near the terminal, look for the sign *Passenger Drop Off, which* is to the left of the ferry vehicle tollbooths and line-ups. Passengers can purchase tickets and check baggage in the terminal. The terminal has both a cafeteria and vending machines. To get to the new Tsawwassen Quay concession, passengers must walk across the ferry line-up area.

BUS

Translink in Vancouver offers public bus service that stops at Tsawwassen, but it can be a time consuming process. The approximate fare is $3.25 between Tsawwassen and Vancouver Airport (YVR), or $4.50 to the downtown area and Canada Place cruise ship terminal. For specific information on routes, times, and current fares consult their web site **www.translink.bc.ca** or call 604.953.3333. On line, click on *Trip Planning*, and then enter your desired departure or arrival time, and other information. For the ferry terminal, enter *Tsawwassen Ferry Terminal*. For the airport, enter *Airport - YVR*. For the cruise ship terminal, enter *Canada Place*. A typical trip to Tsawwassen terminal from the airport will require one or two transfers and take about 50 minutes to two hours, depending on day and time. A trip to and from Canada Place and Tsawwassen terminal typically involves a transfer between a bus and the Sky Train light rail system, which runs through downtown Vancouver to the waterfront.

Pacific Coach Lines (PCL) operates scheduled private coach service between Vancouver (downtown, the airport, and the Canada Place cruise ship terminal on cruise ship days) and Tsawwassen. Call 604.662.8074 (Vancouver), 250.385.4411 (Victoria), or 1.800.661.1725. Check **www.pacificcoach.com** for current schedules and fares.

Meet the bus at the following locations: Downtown: 1150 Station Street; Vancouver International Airport: Domestic Terminal (kiosk across from Baggage Claim #6), or International Terminal (kiosk across from Bay #2). Buses leave every 2 hours. Buses also meet cruise ships at Canada Place, once per Saturday as needed at 11:00 am.

Once the bus arrives at Tsawwassen, one can either: 1) Depart the bus and board the Southern Gulf Islands Ferry to the Pender Islands; 2) Stay with the bus through Swartz Bay terminal on Vancouver Island, or 3) Continue on with the bus to downtown Victoria. Fares vary seasonally. Summer 2006 rates are $41.50 one way from Vancouver Airport to downtown Victoria Depot, or $29.75 to the Gulf Islands. Fares include the ferry tariff. You can also catch the bus on the Tsawwassen to Swartz Bay ferry, by going to the shuttle bus counter behind the gift shop during the first 30 minutes of the sailing. When you board from the passenger terminal, you can check your baggage using a Pacific Coach Lines tag. If you discover once on board that there is no room on the bus, they will send you on a later bus. Payment accepted on the ferry is cash only, whereas they also accept MC and Visa at their kiosks on land.

When returning to Tsawwassen, you may also be able to use PCL. If your schedule works out, you can meet the PCL bus at Tsawwassen to return to downtown

Vancouver or the airport (YVR). Meet the bus under the arrival building between berths 3 and 4. Prepare to pay cash. If you are touring the southern BC area, you can plan your trip to end in downtown Victoria, and take PCL all the way to Vancouver from their terminal, which is located behind the Empress Hotel at 700 Douglas (at Belleville). MC and Visa are accepted there. This may be your best bet to ensure catching a flight that is before noon, without having to stay overnight near Vancouver airport. You can also take the ferry from the Pender Islands to Swartz Bay and pick up the PCL bus there. At the passenger terminal, check your baggage with a PCL tag, then once on board the ferry, find the shuttle bus desk near the gift shop within 30 minutes of sailing to reserve a space on the bus. Only cash is accepted on the ferry. Contact PCL regarding options if the buses are running near capacity.

TAXI

Most taxi companies will take you from all points in Vancouver to the Tsawwassen passenger terminal (About $40 from the airport). Ample cabs wait at the airport. Following are some local taxi companies (Area code 604):
Tsawwassen Area: **Tsawwassen Taxi:** 594.5444; **White Rock Taxi:** 536.7666
Vancouver: **Yellow Cab:** 681.1111; **North Shore Taxi:** 1.800.668.7774;
Black Top and Checker: 681.3201; **Sunshine Cabs:** 922.3333; **McClure's:** 731.9211;
Vancouver Taxi: 871.1111; 255.5111; **Imperial Limousine:** 687.5466

Upon returning to Tsawwassen, a few taxis may be waiting at the terminal, but to avoid waiting, you may want to call Tsawwassen Taxi at 604.594.5444 when your ferry is about to leave Otter Bay, giving them your name, so that they will hopefully be there and watch for you.

RAIL

Canada's **Via Rail** and the U.S.'s **Amtrak** both service Vancouver, but transfers by bus or taxi are required to get to Tsawwassen Ferry Terminal. Also, a new Vancouver-Whistler tour train began in 2006. See **www.whistlermountaineer.com**.

Via Rail: www.viarail.com, 1.888.VIARAIL. (1.888.842.7245). Downtown Vancouver Pacific Central Station (VAC), 1150 Station Street, corner of Main Street and Terminal Avenue, east edge of downtown adjacent to Chinatown. From Vancouver, the western Transcontinental line travels to Toronto via Kamloops, Jasper, Edmonton Saskatoon and Winnipeg. Via Rail also operates the Malahat line on Vancouver Island once daily between Victoria and Nanaimo (2 hours 25 minutes, about $15 one way) or Courtenay (4 hours 30 minutes, about $28). Reservations are recommended. The Victoria station is located at the east end of the Johnson Street Bridge at 450 Pandora (**Map 11**).

Amtrak: www.amtrak.com, 1.800.USARAIL (1.800.872.7245). The journey from Seattle (SEA- King Street Station, 303 South Jackson Street) to Vancouver (VAC - See VIA Rail above) takes about 4 hours and costs about $26USD each way.

Gas Food and Lodging

Food at the Terminal

The 16,000 square foot Tsawwassen Quay marketplace opened in June 2005 at the terminal, replacing the old outdated facilities in the middle of the ferry vehicle line-up area. Food choices include **Wok 'n Roll** Asian food, **Crepe Expectations, Oh Gelato** ice cream, **Salt Spring Organic Coffee, Starbucks Coffee, Skyway Gourmet** sandwiches, **Salty's** hot dogs etc., **Rocky Mountain Chocolate, Ali Baba Pizza, Taste of BC** salmon products and chowders, and **SPUD** organic grocery. Several gifts shops are available for browsing, as well as a bookshop, an Internet and game shop, a currency exchange, a Lotto centre, and independent kiosks. The passenger terminal has a cafeteria and vending machines, or passengers can walk across to Tsawwassen Quay while waiting. Announcements of departing ferries are made via loudspeaker around the terminal and inside of the terminal buildings.

Food Near the Terminal

The terminal is not located within walking distance of commercial zones, so it is not practical to park your vehicle in the ferry line and walk to a restaurant outside of the terminal. The town of Tsawwassen (Area Code 604), located several kilometres from the terminal, has numerous restaurants. The closest restaurants are on 56th Street. On your way to the terminal on Highway 17, turn left (south) onto 56th Street (or right if you have just left the terminal). Drive south on 56th Street for 800 metres (.5 mile) to 18th Avenue where a **McDonalds** is located. Continue to 16th Avenue for **Dairy Queen** or to 12th Avenue for **Tim Horton's, White Spot** and a **Safeway** supermarket. Between 12th and 10th Avenues, on the right are **Robbs Fish Restaurant**, 943.1783; **Alfa Greco Roman Cuisine**, 946.7471; **Mario's Kitchen**, 943.4442; and **Ocean Palace Chinese Seafood**, 948.9338. Also in town are **Bay Area Gourmet**, 1299 56th St, 943.2126; **Beaches**, 1665 56th St, 943.8221; and **Best Garden Restaurant**, 1284 56th St, 943.3818. See www.tourismdelta.bc.ca for additional area listings of all kinds, including restaurants in nearby Ladner (which also has supermarkets) and accommodations as well.

Fuel

The nearest vehicle fuel stations to the terminal are in Tsawwassen, south on 56th Street from Highway 17, near the restaurants described above.

Accommodations

If you arrive too late to catch a ferry, a few options for accommodations are available in the Tsawwassen area (or plan ahead and stay in Vancouver). The area code here is 604. A full service hotel that even advertises as being dog friendly is the **Coast Hotels Tsawwassen Inn** at 1665 56th Street (left from Highway 17 if you are heading toward the ferry terminal); 1.800.943.8221, 943.8221. The **Delta Town & Country Inn** is at the junction of Highway 99 and Highway 17; 946.4404. Other older hotels in the area may have more reasonable rates, including the **Tsawwassen Motel at Sundance Place** at 6574 Ladner Trunk Road; 946.4288. Numerous B&B's are also located in this area.
The **ParkCanada RV Park** is located just north of the ferry terminal causeway along Highway 17 at 4799 Nulelum Way; 943.5811.

Ferry Service To the Pender Islands

Typically two ferries run daily between the Pender Islands and Vancouver's Tsawwassen terminal. These ferries stop at Galiano and/or Mayne Island, and some require a transfer at Mayne Island. The transfer is easy; just follow the signs or watch for the ferry workers' signals. This route is 100% reservable and can be full, especially on summer and holiday weekends. During these times, reservations should be made for travel to the Pender Islands Thursday, Friday, and Saturday (morning); and for the return trip on Sunday, Monday, and Tuesday following a holiday Monday. Also, due to the number of Vancouverites that have weekend places on the Gulf Islands, the weekend ferries can be booked to Pender Island any time of year on Friday nights as well as the return to Vancouver on Sunday nights or holiday Mondays. Make sure to check to see if you will be traveling on a Canadian or U.S. holiday. Note that Sunday schedules are in effect on Canadian holiday Mondays. A waiting list may be available for this route. Ask your BC Ferries representative.

If the Tsawwassen-Pender Islands ferry is sold out, or if the scheduling works better, you can take the ferry from Tsawwassen to Swartz Bay, then transfer to a ferry to the Pender Islands for the same fare as the Tsawwassen-Pender Island route. You may want to make a reservation on the Tsawwassen to Swartz Bay route to ensure that you make your connection to Pender. The Tsawwassen-Swartz Bay ferries sail hourly, with a few gaps depending on the season, and take 1.5 hours. Although this route is only partially reservable, it may fill up at peak periods and you may have a wait of one or more sailings. When you purchase your ticket at Tsawwassen, tell them that you are going to the Pender Islands so that they will give you a throughfare ticket. You must take the next available sailing to the Pender Islands for it to be valid. Similarly, if you are returning from the Pender Islands to Tsawwassen via Swartz Bay, ask for a throughfare ticket at the Pender Island kiosk or on board the ferry to Swartz Bay, then take the next available sailing to Tsawwassen. Check the schedules to work out your itinerary, or call a BC Ferries representative who can explain your best itinerary depending on the status of the ferries. The ferries between the Pender Islands and Swartz Bay are non-reservable.

Fares
The Peak Season (June 29 to September 10, 2006) fare from Tsawwassen to the Pender Islands for a vehicle with a driver and one passenger in an undersize vehicle is $64.00 ($41.50/vehicle and $11.25/each passenger) plus at least $2.05 in fuel surcharges. The fare to return to Tsawwassen is $31.95 ($21.45/vehicle and $5.25/each passenger) plus at least $2.05 in fuel surcharges. The fares are discounted mid-week in the off-season. Discount books are not sold for this route. Two persons in one vehicle can expect a roundtrip summer 2006 fare of about $100 plus any additional fuel surcharges that are approved.

Ferry Food
Food services may change as a result of the ferry ownership change in 2003. At time of writing, food on the Queen of Nanaimo that serves the Tsawwassen – Pender Islands route is typically available on all of the sailings, and includes breakfast platters in the

morning, and then a menu for both lunch and dinner which consists typically of hot and cold sandwiches, burgers, fries, chili, soup and salads. If the smaller Bowen Queen is used, food service may not be available, so check on this before setting out.

A step up in food service occurs on the two Spirit series superferries, which handle about half of the sailings between Tsawwassen and Swartz Bay. (Check with BC Ferries to see which times they will be sailing). They feature the Pacific Buffet, which is an all you can eat buffet that contains food of above average quality. The best part is spending the journey at a table, hopefully next to the window, for the entire trip, with the ability to amble up for food and drink at your leisure, unless there is a huge crowd waiting to get in. The extra cost (about $11 to $15) usually limits the amount of diners, however, and the ambience is more cruise ship and less cattle call. Another option is the lounge on the ship's bow on the top deck, where for a $7 admission fee, one gets a newspaper, coffee and great view. Staterooms are also available on the larger ferries.

HORSESHOE BAY TERMINAL NORTHWEST OF VANCOUVER

The other Vancouver ferry terminal is at Horseshoe Bay, north of West Vancouver on Canada Highway 1. *Ferries departing Horseshoe Bay do not service Victoria or the Pender Islands.* They service Nanaimo (Departure Bay Terminal) on Vancouver Island, Langdale (Gibsons/the Sunshine Coast, including Pender Harbour), and Bowen Island. The Horseshoe Bay to Nanaimo Route is considered part of Canada 1, which continues south to *Milepost 1* in Victoria. One can do a circle route by taking the ferry to Nanaimo, driving to Victoria, then taking the ferry from Swartz Bay to the Pender Islands. Note that the drive from Nanaimo to Victoria is mostly non- freeway and takes about 2 hours to drive the 90 km (54 miles). Then, add another 25 to 45 minutes to get to the Swartz Bay Ferry Terminal. An option to cut some mileage, and perhaps some time off this drive is to take the Mill Bay to Brentwood Bay ferry, which allows you to bypass the Victoria area. The Horseshoe Bay area is very picturesque, and the town adjacent to the terminal contains several good waterfront restaurants.

SWARTZ BAY TERMINAL NORTH OF VICTORIA

The most frequent and convenient, non-stop ferries to the Pender Islands run from the Swartz Bay/Victoria terminal. The best way to visit the Pender Islands by ferry is by taking a sailing from the Swartz Bay terminal.

The terminal that services the Pender Islands from Vancouver Island and Victoria is at Swartz Bay, located about 32 km (20 miles) north of Victoria, and 5 km (3 miles) north of Sidney at the north end of the Patricia Bay Highway (Highway 17). Swartz Bay is also the terminal for ferries to Vancouver's Tsawwassen terminal, Salt Spring Island's Fulford Harbour, and three other Southern Gulf Islands (Mayne, Galiano and Saturna). Announcements of departing ferries are made via loudspeaker around the terminal and inside of the terminal building. A pet walk is located to the right as you face the ferries.

Getting to and From Swartz Bay

CAR

The Swartz Bay Ferry Terminal is easy to find. Signs direct motorists to *Ferries* throughout the Victoria area and the Saanich Peninsula (the area north of Victoria where Butchart Gardens is located). Make sure not to follow signs directing you to the other ferry terminals in Brentwood Bay (Mill Bay Ferry), Sidney (Washington State Ferry) or downtown Victoria (private ferries to Washington). Drive north on the Patricia Bay Highway (17) (not Canada 1) that ends at the BC Ferries terminal, 32 km (20 miles) north of Victoria. Driving times can vary depending on traffic, with the average being 30 minutes. The right lane (new in 2005) near the ferry terminal is dedicated for *Gulf Islands* traffic as an overhead sign indicates.

From Downtown Victoria Blanshard Street turns into Highway 17 as you travel northbound, while Douglas Street turns into Highway 1. So, if you are on Douglas Street you will need to take a connector street to your right (east) to get to Blanshard and Highway 17. If you are on Canada 1 and come to McKenzie Avenue, this is your last chance to cut over, so be sure to make a right, then head north on Highway 17 when you reach the highway interchange. From the Langford Area, take Canada 1 to Mackenzie, turn left, then north on Highway 17.

From Victoria Airport Exit the terminal by heading east (left) on Willingdon Road until it ends at McTavish Road. Make a left and then another left to head north on Highway 17. The terminal is less than a 10-minute drive from the airport if there is no traffic backup.

From Butchart Gardens Exit heading east on Benvenuto Drive that turns into Keating Cross Road. Turn left on Central Saanich Road, right at Island View, and left on Highway 17 at the signal. Allow about 25-30 minutes, more on busy weekends and holidays.

When arriving at the Swartz Bay tollbooths look to the right for the kiosk illuminated with *Outer Gulf Islands* or *Salt Spring/Gulf Islands* and ask for Pender Island. If you do not already have one, ask for a cardboard placard for your windshield with *Otter Bay* on it. The line-up lanes for the ferries bound for the Gulf Islands are to the right of the main terminal building (Vancouver traffic is to the left of it). After leaving the tollbooths, drive to the far right lane and look for a lane that curves off to the right that is signed *Gulf Islands*. Proceed to the lane assigned to you, as printed on your ticket.

Connecting Ferries

If you are traveling between Vancouver and the Pender Islands with a transfer at Swartz Bay, this is called a *throughfare*. Request a *throughfare pass* when you begin your ferry travel, which will save you money. Upon disembarking the ferry, you must (unless you are a foot passenger) exit the terminal. Look for a turnaround lane in the centre median after you pass the tollbooths, and make a U-turn there. If the turnaround is closed, continue to the first exit, McDonald Park/Wain Road. Make the first left to cross over Highway 17. Make a left at the stop sign at McDonald Park Road, which returns to Highway 17, and back to the terminal. You must catch the next avail-able ferry to your destination for the throughfare pass to be valid.

Parking
Swartz Bay terminal has 596 parking spaces available. Call BC Ferries or check their web site for parking availability. Short term parking is $1 for 30 minutes or $12 per day. Pay at the machine and place the ticket on your dashboard. Long term parking is $5.00 for 6 hours or $10 for 24 hours. Payment is space-specific and is made at machines in the parking area or by calling toll free 1.866.277.5446 with a credit card (AE, MC, VI). Machines accept credit cards and cash. After parking, remember your space number and pay for the estimated time needed with either method. Keep your receipt in the event you need to extend your time, which can be done by phone. Using this method, you do not need to display your receipt in the vehicle. To find the parking lot by car, stay in the right lane on Highway 17 as you approach the terminal area, and follow the signs for parking and the passenger terminal, which will take you onto the last exit before the tollbooths. Make a left to go over the highway, then a right to get to the parking lot and terminal.

Passenger Drop-Off and Pick Up
A separate foot passenger terminal is adjacent to the ferry berths, where foot passen-gers for all ferries must go to purchase the required boarding pass. Follow the same directions as to the parking lot, described above. Passengers have the option of checking their luggage here for sailings to Vancouver (but not the Gulf Islands). Tsawwassen-bound passengers board from the second level, while Gulf Islands passen-gers must go downstairs and outside of the building to board. Vending machines and a small snack bar are available. To pick up passengers, you can park in the short-term parking lot and meet them in the *Arrivals* area, then retrieve their luggage outside in the baggage claim area, or you can pick them up from the curb using the free pas-senger loading parking spots. Buses and taxis drop off foot passengers at the Passenger Terminal as well.

TAXI

Take a cab from downtown Victoria or Victoria Airport to Swartz Bay. Call for rates; a typical fare to Swartz Bay is $42 from the Inner Harbour or $16 from the airport. Some local companies include (Area code 250):
Sidney Area:
Peninsula Taxi: 656.1111; **Beacon Taxi/Sidney Taxi:** 656.5588
Victoria:
AAA Airport Taxi: 727.8366; Alpine **Westshore Taxi:** 478.7888;
A-1 Airport Taxi: 389.0090; **Atlas Taxi:** 213.6942; **Ambassador Taxi:** 812.9000;
Blue Bird Cabs: 382.4235; **Concorde Taxi:** 598.5655;
Empress Taxi: 1.800.808.6881, 381.2222; **Esquimalt-Saanich Taxi:** 386.7766;
Global Cabs: 216.7575; **Skyline Taxi:** 881.2429; **Victoria Taxi:** 1.800.842.7111, 383.7111

BUS

At time of writing the options for traveling between Swartz Bay Ferry Terminal and Victoria International Airport include a limited number of public bus runs (Route 70 Airport) and taxi. All other transport methods described below connect Swartz Bay with downtown Victoria. Other options are available using transfers.

Public Transit   The public transit system is **Victoria Regional Transit System** (under BC Transit). For information on schedules and service, contact them at 250.382.6161 or visit their web site at **www.transitbc.com/regions/vic**. To determine the best route from their web site, click on *Maps and Schedules,* and then click on either *Popular Destinations* or a map and the attraction you intend to visit, such as Butchart Gardens. About six trips in each direction run daily between downtown Victoria and the Victoria Airport terminal, with about half of those also connecting with the Swartz Bay Ferry Terminal. Bus routes also connect to points near the other ferry terminals at Victoria Inner Harbour (ferries to Port Angeles, Bellingham and Seattle) and Sidney (Washington State ferry to the San Juan Islands and Anacortes - except for the *70 Via West Sidney* buses). One-way fare between the Swartz Bay Ferry Terminal and downtown Victoria (two zones) is $2.75 for adults, $2.00 for those 18- or 65+. Exact fare is required. Sidney to Swartz Bay (one zone) is $2.00 ($1.25 youth/senior). Children under age six are free. Fares are subject to change. Day Passes can be purchased from a vending machine at Swartz Bay terminal or at outlets in downtown, including Tourism Victoria for $6 ($4 youth/senior). Discounted multi-ticket books are also available. The **Airport Shuttle Bus** described below supplements the BC Transit service.

TIPS ON USING BC TRANSIT TO VICTORIA

BC Transit Travel FROM Swartz Bay Ferry Terminal: Board the *70-Pat Bay Highway* bus upstairs in front of the main passenger terminal arrival/departure area upon disembarking the Ferry. This bus will take you to downtown Victoria. To visit Butchart Gardens transfer in Sidney from the 70 bus to the *75-Central Saanich* bus. The driver can assist you with directions. If a bus is signed *70 Airport* or something similar, it stops at Victoria International Airport along its route. These run during peak travel times. Pick up a free *70/75 Bulletin* for additional information.

BC Transit Travel TO Swartz Bay Ferry Terminal: Board the *70 Pat Bay Highway* bus in downtown Victoria at Douglas north of Belleville, or Douglas at Courtney, Broughton, Johnston or Fisgard. It also stops at all bus stops between Fisgard and the Ferry Terminal. From Butchart Gardens, take the 75 and transfer to the 70 northbound in Sidney. If arriving at Victoria Airport, check the schedule to see if a 70 Airport route bus is available.

Victoria Airport Shuttle Bus   The Airporter runs from various locations in downtown Victoria to the Victoria Airport terminal, but not from the Swartz Bay Ferry Terminal. The Airporter also provides service between the Airport terminal and BC Transit's

McTavish Park and Ride site where transfers can be made to downtown and other public transit destinations such as Swartz Bay Ferry Terminal. The Airporter runs every 30 minutes from approximately 7:00 am to 9:00 pm, with summer hours extended to 4:00 am to midnight. One-way fare between the Airport and downtown is $15.00 ($8 for children 6-12 years). One-way fare from the Airport to BC Transit's McTavish Park and Ride is $2.00. Phone 250.386.2525 for the most current fares.

Pacific Coach Lines (PCL) offers scheduled service from downtown Victoria, leaving from the terminal at Belleville and Douglas, across from the rear of the Fairmont Empress Hotel. Buses leave approximately every two hours. You can ride the PCL bus to the Swartz Bay Terminal, the Tsawwassen Terminal south of Vancouver, Vancouver Airport, or downtown Vancouver. You may have to transfer buses, depending on your destination. The cost from downtown Victoria to Vancouver Airport is approximately $41 per person and includes the ferry tariff. See the section *Getting to the Tsawwassen Ferry Terminal* for further information. **www.pacificcoach.com**, 1.800.661.1725.

Gray Line of Victoria operates between Victoria, Nanaimo, Campbell River and Port Hardy, **www.grayline.ca/Victoria,** 1.800.318.0818.

PRIVATE BOAT

A red government dock is located just to the east (to the left if approaching by boat) of the ferry berth area, where you can dock temporarily to drop off ferry passengers headed to Tsawwassen/Vancouver. Free moorage for up to 4 hours is available, but you may have to raft up. A new float installed in 2004 alleviated the overcrowding situation somewhat. Be aware that vandalism has been a concern here. From the drop-off point, passengers need to walk up Barnacle Road and make a right onto Dolphin Road (with no sidewalks). After about 10 minutes of walking at a steady pace, they will see a pedestrian walkway across from Canoe Cove Road that leads to the ferry ticket booths. From there, they can carefully make their way through the ferry line-up area (use the cross walks) to the passenger terminal on the left to purchase tickets. They should allow at least 20 minutes from the government dock to the passenger terminal. This option may not be a good idea if the passengers have a lot of baggage.
Boaters note: Use extreme caution navigating around this active ferry terminal where ferries move quickly and collisions have occurred. Also, the red-right-return navigation rule does not apply to Swartz Bay ferry terminal area as it is not considered a harbour.

Gas Food and Lodging

Food At the Terminal
You can purchase limited hot items (typically pizza or sausage rolls) and interesting pre-made cold sandwiches and wraps at Swartz Bay terminal while you are waiting. In peak season artisans set up booths adjacent to the terminal building, which may also include food stands that sells smokies, chocolates, and smoked salmon.

Food Near the Terminal

If you have a ferry deadline, always inform the maitre d' before entering and the server before ordering to ensure that they can accommodate you. Even better, call in advance. The closest eating establishments, and the only ones within a reasonable walking distance of the terminal are down Canoe Cove Road. If you are on the way to the ferry, take the last exit before the toll booths (Lands End Road), cross Lands End and take Dolphin Road briefly to the north, then make a quick right on Canoe Cove Road. The **Stonehouse Pub** on the right is a beautiful renovated heritage stone building with outdoor patios that serves very good food for lunch and dinner; 250.656.3498. To walk there from the ferry line-up, carefully make your way out past the tollbooths, to the path on the left. Walk up the path to its end, then carefully cross the street to Canoe Cove Road. As signs indicate, **Stonehouse Pub** is a 5-minute walk from that point, or a total of 10 to 20 minutes from your car in the ferry line-up. Also, at the end of Canoe Cove Road is the **Canoe Cove Marina Coffee Shop**, about 5 minutes further 250.656.5557, serving basic fare for breakfast through lunch.

Sidney is your best bet for getting food to-go for the ferry. For fast food, drive-through service is available at **McDonalds** (if you go east on Beacon Avenue at the traffic light, it is immediately on the left) and **Dairy Queen** (on Bevan Avenue if you veer off to the right at the very first fork). A **Kentucky Fried Chicken** is in the **Safeway** shopping centre down Beacon on the right and **Subway** is on the left in the **Thrifty** centre. Better yet, call in advance for take out at some of the more interesting Sidney restaurants. See *Dining Out - Sidney to Victoria* in Chapter 8: *Nearby Attractions Off Island*.

Fuel

The closest vehicle fuel is in Sidney, at the Mt. Newton X and Beacon Avenue intersections along Highway 17. Both **Shell** stations sell diesel and have similar pricing.

Accommodations

If you missed the last ferry and need overnight lodging, here are some options in nearby Sidney, mostly in the $100-$200 range in peak season:
On Beacon Avenue just east of Highway 17:
Best Western Emerald Isle: 1.800.315.3377
Victoria Airport Travelodge: 250.656.1176
At the end of Beacon Avenue: **Sidney Waterfront Inn**: 1.888.656.1131
At 9724 3rd Street: **Beacon Inn**: 1.877.420.5499
Just south of the Washington State ferry terminal for $110 or less are:
Cedarwood Inn and Suites: 9522 Lochside, 250.656.5551
Driftwood Beach Resort & Motel: 9115 Lochside, 250.656.4419
Also check the website **www.sidneybc.com** for links to the web pages of these accommodations and a list of others in the Sidney area. See also **www.spcoc.org**, the Saanich Peninsula Chamber of Commerce website. The Victoria area has numerous options for budget hotels, especially in the off-season. A favourite of Penderites in downtown Victoria is the **Hotel Douglas** where off-season rates start at $46; 1.800.332.9981.

Ferry Service To The Pender Islands

The most frequent and convenient ferries to the Pender Islands are from Swartz Bay. Swartz Bay is also the terminal for ferries to Vancouver's Tsawwassen terminal, Salt Spring Island's Fulford Harbour, and Mayne, Galiano and Saturna Islands. One can do a day trip of various lengths to the Pender Islands from Swartz Bay, or vice versa. No reservations are accepted on the Swartz Bay to Gulf Island ferries, so arrive at least a half-hour early at peak periods to be assured of a spot. Be aware of ferry substitutions since overflows are more common if a small vessel is substituted. You can sign up with BC Ferries on their web site for email service alerts, as described previously in *Overview, Reservations and Service.*

Most ferries between Swartz Bay and Otter Bay are non-stop and take 40 minutes. Be careful not to choose one that goes to other islands first, which can take 2 to 3 hours to get to Otter Bay

Fares

Travelers are only charged one way, from Swartz Bay to the Pender Islands. Summer 2006 fares are $40.05 round trip for a vehicle with two passengers (plus $2.10 fuel surcharge at time of writing). This breaks down as $25.35 per undersize vehicle, $7.35 per passenger plus surcharges.

LOCALS TIP
If you will be a frequent traveler on the route between the Pender Islands and Swartz Bay, purchase a ticket book of five or ten, which results in a significant savings. These books are not available for the Swartz Bay to Tsawwassen route, or for traveling between Pender Island and the other Gulf Islands. Books cover undersize vehicle only, undersize vehicle and driver, motorcycle or passenger. The books are transferable. The cost of ten-ticket round-trip books in 2006 are $202 for a vehicle with driver, and $48 for passenger only. The per round-trip price equates to about $25 for a vehicle with a driver and one passenger, versus the $40 (plus $2.10 fuel surcharge) regular price.

Ferry Food and Amenities

The refreshment stand on the Queen of Cumberland is typically open, and carries cold pre-made items, although you can have your bread or bagel toasted. They also serve hot dogs on occasion. A large upper view deck is available for sightseeing on beautiful days. The smaller, older Mayne Queen has no snack bar, and may have operational vending machines if you are lucky. It does have a row of work cubicles with *use at your own risk* electrical outlets.

Part Two: U.S. Ferry Services
From Washington to Vancouver Island

Several U.S.-based ferry companies operate runs between the State of Washington and the Victoria area on Vancouver Island, where travelers can then connect to BC Ferries service to the Pender Islands from Swartz Bay. Some services operate only in summer. None of the U.S. ferries dock at Swartz Bay, so if you are not driving you will need to take a bus or cab to make the connection to any BC Ferries destination such as the Pender Islands or Vancouver.

For cyclists, bike routes and trails connect the ferry terminals in downtown Victoria, Sidney and Swartz Bay. See the *Bicycling Guide*. The northern portion of the trail is called the Lochside, and the southern portion is called the Galloping Goose, which continues through Victoria to Sooke. You can therefore take a bike tour from the Olympic Peninsula, Seattle, northwest Washington, or the San Juan Islands, cycle the Saanich Peninsula (Sidney or Victoria to Swartz Bay) on bike trails, and continue to the Pender Islands or the other Southern Gulf Islands. The Lochside Trail begins near the Swartz Bay terminal and skirts the Sidney Terminal (Washington Ferry to San Juan Islands/Anacortes). A spur of the Galloping Goose trail ends in downtown Victoria, about a kilometre from the ferry docks (ferries to Port Angeles, Bellingham, Friday Harbor, and Seattle).

Port Angeles to Victoria

Vehicle Ferry **Blackball Transport, Inc.** operates the **M.V. Coho**, a vehicle ferry that runs all year between Port Angeles, Washington, and downtown Victoria. The ship built in 1957 travels back and forth during the day, more frequently in the summer months, taking about one and a half hours. Fares (Summer 2006), each way, are $42.50 USD for vehicle (up to 18 feet; $3/foot extra for oversize) including driver, plus $11 for passengers in the vehicle or walk-on; bicyclists are $16 USD, and motorcyclists (driver only) are $23. Children 5-11 are half price and under 5 are free. Depending on the season, between two (winter) and four (peak summer) sailings depart each port. Customs is handled upon exiting the ship at either port, although the U.S. Customs also pre-screens everyone leaving Victoria. The Coho's web site is **www.cohoferry.com**. Phone numbers are 360.457.4491 (Port Angeles) and 250.386.2202 (Victoria). At time of writing a new reservation system has been initiated. Non-refundable reservation fees per vehicle are $10 USD ($15 USD roundtrip) if made on line or $15 ($25 roundtrip) via phone (to either office), up to day of travel. The actual ferry tariff is charged upon arrival. Foot passengers can also reserve for no extra charge although the fare is charged in advance. A portion of the ship may remain first come first served for vehicles. If you do not have a reservation, contact them to find out how early to arrive to ensure a spot on the ferry. In the summer the wait is typically several hours ahead of sailing time. In either port you can park your vehicle in the queue area, and then dine or sightsee in the surrounding neighbourhood. In Victoria, however, you need to be back to your vehicle 60 to 90 minutes before sailing due to the U.S. Immigration screening. The crossing can be rough since the Strait of Juan de Fuca is fairly exposed to the Pacific Ocean. You are not permitted to stay on the car deck during the crossing. Food choices aboard the Coho are limited to very basic hot and cold pre-made sandwiches and snacks. In Port Angeles, a great place for breakfast is **1st Street Haven** near Laurel Avenue. You can stay overnight in Port Angeles, park your vehicle on

M.V. Coho docks at Victoria Inner Harbour

line at the ferry terminal early in the morning, and walk over for a hearty breakfast there. An Indian Buffet across from the ferry terminal offers take-out. The Duty Free Shop is in the wharf building. They deliver the goods to your vehicle prior to departure. In Victoria, the terminal is in the Inner Harbour area, so with sufficient time, you have endless dining options. An Internet café is across the street from the terminal. The harbour area has subscription wi-fi service available.

Passenger Ferry **Victoria Express** operates a summer-only ferry between Victoria and Port Angeles that takes one hour. Either two or three sailings are scheduled each day. Summer 2006 fares are $12.50USD each way plus $5USD for bicycles or kayaks. Canada: 250.361.9144; U.S: 360.452.8088; 1.800.633.1589; **www.victoriaexpress.com**

Friday Harbor, San Juan Island to Victoria

Passenger Ferry **Victoria Express** (described above) began a new summer service between Victoria and Friday Harbor (San Juan Island, Washington) in 2004. Fares are $35USD each way with no extra charge for bicycles or kayaks. One sailing per day leaves Victoria in the morning, docking in Friday Harbor 2.5 to 3 hours later. The boat returns to Victoria in the afternoon.

Seattle to Victoria

Passenger Ferry **Victoria Clipper** provides year-round passenger-only ferry service between Seattle and Victoria Inner Harbour, offering regularly scheduled service and tour packages. The high-speed catamaran takes two hours if non-stop or three hours if it stops in the San Juan Islands. Peak (2006) round trip fares are $100 - $140 USD; **www.victoriaclipper.com.** Phone 206.448-5000 (Seattle), 250.382.8100 (Victoria) or 1.800.888.2535 (elsewhere). If you fly into SeaTac airport, you can taxi (about $32USD) or take Bus 194 then transfer to Route 99 Trolley to the Pier 69 slip ($1.50/1 hour).

Anacortes to Sidney (North of Victoria)

Vehicle Ferry **Washington State** Department of Transportation (WDOT) Department of Ferries operates this route; **www.wsdot.wa.gov/Ferries**. General Schedule Info and Reservations in Seattle: 206.464.6400; From Washington State: 511; 1.888.808.7977 (toll free) or 206.464.6400. Washington Automated Info Line: 1.800.843.3779.

Anacortes is about a 90-minute drive north of Seattle. Sidney is a 10-minute drive to the Swartz Bay ferry terminal that services the Pender Islands. The summer 2006 fare is $49.50 USD each way for a car with driver plus $14.70 per additional passenger. Vehicles that are 20 feet or greater in length are subject to a significant surcharge. Summer reservations (on line or by phone) are recommended.

This ferry stops at two U.S. San Juan Islands, Orcas Island and San Juan Island (Friday Harbor) and takes about three hours. The ferries between Anacortes and the San Juan Islands are frequent and sail year round. The Anacortes to Sidney route typically has two sailings each way in the peak summer season, one sailing in the shoulder seasons, and does not operate January through March. One of the summer sailings is an express that takes only two hours. Note that WDOT has promised to cut back service on this route due to funding issues. The crossing to Sidney may be discontinued by 2009, possibly replaced by a private service. Check for current schedules, fares and status of the ferry in advance. It is generally more expensive than its BC Ferry counterparts, although they have recently been offering significant discounts to RV's and buses. The crossing is very beautiful, traversing numerous San Juan Islands. In the past there has been a snack bar on board, however the current information from their web site indicates that only vending machines are available. There is a duty-free shop on the ferry (check before hand to verify that it will be open), and alcohol prices are significantly lower than in Canada. Canadian customs are in Sidney upon exiting the vessel. U.S. customs checks include a preliminary interview and ID check in Sidney, and a customs check upon arrival in Anacortes.

Once you arrive inside the gates of the Sidney ferry terminal for your sailing to Anacortes, you are not permitted to leave again, even on foot, due to U.S. Customs requirements. Inside the terminal is a small souvenir shop with snack bar that accepts credit cards and Interac (ATM).

In the past, only the Anacortes terminal accepted credit cards for the ferry fare, while the Sidney, BC and San Juan Islands terminals accepted only US or Canadian cash. At time of writing the WDOT web site states the Sidney terminal now accepts credit cards. Check for the current policy. Also, WDOT is much pickier about measuring and charging for overlength vehicles than their BC Ferries counterparts. You can calculate your actual fare on their website.

Other Washington State ferry routes create shortcuts across Puget Sound between the Seattle area and the Olympic Peninsula, including Whidbey Island - Port Townsend, and Seattle - Bremerton. See **www.wsdot.wa.gov/Ferries** for details on these sailings, and the *Port Angeles to Victoria,* heading, above, for details on the ferries to Victoria.

PORT AMENITIES

Anacortes Accommodations near the Anacortes terminal include a host of hotels and restaurants in the central part of town along Commercial Street, about a 10-minute drive to the ferry terminal. The **Ship Harbor Inn** is a pleasant hotel with water views that is just two blocks from the terminal; 360.293.5177. The 387-metre (1,270-foot) Mount Erie, five miles south of town via Heart Lake and Mount Erie Drives, offers spectacular vistas of the Olympic and Cascade Mountains and the San Juan Islands. The town of La Conner, located 30 minutes south of Anacortes, is worth checking out with its restored heritage riverside street full of restaurants and shops.

Sidney Since the Sidney sailing is later in the morning, one can easily stay in Victoria, and drive the 20-30 minutes to the terminal the following morning, or stay in peaceful and quaint Sidney-By-The-Sea. See the *Swartz Bay Ferry Terminal* section for information on Sidney accommodations. Most are within walking distance to restaurants, including several along the waterfront, and stores, which include large **Safeway** and **Thrifty** supermarkets. Sidney is known for its many independent bookshops. In summer, Beacon Avenue is closed for a large street market, 5:00 - 9:00 pm Thursdays.

Bellingham to Victoria and the San Juan Islands

Passenger Ferry **Victoria-San Juan Cruises** operates between Bellingham, Washington, the San Juan Islands and Victoria. One boat makes the 3-hour trip each day, mid-May to mid-October, leaving Bellingham at 9:00 am and leaving Victoria at 5:00 pm. Cruise-only adult fares are about $69 - $89 round trip. An optional evening buffet is available. From I-5 in Bellingham take exit 250, Old Fairhaven Parkway. Head west to *Alaska Ferry/Fairhaven Terminal*; **www.whales.com**, 1.800.443.4552, 360.738.8099.

Pender Water Taxis

Gulf Islands Water Taxi transports Pender Island children from the Port Washington Dock to High School on Salt Spring Island during the school term, and is also available to the general public ($25 round trip) if there is room. In summer they service Mayne, Galiano, and Salt Spring Islands. Pender Islands summer service was discontinued due to poor turnout; 250.537.2510, **www.saltspring.com.watertaxi/**

Sound Passage Adventures, based out of Port Browning Resort, began operation in 2004, and offers water taxi service between Sidney, Poets Cove Resort and Port Browning Resort. They also offer excursions to nearby islands, as well as fishing and diving trips; 629.3920, 1.877.629.3930, **www.soundpassageadventures.com**.

Car Rentals

No car rentals are available on the Pender Islands at time of writing. If you are flying in, some rental car options near the Vancouver and Victoria airports are listed below. For additional locations, such as downtown Vancouver or Victoria, you can contact some of the major companies by toll free number or on-line, also listed in the following:

Victoria (Area Code 250)
At Airport **Avis:** 656.6033; **Budget:** 953.5300; **Hertz:** 656.2312; **National:** 656.2541
Off Airport (Sidney) **Thrifty:** 2280 Beacon, 656.8804; **Discount,** 2440 Bevan 657.2277

Vancouver (Area Code 604)
At Airport **National:** 273.3121; **Alamo:** 231.1400; **Hertz:** 606.3781; **Avis:** 606.2847
Thrifty: 606.1655; **Dollar:** 279.0045; **Budget:** 668.7000
Off Airport (Richmond): **Enterprise:** 303.1117; **Discount:** 207.8180

Web Sites and Toll Free Reservation Lines
Avis: www.avis.com, 1.800.272.5871
Hertz: www.hertz.ca, 1.800.263.0600
National: www.nationalcar.ca, 1.800.CAR.RENT, 1.800.522.9696
Budget: www.budget.com, Canada: 1.800.472.3325; U.S: 1.800.527.0700

Air Travel

The most convenient way to get to Pender Island, if you are not renting a car and have a way to get around the island, is to fly into Vancouver International Airport (YVR), and connect to a floatplane from YVR's South Terminal to Pender Island. The most convenient airport if you are renting a car is Victoria International Airport (YYJ), since the ferry service is much better from Victoria to Pender Island than from Vancouver. YVR offers many more airline options than YYJ, and generally lower fares as well. If you are using airline miles, however, it probably takes the same number of miles to fly out of Victoria as Vancouver, although availability may be quite limited. From YYJ to the U.S. the only non-stop option at time of writing is Horizon Air to Seattle or occasional flights by Delta to Salt Lake City and Harmony Air to Hawaii.

Major Airlines and Destinations

Check YVR's (Vancouver Airport) website **www.yvr.ca** for a summary of all airlines that fly into YVR. You can also search by destination. The general information number is 604.207.7077. Vancouver Airport offers email notifications to home or cell phones for delayed or cancelled flights. YYJ's (Victoria Airport) website **www.cyyj.ca** contains a link to the airlines that service that airport. The general inquiry number is 250.953.7500.

AIRLINE SERVICE FROM YYJ (VICTORIA) AND YVR (VANCOUVER)
See also *Destinations* at www.yvr.ca

Air Canada 1.888.247.2262, www.aircanada.ca, YVR, YYJ: Worldwide
Air China 604.685.0921, www.airchina.com.cn, YVR: Beijing
Alaska Airlines 800.252.7522, www.alaskaair.com, YVR: Anchorage, Las Vegas,
  Los Angeles, Palm Springs, Portland, San Francisco, Seattle
Aloha Airlines 1.800.367.5250, www.alohaairlines.com, YVR: Honolulu
All Nippon Airways 1.888.422.7533, www.ana.co.jp, YVR: Osaka/Kansai, Tokyo
American Airlines 1.800.433.7300, www.aa.com, YVR: Chicago, Dallas
America West 1.800.235.9292, www.americawest.com, YVR: Las Vegas,
  Los Angeles/LAX, Phoenix
British Airways 1.800.247.9297, www.british-airways.com,
  YVR: London/ Heathrow
Cathay Pacific 604.606.8888, www.cathaypacific.com, YVR: Hong Kong,
  New York/JFK
China Airlines 604.682.6777, www.china-airlines.com, YVR: Taipei
Continental Airlines 1.800.231.0856, www.flycontinental.com,
  YVR: Houston, Newark
Delta Airlines 1.800.221.1212 www.delta.com YVR: Atlanta, Salt Lake City
Harmony Airways 1.866.868.6789 www.harmonyairways.com, YYJ: Honolulu,
  YVR: Honolulu, Kahului, Las Vegas, Palm Springs, Toronto
Horizon Air 1.800.547.9308 www.horizonair.com, YYJ: Seattle;
  YVR: Portland, Seattle
Japan Airlines 1.800.525.3663 www.japanair.com, YVR: Tokyo, Mexico City
KLM 1.800.447.4747 www.klm.nl, YVR: Amsterdam
Lufthansa 1.800.563.5954, www.Lufthansa-ca.com, YVR: Frankfurt, Munich
Mexicana 1.800.531.7921, www.mexicana.com, YVR: Mexico City
Northwest Airlines 1.800.225.2525, www.nwa.com, YVR: Minneapolis, Detroit
United Airlines 1.800.241.6522, www.ual.com, YVR: Chicago, Denver, Seattle,
  San Francisco
Western Express Airlines 1.877.293.7839, www.westex.ca, YVR: Masset, Tofino
WestJet 1.800.538.5696, www.westjet.ca, YVR, YYJ: Most major Canadian cities

Float Planes To The Pender Islands

Float plane carriers and their service to the Pender Islands have changed over the years, and the following are the carriers that serve the Pender Islands at time of writing. They will not stop at any particular island unless it has been arranged in advance. The planes typically serve all of the Gulf Islands, so you may have to make multiple stops along the way. Find out in advance about luggage restrictions and/or supplemental charges for excess baggage.

North Pender Island to Vancouver Airport YVR

Seair offers float plane service year round between the Port Washington government dock on North Pender Island and the South Terminal at Vancouver International Airport (YVR). Seair provides a free shuttle to the main terminal (call to verify). One-way fare: Approximately $80. About 3 daily departures; must reserve in advance. They also offer charter service.
604.273.8900, 1.800.447.3247.
www.seairseaplanes.com

South Pender Island to Vancouver Airport YVR or Downtown Vancouver

Harbour Air provides service during March – September between Bedwell Harbour (Poets Cove) and downtown Vancouver (2 or 3 flights daily, $74+tax each way), or Vancouver Airport (YVR) South Terminal (1 or 2 departures daily, $69+tax each way). No shuttle is provided to the main airport terminal, which is a 10-minute taxi ride away; www.harbour-air.com. Victoria: 250.384.2215, Vancouver: 604.274.1277.

South Pender Island to Seattle (Summer Only)

Kenmore Air provides floatplane service to Bedwell Harbour (Poets Cove) on South Pender Island from Lake Union, Seattle, when the Bedwell Harbour Customs dock is open during May through September. One afternoon flight daily, $291 USD roundtrip; www.kenmoreair.com. Seattle: 425.486.1257, toll-free: 1.866.435.9524.

Pender Island Airstrip and Helipad

Hastings Airstrip is a lightly used private grass landing strip located just north of the Driftwood Centre on Bedwell Harbour Road. Private aviators and charter services use the airstrip after gaining permission from its owner, Earl Hastings. A heliport used by medevac helicopters is also located at the airstrip.

Arriving by Private Boat

See the *Boating Guide* for a description of anchorages and the public marinas on the Pender Islands: Otter Bay, Port Browning, and Poets Cove. In summer months, reservations may be required for all the marinas. Once docked at the marinas, shuttle service may be available to the Driftwood Centre for supplies (check before arriving) or other locations. A taxi service may also available. See *Getting Around the Pender Islands* below. An unmanned Canada Customs dock is open adjacent to the Poets Cove Marina from May through September. When that facility is closed, boaters coming from the U.S. (without CANPASS permits) must first check in at open stations, such as Port Sidney Marina or Van Isle Marina in Sidney. CANPASS permit holders (if everyone on board is a CANPASS member) can check in at either Poets Cove or Port Browning marinas year round. A marine fuel dock is located at Poets Cove Marina (Bedwell Harbour). The next closest fuel docks in the Southern Gulf Islands are at Ganges and Fulford Harbours on Salt Spring Island, the CRD Dock at Miners Bay on Mayne Island, Lyall Harbour on Saturna Island, or Montague Harbour on Galiano Island. Fuel docks in the Swartz Bay/Sidney area on Vancouver Island are north of Port Sidney, and include Van Isle Marina (at the customs dock), North Saanich Marina, and Canoe Cove Marina. Gulf Islands fuel costs are typically higher than those on Vancouver Island or in the U.S.

Getting Around the Pender Islands

Transportation
Most visitors come to the Pender Islands via ferry with their automobile, and others on bicycle or on foot. Many arrive by private boat or float plane service. Since there is no public transportation on the Pender Islands, most pedestrians either have left a car near the ferry terminal, have arranged for a ride, or hitch hike. See maps on next page.

Rental Cars
At time of writing, there are no car rental services on the Pender Islands. The closest place to rent a car is at Victoria Airport. See the *Car Rental* section for rental agencies serving Victoria and Vancouver airports.

Taxi
Pender Island Taxi & Tours Ltd. began operations in 2004 with two Land Rovers in its fleet; 629.3555. Fares are $5.00 trip fee plus $1.50 per kilometre, or approximately $20 to Magic Lake or $30 to Poet's Cove Resort from the ferry terminal. Always call in advance before arriving on Pender to make sure a taxi service will be available.

Tours
Pender Island Taxi and Tours offers island tours; 629.3555. **Poets Cove Resort** offers tours through its activities department, available to the general public. 629.2100.

Shuttles
Otter Bay Marina has offered its guests shuttle service to the golf course, **Islanders** restaurant, and Driftwood Centre in the past, but this is not a guaranteed service, so call in advance. **Tru Value Foods** at Driftwood Centre has offered free summer shuttle service back to Port Browning Marina with $25 minimum purchase. **Poets Cove Resort and Marina** offers shuttle services to its guests to most locations for a fee; 629.2100. See also the *Boating Guide - Marinas*. Accommodations may provide transportation to or from various docks or Pender destinations. See the *Accommodations Guide*.

Bicycle
Although there are no bike lanes and plenty of hills, many folks choose to ride their bikes around the Pender Islands. See the *Bicycling Guide* regarding rentals and routes.

NORTH PENDER ISLAND

SOUTH PENDER ISLAND

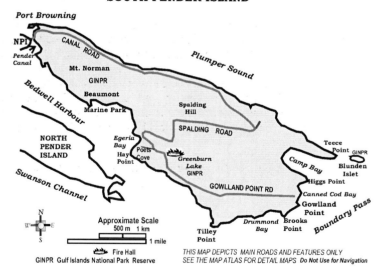

4   ACCOMMODATIONS GUIDE

PENDER LODGING & CAMPING

The Pender Islands contain two resorts, one new and luxurious, and the other a Pender classic. Several Inns and numerous bed and breakfasts are located throughout the islands. In addition, a multitude of private cottages, homes and two resort compounds are available for rent. These are not described here, but agencies that represent them are listed at the end of this chapter. Primitive camping is also available with access by car or boat. Map references are provided to locate the accommodations and campgrounds in the *Map Atlas*. Information regarding off-island accommodations near ferry terminals is found in Chapter 3 - *Travel Guide*. Additional information is found in Chapter 8 - *Nearby Attractions Off Island*.

Resorts, Inns and B&Bs

To obtain the information for the *Accommodations Guide*, a questionnaire was sent to innkeepers and resorts on the Pender Islands. Of these, 16 completed the questionnaire and are included. The facilities were not inspected, and they did not pay to have their listings included. The information is current as of Winter 2006. The properties known to be for sale are noted on the appropriate listings. The names of the hosts (typically owners of B&B's or Inns) and managers are included for reference, since aspects of the lodgings may change along with changes in ownership or management.

The accommodations are listed according to their location. All but two of the accommodations are on North Pender Island, as indicated. The survey revealed that there is a scarcity of wheelchair-accessible accommodations, as only **Poets Cove Resort** and one room in **Sahalli Serenity B&B** are fully accessible, and **Ferndale on Pender B&B** is partially accessible. Pets fare better, with half of the accommodations stating that they will accept pets, some with conditions. For gay and lesbian travelers, a *Gay-friendly Accommodations* list is found in the *Wedding Guide - Same-Sex Weddings* subheading. Of the 16 accommodations completing the survey, 12 requested to be placed on the list.

Price Range: $ <100 $$ 100-199 $$$ 200-299 $$$$ 300-399 $$$$$ 400 +

Hope Bay Area

The charming northeast sector of North Pender Island features bucolic farmland and scenic ocean coves with several public beach access points. The new Hope Bay Store contains a waterfront restaurant open for all meals, galleries and shops. One accommodation is operating here, on the waterfront. The historic **Corbett House** has occasionally been operated as a B&B, but not at time of writing. **Map 1C.**

OCEANSIDE INN $$ - $$$
Open April to October
Box 50, 4230 Armadale Road, North Pender Island, BC V0N 2M0.
From Clam Bay Rd, turn onto Coast Shale Rd then left on Armadale Rd.
Phone: 629.6691; Toll free 1.800.601.3284; Hosts: Bill & Maggie Rumford.
Email: Oceanside@penderisland.com, Web site: **www.penderisland.com**
Located on high bank forested waterfront with beach access.
Four rooms with private baths, all non-smoking (no smoking on entire property).
Views are to the ocean. Refurbished in 2003. Each room has private patio with hot tub, CATV, hair dryer, bathrobe, bar fridge; 2 have VCR's. No phone or Internet.
Common room has computer with cable Internet access.
Meals included: Gourmet breakfast in oceanfront dining room.
Typical Clientele: Couples. No children: Age 18+ only. No pets.
No wheelchair access. No transportation provided. Not a wedding venue.
Terms: Rates: $159-$239; 2-night minimum or $20 surcharge.
Reservation deposit: 50%; Penalty: (call); Payment: VISA, MC, debit.
Notes: Canada Select 4 stars; Beautiful waterfront acreage on Navy Channel;
Walk to Hope Bay (1 km). Short walk to Bricky Bay ocean access.

Otter Bay Area

Two waterfront B&B's and one wellness retreat are located on MacKinnon Road north of the Otter Bay ferry terminal. During the summer, orcas frequently swim past this area in Swanson Channel, creating a flurry of excitement. **Islanders** Restaurant is located near the B&B's, and **The Stand** burger stand is at the ferry dock (see the *Dining Guide*). Bicycle and scooter rentals may be available at Otter Bay Marina near the ferry terminal. **The Pender Island Golf Club** is located about 1.5 - 2 km from the B&B's. **Map 1A.**

SUN RAVEN WELLNESS RETREAT AND B&B $-$$
Open All Year
1356 MacKinnon Road, North Pender Island, BC V0N 2M1
From the ferry terminal, turn left on MacKinnon Road, and look for the *Sunraven* sign on the right in about 40 yards. Follow the long paved driveway up the hill to the B&B on the right. Host: Chris Poellein
Phone: 629.6216; **www.sunrvaven.com**; info@sunraven.com.
Located on south facing Dent Hill just north of the Otter Bay Ferry terminal.
Two ocean-view non-smoking guest rooms with private entrance, last refurbished 2003 - 2005. Large ocean-view common room with wood stove, library, TV, phone, stereo, fridge, hot plate, toaster. No Internet. Breakfast is included. Outdoor pool, sauna, walking trails with benches. Typical Clientele: Nature lovers, holistic minded with a touch of spirituality. Only children who can swim are allowed due to unfenced pool. No

pets. No wheelchair access. Can be used as a wedding venue. Transportation provided to and from ferry or floatplane dock.

Terms: Rates Per Room: $120 per night (min stay 2 nights) or $500 for 5 nights. Deposit required with cancellation penalty. Accepts cash, traveler's cheques.

Notes: Staff helps you experience wellness for your body, mind and soul. Assists in arranging for kayak or orca-watching trips, spa, fitness workout. Reiki treatment available. Offers *self-catered* stays. Free accelerated learning programs for 5+ night stays.

BEAUTY REST BY THE SEA B&B $$

Open April to October

1301 MacKinnon Road, North Pender Island, BC V0N 2M1

Left from the ferry terminal about 1 km to end of the road.

Phone: 629.3855; beauty@penderisle.com; **www.penderisle.com**,

Hosts: Barry & Norah Jean Lynd. Occupies beautiful James Point, high and low-bank waterfront on a prime property along summer orca route.

Three non-smoking rooms, private baths; Views to ocean (southwest). In rooms: Coffee maker, fridge, private balcony, wi-fi signal. No phone. Rooms refurbished in 1999.

Full breakfast included.

Common room/area: Phone/Internet, satellite TV, solarium, reading room.

Typical Clientele: Couples 40-70. Not a wedding venue.

Infants and older children only. No pets. No wheelchair access.

Transportation provided to Otter Bay Ferry Terminal within reason.

Terms: Rates $140-$150/couple/night; 2-night minimum stay; Shoulder season discounts. Reservation deposit: VISA. Payment: VISA, cheque, cash.

ARCADIA-BY-THE-SEA $$

Open Victoria Day to September

1329 MacKinnon Road, North Pender Island, BC V0N 2M1

Left from the ferry terminal; proceed about 500 m to property on the left.

Phone/fax: 629.3221; 1.877.470.8439. Hosts: Peter & Tessa Emmings,

peterortessa@arcadiabythesea.com; **www.arcadiabythesea.com.**

Situated on 4 acres of accessible medium bank Swanson Channel waterfront.

Three non-smoking cottages with private baths; Views to ocean.

In cottages: Kitchen, TV/VCR available. No phone or Internet. Cottages refurbished at various times during last 10 years. Common room/area features: Tennis court, hot tub, heated pool, shuffleboard. Orca-watching and beachcombing.

No meals included. Typical Clientele: Couples, some groups.

No children, except for group bookings. No pets. No wheelchair access.

Not a wedding venue. Transportation provided to Otter Bay Marina and Ferry.

Terms: Rates: $132 to $186; Discount for singles, longer stays.

50% deposit/cancellation penalty. Payment: VISA, MC, cheque, cash.

Note: BC Accommodations approved.

CURRENTS AT OTTER BAY

The quarter-share ownership vacation home development constructed during 2005-2006 around the Otter Bay Marina will have accommodations available for rent to the general public starting July 2006. Many are waterfront units with views out to Otter

Bay and across to Roe Islet, the ferry terminal, and Swanson Channel. Facilities include two swimming pools. Specific rental information was not available at time of writing. Check their website **www.otterbay.ca** or call 629.2150. *Note:* This new accommodation did not complete the information survey completed by the other accommodations.

Central Area
Downtown Pender Island is where you'll find The Driftwood Centre, hub of island activities, with a supermarket, restaurants, shops and most services. Three diverse accommodations in the area include a B&B in the hills, an Inn with dinner restaurant along the main road and a rustic resort with a pub and marina on the beach at Port Browning. **Maps 5, 5B.**

EATENTON HOUSE BED & BREAKFAST INN $ - $$
Open All Year
4705 Scarff Road, North Pender Island, BC V0N 2M1. **Map 5.**
Continue south past Driftwood Centre to Scarff Road. Inn is up hill on left.
Situated on hilltop in forest with view to ocean. Host: William Childs
Phone: 629.8355,Toll Free: 1.888.780.9994, Fax 629.8375
Email: eatenton@penderislands.com; Website: **www.penderislands.com**
Three non-smoking rooms with ensuite baths, refurbished 2000, views to forest.
In rooms: Silk robes, hair dryer, Cable TV, VCR. No phone or Internet.
Common room/area features include panoramic view over forest to ocean (about 300 m away), outdoor hot tub. Two-course hot breakfast included.
Typical Clientele: Mixed. Children over 12 only. No pets.
No wheelchair access. No transportation provided. Not a wedding venue.
Terms: Rates $95 - $135; Prefer 2-night minimum. Reservation deposit: VISA.
Room payment: VISA, cheque, cash.
Nearest ocean access is Hamilton Beach and Medicine Beach within 1.5 km.
Note: Featured in New York Times and Los Angeles Times travel sections.

THE INN ON PENDER ISLAND $-$$
Open All Year
4709 Canal Road, North Pender Island V0N 2M1 Mail: Box 72 Pender Island V0N 2M0
Located south of Driftwood Centre adjacent to GINPR Prior Centennial Campground.
Map 5. Set in forest. Owner: Dave Dryer. *For sale at time of writing.*
www.innonpender.com, 629.3353, Toll Free 1.800.550.0172, Fax 629.3167
Nine rooms and 3 cabins, all non-smoking and with private baths, refurbished 1999.
Views to forest. In room/cabins: Cable TV, VCR; Cabins have partial kitchenette, hot tubs, fireplace. No phone or Internet. Lodge rooms share large hot tub on deck.
Meals not included. **Memories** restaurant on the premises (See the *Dining Guide*).
Typical Clientele: Mixed. Children and pets are allowed. No wheelchair access.
No transportation provided. Not a wedding venue.
Terms: Rates: $79-$99 lodge; $149 cabins. Deposit required, 14 days cancellation.
Discount: Off season; Payment: VISA, MC, debit, cash.
Nearest ocean access is Hamilton Beach and Medicine Beach within 1 km.
Notes: BC Tourism Approved, Canada Select 3 stars (room) 3 1/2 stars (cabin).

PORT BROWNING RESORT $
Open All Year
4605 Oak Road (off Hamilton Road), North Pender Island V0N 2M1
From Driftwood Centre, south to Hamilton Road. **Maps 5, 5B.**
Phone: 629.3493, Fax 629.3495. Manager: Kerry Thompson
Email: portbrowning@cablelan.net, **www.portbrowning.com**
Situated at Port Browning with low-bank waterfront.
Three rooms with shared baths, TV, common area with full kitchen; Two cabins with private baths, TV, kitchenette. No phone or Internet. Smoking OK.
Last refurbished in 1998. Views southeast to Port Browning.
Typical clientele: Mixed. Children and pets are allowed. No wheelchair access.
Meals not included. Available as wedding venue.
Resort facilities: Pub, café, tennis court, swimming pool, playing field, marina, located on Hamilton Beach. 10-minute walk to Driftwood Centre.
Terms: Rates: $50 rooms; $80 cabins. No deposit or minimum stay.
Discount: Extended stay; Payment: Visa, MC, Debit, Cash.
Transportation available by request to various points. Also, water taxi to Poets Cove Resort and Sidney via Sound Passage Adventures, who also does fishing, diving, eco tours and excursions.
Note: Resort is for sale at time of writing.

Magic Lake Estates
The Pender Islands' *neighbourhoo*d is where the majority of its residents live. It is a scenic area with forested hillsides, serene lakes and picturesque seaside parks. The popular Golf Island Disc Park is located here, and tennis courts are also available for a fee. Several B&B's are in this area and are listed below. The closest food provisions are located 1.5 km from the entrance to the subdivision. **Maps 4, 4A, 4B.**

BETTY'S B&B $-$$
Open All Year
4711 Buccaneers Road, Pender Island, BC V0N 2M2; Hosts: Tom & Betty Smith
Follow signs from ferry to Magic Lake. Follow Schooner to the left at the entrance to Magic Lake Estates and make the first left on Buccaneers. B&B is on the right. **Map 4.**
Phone: 629.6599; **www.gulfislands-accom.com.** Email: bettysb-b@direct.ca
Located in residential neighbourhood on the shore of Magic Lake.
Two rooms with large shared bath and large common room. Views to garden/lake or garden/ball field. No smoking. Common room has DVD & VCR with video library, books, fridge and electric kettle. Dial-up Internet access.
Elaborate English garden on lake side of property. Rowboat available to access swim float. Four high-quality mountain bikes available to explore the byways.
Breakfast included with choices of hot items. Free pickup from ferry.
Children over 12 allowed. No pets. No wheelchair access. Not a wedding venue.
Terms: Rates $115 high season, 1 or 2 persons; $90 - $100 Oct - April.
Deposit (Visa); Penalty to cancel. Payment: Visa, cash, cheque, traveler's cheque.
Notes: BC Accommodations approved; Near Catholic Church and trailhead to Golf Island disc golf course (10 minute walk).

FERNDALE ON PENDER B&B $-$$
Open All Year
2711 Privateers Road, North Pender Island, BC V0N 2M2. **Map 4A.**
Host: Carol Hoffmann
From the entrance to Magic Lake Estates, turn left on Schooner Way, right on Privateers Road, and proceed about 1 km, just past Brigadoon to B&B on the left.
Phone: 629.6810, **www.gulfislandsguide.com/accommodation/ferndale-BB.html**
Email: ferndale@cablelan.net
Situated in a forested residential area with views over trees to the ocean.
Three rooms: Two with king bed/ensuite bath, one with queen bed, private bath. All non-smoking. Views toward ocean or to garden. Rooms refurbished in 2005.
In rooms: tea/coffee maker with selection of teas, bar fridge, cable TV, DVD/VCR. No phones. Common areas: Large fenced yard, patio with barbeque and ocean view, guest lounge with TV overlooking garden and cable Internet access, treatment room for reiki, massage, reflexology (fee).
Breakfast included: Choose English or continental; with fresh fruit & muffins. Children are allowed by arrangement. Pets welcome. No transportation provided.
Some wheelchair access (call). Available as a wedding venue.
Terms: Rates $115 year-round; no minimum stay. Reservation deposit $50 with Visa (non-refundable). Payment: Visa, cheque, cash.
Boat Nook, Thieves Bay Park; disc golf, tennis (fee) all 10-15 minutes walk.

SUNSHINE HILLS B&B $
Open All Year
4723 Captains Crescent, North Pender Island V0N 2M2. **Maps 4, 4B.**
From Magic Lake Fire Hall (Schooner & Ketch), right on Ketch, right on Captains Crescent, B&B at the end on right. Hosts: Putzi & Wim Honig
Phone 629.6497; Email: **sunhills@cablelan.net; www.sunshinehillsbb.com**
Situated on a sunny hilltop in forested residential neighbourhood with nice view to trees and panorama to Olympic Mountains to the southwest.
Two rooms are non-smoking with private baths. One has TV. Views are through trees to ocean (1 km away). No phone or Internet. Home constructed in 2002.
Common area includes deck, room with TV, fridge, microwave, toaster.
European breakfast in fridge. No transportation provided. Not a wedding venue.
Typical Clientele: Mixed. Children are allowed. No pets. No wheelchair access.
Terms: Rates $80-$85. No min stay or deposit. Payment: Cash, traveler's cheque.
Nearest water access: Magic Lake 1.5 km (Swimming hole about 2.2 km).

GNOMES HOLLOW B&B $-$$
Open All Year
4844 Cutlass Court, North Pender Island V0N 2M2. **Map 4.**
From Magic Lake Estates entrance, continue left on Schooner Way past Pirates Road, left on Cutlass Court to the end. Hosts: Dave & Tania Schissler
Phone 629.3844; Email: info@gnomeshollow.com; **www.gnomeshollow.com**
Whimsical establishment situated in forested residential neighbourhood. Three theme rooms, all private bath and entrance, all non-smoking. View to garden with waterfall or forest. Home built in 2001. No TV, phone or Internet in rooms.

Common area includes lounge with fireplace, cable TV, stereo, fridge, hot tub by water-fall in backyard. Full course breakfast included; vegan option.
Typical Clientele: Mixed. Children <2 and >12 only; Pets allowed on approval.
Available as wedding venue: Common room for small reception if party rents all 3 rooms. No wheelchair access. No transportation provided.
Terms: Rates $100 - $110; 2 night minimum summer weekends; Deposit: Half rental; Payment via cash or cheque; Discount: $10 off October 15 to April.
Access to Boat Nook 1.5 km, Magic Lake 1 km (swimming hole 1.5 km)

CEDAR COTTAGE GUEST HOUSE $
Open All Year
4870 Pirates Road, Pender Island, B.C. V0N 2M2 **Map 4.**
Follow signs from ferry to Magic Lake. Left at entrance to Magic Lake Estates, continue on Schooner Way past north end of lake, left on Pirates Road, property is on the left.
Phone: 629-3555; Email: cedarcottage@penderislands.info; **www.penderislands.info**
Hosts: Lorelle and John Roberts
Located in residential neighbourhood on the shore of Magic Lake.
Bachelor style guest cottage with full kitchen, bath, and sunroom. Non-smoking, phone for local calls, CATV, cable Internet (computer available). Refurbished in: 2004. Views to garden. Typical Clientele: Best suited for singles, couples, small families.
Common Area: Lakefront property has Magic Lake access, deck over lake, swim dock. Gas barbeque, canoe and two mountain bikes available.
Meals included: Welcome basket with granola, tea, coffee, fruit, brownies, water and sparkling fruit juice. Emergency pizza in freezer.
Children and pets are allowed. Pets have access to fenced yard. Wheelchair access to all except one step to bathroom and lake access. Not a wedding venue.
Terms: Rates: $200 for two night weekend (minimum); No check in or check out restrictions: Arrive anytime on Friday for two night weekend through dusk Sunday. $525 per week. 30% deposit for weekly booking. Payment via: cash, travelers' cheques, Visa and personal cheques (for Canadian residents).
Transportation: Complimentary taxi ride from ferry or point of arrival on Pender. Other rides are regular rate. Owners operate Pender Islands Taxi & Tours.

Oaks Bluff
This magical perch is situated halfway between the Magic Lake Swimming Hole and the Trincomali neighbourhood on North Pender Island. If you hike up to the 100-meter high Oaks Bluff Park viewpoints, you will get an idea of the spectacular views enjoyed by the two B&B's located in this area, probably the best view from any accommodation on the Pender Islands. One of the B&B's, Sahhali Serenity, is for sale at time of writing. Views are to the south and southwest toward the Gulf Islands, the San Juan Islands, the Victoria area and Vancouver Island, and the Olympic Mountains beyond. Orcas can be seen swimming far below in Swanson Channel on many summer days. You will need transportation to get to beach accesses from these B&B's, as there is no public beach access in the Oaks Bluff area. The nearest ocean accesses are about 3 km away in the Trincomali area. Magic Lake swimming hole is about 2 km away. No restaurants or groceries are within walking distance. (See **N. Pender Index Map**, northwest of **4C**).

DELIA'S SHANGRI-LA OCEANFRONT B&B $$ - $$$
Open All Year
5909 Pirates Road, North Pender Island, BC V0N 2M2
From Magic Lake Estates entrance, follow Schooner Way to Pirates Road and look for
Oaks Bluff sign on right in about 2 km. See web site for detailed directions.
Host: Delia Laurencelle. 629.3808, 1.877.629.2800, Fax 629.3018.
Email: info@penderislandshangrila.com, **www.penderislandshangrila.com**
Situated in rural, high-bank Oaks Bluff waterfront area (No ocean access).
Panoramic views to Olympic Mountains, nearby islands and Vancouver Island.
Three non-smoking rooms with private baths, each has satellite TV, VCR, microwave,
bar fridge, wireless Internet access, fireplace, hot tub, private deck.
Views are ocean panoramas. Rooms refurbished in 2001.
Common room is large size with 360-degree views to the Olympic Mountains, nearby
islands, Vancouver Island, the Vancouver area and North Shore Mountains. Choice of
breakfast included. Typical Clientele: Couples. Children and pets (extra fee) are
allowed. No wheelchair access. Transportation not provided. Wedding venue available
in large common room, on the deck, on the cliff, or elsewhere on property.
Terms: Rates $150 - $220; Deposit: 50% - 100%; Payment: Visa, MC, AmEx, Interac,
Certified Cheque. Discounts: 7th night free, seasonal specials and others.

SAHHALI SERENITY LUXURY OCEANFRONT B&B $$$
Open All Year
5915 Pirates Road, North Pender Island, BC V0N 2M2
From Magic Lake Estates entrance, follow Schooner Way to Pirates Road and look for
Oaks Bluff sign on right in about 2 km. See web site for directions.
Hosts: Penny Tomlin and Wally Skillen; 629.3664, 1.877.625.2583, Fax 629.3667.
Email: sahhali@gulfislands.com; **www.sahhali-serenity.com**
Situated in rural high-bank Oaks Bluff waterfront area (No water access).
Panoramic views to Olympic Mountains, nearby islands and Vancouver Island.
Rooms: Three non-smoking rooms with private baths, each has satellite TV, VCR, mini
microwave and fridge, fireplace, hot tub, private deck; see web site for more. No
phone or Internet access. View to ocean and night-lit quarry pond. Rooms last refur-
bished in 2002. Breakfast included. Common room is a lounge with high bank water-
front panorama. Binoculars, crab pots, canoe, telescope available.
Typical Clientele: Couples. Children over 10 only. Dogs by arrangement (fee). No cats.
Wheelchair access in Bonsai Suite only. No transportation provided.
Swedish massage and light reiki available.
Wedding venue options: On bluff, in gazebo or guest lounge.
Terms: Rates: $295. Deposit required with cancellation penalties.
Payment: Visa, Travelers Cheques, Cash, Money Order, Bank draft.
Discount: Off-season; repeat customers; seniors; and more, see web site.
Notes: Canada Select 4-stars; BC Accommodations Approved.
For sale at time of writing.

South Pender Island

South Pender Island contains some of the best hiking on the Pender Islands at the Gulf Islands National Park Reserve lands containing Mount Norman, Beaumont Marine Park and Greenburn Lake, as well as the beautiful Brooks Point Reserve. The only restaurants on South Pender Island are at **Poets Cove Resort,** which also maintains a small general store. Accommodations on South Pender consist of one high-end resort and a rustic seaside B&B. **Maps 8 and 9.**

POETS COVE RESORT $$$-$$$$$
Open All Year
9801 Spalding Road, South Pender Island V0N 2M3. **Map 8.**
Located where Spalding Road ends at Gowlland Point Road (16 km from ferry).
Phone 629.2100, Toll Free 1.888.512.7638, Fax 629.2105
www.poetscove.com, reservations@poetscove.com. On line reservations available.

Faces west along Bedwell Harbour low-bank waterfront with marina. Lodge Rooms: 22; Cottages: 15; Villas: 9. All have private baths. All non-smoking. Rooms have phone, Internet connection, cable TV, soaker tub, separate shower, open fireplace, balcony with marina and Bedwell Harbour view. Cottages also have 2-3 bedrooms, kitchen, washer/dryer, BBQ, hot tub. Villas also have second level with balcony. Resort was constructed during 2003-2004. Grounds contain a waterfront promenade with waterfall fountain.

Resort contains Aurora Restaurant and Syrens Lounge, marina with small store, two heated pools, tennis, Jacuzzi, fitness centre, Susurrus full service spa (fee), Activities Centre offers boat and bike rentals and excursions. Floatplane dock (Bedwell Harbour) with Canada Customs post (summer only; winter CANPASS station).
Continental breakfast included. Typical Clientele: Mixed. Children allowed.
Pets allowed in cottages and villas only for $25 fee. Wheelchair access available.
Transportation is available to the ferry and various activities for a fee.
Resort is available as a venue for weddings, conventions and conferences.
Terms: Summer Rates: Lodge Rooms $279; Cottages $529-$729; Villas $479-$579.
Deposit required with cancellation penalty; Payment by Visa, MC, AMEX, Interac, cash.
See web site for information on discounts, packages and off-season rates.
Notes: The resort consists of quarter-ownership units that are also rented to the general public when not used by the owners.

WHALEPOINTE STUDIO & B&B $
Open 10 Months/Year
9929 Southlands Road, South Pender Island, BC V0N 2M3. **Map 9**.
From Spalding and Gowlland Point Roads, continue on Gowlland Point Road until Craddock Road; Turn right, and left on Southlands to the end.
Host: Joy McAughtrie; Phone: 629.6155. Situated on south-facing high bank waterfront between Tilley Point and Brooks Point.
Accommodation in separate 2 bedroom non-smoking cottage with shared bath (with shower). Bar fridge, microwave for snacks. Full breakfast included with local eggs and fruit in season. No TV or phone in cottage. Views to garden with ocean glimpse. Beautiful grounds with orca and eagle watching.
Typical Clientele: Quiet couples. Children allowed if supervised. No pets. No wheelchair access. No transportation provided. Not a wedding venue.
Terms: Rates $85/night double; $70/night single. Deposit required, minimum stay 2 nights on long weekends. No walk-ins; reservations only. Payment via cash or cheque. Nearest water access: Craddock Road, a few minutes walk. Studio visits by chance or appointment to Whalepointe Studio, featuring Joy McAughtrie's paintings and drawings reflecting travel influences and island life.

Vacation Rental Agencies

The majority of accommodations on the Pender Islands are non-hosted homes, cottages, or even entire compounds. There are too many of them to list in this book, but you can easily find a variety to choose from on the rental agencies' websites listed below, other Pender Island information websites found elsewhere in this book, or in the Pender Post or Lions Club Phone Directory.

GULF ISLAND VACATION RENTALS, INC. 1.877.662.3414
info@gulfislandvacationrentals.com, www.gulfislandvacationrentals.com
Specializes in short-term vacation rentals on Pender and other Gulf Islands. Also is a rental agent for **Clam Bay Farm** retreat (**www.clambay.com**) and **The Timbers** resort (**www.thetimbers.net**) on North Pender, which are popular for weddings, family reunions, corporate retreats, etc. Both have docks.

ISLAND EXPLORER PROPERTY MANAGEMENT   1.800.774.1417, 250.654.0230
bgerry5@shaw.ca, www.island-explorer.com. Handles short and long term vacation rentals on Pender and other Gulf Islands, including **The Timbers** resort.

BREAKAWAY VACATIONS (BC) LTD 1.800.800.7252;
breakaway@lloydstravel.com, **www.breakawayvacations.com**. Vancouver-based agency lists Pender properties.

VACATION RENTALS BY OWNER
www.vrbo.com
This international service enables homeowners to rent their own properties.

Campgrounds

All campgrounds on the Pender Islands are primitive with no utility hook ups for RVs. Currently, both drive-in and boat-in/hike-in campgrounds are operated by Parks Canada, and a lawn is available for camping at a rustic resort.

GULF ISLANDS NATIONAL PARK RESERVE - PRIOR CENTENNIAL CAMPGROUND
This centrally located drive-in campground is open seasonally, May 15 - October 15. See **Maps 5** and **5A**: Proceed about 2 km south from Driftwood Centre on Canal Road. The fee is $14/night per site ($7 for seniors in shoulder season). Reservations can be made for twelve of the seventeen sites from **www.discovercamping.ca**, which handles BC Parks. Reserve on line or call 1.800.689.9025, or 604.689.9025 in Vancouver. The National Parks campground reservation website may take over this service in the future. If so, reserve on line at **www.pccamping.ca** or call 1.877.737.3783. Additional reservation service fees apply. The seventeen vehicle-accessible sites are set amongst a thick second-growth forest of fern, maple and red alders. Each spacious campsite allows up to a total 45 feet for 1 vehicle and 1 accommodation unit (tent, camper, trailer or motorhome). The campground is primitive, with cold water available only from a single hand pump, but it may have to be boiled before use. There are pit toilets, but no showers, washrooms, or dump station. A campfire ban may be in place during the dry summer season. For current information, consult the Parks Canada website **www.pc.gc.ca/gulfislands**, or phone 250.654.4000.

A hiking trail (**53**) leads from the campground and beyond the National Park boundary to Golf Island Disc Park, about 3 km away. Ocean swimming and kayak launching is available at Medicine Beach approximately 400 meters from the park. Magic Lake is approximately 3 km away (4.5 km to the swimming hole). The **Memories** restaurant at the **Inn on Pender** is located adjacent to the campground and is open for dinner or take-away pizza all through the season that the campground is open. **Magic Lake Market** is located near Medicine Beach. The main Pender Island shopping centre (Driftwood Centre) and **Port Browning Resort and Pub** are both about 2 km away, each with pay showers and a Laundromat.

GULF ISLANDS NATIONAL PARK RESERVE -
SOUTH PENDER ISLAND/BEAUMONT MARINE PARK
See **Maps 6** and **7**. The former Beaumont Provincial Marine Park became part of GINPR in 2004. It occupies 58 hectares (143 acres) on the west shore of South Pender Island, and is contiguous with the former Mount Norman Regional District park, now also part of the GINPR. The campground is primarily reached by boat, although it can also be accessed by a steep hiking trail (**84**) from the Pender Bridge area in less than one hour.

The scenic primitive campground contains 15 campsites and several pit toilets. The water well was shut down in 2006. Fees ($5/person) are charged from May 15 to September 30. Two information boards contain payment boxes. No campfires are allowed in the park year-round. For boaters, access to the campground is available up a set of stairs from the eastern end of the park where there are several campsites and pit toilets. A short trail runs along the shore to the west to a scenic isthmus with twin shell beaches, also a good boat landing spot. Inland from the isthmus are the remaining campsites set in the forest and more pit toilets. Benches and a few picnic tables are also distributed along the trails and in the campground areas. A trail (**82**) continues along the scenic arbutus-fir shoreline, and eventually leads to the summit of 244-metre Mt. Norman and its spectacular vista in about 3.2 km.

If you arrive at the campground on foot, you will need to bring all of your provisions, as no stores or restaurants are located nearby. If you have boated in, you can easily reach **Poets Cove Resort** from the campground, about .5 Nautical Mile (NM) away. Port Browning Resort is also reachable (about 2 NM away), but be aware of strong currents through the Pender Canal. From Port Browning Resort it is a 10-minute walk to the Driftwood Centre, the main

shopping centre on the Pender Islands. Pay showers and laundromats are available at **Poets Cove Resort**, **Port Browning Resort**, and the **Driftwood Auto Centre**. For kayakers, this campground is a good base for exploring the Pender Islands as well as Saturna Island. See the *Boating Guide's Kayaking, Anchorage* and *Boat Launching* sections *and the Coastal Access and Hiking Guide* for further informa-

tion. Also see **www.pc.gc.ca/gulfislands**.

GINPR reminds: This area has been used by First Nations people for thousands of years, and continues to hold much significance for them. Please do not disturb or remove any cultural artifacts, and camp only in designated areas.

PORT BROWNING RESORT
The resort on North Pender Island has a large open lawn/orchard near Hamilton Beach for camping for tents, trailers or campervans. No utility hookups are available. A couple of the tent sites perched atop a hillock next to the water are prime. The fee is $15/night. **Maps 5, 5B**. 629.3493, **www.portbrowning.com**
Note: The resort is for sale at time of writing.

5   DINING GUIDE

RESTAURANTS GROCERIES
FARMS AND WINERIES

Pender Islands Restaurants

The Pender Islands' restaurants have evolved over the years, but there is definitely a trend toward high quality cuisine, and you are likely to have delicious meals while you are on island. Three of the restaurants are at the high or higher end of the price spectrum and serve continental cuisine with interesting flair. A new waterfront café is high quality but casual, a cozy inn serves a variety of entrees, and a pub specializes in fish and chips with nightly specials. The bakery has recently expanded and serves breakfast and lunch items. Good pizza is available from at least two sources. A popular burger stand is located at the ferry terminal, and the casual restaurant at the Golf Course keeps finding new incarnations. Changes may be on the horizon with local businesses, since at time of writing, several properties are for sale.

The cuisine on the Pender Islands can be described as variations on continental Canadian, from basic to gourmet. Ethnic cuisine is mostly limited to occasional dinner specials at the various restaurants. Most Penderites satisfy their cravings for ethnic food in Vancouver or Victoria (See Chapter 8, *Nearby Attractions Off-Island* for Victoria-Sidney area restaurants).

As in all locales, restaurants on the Pender Islands can change ownership, hours, and menu items. There tends to be a lot of turnover in the food services field. Call first to find out what their situation is if you have not been there in a while, or are new to the island. If you are on a schedule, especially with regards to catching a ferry, make sure to ask in advance how long it will take to get served, as some restaurants can be on what is referred to as *On Pender Time*. On busy weekends reservations are a must at many of the restaurants, and a reservation couldn't hurt on any summer evening or winter weekend.

Port Browning Resort's Pub. A Pender Tradition.

Overview

At time of writing, the following describes where to go for your various culinary needs:

Meals Throughout the Day

BREAKFAST options may include **Hope Bay Café, Pender Island Bakery, Port Browning Café, Aurora at Poets Cove Resort** and **The Stand.** On weekends check for **Chippers** and occasionally **Islanders.**
LUNCH spots include **Hope Bay Café, Pender Island Bakery, Pistou Grill, Port Browning Pub (Sh-Qu-Ala Inn)** and **Café,** and **Syrens at Poets Cove.** Other options, which are more seasonal or have limited winter hours are **Chippers, The Stand,** and sometimes **Islanders.**

MID-DAY MEAL OR SNACK options may include **Pender Island Bakery, Syrens at Poets Cove, Port Browning Pub and Café, Chippers, The Stand, Hope Bay Café** and **Tru Value Foods.** Places where you can get a quick take-away sandwich include the **Pender Island Bakery, Moorings Market at Poets Cove Marina, Tru Value Foods,** and new for Summer 2006, the take out stand at the **Hope Bay Café.**

DINNER houses include **Hope Bay Café, Islanders, Pistou Grill, Memories, Port Browning Pub,** and both **Poets Cove** restaurants. **Chippers** may be open for dinner in summer and on select off-season nights. The Legion Hall has special dinner nights, announced in the Pender Post.

Coffee Houses

Espresso Coffee Bars at time of writing are found at **Pender Island Bakery, Hope Bay Café, Otter Bay Marina, Southridge Farms Country Store, Port Browning Resort Café,** and **Moorings Market at Poets Cove Marina. Islanders** advertises to come for coffee and dessert. **Tru Value Foods** serves regular coffee. Pender's own excellent **Moonbeans Coffee** is served at **Hope Bay Café** and the **Poets Cove Resort** restaurants.

Pubs

The pub at the **Port Browning Resort** is the islands' only pub. It features live music on summer weekends, contains the only public pool table on the Pender Islands, and a deck overlooking Port Browning. **Chippers** at the **Pender Island Golf Club** is fully licensed. **Syrens** at **Poets Cove Resort,** South Pender Island, is an imaginatively designed *lounge* and serves beer, wine, ale and cocktails. Views are out to Bedwell Harbour and live music can be heard on many summer weekends.

Prepared Foods

Tru Value Foods at Driftwood Centre makes sandwiches daily that are kept in a cooler next to the deli, but they are not made to order. They also have hot dogs and sausages, fresh whole BBQ chickens (in limited supply), and a small selection of miscellaneous items such as spanikopita and sausage rolls that they can heat for you. The full deli has cold cuts, salads and bulk rolls. Prepared foods can also be found at **Pender Island Bakery, Moorings Market at Poets Cove Marina,** and **Hope Bay Café.**

On the Waterfront

The prize for being closest to the water goes to **Hope Bay Café**, which is perched over Hope Bay at the dock. Other North Pender restaurants with water views include **Islanders, Port Browning Pub**, and **The Stand** take-away at the ferry dock. These eateries also have outdoor patios. On South Pender Island, the **Poets Cove Resort's Aurora** restaurant and **Syrens** lounge have marina/water views and outdoor waterfront patios.

Caterers

Several caterers operate on the island. See the restaurant listings below and also Chapter 7, the *Wedding Guide*.

Restaurant Listings

Listings are from north to south, and are all on North Pender Island except for the **Poets Cove Resort** restaurants, which are on South Pender Island. See the *Pender Islands Map Atlas* for locations of the establishments on the referenced maps.

A la carte entrees: $ Under 10 $$ 10-15 $$$ 15-20 $$$$ 20-30 $$$$$ 30+

HOPE BAY CAFÉ $-$$$$
629.6668
Located at the Hope Bay Dock, north end of Bedwell Harbour Road. **Maps 1, 1C**. This casual dining room is perched over the waters of Hope Bay, and has a small deck for al fresco dining. The dining room is all windows, so you can watch the seals, otters and eagles as you dine. One cozy corner has a fireplace and frequently local musicians perform there. The chefs emphasize home cooking with local ingredients. They are typically open for breakfast, lunch, and dinner, closed one day each  week. Hours vary so check before going. Breakfast includes various egg dishes. The popular a la carte Sunday brunch features various egg bennies. Fresh baked goods are offered all day, including Vanna's famous scones. Beverages include cappuccino, Moonbeans coffee, beer and wine. The Summer 2006 lunch and light dinner menu includes chicken, beef or veggie burgers with fries or salad ($8-$10), and Fish and Chips with cod or salmon ($7- $11). Dinner (served until 9 pm) includes soup or salad, veggies and a starch: Seafood platter for two ($58), Full Dungeness Crab ($28), Wild Salmon ($18), Bouillabaisse ($18), Pork Tenderloin ($17), Half Free Range Chicken ($18), Stuffed Duck Breast ($19), Vegetarian Wellington ($16), Seafood Fettucini Alfredo ($15) and New York Steak ($24). Boaters may be able to pull up to the government dock if there is availability (which is limited), use one of two mooring buoys now available, or

anchor nearby and dinghy in. *Note:* Check your chart for safe anchorage areas. This area can also be very blustery. Call for dinner reservations and latest hours. Off-season brings ethnic nights, and theme parties. Accepts Interac, MC, Visa. *New for 2006* is an ice cream parlour with take-out ice cream, shakes, pre-packaged sandwiches and wraps, canned drinks, and coffee.

ISLANDERS $$$-$$$$ (Dinner) *Georgina is at the Pub now*
629.3929
1325 MacKinnon Rd; Left from ferry terminal, left side, past the Legion Hall. **Map 1A.** georgina@islandersrestaurant.com, **www.islandersrestaurant.com**. Enjoy casual fine dining in their cozy Provence dining room or enclosed summer patio with an ocean and sunset view. They typically post their open hours on a sandwich board across from the Driftwood Centre. Dinner hours have been daily except Tuesday (also closed Wednesdays in winter). They have on occasion also been open for breakfast and lunch. Call for dinner reservations for this popular spot. Off-season special events include guest server night, starving artist dinner and the annual pajama dinner. Examples of Georgina's creative and delicious a la carte selections include Apple Pecan Mixed Green or Spicy Caesar Salad ($7), Seafood Chowder ($8), Curried Butternut Squash Soup ($7), Salmon with Sambal Aoli ($20), New York Steak with Peppercorn Cream Sauce ($22), Seafood Linguini ($20) and Duck Breast with Cranberry Jus ($22). Her Halibut with Horseradish Sauce special is outstanding. A varied selection of wine and dessert (*"come just for desert"*) is available. Islanders also operates **Every Last Crumb Catering**. Check out Islanders website for further information. Accepts Interac, MC, Visa.

PISTOU GRILL $$$-$$$$ (Dinner) $-$$ (Lunch)
629.3131
Driftwood Centre. **Map 5B.** Skilled French Chef Pierre Delacôte offers imaginative gourmet cuisine for lunch and dinner at Pistou Grill. The lunch is a good value, offering delicious sandwiches, memorable soups, salads and daily specials at reasonable prices. Some highlights are the Wild Salmon Burger ($8), Sirloin Tip Hamburger ($7), Lamb Burger with goat cheese and cured lemon ($9.50), Pistou Soup ($6.50) and Smoked Sockeye Salmon Salad ($8). Dinner is typically sumptuous, and features six or seven artistically designed creations to choose from. Appetizer favourites include Grilled Local Lamb & Mint Sausage ($7.50) and Warm Marinated Calamari Salad. Some ala carte entrees include Seared Black Thai Prawns & Scallops in red Thai curry ($22), Braised Shank of Lamb ($21), and Medallions of BC Venaison ($25). A selection of wines and homemade desserts are available. The interior is artsy-bistro, and the summer outdoor courtyard is available for al fresco dining. Restaurant capacity for special events is about 30 persons. Pistou also does catering, and offers an expanded version of the Lunch menu for Dinner take-out from fall to spring. Hours are typically Tuesday through Saturday 11:30 am - 2:30 pm and 5:30 pm - 8:00 pm. Call for dinner reservations. Accepts MC, Visa and Interac.

MEMORIES AT THE INN $$-$$$$
629.3353
Canal Road at **The Inn on Pender Island,** next to Prior Centennial campground, south of Driftwood Centre; **www.innonpender.com, Map 5.** *For sale at time of writing.* Dinner only, open 7 days summer, Wednesday-Sunday rest of year. Closed December through March. The Inn contains a licensed dining room that is open to the public for dinner. It is popular and offers a wide selection. Prices are generally less than Pistou Grill, Islanders and Aurora, and the ambience and food quality are that of a cozy family restaurant. Entrees are mostly a la carte and many include veggies and starch. A few examples are Lasagna (meat or veggie) ($13), Island Chicken ($16), Wild Salmon ($18), Baby Back Ribs ($20) and New York Steak ($23). Add $5- $6 for soup or salad. A wide variety of pizza is offered to eat in or take out, from $8 - $10 small to $18 - $22 large. Their banquet room seats 20-24 persons. Accepts Interac, MC, Visa.

PORT BROWNING RESORT $-$$ 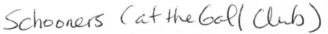 *Georgina is Chel here now*
629.3493
Located at the end of Hamilton Road near Driftwood Centre. **Maps 5, 5B.** *For sale at time of writing.* The café is open for breakfast (most items $4-$8) and lunch and has a summer ice cream stand. The pub (Sh-Qu-Ala Inn) opens for lunch and dinner. The view is out to a bay and marina. It is the only pub on Pender (as Syrens at Poets Cove is a *lounge),* and features live entertainment and dancing on selected evenings and on most summer weekends, the only public billiards table on the Pender Islands, and a deck overlooking Port Browning. Examples of food items are cheeseburger $7, oyster-burger $9, Caesar salad with Louisiana chicken $9, fish 'n chips with cod ($7-$8.50), fried oysters 'n chips with salad $11, and New York Steak $15. Check their web site **www.portbrowning.com** for their full menu and for nightly specials, including Turkey Tuesdays, Pizza Wednesdays, and Roast Beef Sundays. Interac, MC, Visa.

~~**CHIPPERS**~~ $ - $$ *Schooners (at the Golf Club)*
629.6665
Located at the Pender Island Golf and Country Club on Otter Bay Road. **Maps 1, 1A.** This fully-licensed restaurant has a golf-course atmosphere with plain decor inside and a scenic outdoor patio that overlooks the first tee and across most of the course. Summer 2006 hours are expected to be 8am to 8pm everyday; 3pm Sundays. Breakfast incudes a $5.50 special Monday-Saturday until 9:30, Omelettes ($9), and Sunday brunch specials ($7-$12). Lunch includes several types of burgers and sandwiches  ($8- $10), West Coast Chowder ($9), etc. with various sides included. In addition, evening dinner specials are offered in summer. Watch for the nine (golf holes) and dine specials on summer Wednesdays. Interac, MC, Visa.

THE STAND $
629.3292
Located at the Otter Bay ferry terminal. **Map 1A.** Get in the ferry line-up early and enjoy hot sandwiches for breakfast or lunch. They have been written up in BC newspapers for their hamburgers, and they make a good breakfast sandwich. Other items include various seafood burgers, sausages, and ice cream. You can sit on outdoor tables on the waters edge while you watch your ship come in. Allow plenty of time for grilled items though, especially if others are waiting in front of you, since food is made to order. Or, call in advance. You may wonder what happens if the ferry arrives before your food is ready? The closest I came involved running to my car with a dripping burger just as my lane began to board. However, it seems that the more nervous you seem, the slower your food is prepared, so, stay calm! You can also pick up food here and take it to picnic. Try the nearby beach access, 1 km west on MacKinnon Road. Either park in the BC Ferries lot and walk down to *The Stand*, or tell the BC Ferry attendant at the kiosk you are picking up food there, and they will direct you to a traffic lane. Hours vary; reduced in off-season. Cash only. Items range from about $4 to $12.

PENDER ISLAND BAKERY CAFE $
629.6453
Located in Driftwood Centre. **Map 5B. www.penderislandbakery.com**. The latest incarnation of this bakery is sumptuous. They bake top quality breads, rolls, pies, pastries, and sausage rolls on premises, and import items like meat pies and pasties. They carry grilled panini sandwiches, pizza slices, breakfast items including frittatas, and daily specials. They also feature a summer ice cream stand, and make gourmet pizzas to go. A successful 2004 expansion provided indoor table seating, a cappuccino bar, a deli case with gourmet items and an Internet station (fee). Cakes are available made to order. *Also on site:* **Creative Cuisine Catering**. Accepts Interac, MC, and Visa.

POETS COVE RESORT - SOUTH PENDER ISLAND
629.2100, 1.888.512.7638, Fax 629.3212, **www.poetscove.com,**
reservations@poetscove.com, **Map 8.** The resort has two restaurants, described below. The marina store sells sandwiches and other pre-made items. They also have had weekend summer barbeques. *Locals note: Ask for a possible local's discount.*

AURORA $$$$-$$$$$ (Dinner) $-$$ (Breakfast)
629.2115
With an ambience that evokes a cozy yet elegant seaside lodge, Aurora is perhaps Pender Islands' premiere dining room. West Coast Cuisine is served at this second-story restaurant and al fresco terrace overlooking Poets Cove Marina and Bedwell Harbour beyond. Breakfast is served daily 7:00 am - 10:30 am, with items ranging from around $9 to $16 and including omelets, wraps, eggs bennie and French Toast. Dinner is served 5:00 pm - 9:00 pm. At time of writing, a new chef has created a menu for 2006 featuring local ingredients including starters Chili Seared Wild Spring Salmon ($11), Goat Cheese Tart ($10), Clam Chowder ($9) and Watermelon Salad ($8). Entrees include Pender Island Lamb ($35), BC Seafood ($34), Pacific Salmon ($25), Cowichan Bay Chicken ($29), Oxtail with Lobster Tail ($33), and Eggplant Parcel ($22). Gourmet desserts ($9) include Tarte Tatin and Warm Apple Cake. See their web site for further

details and the latest menu. Despite several chef changes during its first couple of years, the food has typically been delicious. Advance reservations are recommended, especially in summer. Accepts Interac and most credit cards.

SYRENS $-$$$
629.2114
This 75-seat unique casual seaside lounge with 30-seat patio serves classic comfort food and inventive seasonal fare. A good selection of wines, alcoholic and non-alcoholic drinks and a selection of local and international ales and lagers are available. Syrens' menu tends to change, and offers a more casual alternative to Aurora. An example of menu items include Spicy Pender Wings ($8), Caesar Salad ($7), Soup du Jour ($7), and pastas ($15-$18). A selection of burger options may include fish, chicken or beef ($9 - $12) accompanied by yam or regular fries, soup, or salad. Other options include Halibut Fish 'N' Chips ($12-$15) and sandwiches du jour ($11-$16). The atmosphere on the patio on a nice day is nautically exhilarating, while the interior is unique and fun, with a beautiful fireplace. Prepare for crowds from the resort and a possible wait during the summer. Open from 11:00 am to midnight (1:00 am weekends), but the kitchen closes earlier (call for hours). No reservations. Accepts Interac and most credit cards.

Groceries and Produce

Pender Islands Groceries and Fresh Foods

TRU VALUE FOODS
Located in Driftwood Centre, Pender's main market is an attractive full service grocery store with a deli, bakery, butcher, and fresh produce section. The store is stocked well and prices are fairly reasonable, although selection is appropriately less than a large urban supermarket. The butcher accepts special requests for cuts of meat. When you check out, select a local charity from the Community Spirit Board list on the front wall, and the store will donate 1% of your purchase to it (over

$120,000 has been raised to date). Open every day until the early evening, usually 8:00 pm. A free return shuttle has been offered in summer to Port Browning Resort with $25 purchase.

MAGIC LAKE MARKET
This market is located 1.3 km from the entrance to Magic Lake Estates at 5827 Schooner Way and Aldridge Road (**Map 5A**). The store is well stocked with the essentials, and features organic and international foods, natural cleaning products, and local

eggs and produce. They have a respectable DVD/VHS video rental section and a spa supply centre. A good place for a cold beverage or snack while you are out and about. Open 8:30 am - 9:00 pm Sunday - Thursday, and until 10:00 pm Friday and Saturday; 629.6892.

SOUTHRIDGE FARMS COUNTRY STORE
This small and charming store is located at the north end of North Pender Island, at 3327 Port Washington Road across the street from **Pender Island Home Building Centre**. **Maps 1, 1C**. It features essentials, unique international items, organic produce, bulk foods, feed & pet foods, and natural cleansers. It operates a small video rental (VHS only) section, and an espresso bar; 629.2051. Also throws occasional summer barbeques.

POETS COVE MARINA "THE MOORINGS"
Located at Poets Cove Resort on South Pender Island. **Map 8**. The small general store sells a few groceries, deli, ice cream scoops, sandwiches, baked goods, and coffee drinks, as well as non-food essentials.

ORGANIC ISLANDS delivers a box of organic produce to your door; 629.6698.

SEAFOOD

Fishermen at the Hope Bay dock and Port Browning Marina sell fresh catch. Look for signs advertising the catch type and sales times around the island, especially across from the Driftwood Centre and in front of the Community Hall. The catch can include crab, varieties of salmon or other fish, smoked fish of various types, oysters, or prawns. Sometimes the seafood is frozen and brought from other locations. Cash only.

BAKED GOODS

Ewa's European Cakes
A Pender Island treasure, Ewa (at Christmas Craft Fair, right) puts her heart into her custom-made cakes that are the highlight of many Pender special occasions, yet are priced for the everyday sweet tooth. She also makes cabbage rolls or crepes with interesting fillings. Ewa is usually at the Saturday Farmer's Market, selling a variety of cake slices. Call 629-3119 or Email **jarose@cablelan.net** for special orders of cakes like those available at the Saturday market, or her  fabulous rich European style specialty festive tortes. Cash only.

See the *Restaurant Listings* for the following:

Pender Island Bakery Café at the Driftwood Centre is the place to get your fresh Pender pies, as well as a variety of pastries, cookies, breads, and cakes. Special occasion cakes are made to order.

Hope Bay Café has fresh baked goods available, including Vanna's famous scones.

Groceries - Nearby Off-Island

It is common custom for islanders to support Pender Islands businesses whenever possible. Some things, however, are just not available on island, and many Penderites supplement their Pender purchases with items obtained on shopping trips to Van Isle. Following is some helpful information for those shopping trips.

Sidney
The closest supermarkets to the Swartz Bay terminal are in Sidney, including a large **Safeway** at 2345 Beacon Avenue, which sends sales fliers to Pender postboxes. From Swartz Bay, head south on Highway 17 about 5 km (3 mi), turn left at Beacon Avenue, and look for the store on the right; 1.800.723.3929. A large **BC Liquor** store and a **PharmaSave** are located adjacent to **Safeway**. **Sidney Soopers** is a smaller but ample market down Beacon Avenue near the waterfront, and is a favourite for boaters moored at Port Sidney Marina. A **Thrifty** supermarket is located north of Beacon Avenue (at 8th Street). Sidney also has an excellent fresh seafood market on the pier, and several bakeries, including **Italian Bakery**, 2360 Beacon Ave, and **Sidney Bakery**, 2507 Beacon.

Saanich and Victoria
The next supermarket down Highway 17 is at Broadmead Centre, left at the Royal Oak Drive exit, about 22 km (14 mi) from Swartz Bay. This centre features a large, excellent **Thrifty** supermarket with bakery, deli and butcher, as well as a **PharmaSave, Canadian Tire, BCAA (Auto Club), Pets West,** and various other stores. Numerous food markets are located in the Victoria area, including the **Save On Foods** chain.

Langford
Located about 7 km (4 mi) west of Victoria on Canada 1, Langford is an area of explosive new development referred to by Penderties as *Big Box Land* because of its plethora of large chain stores. From Swartz Bay, take Highway 17 south about 25 km (16 mi) to McKenzie Avenue. Turn right, and follow it past several traffic signals until it intersects with Canada 1. Turn right, and proceed about 6 km (4 mi) to the Millstream Exit/Langford. To find **Costco Wholesale** membership warehouse, stay to the right at the ramp and follow Millstream north to the first traffic light at McCallum Road. Make a left. **Costco** is up the hill on the left, past the **Staples** store. Other stores in this complex include **Home Depot, Future Shop, Home Outfitters,** and **Sleep Country.** To find the other Big Box area in Langford, upon exiting on Millstream, keep to the left, which leads to Millstream Avenue south. Follow Millstream past the intersection with

Goldstream until you see a complex of large stores approaching, and make a right at the light on Attree. You will see a **WalMart** straight ahead, and to the left a large **Canadian Tire, Zellers,** and a **Real Canadian Superstore**, another excellent place to stock up on groceries, as well as cosmetics. Need a loonie for the cart deposit? The greeter inside keeps change. See the *Shopping and Services Guide* for information on the large stores.

Farmers and Roasters

Pender Islands Farmers Market

The Pender Island Farmer's Institute's Farmers Market is held on Saturdays 9:30 am - 1:00 pm, in the summer months and portions of the spring and fall, at the grounds of the Community Hall at the intersection of Otter Bay and Bedwell Harbour Roads. Some community groups set up booths here. Local farmers bring fruits, vegetables, eggs, cheeses, and offer fresh lamb and meat chickens for sale. Many locals offer home made baked goods, jams, sauces, and various arts and crafts. Some may set up food stands to sell smoothies or smokies. Coffee and beverages are served inside the Community Hall. Arrive early to grab *the best stuff* and to chat with your friends and neighbours.

Pender Islands Farm Stands

Farm stands are located throughout the Pender Islands, in season, where you can purchase locally grown fruits, vegetables, and eggs. Carry change so that you can pay in the honour boxes. It is a fun way to buy food, though you definitely cannot count on the inventory. Stands on North Pender Island are found along Port Washington Road, Clam Bay Road, South Otter Bay Road and Pirates Road, among others. On South Pender Island, a stand or two may be open along Spalding Road.

Pender Islands Coffee Roasters

Moonbeans Coffee roasts high quality beans into a variety of blends on North Pender Island. Their decaf is a true Swiss Water process, and tastes as good as regular. Pender Blend is a great Pender Island souvenir, which is "smooth yet strong with florally hints." Organic blends like Peruvian are reminiscint of Kona or Blue Mountain coffees, but much less expensive. Espresso is "smooth with excellent crema." Check their website **www.moonbeanscoffee.com** for a full summary of all of their blends. They are not open to the general public, but you can purchase their coffee beans at **Tru Value Foods,** and the **Moorings Market at Poets Cove**. At time of writing all **Poets Cove** establishments and **Hope Bay Café** serve Moonbeans; 1.866.44.BEANS, 629.6448, info@moonbeanscoffee.com.

Pender Islands Farms

The following farms are frequently represented at the Saturday Farmers Market at the Community Hall grounds, or can be contacted individually for orders. Some of the farms are certified organic by the Islands Organic Producers Association (IOPA), which falls under the Certified Organic Associations of British Columbia (COABC); **www.certifiedorganic.bc.ca.** All farms are on North Pender except as indicated:

Charman Farms at 5914 Pirates Road, grows and sells a variety of gourmet organic garlic and garlic preserves, and puts on a garlic day/open house in August; 629.6559, **www.charmanfarms.com,** info@charmanfarms.com.

Photo of Garlic Day by Charman Farms

Fir Hill Farm organically raises and sells premium spring lamb that they custom cut. Also sells wool products and yarn; 629.3819.

Iona Farms, 3403 South Otter Bay Road is certified organic by the IOPA. They produce a variety of fresh goat cheeses, meat chickens, eggs, vegetables, fruit, flowers, garlic, lamb and chevon; 629.6700, **iona@cablelan.net.**

Jane's Herb Garden, 3719 Rum Road. Jane specializes in herbs for garden and kitchen, and also makes jams, jellies, chutneys, toffee, fudge, soap from local goats milk, all made naturally. Jane can be found at the Farmers Market or call and visit; 629.6670, **janesherbgarden@cablelan.net.**

Shepherd's Croft Farm, 2234 Port Washington Road; 629.6644. Sells free range farm fresh eggs, apple juice and nuts.

Other Farms: Some of these farms have stands at the Saturday Farmers Market (Photo, right):
Kenta Farm (certified organic by IOPA) on Port Washington Road is usually at the Market; Historic **Old Orchard Farm** near the junction of Otter Bay and Port Washington Roads has a roadside stand that sells orchard fruit. **Hope Bay Farm** has a stand on Clam Bay Road across from Mt. Elizabeth Park. **Whalewytch Farms** on South Pender Island near Gowlland

Point grows a variety of produce for sale at the Farmers Market. Also, a rare Canadian olive grove was planted at the Waterlea homestead near the end of MacKinnon Road with 70 olive trees from Italy and California, with hopes of producing olive oil by 2007 (Neering, 2003).

Nearby Off-Island Produce

Locally-grown produce can be found in season throughout the Gulf Islands and Vancouver Island. You can find a bounty of nicely stocked fresh produce stands along the country roads of the Saanich Peninsula between Swartz Bay and Victoria. Pick up the free annual brochure *Farm Fresh* (available in the lobby of many Vancouver Island supermarkets) that shows the farms of the Saanich Peninsula and Gulf Islands on a map with cross-referenced produce type and growing season, or check their website **www.islandfarmfresh.com**. Try **Silver Rill Corn** at 7117 Central Saanich Road (from Hwy 17, west on Island View, make first right, then immediately bear right). **Michell Brothers** is conveniently located just east of Hwy 17 at Island View. The book *Eating Up Vancouver Island* by Rosemary Neering (2003) summarizes the best places to find fresh farm produce on the Saanich Peninsula, including Blenkinsop Road between Mackenzie and Royal Oak, Stelly's Cross Road and its side roads, East Saanich Road, West Saanich Road between Royal Oak and Deep Cove, Wallace Drive west of West Saanich Road, Mount Newton Cross Road and the Deep Cove area.

Wine and Spirits

In British Columbia, spirits are sold only at BC-run liquor stores. Wine and beer is also sold at these stores, as well as in wine shops. Grocery stores cannot sell alcoholic beverages. Restaurants are *licensed* if they serve beer and wine, and are *fully licensed* if they also serve cocktails. The region is fast becoming a top-notch wine-making region, and a fledgling winery is in operation on North Pender Island.

Pender Islands Liquor Stores

Pender Island Liquors (a BC Liquor Store) is located in the Driftwood Centre (**Map 5B**). Open Monday through Saturday 10:30 am to 6:00 pm. Offers good selection of wine and spirits. Return empty alcoholic beverage containers here for deposit refund.

Port Browning Resort operates a licensed liquor store, open every day, 10:00 am to 8:00 pm (to 9:00 pm Saturday and Sunday). **Map 5B**.

Poets Cove Resort on South Pender Island operates a licensed beer and wine store next to **Moorings Market** in the marina. **Map 8**.

Liquor Stores Off-Island

In Sidney, a large **BC Liquor** store is in the **Safeway** centre, a liquor store is located next to the **West Marine** store at the intersection of Highway 17 and Beacon Avenue, and another in the new Cannery building near the public pier at the end of Beacon. Liquor and wine shops are located throughout the Saanich and Victoria area. Ganges on Salt Spring Island has a **BC Liquor** store. Or, make your own wine at facilities such as **Wine Kitz** at 203-9810 Seventh Street in Sidney; 250.654.0300, **www.winekitz.com**.

Washington State has similar liquor laws as BC regarding spirits, however beer and wine are sold in grocery stores. The closest supermarkets that sell beer and wine are in Point Roberts and Blaine. Bellingham has a **Costco** (which tends to have good prices on wine and beer), state-run liquor stores, and numerous grocery stores. The nearest **Trader Joe's** to British Columbia is in Everett, Washington (and several others in the Seattle area), where there is a large selection of discounted wine and beer from around the world. The Anacortes to Sidney WDOT ferry has a duty-free shop that sells liquor, and a duty free shop is also located near the Coho ferry terminal in Port Angeles (but not in Victoria). Duty free shops are located at many border crossings. Consult the Canada Customs website for the quantity of liquor allowed back into Canada without payment of duty. Some policies are fairly ambiguous. For example, one customs officer stated that above the allowed limit, they charge duty based on a formula related to the price of the wine, but a minimum of $5CDN/per bottle to account for home-made or inexpensive wine.

Wineries

Southwest Vancouver Island and the Gulf Islands have become known as BC's fastest growing wine country. Some produce wines from grapes grown locally, while others import grapes from other locales such as the Okanogan. Check the Wine Island Vintners Association website at **www.islandwineries.ca**.

THE PENDER ISLANDS

Morning Bay Vineyard is a fledgling winery located in the Harbour Hill area of North Pender Island, 6621 Harbour Hill Road; 629.8351. Their wine is also available for sale via their website, **www.morningbay.ca**. From the Driftwood Centre, proceed down Razor Point Road for about 2 km, make a left on Harbour Hill Road, and look for the entrance on the left, at the top of the hill near the end of the paved road. See **Map 5**. Park near the new winery building. For open days and hours, look for the sandwich board sign in front of the Driftwood Centre. At time of writing they are open Wednesday through Sunday during peak season, with off-season schedule reduced. The wine shop offers for tastings and sales a range of varietal wines made by Morning Bay's winemaker at an Okanogan winery. Wine from their vineyard, a six-acre planting established in 2002, should be available after the first harvest in the fall of 2005. Their goal is to be a producer of high quality wines. Outdoor tables are available on a lovely licensed patio for your picnic if you purchase a bottle of wine from them to go with it. Check their website for updates on hours of operation, types of wine available, and upcoming festivals or performances. Also check the Pender Post for events. The winery invites guests who visit their wine shop to access Gulf Islands National Park - Mount Menzies from their property. The public access to this area of the National Park is from the end of Hooson Road (See the *Coastal Access and Hiking Guide*). Ask the proprietors for details when you visit the winery. Note that the ocean viewpoint at the end of the trail is precipitous with no guardrails, and is a dangerous place for young children or intoxicated adults.

WINERIES - OFF ISLAND

Saturna Island
Saturna Vineyards is located directly across Plumper Sound from Port Browning. The winery produces award winning wines from imported grapes as well as grapes grown at its vineyard. They offer tastings, a bistro with tasty lunches, and winery tours. To access the winery, take a BC Ferry to Lyall Harbour (limited service from the Pender Islands) and drive across the island. The winery is accessible by private boat (see the *Boating Guide*) or by excursions using Pender boat charter companies. The wine shop and bistro are open seven days a week May through September and October weekends. Wine shop: 11:30 am - 4:30 pm; Bistro 11:30 am - 3:30 pm. Call the day before your visit to verify hours; 539.5139, **www.saturnavineyards.com** wine@saturnavineyards.com. *For sale at time of writing.*

Other Gulf Islands
Wineries have been established on Thetis Island with the new **Thetis Island Vineyards**, and Salt Spring Island: **Salt Spring Vineyards**, 151 Lee Road, 250.653.9463, **www.saltspringvineyards.com**; Garry Oaks Winery, 1880 Fulford-Ganges Road 250.653.4687, **www.garryoakswine.com**.

Vancouver Island
The Van Isle wine-growing region lies between Nanaimo and Victoria. If your visit to the Pender Islands begins and ends in Vancouver, you can do a circle tour incorporating the Wine Route. Arrive on Pender Island via the ferry from the Tsawwassen/South Vancouver ferry terminal. After your Pender visit, take the ferry from Pender to Swartz Bay. The Wine Route begins nearby, and ends near Nanaimo where you can take the ferry to Horseshoe Bay/northwest Vancouver to return to the mainland. Pick up a *Wine Route* brochure at various information kiosks that describes the diverse wineries of the region, or check **www.islandwineries.ca**, then convince someone to be your designated driver. The closest wineries to Swartz Bay are **Marley Farm Winery** in Saanichton (**www.marleyfarm.ca**, 1831 Mount Newton Cross Rd, 250.652.8667), and **Victoria Estate Winery** in Brentwood Bay (1445 Benevenuto Ave 652.2671, **www.victoriaestatewinery.com**). From there, you can hop on the Brentwood Bay - Mill Bay ferry to the Cowichan Valley, whose climate and soil conditions are similar to that in the cider-growing regions of France and England. Mill Bay is home to **Merridale Ciderworks** (**www.merridalecider.com**, 1230 Merridale Rd, Cobble Hill, 743.4293). Further north is Cowichan Bay/Cobble Hill and **Cherry Point Vineyards** (**www.cherrypointvineyards.com**, 840 Cherry Point Rd, 743.1272). Continue to **Venturi-Schulze Vineyards** (4235 Trans Canada Hwy, Cobble Hill) and the nearby **Blue Grouse Vineyards** (4365 Blue Grousse Road, Duncan, 743.3834, **www.bluegrousevineyards.com**). About fifteen minutes further north, just before Duncan, are **Echo Valley Vineyards** (**www.echovalley-vineyards.com**, 4651 Waters Rd, 748.1470), **Zanatta Winery** (**www.zanatta.ca**, 5039 Marshall Rd, 748.2338), and **Godfrey Brownell Vineyards** (**www.gbvineyards.com**, 4911 Marshall Rd, 715.0504) Just north of Duncan is **Alderlea Vineyards** (1751 Stamps Rd, 746.7122.) The tour ends at Nanaimo and the **Chateau Wolff Vineyard** (2534 Maxey Rd, 753.4613).

6   SHOPPING AND SERVICES GUIDE

SHOPPING, SERVICES AND COMMUNICATIONS

Shopping On the Pender Islands and Beyond

The Pender Islands offer a surprising variety of shopping opportunities for both locals and visitors. Several stores can also order additional items that are delivered to the store free of charge. In such a small community it is important to support the local merchants whenever possible to ensure their livelihoods. In this chapter, listings from each category begin with the local shopping opportunities on the Pender Islands. In reality, many items are only available off-island, and selected retailers in nearby communities on Vancouver Island are also listed. The main shopping centre on the Pender Islands is Driftwood Centre. The diagram below depicts its layout and **Maps 5** and **5B** shows its location. Other shopping is located on Port Washington Road, at the Hope Bay Store (**Maps 1, 1C**), and Magic Lake Market (**Map 5A**). Various individual shops and galleries are also dispersed around the islands. See **Maps 10** and **11** for Van Isle.

1 Pender Island Pharmacy 6555
and Sears Catalogue Pickup
2 HSBC Bank SatelliteOffice 6516
3 Pender Island Bakery & Café 6453
4 Pistou Grill 3131
5 CRD Office 3424
6 Message Boards
7 BC Liquor Store 3413
8 Restrooms & Phone
9 Islands Trust (Limited Hours)
10 Talisman Books & Gallery 6944
11 Gwen's Fine Arts 6647

Driftwood Centre
With Phone Numbers 629.xxxx

Razor
Point Rd
Shade for Pets ➔

Bedwell Harbour Road

12 Shear Delight Hair Design 3582
13 Pender Island Realty 3383
14 Casual Pender Gifts 3932
15 Tru Value Foods
16 Pender Island Insurance 3336
17 Canada Post 3222

18 The Spa at Driftwood Centre 9969
19 House on Pender 9950
20 Pender Island Cable & Internet 3075
21 Revolution Fitness & Dance Studio 3122
22 Laundromat & Showers (Auto Centre)
23 Driftwood Auto Center: Gas & Diesel,
Car Repairs, Store, Rogers Video Rental 3005

Lumber and Hardware

Pender Islands
Pender Island Home Building Centre (a **Home Hardware** affiliate) is the Pender Islands' hardware store and lumberyard. It serves as Pender's *General Store*, selling a wide variety of items. Although the inventory may not be huge, they can order most anything you need from **Home Hardware**'s catalogue. They have a paint-mixing department, equipment rental and a garden centre. They also carry miscellaneous marine and fishing supplies, electronics accessories, housewares, sporting goods, and are the only propane supply on the Pender Islands for portable tanks. Located at 3338 Port Washington Road, between Clam Bay and Corbett Roads; 629.3455, Fax 629.2036. Closed Sunday. They also operate **Island Home Nursery** at the corner of Otter Bay and Bedwell Harbour Roads across from the Community Hall (see *Nurseries*).

Nearby Off-Island
Slegg Lumber: 2030 Malaview Ave, Sidney; 656.1125, 388.5443.
Do-It Centre: 1720 Cook St; 384.8181.
Home Building Centre: 2046 Keating X, Saanichton; 652.1121.
Home Depot: www.homedepot.ca, 2400 Millstream at McCallum, Langford; 391.6000.
Canadian Tire: For hardware. See *Department Stores* below.

Department/Variety Stores and Malls

Pender Islands
Pender Island Home Building Centre carries a variety of items. **Sears** has a catalogue outlet window in the **Pender Island Pharmacy**. Shop through their catalogue, or on line at **www.sears.ca**, and the merchandise will be delivered free of charge to the Pharmacy (629.6505), or to your home for a fee.

Department Stores and Malls - Nearby Off Island
Only a precious few Department Stores remain in Victoria after the demise of **Eaton's** and **Marks & Spencer**. These are listed below, along with multi-department stores like **Canadian Tire**, **Costco**, **London Drugs** and **Real Canadian Superstore**. A new Superstore may be built in the Mayfair area of Victoria. Stores tend to be concentrated in central Victoria and Langford.

VICTORIA MALLS
The Bay Centre (Downtown, Formerly The Eaton Centre), 1150 Douglas Street
Mayfair Mall (North end of town), 3125 Douglas (access also off Blanshard)
Tillicum Centre (West of town), 3170 Tillicum
Hillside Centre (East of town), 1610 Hillside Avenue/3190 Shelbourne Street

DEPARTMENT STORES
The Bay: www.hbc.ca: The Bay Centre, 385.1311 and Mayfair Mall, 386.3322
Canadian Tire: www.canadiantire.ca: Broadmead Village (Hwy 17 & Royal Oak),
727.6561; Downtown: 2959 Douglas, 361.3152; Gordon Head: 3993 Cedar Hill Rd,
721.1125; View Royal: Admirals Rd/Old Island Hwy, 381.3111;
Langford: 855 Attree (Canwest Mall- largest of the stores) 474.2291
Capital Iron: Downtown: 1900 Store St., 385.9703; Sidney: 2353 Bevan, 655.7115
Costco membership warehouse, **www.Costco.com**: 799 McCallum Rd, Langford,
391.1151; M-F 11-830, Sat 930-6, Sun 11-5. Business members M-F 10-11am
Fields: 1420 Douglas, 386.7554; 1153 Esquimalt Rd, 383.4229
London Drugs: www.londondrugs.com, Tillicum Cntre, 360.2654; Quadra/Mackenzie,
727.0246; 911 Yates, 360.0880; Colwood/Langford: 1907 Sooke Rd, 474.0900
Real Canadian Superstore: www.superstore.ca: Langford: 835 Attree Ave, Pharmacy:
391.3135; Hours daily 9am-10pm (Saturday open 8am)
Sears: www.sears.ca: Hillside Centre, 595.9111 (see also *Large Appliances*)
Wal-Mart: www.walmart.ca: 3601 Douglas at Saanich, 475.3356; Langford: 860 Attree
at Phipps, 391.0260. *Note:* RV Camping not allowed at Douglas store.
Zellers: www.hbc.ca: Hillside Centre, 595.2141; Tillicum Centre, 384.6352;
Langford: 100-2945 Jacklin Rd, 474.3148

Housewares and Home Furnishings

Pender Islands
Pender Island Home Building Centre sells housewares.
Sears has a catalogue outlet at **Pender Island Pharmacy;** 629.6505.
Sladen's at the Hope Bay Store sells various household items including linens,
furniture and notions. Also offers interior design services; 629.6823.
House on Pender at Driftwood Centre sells flower arrangements, tile and stone, and
decorating accents; 629.9900.
Housewares and Home Furnishings - Nearby Off-Island
Sidney has various shops including a **Capital Iron** next to **Safeway**.
Pier One Imports, www.pier1.com, 755 Finlayson St, 381.9190
United Furniture Warehouse, www.UnitedFurnitureWarehouse.com,
Saanich: 1949 Keating X Rd, 652.1555; Victoria: 2835 Douglas, St, 360.2300
ScanDesigns (Furniture) **www.scandesigns.com**, 574 Culduthel Rd, 475.2233
The Brick, www.thebrick.com, 2635 Quadra St, 1.800.991.2727
Home Outfitters, www.hbc.com, Langford: 759 McCallum Rd, 474.9700
Linens 'n Things, www.lnt.com, Tillicum Centre, 3170 Tillicum Rd, 381.3133
Illuminations (Lighting), www.illuminationsbc.com, 2885 Quesnel St, 384.9359
Also check various independent stores in downtown including Chinatown.
Ganges, Salt Spring Island: **Mouat's Trading Company**; 537.5551.

Home Electronics

Pender Islands

Pender Island Home Building Centre has limited selections of electronic equipment and accessories (cables, blank tapes, CDRs, ink cartridges, etc). Also try **Pender Island Pharmacy** and **Sears** catalogue outlet.

Nearby Off-Island

The Source by Circuit City (formerly Radio Shack Canada) has stores at Broadmead Village, Tillicum Centre, Hillside Centre, Mayfair Mall, The Bay Centre, Canwest Centre. See *Department Stores* for **Costco, Real Canadian Superstore, London Drugs, Canadian Tire, Wal-Mart.** See *Media: CDs* for **A&B Sound** and **Future Shop.** See *Home Furnishings* for **The Brick.**

Major Appliances

Pender Islands

You can order appliances on line from **www.sears.ca** and have them delivered free of charge to the **Pender Island Pharmacy** or for a fee to your door.
Installation and repair on Pender is available from Pender Electric, 629.6523.

Nearby Off-Island

In Victoria, major appliances are sold by **Sears** at the Island Home Centre, 800 Tolmie Ave, 380.7100 (and their Hillside Mall store), **Home Depot** and **Costco** in Langford, **Future Shop** (both locations), and **The Brick.** Also try **Lalani's Appliance Centre,** 776 Cloverdale, 475.1511, and for reconditioned units try **McFarland Appliances** at 1917 Quadra, 383.8233, and **Westcoast Appliance,** 370 Gorge Road/Jutland, 382.0242.

Media: CDs and DVDs

Pender Islands

Talisman Books & Gallery in Driftwood Centre has a small new CD section featuring local artists, and a used CD bin. Some of the gift shops on the island tend to stock a few new age or local artist titles.

Nearby Off-Island and the Internet

A&B Sound in downtown Victoria has a large selection and typically knowledgeable staff. 641 Yates, 385.1461. Or, order online at **www.absound.ca.**
Future Shop at 805 Cloverdale (at Blanshard), 380.9338, has a larger selection than their Langford store at 779 McCallum, 391.4514. For best selection, try their website **www.futureshop.ca.** They sometimes have free shipping on CDs.
HMV Canada, www.hmvonline.com, is at Mayfair Mall, 388.9859 and Hillside Centre, 370.5066. Department stores may also sell CD's (see that section). **Costco** has good prices on most mainstream new releases, but a limited selection otherwise. Others include **Real Canadian Superstore, London Drugs,** and **Wal-Mart.**

A number of independent new and used CD shops are located in the Victoria area, as listed below:

Amadeus Used CD's, Tapes & Videos, A-644 Yates, 361.1996
Boomtown Import Records, 561 Johnson, 380.5090, **www.boomtownrecords.com**
Ditch Records & CD's, www.ditchrecords.com, 635 Johnson, 386.5874
Galliard Music, Folk & World, www.galliardmusic.com, 101-Fan Tan Alley, 920.5575
Lyle's Place, 770 Yates, 382.8422; **Roger's Jukebox,** 1071 Fort, 381.2526
Mainly Music 2417 Beacon Ave, Sidney, 656.4818; **Whitebird,** 769 Yates, 380.7040
Oak Bay Books, 1964 Oak Bay Ave, 592.2933
The Turntable, 107-3 Fan Tan Alley, 382.5543

Canadian web sites include **www.amazon.ca,** and **www.ebay.ca** (where you can cross-reference independent on-line sellers), and **www.mymusic.com.** The site **www.djangos.com** accesses a large network of US independent new/used CD dealers at good prices, and they have reasonable shipping to Canada. To support local artists, it is usually best to order their CDs from their respective web sites.

Book Stores and the Pender Island Library

Pender Islands

Talisman Books & Gallery in Driftwood Centre features an extensive selection of local guidebooks and books by local authors as well as bestsellers and used books. If they do not stock a particular book, the helpful staff can order it for you. They also do valuations of book collections; 629.6944, talismanbooks@cablelan.net.

On Line: Pender Island web shoppers can try **www.amazon.ca, www.ebay.ca, www.bookcloseouts.com,** and **www.indigo.chapters.ca.**

The **Pender Island Public Library** is located on Bedwell Harbour Road between Otter Bay Road and Corbett Road, next to the Nu-To-Yu store (**Map 1**). Pender Island residents can obtain a free library card. Non-residents can obtain a visitors card for a fee. The library is run mostly by volunteers, and is one of the most popular places to volunteer on the island. New featured books are described each month in the Pender Post.

Five high-speed Internet computer terminals and a modem port for a laptop are available for a nominal fee. A meeting room is available for rent. Summer Story Time is a popular kids' program. Staff can photocopy or print out pages from the computer ($0.20 each) and can send or receive faxes for $1.00 per page. Open 10:00 am to 4:00 pm Tuesday, Thursday, Friday and Saturday; 629.3722, Fax: 629.3788; **www.penderislandlibrary.ca;** Email: info@penderislandlibrary.ca.

Nearby Off-Island

If you are the type that needs to browse lots of books to find what you want and you've already been through **Talisman**, your next stop can be to Sidney, which is known as *Booktown* for its numerous independent bookshops (ten at last count), mostly along Beacon Avenue. See **www.sidneybooktown.net.**

SIDNEY BOOKTOWN
Tanners (New), 2436 Beacon Avenue, 656.2345
Beacon Books (Used), 2372 Beacon, 655.4447
Children's Bookshop, 2442 Beacon, 656.4449
Time Enough for Books (Used), 2424 Beacon, 655.1964
Haunted Bookshop (Rare/Used), 9807 Third St, 656.8805
Galleon Books (Used), 9813 3rd St, 655.0700
Lifetimes Books (Biographies, New/Used), 9768 Third St, 656.5495
Country Life Books (Used/Collectible), 2378 Beacon, 655.4447
The Book Cellar (Military), 2423 Beacon, 655.3969
Compass Rose (Nautical), 9785 Fourth St, 656.4674
Nautical books are also sold at the marine shops in Sidney, including **West Marine** and **The Boathouse**. The **Institute of Ocean Sciences** at 9860 West Saanich Road also sells local nautical charts.

VICTORIA
Munro's Books at 1108 Government Street in downtown Victoria is the premier local shop, worth checking out; 382.2464, **www.munrobooks.com.**
Chain Stores: **Chapters (Indigo Books & Music)**, 1212 Douglas, 380.9009;
    Coles, 3147 Douglas, 388.3199 and 1150 Douglas/The Bay Centre, 385.3077;
    Smith Books, Tillicum Centre, 381.3034
University of Victoria: www.uvicbookstore.ca, Finnerty Road, 721.8311
Costco in Langford has the most discounted prices but carries mostly bestsellers.
Bolen Books: www.bolenbc.ca, 1644 Hillside, 595.4232
Crown Publications: www.crownpub.bc.ca: Maps, BC books, 521 Fort St., 386.4636

Office Supplies

Pender Islands
Pender Island Pharmacy stocks limited office supplies; 629.6555.

Nearby Off-Island
Monk Office Supply: www.monk.ca: 9769 5th St, Sidney, 655.3888
    Also at Broadmead Village; University Heights Centre; 794 Fort Street
Office Depot: www.officedepot.ca: 775 Finlayson, 385.0001
Staples: www.staples.ca: Victoria: 780 Tolmie, 383.8178;
    Langford: (Next to Costco), 391.3070.
Costco: Langford

Pharmacy

Pender Islands
Pender Island Pharmacy, Driftwood Centre: The full service pharmacy has a full-time pharmacist. Also sells over the counter health-related products, cosmetics, stationary, office supplies, cards, gifts, souvenirs, toys, games and pet supplies. Other services include photo finishing (sent-out) and a **Sears** Catalogue pick-up window. Blood pressure and cholesterol clinics are held twice monthly. Closed Sunday; 629.6555, Fax 629.6533, pharmacy@swan.ca.

Nearby Off-Island
Sidney has a **PharmaSave** and a **Shoppers Drug Mart** on Beacon Ave. Victoria has many of these franchises, plus several **London Drugs,** which sends sales flyers to Pender post boxes. See *Department Stores* for **London Drugs** Locations, and for the pharmacies at **Real Canadian Superstore** and **Costco** in Langford.
Pharmasave: www.pharmasave.com, Sidney: 9810 7th St, 656.1348;
   Broadmead Centre, 727.2284; 1641 Hillside Ave; 1775 Fort St; 230 Menzies St;
   2220 Oak Bay Ave; 2020 Richmond Ave; 1153 Esquimalt Rd.
Shoppers Drug Mart: www.shoppersdrugmart.ca: Sidney: 2341 Beacon Ave,
   656.1102; 4440 West Saanich Rd (North of Quadra), 881.1980; 3575 Douglas St (Town & Country Centre), 475.7572; 101 Burnside Rd; 1644 Hillside Ave; 2947 Tillicum Rd;
   1627 & 1990 Fort St; 870 Esquimalt Rd; 1222 Douglas St.

Gift Shops

Pender Islands
A visitor can make a very enjoyable day out of exploring Pender's shops and galleries. See also the *Arts on Pender* chapter for art galleries.

NORTH PENDER ISLAND'S DRIFTWOOD CENTRE
Casual Pender has gift items, clothing and many Pender Island-themed items such as tee shirtsand hats; 629.3932.
Talisman Books & Gallery carries arts and crafts by local artisans and various gift items; 629.6944.
Gwen's Fine Art & Native Collectables is a great place to shop for Native jewelry, masks, antique furniture, baskets and collectables; 629.6647.
Pender Island Pharmacy carries a few gifts items; 629.6555.

HOPE BAY STORE
Pender Treasures: Ladies consignment clothing; local crafts, body care; 629.3201.
Sladen's carries housewares, notions, linens, and furniture; 629.6823.

PORT WASHINGTON ROAD
Pender Island Home Building Centre carries gift items.
Renaissance Studio at 3302 Port Washington Road is worth a browse for jewellery, antiques and art; 629.3070.

SOUTH PENDER ISLAND
Poets Cove Resort's Moorings Market sells some gifts; 629.2112.

Nearby Off Island
Sidney has numerous shops along Beacon Avenue. Neighbourhoods in Victoria worth strolling and shopping include Government Street north of the Inner Harbour, Market Square at 560 Johnson Street, and the Shops in the **Fairmont Empress**. Also try the Douglas and Yates corridors and Fan Tan Alley in Chinatown. The 800 to 1100 block of Fort Street is known as antique row. The Oak Bay neighbourhood has several shops and restaurants. On Salt Spring Island, Ganges has numerous galleries and gift shops.

Thrift Shops

Pender Islands
Nu To Yu, 4409 Bedwell Harbour Road, next to the Library, **Map 1**, 629.2070, Photo, right. The popular volunteer-run thrift shop sells donated goods, and proceeds (over $500,000 since 1984) go to Pender Island charities. Donate goods on Tuesday and Thursday: (9:00 am -12:00 pm), and shop on Friday and Saturday (10:00 am - 4:00 pm). Watch for $5 a bag days.

Pender Treasures: Ladies clothing and other items on consignment, as well as local crafts. Hope Bay Store; 629.320, **Map 1C**.

Nearby Off Island
A number of thrift stores are located in downtown Sidney. Victoria also has many.

Marine and Fishing Supplies

Pender Islands
A selection of boating and fishing supplies, including rods and reels, can be found at **Pender Island Home Building Centre**. **Driftwood Auto Centre** sells fishing licenses and various bait and tackle, and Otter Bay and Poets Cove Marinas have small stores with marine supplies. See the *Boating Guide - Fishing* for information on licenses.

Nearby Off Island
In Sidney, walk from Port Sidney Marina to:
Boathouse Marine Centre: 2506 Beacon Ave, 655.3682
West Marine Superstore: www.westmarine.com, 2210 Beacon (at Hwy 17), 654.0045
Walk from Tsehum Harbour to:
All Bay Marine: 2204 Harbour (at Resthaven), 656.0153
In Central Saanich:
Sherwood Marine: 6771 Oldfield, 652.6520, www.sherwoodmarine.com
Department stores near Victoria: Try **Canadian Tire** and **Wal-Mart**
In Ganges, Salt Spring Island, walk to **Mouat's Trading Company**, 1.877.490.5593, or the **Ganges Marina** store, 537.5242.

Sporting Goods

Pender Islands
Some sporting goods are sold at the **Pender Island Home Building Centre** and perhaps the pharmacy or auto centre, including necessities such as golf discs and tennis balls. Golf balls and limited golf accessories are sold at the Pender Island golf course.

Nearby Off Island
Several chain stores and numerous independent shops are situated in the Victoria area. Department stores that carry various sporting goods include **Canadian Tire, Costco, Capital Iron, Sears, Wal-Mart, Real Canadian Superstore**, and in Ganges **Mouat's Trading Co.** Chain sporting goods stores include:
Mountain Equipment Coop, www.mec.ca, 1450 Government St, 386.2660.
SportChek, www.sportchek.ca, The Bay Centre Downtown, 388.5103
   805 Cloverdale, 475.6851
Sport Mart, www.sportmart.ca, Tillicum Mall, 386.5536; 3593 Douglas, 475.6278

FOR BICYCLING EQUIPMENT AND RENTALS *See the Bicycling Guide, Chapter 14.*
FOR TENNIS AND GOLF EQUIPMENT *See the Recreation and Golf Guides, respectively.*

Nurseries

Pender Islands
Island Home Gardens is located at the corner of Otter Bay and Bedwell Harbour Roads across from Community Hall. Operated by the **Pender Island Home Building Centre**, the nursery is open seasonally 10:00 am to 4:00 pm, and sells annuals, perennials, trees, containers, soil, pots, baskets, and shrubs. The main **Home Building Centre** on Port Washington Road sells gardening supplies and plants, 629-3455.

See the *Gardening Guide* in Chapter 17 for a list of nurseries and garden supply centres in the Sidney-Victoria area.

Pender Islands Services

A variety of services are available on the Pender Islands. Check the Lions Club local phone directory, the Pender Post, and message board postings for availability. In addition, the morning ferry from Swartz Bay is filled with contractors and service persons of all types who are willing to make the trip over to do work on the Pender Islands.

Banking

A small branch of **HSBC Bank Canada**, a satellite of the HSBC Saanich branch, is located in Driftwood Centre and is open Tuesday through Friday 10:00 am - 4:00 pm and Saturday 10:00 am - 3:00 pm; 629.6516. It has no ATM (Interac), but there are three private ATM's, in the Driftwood Automotive Centre, Pender Island Pharmacy, and Poets Cove Resort (lower level lobby next to Syrens). The nearest off-island communities with banks that are easily reachable by private boat are Sidney and Ganges. In addition, check the latest Lions Club phone directory under Financial Services.

Automotive Service, Towing and Licensing

Fuel
The only vehicle fuel station on Pender Island is **Driftwood Auto Centre**, which sells diesel and two grades of gasoline. Fuel prices tend to be 10-20% higher than on the Saanich Peninsula. A repair garage is also located at the service station. They do many repairs and certified government inspections, although they do not have much in the way of advanced diagnostic equipment; 629.3005. The facility also has an ATM machine, Laundromat, showers and a convenience store that sells fishing supplies and licenses.

Towing
Pender's towing service is **Pro Stock Automotive**, which is contracted by BCAA (see below), and also does automotive repairs; 629.6692. Wait time will vary depending on the availability of the one truck, and it can be many hours. If the repair cannot be done on-island and a tow into Victoria is required, it can cost about $275, even with BCAA extended coverage, due to the tower's surcharge associated with the ferry ride. The cost without BCAA can be about $300. Pro Stock is available most of the year for towing except for an annual 2-week summer vacation. When they are not available, a tow from a Victoria outfit may cost even more.

Auto Club
British Columbia Automobile Association (BCAA) is the local club; **www.bcaa.com**; Roadside Assistance: 1.800.CAA.HELP, Cellular *22.
Members of AAA can utilize BCAA's services.
Main Victoria Office: 1075 Pandora Avenue, 389.6700
Saanich Office: In Broadmead Centre, from Hwy 17, east on Royal Oak Avenue, located next to **Thrifty** supermarket.

Automotive dealerships and repair facilities of most types are located around Victoria. area. **Sidney Tire** at 9817 Resthaven Drive north of Beacon Avenue has been recommended by several Penderites for routine repairs and tires, 656.5544.

Drivers License and Insurance
www.icbc.com/Licensing/index.html; The closest licensing office is in Sidney at 2440 Sidney Avenue (North of Beacon Ave between 3rd and 4th Streets), 656.1184, Open 8:30 am - 4:00 pm Monday to Friday.
Insurance: Check with **ICBC** at **Pender Island Insurance Agency,** 629.3336.

Postal Service and Courier

A **Canada Post** branch is located at the Driftwood Centre, which is open Monday through Friday 8:30 am - 4:00 pm, and 8:30 am - 12:00 pm on Saturday; 629.3222. Last mail pickup at the post office is 3:30 pm weekdays and 11:30 pm Saturday. Mail delivery on the Pender Islands is Monday through Friday. Mail is delivered to neighbourhood lock boxes, which all contain a drop-off slot, usually in the middle of the left group of boxes. Sign up for a lock box for no charge at the post office. Customers supply their own lock. If you do not want sales flyers delivered, leave a note in your post box specifying this. This is not an on-and-off option for seasonal residents. Post Office boxes located in the **Canada Post** branch are also available for a fee.

Mail that is collected around the Pender Islands and from the **Canada Post** office is sorted in the afternoon and travels to Sidney early the following morning via water taxi. Therefore, you can give your mail a head start if you can post it on your trip into Sidney or Victoria.

To look up postal outlets, rates and postal codes, go to **www.canadapost.ca.** In Sidney, the Post Office is located on Beacon Avenue between 1st and 2nd Streets, (no longer in the old *Sidney Post Office* building). **Monk's Office Supply** at 9769 5th Street and **Pharmasave** on 9810 7th Street have **Canada Post** substations.

Four Postal Codes cover the Pender Islands. V0N 2M0 is for post office boxes. For North Pender Island, V0N 2M2 covers the south end including all of Magic Lake Estates and Trincomali, while V0N 2M1 covers everything else, from Hope Bay, down to the Driftwood Centre and along Canal Road to the bridge. V0N 2M3 covers South Pender Island.

Expedited delivery is available through **Canada Post** via their XPress Post service. For courier service, **Canada Post** offers Priority Courier Service within Canada. For international service, you can ship via **Purolator International** through **Canada Post.** **Purolator** also offers some domestic service, depending on the item to be shipped. **Purolator:** www.purolator.com; 1.888.SHIP123. Shipping centre, Victoria: West on Kelvin from Douglas to 3330 Tennyson Ave, 475.9562. Authorized agent: **Cloverdale Paint,** 9768 5th St, Sidney, 656.9781.

You cannot send out a **Federal Express** (FedEx) parcel via **Canada Post**, although you can pay **Pender Island Courier** (see below) to drop it off for you in Sidney. However, you can receive **FedEx** parcels on Pender Island. Incoming parcels are transferred in Richmond to another agency for delivery at their discretion, which could be either **Canada Post** or a local courier service. Fed Ex: **www.fedex.com**, 1.800.GO.FEDEX; Closest staffed centre: Victoria Airport in Sidney, 1541a Kittyhawk Road, open M-F 8-4.

Incoming parcels requiring a signature that are being handled by **Canada Post** may be brought directly to residences that are within one-half kilometre of the postal route. Otherwise, a note is left in the lock box to sign for it at the post office.

United Parcel Service (UPS) delivers to residences via **Pender Island Courier**. Note that if you have a package shipped from the USA using UPS, they charge customs brokerage fees and GST, regardless of the shipping charges you already arranged with the vendor. **Pender Island Courier** collects those fees C.O.D; **www.ups.ca**, 800.742.5877, Mail Boxes Etc. stores around Victoria are drop off locations. UPS Customer Centre: 4254 Commerce Circle, Victoria.

Pender Island Courier will drop off courier packages for you in Sidney. They can also pick up or deliver various items in Victoria and the Saanich Peninsula. Call 629.3366 or 250.889.0225 for fees and scheduling.

Pender Island Freight Service offers freight and courier service to the Mainland and Vancouver Island; 629.6424.

United States Postal Service: www.usps.com has zip code look-up.

Trash Disposal and Recycling

Trash disposal is a challenge for Pender Island residents as there is no landfill or public trash collection service on the islands. Visitors should help out by taking their trash with them and disposing of it off island. For residents, private services are available to dispose of trash for a fee. These are individual businesses and not a community system. See the local telephone directory, the Pender Post, or notices posted at the Driftwood Centre or **Magic Lake Market** for these services. **Spalding Garbage Service** has been in operation for 15 years; 629.3544. Penderites tend to become proficient at sorting and disposing of trash. Most beverage containers can be easily returned on-island to the food markets and liquor containers to the liquor store for a deposit refund, while other materials can be recycled on-island at the recycling centre. Many people compost a lot of their organic materials, leaving only protein to dispose of.

The **Pender Recycling Society** on 4402 Otter Bay Road is open Saturday 10:00 am - 3:00 pm, Sunday 3:00 pm - 5:00 pm, and Tuesday 8:00 am - 3:00 pm. They may also have Friday hours in summer. No after hours drop offs are allowed. Recycling hotline: 1.800.667.4321; Office: 629.6962. Family annual membership fee is $10. It is a quaint and funky operation, making recycling enjoyable (Just make sure to follow the rules).

Pick up a brochure from the office that describes which materials can be recycled there, and where to dispose of materials that they do not accept. This information is also sometimes published in the Pender Post. In general, accepted materials are clean glass, dry corrugated cardboard, mixed paper, tin, aluminium (cans, foil, plates), copper, brass, zinc and lead, ferrous scrap metal, white goods (fridges, freezers, etc. $20 fee), lead acid, Ni-Cd and alkaline batteries, latex and oil paint, plastics, and plastic bags.

Trades

Numerous tradespersons reside on the Pender Islands, and even more commute to jobs here from off-island, predominantly the Victoria area. Find information on local tradespersons in the Lions Club phone book, the Pender Post, and notices posted at the Driftwood Centre and **Magic Lake Market**. Make sure to ask for references.

Property Management and Real Estate

Property Management
Several businesses specialize in looking after homes, especially while they are vacant, and doing routine maintenance and miscellaneous other services. See the Lions Club phone book, the Pender Post, and the message boards for information on these services. Make sure to ask for references. Contact your insurance company for your requirements for home care while you are away. For example, for seasonal resident policies, you may be required to personally visit your property every 90 days for your policy to be valid. **Pender Island Insurance Agency**, Driftwood Centre: 629.3336.

Real Estate
The best way to find out which realtors are practicing on the Pender Islands is to pick up the latest Pender Post, which should contain most of their listings in the back. At time of writing local realtors include **Dockside Realty** (Hope Bay Store, 629.3166), **Newport Realty**, 629.6680, **Pender Island Realty** (Driftwood Centre, 629.3383), and **Sussex Realty**, 629.6417. You can also check on the Canadian multiple listings for real estate at **www.mls.ca**. Although Pender Island is a casual place, use the same due diligence in your transaction as you would anywhere else. A local CRD Building Department office is located in the Driftwood Centre; 629.3424. They should be able to answer many questions about real estate issues on the island, and are the source for building permits. Some of the issues to consider when buying a property on the Pender Islands are whether it has an adequate water supply and septic system. Consult your realtor, solicitor, the CRD, and other sources for other issues to check for. For non-Canadians, buying a home in Canada is relatively straight-forward, but buyers should first research issues such as taxes (especially when selling the house), insurance, immigration, and health care coverage. Some helpful real estate websites include **www.lawsnet.org**, which contains a variety of Canadian legal information, including real estate law, and **www.realtytimes.com**, which contains real estate information and articles.

Other Services

Dry Cleaning: Drop-off at **Magic Lake Market**; 629.6892
Photo finishing: Drop-off at **Sears** window in the Pharmacy; 629.6505
Picture Framing: **Windover Studios**; 629.3863
Propane bottle refill for portable tanks: **Pender Home Building Centre**; 629.3455
Spa Maintenance: **Gulf Island Spas**; 629.3481
See the *Wedding Guide* for services relating to beauty and caterers

Utilities

Electric/Hydro

Electricity (hydro) is provided by BC Hydro. Rates are reasonable, but have been rising annually. Power outages are routine on the Pender Islands after severe storms, but locals say the service has improved over the years. There are also short 1-second outages as a result of a device that instantly reports a potential problem and cuts the power, and then re-instates power instantly if the problem is not real. These outages are frequent enough to wreak havoc to electronic clocks. It is highly recommended to get a full surge suppression device to the incoming electrical line, as well as suppressers and possible battery back-up to electronic devices such as computers. If you experience a power outage, you are urged to call 1.800.POWER.ON so that they are aware of which areas are impacted and can respond. They should be able to tell you the extent of the outage and its anticipated duration. If you rely on the Internet for your livelihood, you may want to consider a backup generator and a dial-up ISP service to back up the cable, since the phone service does not go out as frequently as the hydro. *Note: Do not hook up a generator to your main electrical circuit unless an electrician can do it properly. Instead, plug various devices into it directly with CSA-approved/properly rated extension cords.* When the power goes out island-wide, the cable Internet and television service goes out with it, and sometimes it takes them a while to restart the service after the power is restored. Also, keep a non-electric telephone handy that you can use when the power is out. If you have no way to heat your house, you can go to St. Peters Anglican Church. Check **www.bchydro.com** for additional precautions and procedures. A good summary is found in March 2006's Pender Post. BC Hydro general number: 1.800.224.9376. Automatic bill paying is available.

Gas and heating

No natural gas is available on the island. Some residents maintain propane tanks. This is earthquake country, so secure your tank. Others use wood stoves for heat.

Water

Water conservation is a necessity on the Pender Islands, as the water supply is only from whatever rainfall occurs on the island. Most areas of the Pender Islands rely on individual drilled wells, although some areas are provided with water from reservoirs. See the *Geology and Water Resources* section in Chapter 17 for information on groundwater on the Pender Islands. Magic Lake Estates has a community water system operated by the CRD that is supplied by Buck Lake, a surface water reservoir. The water is treated to drinking water standards at a plant next to the lake. Magic Lake water is used as backup. The water pipes in the subdivision were inadequate and dilapidated since conception, and many of them were replaced in 2002-2003, funded largely by a tax supplement to residents. Fire hydrants were also installed during the reconstruction. During dry years Buck Lake becomes precariously low by the end of summer, requiring severe water restrictions. To report a problem with water or sewer in the Magic Lake jurisdiction call 629.6611 or 250.388.6275, pager 2614. The Trincomali subdivision on North Pender Island has a community water system that consists of wells and water tanks. In dry years they have to truck in water to help fill the tanks. The water use of residents is posted to encourage them to conserve. The Razor Point area also has a small community system from wells.

Sewer
Most of the Pender Islands rely on individual septic systems. Percolation tests must be passed for these to be approved. Portions of Magic Lake Estates are connected to a CRD-operated sewage system. Some areas of the subdivision drain into collective septic fields, while others drain into two water treatment plants. The plant on Schooner Way (north of Boat Nook) treats to disinfected secondary standards, and the Cannon Crescent plant treats to undisinfected secondary standards. The CRD monitors effluent monthly for compliance with regards to flow, total suspended solids (TSS), biochemical oxygen demand (BOD), fecal coliform bacteria and nutrients.

Telecommunications
The local telephone company is Telus: 1.888.811.2323 (residential); 1.888.811.2828 (business). Long distance services are available from Telus, Primus, other carriers and through cable Internet. See the *Media and Communications* below for information on television, Internet access, and radio.

Media and Communications

Internet Access

Public Internet Access At time of writing you can check your email on Pender Island at three locations. Pender Island Public Library offers cable Internet access for $1 for 1-hour sessions at five stations. **Map 1**. Use of one modem connection for your own laptop is also available for $1/hour. Hours are Tuesday, Thursday, Friday and Saturday from 10:00 am to 4:00 pm. **Pender Island Bakery** in Driftwood Centre has one cable Internet station available: $2 for 15 minutes. The Café at **Port Browning Resort** has a station (fee). A wi-fi hotspot was also set up at the resort in 2005.

Dial Up If you need temporary dial-up Internet access while on Pender, check your ISP for dial-up access numbers. Note that calling Salt Spring Island, Victoria/Vancouver Island and Vancouver is long distance. Telus has a local number, 539.2240, for the *Gulf Islands*. Temporary dial-up Internet service is offered by a Salt Spring Island outfit, **www.imagencommunications.com**. Rates are $25 sign up plus $25 per month (+ tax) for 120 hours (maximum of two months); 250.537.1950.

Cable For Pender Islands residents, **Pender Island Cable & Internet** offers cable Internet at several levels of connection speed. For their latest services, consult their web site **www.pendercable.tv,** visit their new office at the Driftwood Centre, or call 629.3075. For customer service, call their office during business hours, and they can help you with certain issues, including service outages. For problems regarding your modem connection and software issues, call Cablelan at 1.888.681.9688 M-F 8-8, Weekends 10-4. You can check your Cablelan email remotely using their website **www.cablelan.net**. Cablelan customers are also offered a free personal webpage. **DSL** access on the Pender Islands is not available or forecast at time of writing.

Television

Cable TV Pender Island Cable & Internet provides both basic and digital cable television. For their latest services, consult **www.pendercable.tv**, call 629.3075, or visit their new Driftwood Centre office Tuesday through Saturday. Mascom Cable TV is the provider of the service; **www.mascom.bc.ca**, 1.800.692.2078.

Satellite TV Another option for television is satellite, except if you live at a location where topography blocks the signal. The Canadian choices are **Star Choice,** www.starchoice.com and Bell ExpressVu, **www.bell.ca**. A description of Canadian satellite services and rules can be found at the Canadian government website **www.crtc.gc.ca/eng/INFO_SHT/b315.htm**. American satellite systems such as **Dish Network** and **Direct TV** are not allowed in Canada. However, Canadian services carry U.S. networks and many premium channels' programs.

Television Listings The Times Colonist has a weekly TV Times magazine in the Friday edition. On line try **www.Canada.com/tvtimes**. Select the postal code, then choose from Antenna, Pender Cable or the two satellite systems. Another option is **www.jam.canoe.ca**, which offers similar options. Most premium channels post their own schedules on their web sites, including **www.moviecentral.ca** (also carries U.S. HBO programming) and **www.showcase.ca**, (also carries many of U.S.'s Showtime programs, but with commercials). The Comedy Network carries many Comedy Central programs (**www.comedynetwork.ca**). Programming of U.S. premium content in Canada is becoming more and more synchronous with the U.S. counterparts.

General Broadcast Channels can potentially be picked up from BC (Cxxx stations) or Washington (Kxxx stations). *Van* = Vancouver. *Vic* = Victoria/Vancouver Island

2 CBUT (CBC, Van)	11 KSTW (UPN)	26 CBUFT (SRC)
4 KOMO (ABC)	12 KVOS (IND)	32 CIVT (CTV, BC)
5 KING (NBC)	13 KCPQ (Fox)	33 KWPX (PaxTV)
6 CHEK (CH, Vic)	16 KONG (IND)	45 KHCV (IND)
7 KIRO (CBS)	17 CIVI (IND, Vic)	51 KWOG (IND)
8 CHAN (Global, Van)	20 KTBW (IND)	53 CIVI (IND, Vic)
9 KCTS (PBS)	22 KTWB (WB)	56 KWDK (IND)
10 CKVU (IND, Van)	24 KBCB (IND)	

Radio Stations

Depending on your location on the Pender Islands, radio signals can be received from numerous locales.

Following are listings in numerical order for:
British Columbia: VIC=Victoria; VAN=Vancouver; NAN=Nanaimo
Washington: SEA=Seattle; BELL=Bellingham; PORTA= Port Angeles.

CBC Radio 1: Canadian news, music and talk radio. **www.cbc.ca**
CBC Radio 2: Classical music and beyond
NPR: National Public Radio (USA) **www.npr.org**

AM RADIO

600 VAN CKFD, Pre Rock Oldies
650 VAN CISL, Oldies
690 VAN **CBC RADIO 1**
710 SEA KIRO News & Traffic
900 VIC CKMO Camosun College
980 VAN CKNW News, Canucks

1000 SEA KOMO News & Traffic
1040 VAN The Team, BC Lions
1070 VIC CFAX News/talk
1090 SEA AirAmerica Liberal Talk
1130 VAN CKWX All News
1140 VAN CFUN Talk Radio

FM RADIO

88.5 or 91.1TACOMA KPLU
Pacific Lutheran Univ (Jazz)
88.9 VIC CBUX French Class/Jazz
89.3 PORTA KVIX NPR
89.7 DUNCAN CJSU "Sun" Rock
90.1 VAN CJSF Simon Fraser U
Variety of arts, music, politics
90.1 PORTA KNWP NPR
90.3 SEA KEXP, UW Students
90.5 VIC CBCV **CBC RADIO 1**
90.9 VAN CBUX French, Class/Jz
91.3 VIC CJZN The Zone, Alt Rock
92.1 VIC CBU **CBC RADIO 2**
92.5 SEA KLSY Soft rock/traffic
92.9 BELL KISM Rock
93.7 VAN JRFM New Country
94.1 SEA KMPS Country
94.5 VAN CFBT Beat,Tech/Rap
94.9 SEA KUOW UofWash, NPR
95.3 VAN Z95 Top 40
95.7 SEA KJR Rock Greatest Hits
96.5 SEA Jack FM Rock Mix

96.9 VAN CKLG Jack FMRock Mix
97.1 VAN Kiss, Adult Contemporary
97.7 VAN CBUF French
98.1 SEA KING Classical
98.5 VIC CIOC The Ocean, Soft Rock
98.9 SEA KWJZ Orca, Smooth Jazz
99.3 VAN CFOX Hard Rock
100.3 VIC CKKQ Old and New Rock
101.1 VAN CFMI Classic Rock
101.7 NAN CHLY Malaspino Rap
101.9 VIC CFUV UVic Radio
101.9 VAN CiTR UBC Radio l
102.3 NAN CKWV The Wave Rock
102.7 VAN Co-Op Radio, Alternative
103.1 VIC Jack FM Rock Mix
103.5 VAN CHQ Soft Rock
104.3 BELL KAFE ClassicRock
104.9 VAN CKCL Easy jazz/contemporary
105.7 VAN CBU **CBC RADIO 2**
106.9 SEA KRWM Soft rock
107.3 VIC CHBE Cool FM, Top 40

Video Rental

Rogers Video operates an outlet inside of the Driftwood Service Station. **Magic Lake Market** on Schooner Way near Medicine Beach maintains a similar selection in their store for rent. Both are good at keeping up with the newest mainstream releases in both DVD and VHS format, but the selection is less than that of a typical urban video store. Also, **Southridge Farms Country Store** across from **Pender Island Home Building Centre** on Port Washington Road has a small VHS rental section featuring art films.

For a larger selection you can try DVD rental by mail outfits. These services can be advantageous if you can watch the movie soon after it arrives, if you watch a lot of movies, and are flexible as to which title you receive at a certain time. If so, you can potentially bring down the average cost of a DVD rental to as little as $2, compared to the $5 of renting from your local video shop. DVDs are mailed via regular Canada Post without the case. No late fees are charged, but if you delay sending back a DVD, it will delay the receipt of your next title. Outfits with operations in Vancouver will be your best bet for a quick turnaround. **www.zip.ca** has a good selection. Some of the services allow for temporary account suspensions that work well for seasonal residents. Others require customers to cancel their account then start anew the following season.

7   WEDDING GUIDE

TRADITIONAL & SAME-SEX WEDDINGS

Island Weddings

What could be more romantic than an island wedding? Pender Island offers a wide variety of venues, both indoors and out. Choose from churches, banquet halls, B&B's, towering cliffs, seaside meadows or quiet forests. Talented Penderites can provide all the services you will need to hold whatever style wedding you desire, including marriage commissioners, florists, caterers, musicians and photographers. A partial vendor list is found in this chapter. Information for those planning a same-sex wedding is also included.

Gwen Davidson marries Keith Laboucane at Gwen's family home at Roesland.

Wedding Venues

CHURCHES

See the *School and Church Guide* (Chapter 18) for additional information on churches.

St. Peters Anglican Community Hall
The largest church on Pender is located at St. Peters, on Canal Road south of the Driftwood Centre (**Map 5**). The Hall is available for weddings and receptions, with catering available independently, or through the Anglican Church Women (ACW). The service can be held in the adjacent St. Peter's Church, an early 1900's building that was moved to this site in the 1990's. See the latest Pender Post for phone contacts. 4703 Canal Road, RR1, Pender Island BC V0N 2M2; Church Office: 629.3634. The pretty Church of the Good Shepherd near Poets Cove Resort on South Pender Island is also part of this congregation.

Pender Island United Community Church
The circa-1907 church building is nestled in a scenic setting just north of the Pender Island Public Library at 4405 Bedwell Harbour Road (**Map 1**). Several wedding services are typically held there each year, with receptions held elsewhere. They require that an ordained Christian minister conduct the service, and the Church board approves weddings. See the latest Pender Post for phone contacts; 4405 Bedwell Harbour Road, RR1, Pender Island BC V0N 2M1.

Chapel of Saint-Teresa
Located on the shore of Magic Lake (**Map 4**), a Roman-Catholic wedding service can be held in their building, with the reception held elsewhere. Non-parishioners must provide a letter from their priest. See the latest Pender Post for contact information.
4705 Buccaneers Road, RR2, Pender Island BC V0N 2M2

Reception Facilities and Caterers

Pender Island Community Hall is located at the intersection of Otter Bay Road and Bedwell Harbour Road (**Map 3**). Built in 1998, the wooden structure features a lower level with a reception area, kitchen facilities and lounge that can handle a large reception. Upstairs is a wheelchair-accessible hall that is used for performances; 629.3669, bookings@penderislands.org, **www.penderislands.org**.

Pender Island Golf and Country Club: **Chippers** cafe has a fully licensed kitchen, which can cater a reception, and a basically appointed restaurant with a deck overlooking the golf course; 2305 Otter Bay Road, Pender Island BC V0N 2M1, 629.6665, **www.penderislandgolf.com**, Maps 1, 1A.

Royal Canadian Legion Branch #239: The meeting hall located on MacKinnon Road (left from the ferry) rents its hall for events and arranges for catering;
1344 MacKinnon Road, Pender Island BC V0N 2M1, 629.3441, **Map 1A.**

Islanders Restaurant: The popular **Every Last Crumb Catering** is associated with this artfully decorated restaurant, which can handle a reception for about 36 guests. A large covered deck has an ocean view to the southwest; **Map 1A**, 629.3929, **www.islandersrestaurant.com.**

Pistou Grill in the Driftwood Centre can handle a smallish wedding party dinner on site and provides delicious catering for weddings; **Map 5B**, 629.3131.

Clam Bay Farm, a working farm on the northern tip of North Pender Island has rental cottages, a central facility available for events, and a dock on Navy Channel; **www.clambay.com**, 1.877.662.3414, **Map 1C.**

The Timbers resort on Pirates Road at the southeast end of North Pender Island has facilities for a wedding and rental cabins, as well as a dock on Bedwell Harbour. See **www.thetimbers.net**, 1.800.656.9418, Near **Map 4C.**

Creative Cuisine Catering is associated with the Pender Island Bakery: www.penderislandbakery.com, 629.6453.

Wedding Venues at Inns, Resorts and B&B's

See the *Accommodations Guide* for details on the following accommodations that are also wedding venues. All are located on North Pender Island except for **Poets Cove Resort**. B&B's may require rent of all guest rooms (typically two or three) in order to use the common room. These establishments should also welcome same-sex weddings:

OAKS BLUFF
Perched high atop a bluff on North Pender Island, two B&B's offer a spectacular setting for a wedding (See **Index Map**/just northwest of **Map 4C**). **Delia's Shangri-La Oceanfront Bed & Breakfast** and **Sahhali Serenity Luxury Oceanfront B&B** each have three guest suites and a common room. See their web sites for details.
Delia's: **www.penderislandshangrila.com**, 1.877.629.2800
Sahhali: **www.sahhali-serenity.com/weddings.htm**, 1.877.625.2583

MAGIC LAKE ESTATES
Ferndale on Pender B&B has a large fenced backyard with garden and a patio, three guest rooms, a small common room, and massage available; 629.6810, **Map 4A**, **www.gulfislandsguuide.com/accommodation/ferndale-BB.html**.
Gnomes Hollow B&B features a waterfall fountain in the backyard, three guest rooms and a common room; 629.3844, **www.gnomeshollow.com**, **Map 4**.

PORT BROWNING RESORT
The property has a beautiful waterfront setting and rustic facilities including a marina and pub. In the summer the lawn may be filled with campers and the facility bustling with boaters, but in the off-season it can be a peaceful setting; 629.3493, **www.portbrowning.com**, **Map 5B**.

OTTER BAY AREA
Sun Raven Wellness Retreat and B&B is located on a wooded hillside near the Otter Bay Ferry Terminal. The ocean-view lodge with swimming pool provides a picturesque setting for a smallish wedding with lots of good karma; 629.6216, **www.sunraven.com**, **Map 1A**.

SOUTH PENDER ISLAND
Poets Cove Resort at Bedwell Harbour is the premier (and priciest) facility on the Pender Islands, offering options for large or small waterfront weddings. Guests can arrive directly to the dock by boat (or yacht), float plane (from Seattle in summer; Vancouver year-round), or possibly water taxi from Sidney. Poets Cove is the best equipped to handle a large turnkey wedding function on the Pender Islands, with a catering service, a beautiful restaurant, a unique lounge, a full service spa (Susurrus), an activities department and other resort amenities; 1.888.512.7638, **Map 8**, **www.poetscove.com**.

Wedding Resources and Vendors

For everything you need to know about the legalities and logistics of marrying in BC, check the website **www.vs.gov.bc.ca/marriage/**. That site has contact information for the current marriage commissioners. Note that marriage commissioners are not wedding planners, and conduct civil marriages only, not religious services. A nominal fee is charged for their services. A list of wedding service vendors is included below. If your wedding is being held through your accommodation, they may be able to recommend additional vendors, since many choose not to advertise. In addition, you can consult the other Pender Island information sources described in the *Introduction* chapter.

VENDORS FOR YOUR CELEBRATION
CATERERS: See the *Reception Facilities and Catering* section.
WEDDING PLANNER: Angela Southward, 629.3229
WEDDING CAKE: Ewa's European Cakes, 629.3119; Angela Southward, 629.3229
  Pender Island Bakery, 629.6453
MUSICIANS: Flute: **Mary Reher,** 629.6431; She sometimes teams with:
  Brad Prevedoros, guitar, 539.5319, **www.manzanitaproductions.com**
  Bagpipes (solo or pipe band): **Jim Dunlop,** 629.6523, **jimdunlop@cablelan.net**
  Classical/jazz guitar and others: **Ptarmigan Music Society,** 629.6219
PHOTOGRAPHY: Kelly Irving, 629.3100, www.kellyidesign.com
FLORIST: **Petals on Pender,** South Pender, 629.3268
  Sherry Willing Floral Design: In House on Pender at Driftwood, 629.9950
HAIR AND BEAUTY (Appointments required for all except for Shear Delight):
  Hair by Diana, 629.3102
  Hope Bay Hair Salon, Hope Bay Store, 629.6911
  Shear Delight Hair Design, Driftwood Centre, M-F 9-6, Sat 9-5, 629.3582
  Susurrus Spa, Poets Cove Resort, Waxing, beauty treatments, 629.2113
  The Spa at Driftwood Centre, Tanning, Aesthetics, Massage, 629.9969

Same-Sex Weddings and GLBT Resources

Perhaps the most remarkable thing about same-sex wedings on Pender Island is just how unremarkable they have become. No longer are politics or controversy involved. The only statement being made is that of love between two human beings. When Arthur MacNeil and Dan Fitzpatrick (Photo, right) became the first same-sex couple to wed on Pender after Canada officially sanctioned such unions in July 2005, all of the elements of any wedding were present. Guests had come from all over

Pender Island and as far away as the Maritimes, relatives gave emotional testimonials of support, the happy couple exchanged vows, the locally-baked cake was cut, and everyone danced afterward.

LEGAL STATUS
Same-sex marriage has been legal in the Province of British Columbia since July 8, 2003, and at the federal level since July 2005. The Conservative party won the federal election in January 2006 on a platform that included trying to ban same-sex marriage at the federal level, but at time of writing the outcome of that effort is pending. In the interim, a flood of same-sex weddings are taking place since existing marriages would be honoured under their plan. If the Conservatives are successful, the result may be a federal civil unions registry. Actually, same-sex common law partners in Canada already have similar benefits as married couples, even with regard to immigration.

Non-residents of the province may obtain a BC marriage license, but it is up to the applicant to determine if it will be recognized at their residence of origin. Canadians should have no problem, but couples should verify particulars with their home province. For Americans, a BC marriage will probably be more of a sentimental bond than a legal one for quite some time, except possibly in a handful of *blue states* like Massachusetts. However, no federal gay marriage rights are on the horizon in the U.S. Other countries that have legalized same-sex marriage to date include the Netherlands, Belgium and Spain, while many European nations have established same-sex domestic partnerships.

Web resources regarding same-sex marriage and other gay rights issues: **www.samesexmarriage.ca**, **www.equal-marriage.ca**, **www.egale.ca** (advances equal rights for GLBT individuals), **www.365gay.com** and **www.advocate.com** (GLBT news) and **www.pflagcanada.ca** for parents and friends of GLBTs.

PENDER ISLANDS PARTICULARS
Check the web site **www.vs.gov.bc.ca** (click on Marriage Licenses & Certificates) for information on marriage license vendors and current marriage commissioners. Make sure to interview the commissioner and ask how they feel about performing same-sex weddings, and go from there.

In BC, like everywhere else in Canada, churches are not required to conduct same-sex weddings in their facilities. Some progressive churches have been conducting same-sex wedding ceremonies in Canada for years, but mostly in large urban areas like Vancouver. To date, I have not heard of any same-sex marriages conducted in Pender churches. For a religious ceremony on the Pender Islands, one must find a clergy member willing to conduct the ceremony, but it probably will not be in a church.

A few Pender Island hosted accommodations welcome the opportunity to host weddings, as described in the *Wedding Venues at Inns, Resorts and B&B's* section. All of the accommodations listed in that section welcome same-sex weddings. For additional details on these venues see the *Accommodations Guide*. There are also plenty of house and cabin rentals that may be appropriate. You should visit the accommodation prior to booking to make sure that it is what you are looking for. Various halls may also be available as well as public beaches or other natural settings that may make for a spectacular setting for an informal service.

Gay-friendly Accommodations

To aid gay & lesbian travelers select accommodations where they may feel most comfortable during their Pender Island stay, each hosted accommodation was asked if they wished to be placed on a *Gay Friendly* list, defined as *openly welcoming gay and lesbian travelers*. Of the sixteen accommodations responding, twelve requested to be placed on the list. The other four stated that they extend a welcome to everyone, including gays and lesbians, but prefered to opt off the list. The *Gay-Friendly* accommodations list follows. None of these accommodations cater predominantly to gay and lesbian guests. The clientele is mixed, and all should feel comfortable staying at them. See the *Accommodations Guide* for detailed information on the establishments.

Cedar Cottage B&B	Poets Cove Resort
Delia's Shangri-La Oceanfront B&B	Port Browning Resort
Eatenton House Bed & Breakfast Inn	Sahhali-Serenity B&B
Ferndale on Pender B&B	Sunshine Hills B&B
Gnomes Hollow B&B	Sunraven Wellness Retreat
Oceanside Inn	Whalepoint Studio & B&B

GLBT ON PENDER

The laid-back and inclusive attitude on the Pender Islands makes it a desirable place for gays and lesbians to live and vacation. Although the small island population does not support any gay establishments per se, there are a number of gay-owned businesses and services on the island. The Pender Islands are also a favourite place for gay professionals from Vancouver and other metropolitan areas to have second homes. No official GLBT (gay, lesbian, bisexual, transgendered) organizations have been formed on the Pender Islands. The following highlights some regional organizations and clubs:

Salt Spring Island: GLOSSI (Gay & Lesbian) **www.saltspring.com/glossi/**
Victoria: GLBT resources with links: **www.gayvictoria.ca**
Choral Society (Gay, lesbian & friends): **www.geocities.com/musaic_Victoria**
Gay men RV'ers (Rainbow Campers): **www.members.shaw.ca/rbcvi/**
Bisexual support group: **www.angelfire.com/bc3/bivictoria**
Transgender support group: **www.transgender.org/transcend/index.htm**
Victoria's Gay Nightclub: Prism Lounge, **www.prismlounge.com**,
642 Johnson Street (at Broad), 250.388.0505
Victoria Pride: **www.victoriapridesociety.org**. Events held in late June/early July.
Pacific Rim Yacht Club (PRYC): Vancouver Gay & Lesbian yachting club features rendezvous around southern BC (including Port Browning): **www.pryc.bc.ca**
Gay-related travel and activities in Vancouver: **www.gayvan.com**
Vancouver Pride is typically the last weekend in July, **www.vanpride.bc.ca**.

8 NEARBY ATTRACTIONS OFF-ISLAND

DAY AND WEEKEND TRIPS

The Pender Islands are centrally located in a wondrous area of natural and cultural attractions. See the *Boating Guide* (Chapter 15) for a sampling of destinations you can visit by private boat. This chapter summarizes destinations available to those without their own boat, including nearby islands and the Saanich Peninsula on Vancouver Island. Emphasis is on the areas most frequently visited by Penderites, including the Sidney (**Map 10**) and Victoria areas (**Map 11**). See the *Dining Guide - Wineries* (Chapter 5) for a Vancouver Island wine tour, the *Bicycling Guide* (Chapter 14) for Victoria cycling highlights, the *Shopping Guide* (Chapter 6) for a list of places to shop in Sidney and Victoria by category, and the *Boating Guide* for a description of Sidney.

Excursions from Pender by Boat Charter

See also the *Boating Guide - Fishing* and *SCUBA Diving* Sections

Sound Passage Adventures offers various sporting tours (diving, fishing, ecotouring) as well as excursions to adjacent islands such as Ganges on Salt Spring Island for the Saturday Market, Saturna Island for the winery, and a water taxi service to Sidney; **www.soundpassageadventures.com**, 629.3920.

Razor Point Boat Charters offers fishing tours and excursions to nearby islands on their 22-foot Wellcraft which seats four. Rates are by the hour with a 2-hour minimum; 629.9922, 250.881.5648 (cell).

The Canada Day Lamb Barbeque on Saturna Island is accessible to Penderites via a non-profit Saturna marine outfit, Viable Marine Services, 539.3200, or by local Pender outfits, **www.saturnalambbarberque.com**.

Island Camping, Ltd. is based in Sidney; 250.656.4826.

Excursions Via Ferry to Vancouver Island/Victoria

Frequent and reasonably-priced ferries between Otter Bay and Swartz Bay make the area between Sidney and Victoria the most common off-island day trip for Penderites. Although Victoria and Butchart Gardens are the main draw, many Penderites never make it past lovely Sidney-by-the-Sea, just a few minutes drive from Swartz Bay Ferry Terminal. This section emphasizes the area between Sidney and Victoria.

Victoria Highlights

Victoria is the most popular attraction that is easily accessible from the Pender Islands. Bustling Victoria Inner Harbour is where the vast majority of visitors spend their time, wandering around the beautiful and active waterfront with a backdrop of the **Fairmont Empress** hotel, **www.Fairmont.com/empress**, the British Columbia Parliament buildings, and The **Royal British Columbia Museum** **www.royalmuseum.bc.ca**, considered to be one of the finest in Canada. The downtown area is resplendent with restaurants and shopping opportunities. Victoria also boasts beautiful waterfront drives and numerous gardens. A highlight is Beacon Hill Park, a short walk from the Inner Harbour, which contains extensive lawns, lilly ponds with stone bridges, mature oaks and endless flower beds. The Strait of Juan de Fuca waterfront along Dallas Road is a fabulous place to stroll or cycle, with the snow-capped Olympic Mountains towering in the distance. See **Map 11** on page 108.

The small but interesting Chinatown (Canada's oldest) behind the ornate Gate of Harmonious Interest on Fisgard Street is lined with Chinese restaurants (see *Dining Out*, in this chapter), shops, food stands, and galleries. Check out the shops along restored Fan Tan Alley, once a gambling hub. The **Silk Road** tea shop and spa around the corner at 1624 Government Street is worth a stop; **www.silkroadtea.com**, 388.6815. See the *Shopping Guide* for other shopping suggestions around Victoria.

> **Tip:** Although the horse-drawn carriage rides that start across from the Wax Museum do not go around the Inner Harbour, some of the routes go through Beacon Hill Park, which is more interesting than the route through the James Bay area.

Festivals held at the Inner Harbour are very worthwhile. The reception for Her Royal Highness 50th Jubilee in October 2002 was exciting, climaxed by an air show by the Snowbirds. The Tall Ships festival in June 2005 was thrilling, though chaotic. Following are some of the highlights in Victoria and vicinity:

May	**August**
Victoria Day Parade	Symphony Splash
June	(See feature, next page)
Oak Bay Tea Party	Dragon Boat Festival
Jazzfest	Victoria Fringe Theatre Festival
July	**September**
Folkfest	Vancouver Island Blues Bash
SKA Music Festival	Saanich Fall Fair
Luminara Victoria	Classic Boat Festival
(In Beacon Hill Park)	**November**
Sidney Days	Santa Light Parade

For a current list of Victoria area festivals, consult the following web sites:
www.city.victoria.bc.ca/residents/artscl_artfest.shtml
www.foundlocally.com/Victoria/Entertainment/FestivalsList.htm

LOCALS TIP: SYMPHONY SPLASH BY BOAT
The most notable annual event is held the Sunday before BC Day (August 6 in 2006). A large barge containing a concert stage is floated into the Inner Harbour, facing the BC legislature buildings. The Victoria Symphony puts on a spirited, full-length evening concert which climaxes with the 1812 Overture complete with fireworks visible across the bay. Government Street closes around 2:00 pm, and other entertainment is provided around the Inner Harbour that afternoon. Spectators situate their chairs or blankets as early as two days before to claim a good spot along the shore. However, if you have a small boat, such as a dinghy, kayak or canoe, you are allowed to float in to the area between the shore and the barge just before show time. Since logistics can change year to year, contact the Victoria Harbourmaster at 250.363.3578 before deciding on your plan of action. The boats all raft together in front of the stage, creating a gigantic joyful picnic. Many of the dinghies are from the yachts moored at the overflowing downtown marinas. Pender boaters can either reserve a spot at a marina for their boat, then dinghy over to the event; trans-

Splash photo courtesy of Victoria Symphony.

port their small boat atop their vehicle to Victoria and launch from a park near the Inner Harbour; rent a boat from a local concession; or join an organized tour group. A popular place to launch a kayak is the Banfield Park dock upstream of Upper Harbour beyond the Selkirk Trestle (**Map 11** - See page 108). Locals warn to not leave your car in front of the park due to vandalism, but rather to park in the adjacent neighbourhood. Also avoid launching upstream of Tillicum Road due to tricky tidal currents. If you launch from along Victoria Harbour, follow the established traffic pattern, which is monitored continuously by the Harbour Patrol for your safety. If you launch from Westbay Marina, remember that the harbour entrance is exposed and can get very rough, and the return in the dark can be dicey. Take a working running light because the concert ends after dark, and after the last ferry back to Pender. Pack a picnic and get ready for the evening of the summer! **www.symphonysplash.ca**.

See the following web sites for information on current events, recreation, food and lodging on Vancouver Island:

www.tourismvictoria.com   **www.webvictoria.com**
www.vancouverisland.com   **www.victoriabc.com**

The site **www.greatmirror.com** has photographs from all over Vancouver Island.

LOCALS TIP: SAVING MONEY IN VICTORIA
Entertainment Publications sells a *Vancouver Island* coupon book that mostly covers Victoria through Nanaimo. The book offers numerous 2-for-1 coupons for restaurants and savings on attractions, recreation and hotels. See their website **www.entertainment.com** for included establishments. Some of these are noted as **E* in this book, but these can change year to year. Local organizations like the Pender Island Elementary Secondary School sometimes sell the books for fundraisers, which are valid from November through October each year, and some retailers including **Costco** may carry them as well. Also, check the Victoria Tourist Bureau at the Inner Harbour for other local coupon books that may be available, resulting in significant savings. Some coupons are also found in the Times Colonist daily newspaper, Monday Magazine and Victoria phone directories.

Dining Out - Sidney to Victoria

Wondering where to eat on your excursion to Victoria? If you feel like exploring beyond **White Spot** or **Tim Hortons**, check out the suggestions in this section that are based on my experience, as well as other Penderites and Victorians.
Listings with **E* have coupons in the 2006 edition of the Entertainment Book.
From Pender phones, first dial 1.250 for the Victoria area.

Sidney and the Saanich Peninsula

NEAR SWARTZ BAY FERRY TERMINAL
Stonehouse Pub, 2215 Canoe Cove Road, 656.3498, serves good food and local brews inside the restored stone heritage building or on the outside patio. *E

DOWNTOWN SIDNEY
On the Way to the Ferry: Call the following restaurants for food to go, but make sure to ask about timing when you order, since it can take 20+ minutes.
Popular Casual Fish: **Fish on 5th** (9812 5th St, north of Beacon Ave across from the bus stop) Great wraps, salads, fried or grilled fish, 656.4022.
Casual Greek: **Maria's Souvlaki Bar**, 9812 2nd St (near Beacon), 656.9944.
Home made food to go: **Chef on the Run**, 9760a 4th St, 655.3141.
Japanese Lunch Specials: **Taste of Tokyo**, 9842 Resthaven (north of Beacon), also Saturday dinner buffet, 656.6862, *E; **Japanese Garden**, 2493A Beacon, also Sunday dinner buffet, 655.1833. Chinese: **Maple Palace**, 9389 Fifth St, 656.8682.

SIDNEY WATERFRONT
The views toward Mt. Baker to the east are awesome, but the food is mostly typical fare at **Rumrunner Pub**, 656.5643 *E; and **Captains Table**, 656.3320. Café fare is served at **Portside Café**, 655.0119; and **Pier Bistro** at the public pier, 655.4995.

TSEHUM HARBOUR
Dock 503, at Van Isle Marina, 2320 Harbour Rd, is perhaps the best restaurant in Sidney, and accessible by boat as well (see the *Boating Guide*); 656.0828.

Latch Dining Room, 2328 Harbour Rd, is another upscale dining option; 656.6622.
Blue Peter Pub, 2270 Harbour Rd. Marina-side deck and good food, 656.4551, *E.

NEAR VICTORIA AIRPORT
The Roost at Highland House Farm, MacTavish Road and East Saanich Road. Popular for fresh baked goods, farm breakfast, awesome salads, soups and sandwiches. Dine in an old school bus and listen to ostriches, 655.0075.

NEAR BUTCHART GARDENS
You can re-enter **The Butchart Gardens** once per day (except summer Saturdays) if you choose to lunch outside of the park. Follow the signs to **Blue's Bayou Café** and their large outdoor deck overlooking Brentwood Bay, serving interesting Cajun food, 899 Marchant Rd, 544.1194. **Brentwood Bay Lodge** has a new and interesting waterfront pub. At the end of Verdier Avenue, off of West Saanich Rd, 544.2079, **www.brentwoodbaylodge.com**. **The Red Barn Market,** 5550 West Saanich Road sells organic meats and vegetables, ice cream, and sandwiches, 479.8349.

Victoria

SUNDAY BRUNCH AND BREAKFAST
Most Popular Waterfront Sunday Brunch: **The Marina Restaurant**, 1327 Beach Drive, Oak Bay. Extensive buffet features shellfish and interesting dishes with a beautiful view, for about $28. Reserve early: 598.8555.
Sunday Brunch at the Fairmont Empress: **Kiplings** offers a bountiful and sumptuous buffet, around $32. Kiplings also has great breakfast, lunch and dinner buffets at reasonable prices for the Empress. Reservations: 389.2727. *E (except brunch).
Upscale Bistro: **Herald Street Café**, 546 Herald Street. Popular west coast cuisine bistro offers a notable Sunday brunch. Reservations: 381.1441.
Dim Sum: **Don Mee Seafood** at 538 Fisgard Street in Chinatown serves popular daily dim sum lunches, and is great for dinner as well; 383.1032.
Homey Diner+: **John's Place** at 723 Pandora (near Douglas) is packed at breakfast for Belgian waffles with cream cheese maple syrup; **www.johnsplace.ca**, 389.0711.
All Day Breakfast: **Blue Fox**, 919 Fort St. Fluffy omelets & thick French Toast, 380-1683.

FOODS FROM ASIA
Quick Lunch: **Sabre's** $7 East Indian lunch buffet ('til 1:30) has good Tandori chicken, 3480 Tillicum Road (across from Tillicum Mall); 388.4655. *E
Best East Indian Food: **Spice Jammer,** 852 Fort Street, 480.1055 *E, and **Da Tandoor,** 1010 Fort Street, 384.6333 (dinner only).
Downtown Asian Lunch Treat: **The Noodle Box**, 626 Fisgard St, 360.1312 (also 818 Douglas): Stir fry, soup, appies and curries from southeast Asia. Reasonable and quick.
Korean: **Korean Gardens**, 3945C Quadra Street, 744.3311,*E.
Sushi: **Ebizo**, 604 Broughton Street, 383.3234. Try the yam tempura roll.
Japanese Lunch Buffet (11-2; $10): **Toku Sushi**, 2706 Government St. 385.6200.
Thai: **Siam Restaurant**, 512 Fort St., 383.9911.

SEAFOOD
Inventive Seafood: **Pescatores**, 614 Humboldt St, near the Empress, 385.4512.
Famous Seafood: **The Blue Crab**, Coast Harbourside Hotel, 146 Kingston St. is
known for excellent seafood. Reserve: 480.1999. Also Sunday brunch.
Late Night Eats: **Ferris's Oyster Bar & Grill**, 536 Yates St, 360.1824.
Romantic Spot: **Wild Saffron**, 1605 Store Street. Seafood and fondue, 361.3150.

FISH 'N CHIPS
Fun Outing: **Barbs Place** on Fisherman's Wharf. Take a harbour ferry from the Empress
dock or walk along the Inner Harbour pathway to this popular outdoor eatery for
great Fish 'n Chips or grilled fish; 384.6515, **www.barbsplace.ca**, Cash only.
Voted "Best Fish 'n Chips": **Haultain Fish 'n Chips**, 1127 Haultain, 383.8332.

ITALIAN
Cozy Locals' Favourite: **Il Terrazzo Ristorante**, 555 Johnson St (in the alley
behind Yates Street); cozy and intimate outdoor terrace; 361.0028.
Italy Meets Pacific Northwest: **Café Brio**, 944 Fort Street. Seafood and pasta; 383.0009.

VEGETARIAN/ORGANIC
Hip & Healthy: **Re Bar Modern Food**, 50 Bastion Street. All three meals. Fresh food
with ethnic flare, Torrefazione coffee, and Cascadia baked goods; 361.9233.
Organic: **Green Cuisine**, 560 Johnson St, 385.1809, *E; **Molé**, 554 Pandora, 385.6653.

ROMANTIC RESTAURANTS
Dine by Candlelite: **Camille's Fine West Coast Dining**, 45 Bastion Square. Serves
interesting choices with local ingredients. Reservations: 381.3433. *E
Upscale Cafe: **Herald Street Café** (see *Sunday Brunch*).

LATE NIGHT DINING & NIGHTLIFE
Popular & Unpretentious: **The Mint**, 1414 Douglas, Open to 2am, live entertainment
and good Nepalese/Tibetan food. Cash only. *E.
Live Irish Music: **Irish Times Pub**, 1200 Government; **www.irishtimespub.ca**
Check Out Velvet on Sundays: **Steamers Pub**, 570 Yates St, **www.steamerspub.ca**, *E
Gay Nightclub: **Prism Lounge**, **www.prismlounge.com**, 642 Johnson Street, 388.0505.

PUBS AND POTENT POTABLES
Waterfront Heritage Brew Pub: **Spinnaker's**, 308 Catherine St. (Off Esquimalt Blvd.)
Great atmosphere, service, food and brew. Accessible by harbour ferry or long
waterside walk. Reservations: 1.877.838.2739, 386.2739.
Seven Rooms: **Sticky Wicket Pub** in Strathcona Hotel, 919 Douglas Street at
Burdett has English ambience inside or rooftop sand volleyball; 383.7137. *E
Large Outdoor Deck Overlooks Upper Harbour: **The Canoe Club** brewpub, 450 Swift
Street features homemade brew and pub fare; 361.1940, *E
Classy Downtown Drink: The **Bengal Room** in the **Fairmont Empress Hotel** is
grand and very British. Their curry buffet is good, though sparse for $25; 384.8111
Many Martinis: **Bravo** restaurant, 1218 Wharf Street, also has good food; 386.2900, *E

INNER HARBOUR WATERFRONT
Dinghy to the Floatplane Terminal: **Blackfish Café** has very good food, 386.2739. *E
Tourist Traps: Plenty of places offer great views if that is your priority.

COFFEE
2% Jazz at Hillside & Douglas gets raves for its espresso. *E
Bean Around the World in Chinatown on Fisgard near Wharf Street is a good place
  to hang out, sip top-notch java and eat their famous seed cookie.
Dutch Bakery & Coffee Shop at 718 Fort Street features homemade chocolates. *E
Jaleens, 1320 Blanshard Street, is popular and artsy.
Murchies (see Tea above) offers a variety of delicious sweets and coffee drinks.
Chains: Never fear, there are over a dozen **Starbucks** around town (including the
former Torrefazione location at 1234 Government Street), as well as other chains such
as **Serious Coffee** (*E) and **Seattle's Best**.

TEA
Afternoon tea is a Victoria tradition. The
most famous is of course the **Fairmont
Empress** high tea, which should be experienced at least once in a lifetime for the $50
(summer) price tag. Although quite the
tourist attraction, the tea sandwiches, pastries, tea, service and atmosphere are in fact
top notch (Photo, right). Reserve at
389.2727. Locals tend to frequent the more
casual tea options that abound around town.
Oak Bay is home to the locals' favourite
White Heather Tea Room (1885 Oak Bay

Avenue; reserve for this small room: 595.8020), which is similar in quality to the
Empress for about $15, and **Blethering Place** (2250 Oak Bay Avenue, 598.1413, full
menu, *E). Near the Inner Harbour, try the historic **James Bay Tearoom** (332 Menzies
Street, full menu, 382.8282), and visit the Saturday market across the street.
Overlooking the Gorge Waterway (a Harbour Ferries stop) is **Point Ellice House &
Gardens**, where period-costumed hosts offer a historic tour ($25 for tour and tea, lunch
also served, 2616 Pleasant Street off Bay Street, east side of Bay Bridge, 380.6506).
Murchie's Tea & Coffee at 1110 Government Street has a wide selection, snacks, sand-
wiches, and bounteous afternoon tea for $25 (381.5451).

Also worth noting is the
afternoon tea at **Butchart
Gardens Dining Room**
which offers elegant décor
and service. Make reservations at 652.8222. After your
tea, stroll around the Sunken
Garden (Photo, left).

Victoria Arts and Entertainment

Local residents can count on interesting arts and entertainment year round, but the vast majority of events occur during the summer tourist season.

PERFORMING ARTS

Save-On Foods Memorial Centre The 7,000-seat indoor arena opened in 2005 with much fanfare and a sold out Rod Stewart Concert. This venue enables big-draw acts to visit Victoria and is the home venue of the ECHL Victoria Salmon Kings. See **www.saveonfoodsmemorialcentre.com** for schedules. Tickets are available on line through their web site or by phone: 220.7777; 1925 Blanchard St. at Pembroke.

The Royal and McPherson Society of Victoria presents a variety of cultural events, including concerts, plays and dance recitals at the Royal Theatre (805 Broughton St), McPherson Playhouse (#3 Centennial Square, 600 block Pandora Ave) and other venues. For schedule and ticket info see **www.rmts.bc.ca** or call 1.888.717.6121 or 386.6121. The box office for all venues is in the McPherson Playhouse lobby.

Belfry Theatre: Produces a varied schedule of quality theatrical productions in a renovated church; 1291 Gladstone Ave, Victoria, 385.6815

Intrepid Theatre: Producers of the Fringe Festival in late summer and the Uno festival. **www.intrepidtheatre.com.**

Kaleidoscope Theatre: Resident programming for young audiences and their families. **www.kaleidoscope.bc.ca.**

Langham Court Theatre and **Victoria Theatre Guild**: 805 Langham Court, 384.2142; **www.langhamcourttheatre.bc.ca**

Theatre Inconnu: Alternative Theatre, 1923 Fernwood Road, 598.4211.

Phoenix Theatre at UVic: 721.8000, http://finearts.uvic.ca/theatre/

Up-Island: **Chemainus Theatre**: Presents a season of plays including dinner theatre. Tickets: 1.800.565.7738, **www.chemainustheatrefestival.ca**

Cinema

MOVIE LISTINGS

Consult web sites such as **www.forreel.com** or **www.webvictoria.com/movies.php**

FILM FESTIVALS AND ART FILMS

Victoria Independent and Video Film Festival: **www.vifvf.com**.

Cinecenta: University of Victoria, **www.cinecenta.com**, 721.8365

Vic Theatre: Downtown at 808 Douglas St/106 Nootka Ct, 383.1988

MAINSTREAM CINEPLEX AND SINGLE THEATRES

Silvercity Tillicum, Tillicum Mall, newest stadium cinema, with a food court; 381.9300

Cineplex Odeon, 780 Yates, 383.0513 (Sometimes shows inde films)

Capital 6, 805 Yates, 384.6811

University 4, 3980 Shelbourne, 721.1171

Star Theatre, 9842 3rd St, Sidney, 655.1171 (Sometimes shows inde films)

Caprice, 777 Goldstream, Langford, 474.3212

IMAX THEATRE Royal BC Museum, **www.imaxvictoria.com**, Tix: **https//sales.royalbcmuseumbc.ca**, 480.4887. Offers $37 annual IMAX pass.

Museums

TOP PICKS

Royal British Columbia Museum: At the Inner Harbour. Also contains IMAX theatre. 675 Belleville St, 356.7226, **www.royalbcmuseum.bc.ca**.

Craigdarroch Castle: Preserved industrialist's mansion, 1050 Joan Crescent (at Fort Street), 592.5323, **www.craigdarrochcastle.com**.

Art Gallery of Greater Victoria, 1040 Moss St, 384.4101, **www.aggv.bc.ca**

OTHER MUSEUMS

Butterfly Gardens, 1461 Benvenuto, Brentwood Bay, 652.3822

Dominion Astrophysical Observatory, 5071 W. Saanich, Saanichton, 363.8262

Hatley Park Castle and Museum, 2005 Sooke Rd, Victoria, 656.0853

Horticulture Centre of the Pacific, 505 Quayle Rd, Victoria, 479.6162

Maritime Museum of BC, 28 Bastion Square, Victoria, 385.4222

Miniature World, Empress Hotel, 649 Humboldt, Victoria, 385.9731

Naval and Military Museum, 17000 Station Forces, Victoria, 363.4312

Pacific Undersea Gardens, 490 Belleville St, Victoria, 382.5717

Royal London Wax Museum, 470 Belleville, Victoria, 388.4461

Saanich Historical Society, 7321 Lochside Dr, Victoria, 652.5522

Victoria Bug Zoo, 631 Courtney St., Victoria, 384.2847

Butchart Gardens

A must-see attraction on the Saanich Peninsula, **Butchart Gardens** is located in Brentwood Bay, between Swartz Bay and Victoria. The gardens consist of walking paths meandering through fifty-five acres of fabulous floral gardens that change with the seasons. In 1904, Jennie Butchart began to beautify a worked-out quarry site left behind from her husband's Portland cement enterprise. The result is an exquisite Sunken Garden and surrounding areas that were dedicated to a Rose Garden and a Japanese Garden. For information, consult their web site **www.butchartgardens.com** or call 1.866.652.4422, 250.652.4422 (Business office), 250.652.5256 (Recorded information) or 250.652.8222 (Dining room reservations - recommended on crowded days). Special events include summer evening illumination of the grounds, spectacular Saturday evening fireworks and live evening entertainment. During the Christmas season the park is open in the evening, and is decorated to the hilt with Christmas decorations and lights. The theme is the Twelve Days of Christmas, and displays such as a carousel are placed throughout the park, while carollers sing at the entrance.

LOCALS TIP: Check on Butchart's annual pass rate, which in 2006 is $42, compared to $23 for summer adult daily admission. Take your admission ticket receipt the same day to the Visitor Services office to get the pass for only $19 additional. You can then frequent the park all year, watching the change of seasons reflected in the flora, a great way to pass the time if you have several hours before the next ferry back to the Pender Islands. Note that there are blacked out days such as summer fireworks Saturdays. However you can purchase an annual pass on summer Saturdays or special event days getting credit for that day's admission. The pass also gives you 10% savings at Butchart Gardens food stands, restaurants, gift shop, and discounted admission on the excluded days.

TIP: BUTCHART'S FIREWORKS SPECTACULAR
The summer fireworks show is actually a fireworks pageant set to music using illuminated props surrounding a pond, and a bounty of fireworks painting the sky. The show is different every year. It is definitely worth the price of admission and putting up with the crowds. You may want to arrive early, say 4:00 pm or earlier, set out your blanket in the prime observation area (signs direct you), then enjoy the gardens. You can reserve a table at the pricy Dining Room Restaurant (well in advance) to pass some of the time (since readmission is not allowed on these special days). Entertainment is also provided on the grounds. You are allowed to bring in your own picnic, or you can purchase one in the park. After the fireworks show is over the gardens are illuminated, giving them an interestingly different perspective. Rather than fight the traffic, stroll through the gardens one more time.

Directions: From Swartz Bay, follow Highway 17 south to McTavish. Turn right, then left on West Saanich, and right on Benvenuto. Bus: Route 70, transfer to Route 75.

Nearby Gulf Islands
The surrounding Gulf Islands are frequently visited by private boat or by boat charter. See the *Boating Guide* for more detailed information on the destinations on the nearby islands. Following is a brief summary of the opportunities available via BC Ferry:

SALT SPRING ISLAND
Ganges is accessible through limited BC Ferries direct service from the Pender Islands, or more frequent service using the connection through Swartz Bay - Fulford Harbour. Private boat charters may also be available for excursions to Ganges. The Saturday summer market is popular.

OUTER GULF ISLANDS
The other developed Outer Gulf Islands are Galiano, Mayne and Saturna. Reasonable BC Ferry service schedules are available between the Pender Islands and Galiano and Mayne Islands, but getting to Saturna Island is more of a challenge. No discount ticket books are offered on the Inter-Southern Gulf Island Routes. Fares (2006) between Otter Bay and the other Southern Gulf Islands are $3.95/person in summer and $3.15 the rest of the year. Undersize vehicles cost $8.10 summer and $7.05 at non-peak times, so that a roundtrip with two persons in peak season costs approximately $32.00 (plus $1.40 in fuel surcharges).

You can drive on and explore the entire islands, or, you can walk on and explore several parks, shops, or restaurants within walking distance of the ferry terminals. A bicycle opens up more options, although all of the islands are hilly with narrow, winding roads. (See the *Bicycling Guide*). Pick up brochures and maps of the islands on the ferries. For maps of the islands and attractions on line check out:
Galiano Island: www.galianoisland.com. A 9-hole golf course is located at St. Andrews Drive off of Linklater Road, 250.539.5533. Several restaurants in Sturdies Bay.
Mayne Island: www.mayneislandchamber.ca A highlight is Dinner Bay Park with its lovely Japanese Gardens, a tribute to the displaced Japanese here during WWII.

Around the corner is the island's premier restaurant at the Oceanwood Inn www.oceanwood.com. You may also boat in using their mooring buoy.
Saturna Island: www.saturnatourism.com. Saturna Vineyards is open for tastings, tours and a bistro May through October. See www.saturnavineyards.com, 539.5139. A large portion of Saturna Island is now part of the Gulf Islands National Park Reserve.

Vancouver and Whistler

Vancouver is your best bet for cultural events, dining, and shopping selection, though the cost of getting there via ferry is several times that of getting to Victoria (assuming use of the discounted multi-ticket book). The summer fireworks competition held over English Bay is a world-class event. Stanley Park is a wonderful place for a walk or better yet, a bike ride on the expansive trail system through the park and Vancouver waterfront. See the *Bicycling Guide*.

The following websites contain information on Vancouver:

www.vancouver-bc.com   www.vancouverbc.ca
www.vancouver.com   www.where.ca/Vancouver/
www.tourismvancouver.com

Whistler is one of North America's premier ski and year round resorts and is accessible via a 2-hour drive from Vancouver. Whistler/Vancouver is the site of the 2010 Winter Olympic Games, www.vancouver2010.com. Consult www.whistler.com or www.whistlerblackcomb.com. See also *Skiing* in the *Recreation Guide*.

Other Destinations

While this chapter has attempted to cover some of the nearby destinations that people living on and visiting the Pender Islands can access relatively easily, there are many more that are beyond the scope of this guidebook.

Up-island on Vancouver Island, Campbell River bills itself as *Salmon Capital of the World* where lodges specializing in fishing abound. www.campbellrivertourism.com.

On the west coast of Vancouver Island is the Tofino-Uclulet area, a wild and beautiful resort area where accommodations tend to get booked solid all summer, and storm-watching is popular in winter. See www.pacificrimtourism.ca, etc.

To the south of the Gulf Islands is the U.S. where the San Juan Islands resemble the Gulf Islands in many ways. This area is described in the *Boating Guide*. A Washington State Ferry accesses these islands from Anacortes, Washington and Sidney, BC.

Downtown Victoria
Duplicate of Map 11 of the Map Atlas

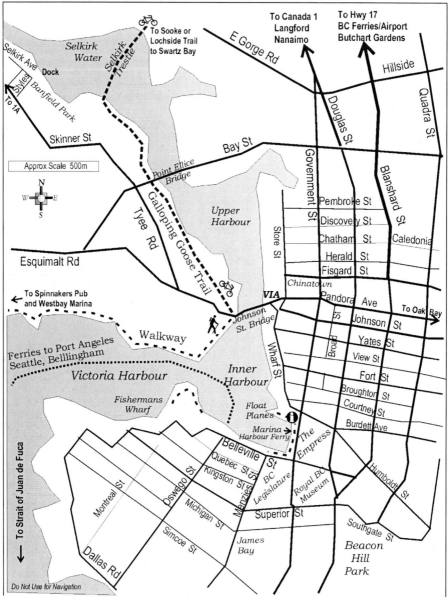

9 RECREATION GUIDE

ACTIVITIES ON THE PENDER ISLANDS

This chapter summarizes recreation opportunities on the Pender Islands that are appro priate for both visitors and locals alike. More detailed information related to golfing, hiking, bicycling, and boating are found in separate *Guides* in subsequent chapters. See the *Shopping Guide* chapter, *Sporting Goods* heading for equipment and supplies.

The Detailed Guides

Hiking and Strolling *See: Chapters 11-13*
Hiking opportunities on the Pender Islands include numerous trails, currently linked by walks along roadways, with hopes for more off-road connections in the future. Trails are situated in lands managed by Parks Canada, the Capital Regional District, and the Pender Island Conservancy. Bicycles are not allowed on any of the island hiking trails. See the *Coastal Access and Hiking Guide* for a detailed summary.

Bicycling *See: Chapter 14*
No public bike trails are found on the Pender Islands, and bicycles are not allowed on the island hiking trails. However, some of the roads are so uncrowded that you may not see many automobiles at all. The Penders are very hilly, and there are no easy routes on the islands, but some routes should be manageable by most. The degree of traffic also varies substantially. The *Bicycling Guide* contains suggested routes from the ferry terminal to all over the islands, details on the three best bicycling areas on the islands, and information on nearby off-island cycling opportunities.

Boating - Kayak, Sail and Power *See: Chapter 15*
The Pender Islands are located in the midst of the one of the premier cruising grounds in North America. Several marinas are situated around the islands, and kayaking is extremely popular. See the *Boating Guide* for detailed narrative information.

Fishing *See: Chapter 15*
The waters off the Pender Islands are not as bountiful as they once were, but there are still ample fishing opportunities, especially during the salmon runs that occur throughout the year. Recent years have seen record runs of Pink salmon. See the *Boating Guide* for further information on fishing.

Swimming   *See: Chapters 11-13*

The waters on and around the Pender Islands are either cold or colder, but some areas warm up enough in the summer to make swimming bearable for the hearty. Several swimming pools are also available to the public around the island. They are located at the marinas at Otter Bay, Poets Cove, and Port Browning. Warmer lake swimming is also an option. See the *Coastal Access and Hiking Guide* for information on swimming.

SCUBA Diving   *See: Chapter 15*

The nutrient-rich waters off of the Pender Islands and the Southern Gulf Islands are teeming with life and offer some world-class diving opportunities. Clarity is best in winter. See the *Boating Guide* for information on diving.

Golf   *See: Chapter 10*

The **Pender Island Golf and Country Club** is a wildly popular asset to the Pender Islands. The picturesque nine-hole course with separate tee boxes to simulate a back nine is open year round, weather permitting. Memberships are available, but the course is open to the general public with no tee times necessary to date. See the *Golfing Guide* for information. **Maps 1, 1A.**

Disc Golf (Golf Island Course)   *See: Chapter 10*

One of the best disc golf courses in British Columbia, and perhaps all of Canada, is located in the midst of the Magic Lake Estates neighbourhood; **Maps 4, 4B.** Fun for all skill levels, this challenging course provides an exhilarating outdoor experience for locals and visitors alike; **www.discgolfisland.com**. See the *Golfing Guide* for information on Golf Island Disk Park. If Pender Island boaters desire a change of disc golf scenery, they can sail over to Ganges on Salt Spring Island and play the 18-hole Hart Memorial course in Mouat Park, a short walk from town.

Other Activities

Picnic

Numerous parks and coastal access areas provide great picnic opportunities. See the *Coastal Access and Hiking Guide* for the best places to picnic. Two of the prettiest and most accessible picnic locations are Roe Islet (**25**) and Brooks Point (**97**). Picnic tables are located in several parks, including Magic Lake (**48**), Thieves Bay (**51**), Shingle Bay (**49**), Lilias Spalding (**90**), and GINPR-Beaumont (**82**). In late summer, wasps (yellow jackets) can be a nuisance, and battery-powered racquet-shaped bug zappers are sold locally to keep them at bay. The severity of the problem varies by location and from year to year. Remember that littering on the Gulf Islands is not tolerated.

Tennis

Tennis courts are available at Port Browning Resort (**Map 5B**) and Poets Cove Resort (**Map 8**) for a fee. Magic Lake Estates has two well-maintained courts on Privateers Road, west of Galleon Way, for residents (**Maps 4, 4A**). A key is required for access. Magic Lake Estates residents pay an optional annual fee of $37 per immediate family for access in addition to their homeowner's association dues. The general public can also gain access for a fee by following the instructions posted on the entrance gate. A group of local residents get together at these courts for an informal weekly *tennis club*.
Resources: Tennis BC site: **www.tennisbc.org**; U.S. tennis site: **www.usta.com**
Comprehensive Canadian tennis site with links: **www.tenniscanada.ca**
International associations: **www.wtatour.com**; **www.itftennis.com**
Supplies: **Centre Court Racquets**, 1543 Pandora, 598.7175; **Courtside Sports**, 1136 Hillside, 386.4236; Also, various Victoria department and sporting goods stores.

Horseback Riding

Bracket Cove Farm at 5611 Razor Point Road on North Pender Island offers a variety of supervised horseback riding opportunities for various levels of experience. They feature pleasure riding along trails on gentle show trained mounts, pony rides, and English and Western riding lessons. Call Laurie Kay in advance at 629.3306.
Email: mythreesons57@hotmail.com.
www.horsecouncilbcsite.com: Horse Council of British Columbia
www.cantra.ca: Canadian Therapeutic Riding Association
www.img.net/erabc/: Endurance Riders Association of British Columbia

Roller Hockey

A roller-hockey rink on the Pender Island School grounds is popular with both students and with roller hockey clubs on island. Adults play on separate men's and women's nights. The season is September through May. Check the Pender Post for current contact information.
www.bciha.com: BC Inline Hockey Assn;
www.whockey.com: Women's hockey website, includes in line roller hockey.
www.mlrh.com: Major League Roller Hockey

Billiards

A coin-operated pool table available for public use is located at the Port Browning Resort Pub. Tournaments are held occasionally.
www.cbsa.ca: Canadian Billiards & Snooker Association. Rules and techniques.
www.billiardsdigest.com: Magazine with free on-line content

Softball

Danny Martin ball field is located between Schooner Way and Buccaneers Road near the entrance to Magic Lake Estates (**Maps 4, 4B**). The ball field is operated under the supervision of the Pender Islands Youth Sports Association (PIYSA) as a result of License Agreements between PIYSA and the CRD. Pender Island Parks Commission plays an overall supportive role within the park. To book the field or to express concerns about it, contact Danny Martin at 629.3739.
www.softball.bc.ca: BC amateur softball association with links.
www.softball.ca: National softball site.
www.svisoftball.ca: Victoria/South Vancouver Island minor fast pitch softball.
Baseball: **www.baseball.bc.ca**: List of leagues. Sidney Little League: 250.656.3994.

Skateboarding

A skateboarding park for Pender's youth has operated at the Community Hall in the past, however a new location is being sought, preferably on CRD land.
www.skateboarding.com: Transworld's site includes BC skateboard parks.
www.exploratorium.edu/skateboarding: The science of skateboarding.

Basketball

The Pender Islands Basketball Association organizes games at the school gym. See the Pender Post for contact and schedule information. Resources: **www.basketball.ca**.

Curling

A group of Pender curlers travel to Sidney for weekly games, except in summer. Beginner and experienced men and women are welcome to participate in the game of fun, exercise and fellowship. Play is at Glen Meadows Curling Club, 1050 McTavish Road, Sidney, 250.656-3136. See the Lions Club Phone Directory (*Sports & Recreation*) for the Pender Island contact. Other curling clubs are located in Esquimalt, Juan de Fuca and Victoria.
www.curling.ca: Canadian Curling Association
www.curlbc.bc.ca: Organization promotes curling in BC and lists clubs

Badminton

Badminton has a long tradition on the Pender Islands. In the past it was played at the old Hope Bay and Port Washington Halls, and later at the school auditorium. For information on where and when the players meet, check the latest Lions Club phone directory under *Sports and Recreation*.

Aerobics and Dance

Aerobics and dance classes are typically announced in the Pender Post. For contacts for evening classes or Rhythmics, check the latest Lions Club phone directory. Also inquire at **Revolution Dance and Fitness** at Driftwood Centre; 629-3122.

Skiing

The only skiing opportunities on the Pender Islands occur every two or three years when the islands are blanketed with a substantial snowfall. Then, Penderites can take out their Nordic skis and cruise along the empty roads or trails. Following are southern BC ski resorts that have more consistent snowpack:

VANCOUVER ISLAND
Mt. Washington Resort, Courtenay: Alpine, Snowboard, Nordic
About 100 km/90 minutes drive north from Nanaimo; **www.mtwashington.ca,**
1.888.231.1499, 250.338.1386; Snow Report: 1.888.833.1515
The Mt. Washington Ski Bus operates daily scheduled bus service between Victoria, Mill Bay, Duncan, Ladysmith, Nanaimo, and the Mt. Washington Resort from December to April; 250.475.6950.

MAINLAND: VANCOUVER AREA
Cypress Mountain, West Vancouver: Alpine, Snowboard, Nordic, Night Skiing
604.419.SNOW, **www.cypressmountain.com**
Grouse Mountain, North Vancouver: Alpine, Snowboard, Night Skiing
604.984.0661, **www.grousemountain.com**
Mt. Seymore, North Vancouver, Alpine, Snowboard, Snowplay, Snowshoe;
604.986.2261, **www.mountseymore.com**

MAINLAND: WHISTLER
Whistler-Blackcomb, Whistler: Alpine, Snowboard, Nordic
About 115 km/2.5 hours drive from Vancouver Airport; 1.866.218.9690, 604.932.3434,
www.whistlerblackcomb.com, www.mywhistler.com

SKIING WEB RESOURCES
www.skicanada.org: Contains links to BC ski areas
www.skicanada.org: Canada Ski Council; Ski/snowboard areas and equipment

Recreation Web Resources

GENERAL
www.sport.gov.bc.ca: Government site on BC sports.
www.athletescan.com: Canada's national team athletes Association.
www.canadiansport.com: Canadian sport information and resources.

HOCKEY

www.canadianhockey.ca: National site.
www.bcaha.org: British Columbia Amateur Hockey Association.
www.canucks.com: Vancouver Canucks official NHL website.
www.nhl.com: Pro team site.
www.salmonkings.com: Victoria ECHL team plays at Save On Foods Arena.

SOCCER LACROSSE AND RUGBY

www.canadasoccer.com: Canadian Soccer Association.
www.bcsoccer.net: BC Soccer Association.
www.whitecapsfc.com: USL soccer team of Vancouver.
Lacrosse **www.bclacrosse.com: www.lacrosse.ca:** BC and National sites.
Rugby **www.bcrugby.com**: BC rugby union.

TRIATHLON

www.triathloncanada.com: National federation for tri/duathlon.
www.tribc.org: Provincial governing body for tri/duathlon.

RUNNING

www.canadianmarathoning.bc.ca: Canadian marathon running.
www.royalvictoriamarathon.com: Victoria's marathon is in October.
www.timescolonist10k.com: The TC sponsors a 10k in April.
www.Canada.com/Vancouver/specials/sunrun/: Vancouver April 10k.
www.vancouverisland.com/sports/runningclubs.html: Running clubs.

MARTIAL ARTS

www.judobc.ca: Governing body for judo in BC.
www.taekwondo.bc.ca: BC Taekwondo Assoc, includes club lists.
www.jjbc.ca: Jiu-Jitsu BC Society.
www.karatebc.org: Governing body for karate in BC; club lists.
www.kungfu.ca: Chinese martial arts in Canada.

FOOTBALL

www.cfl.ca: Official website of the Canadian Football League.
www.bclions.com: Canadian Football League team of Vancouver.

10   GOLFING GUIDE

TRADITIONAL AND DISC GOLF

Traditional Golf

Pender Island Golf and Country Club

2305 Otter Bay Road, Pender Island, BC V0N 2M1. **Maps 1, 1A.**
Business office/fax 629.6614, Golf Shop 629.6659;
Chippers Restaurant 629.6665, **www.penderislandgolf.com**.
Directions: From the ferry terminal, continue to the right onto McKinnon Road until the first intersection at Otter Bay Road. Make a left, and follow the road to the parking lot and clubhouse on the right, about 1 km from the terminal.

The **Pender Island Golf and Country Club** has been in existence since 1937 and was incorporated in 1945. It has operated continuously since then except for a short period during WWII. The popular nine-hole golf course has four separate tee boxes to help simulate a back nine. It is open to the general public all year, except when conditions such as frost, snow, or excess rain render the course unplayable. The course is situated in a pastoral agricultural valley along Otter Bay Road.

A concrete bridge and pond on signature hole 8/17 is modeled after the St. Andrews course in Scotland. (Photo, left). The course can be challenging with several hilly fairways, a few ponds and numerous bunkers. The par for 18 holes is 68 for men and 69 for ladies. Yardage is blue 5049; white 4494. It is rated Men 64.8; Ladies 62.8. Slope index is Men 110, Ladies 106.

THE PENDER ISLAND GOLF COURSE FROM THE MEN'S BLUES

1/10 (Separate tees) Easy par 4, 249/283 yards, straight, downhill, bunkers left.

2/11 Tricky par 4, 322 yards, straight, flat then up steep hill to green with bunkers in front and behind/left.

3/12 (Separate tees) Easy Par 4, 275/303 yards, straight, downhill, pond to right of green, bunkers to the left.

4/13 Short par 3, 137 yards, straight, bunker beyond green.

5/14 Long par 4, 364 yards, straight. Left hookers loose balls to cows over the fence.

6/15 Tricky, long par 3, 190 yards, straight but narrow, bunkers around green.

7/16 Normal par 4, 272 yards, severe dogleg left, bunkers left and right.

8/17 (Separate tees) Tricky par 3, 230/184 yards. Signature hole. Tee off from cliff (#8), or below the cliff (#17). Two ponds along fairway; bunker beyond green. Replica of St. Andrews course bridge.

9/18 (Separate tees) Par 5, 466/485 yards, a long uphill battle with trees and geese. Watch for golfers at practice area to the left and on hole 8/17 to the right. Aim for white post over the hill toward the left. Bunkers to right of green. Contains a manual red signal to alert approaching golfers if others are on the green (the only traffic signal on the Pender Islands!)

Facilities include a newly remodeled golf shop (open May through mid-November and some winter weekends) and **Chippers Café** (see the *Dining Guide*). When the golf shop is closed in winter and after hours the rest of the year, the restaurant handles registration, or else there is an honour box. Golf clubs, push carts, and electric cart rentals are available. Green fees (2006) are weekdays $20 for 9 holes and $32 for 18, and weekends $22 for 9 holes and $34 for 18. Clubs rentals are $10/$15; Pull carts are $3/$4 and golf carts are $16/$25. Twilight rate is $20 for as many holes as you can play. They accept Interac, Visa and MasterCard. Check for discounts for off-season play and golf-and-dine specials associated with **Chippers Café** (usually summer Wednesday *9 and Dine.*). No tee times are necessary except for tournaments. However, the course has been steadily gaining in popularity, and it can be crowded in summer at times, compared to what islanders are used to. Tournaments close the course to the general public for part or full days an average of once per week in summer. Call the course before coming over to make sure that there are no tournaments, and to see if they are expecting a large group from one of the resorts. Also, the course is reserved for members only on Tuesdays for Ladies Day and on Thursdays for Men's Day until 1:00 or 2:00 pm.

About 250 golfers have purchased a membership to the Pender Island Golf and Country Club. The 2006 membership fees are approximately $1,500 to join and $550 annual dues, plus occasional maintenance assessments. This is an active social organization, with many tournaments, men's and ladies leagues, and various social events centered around the Golf Club. A charity Pro-Am tournament is held in July.

A free practice pitch and putt area is located near hole no. 9/18 and accessible from Otter Bay Road (watch out when golfers are teeing off from hole 9/18). A practice net is located at the clubhouse parking lot, but there is no driving range.

Golf Facilities Nearby Off-Island

DRIVING RANGES
The nearest substantial driving ranges are on the Saanich Peninsula: **Island View Golf Centre** (250.652.5215) is visible as you head south from Swartz Bay on Highway 17. Make a right at Island View. Further south is the **Blenkinsop Valley Golf Centre** next to the **Mount Douglas Golf Course**. From Swartz Bay, take Highway 17 south to the Royal Oak exit. Make a left on Royal Oak and follow it for about 2.5 km to Blenkinsop Road. Turn right, and then drive south another 2.5 km to the golf complex on the left. The two-level facility is lighted and is typically open late. A large mini-golf course is adjacent.

GOLF COURSES
Numerous golf courses are located in the Victoria/Saanich peninsula area. See *On-Line Golf Resources* below for information. Note that the Entertainment Book (*E) may contain 2-for-1 coupons for several Vancouver Island Golf courses including **Prospect Lake** and **Olympic View**.

The other golf courses on the Southern Gulf Islands are on Galiano and Salt Spring Islands, all 9-hole courses. **Galiano Golf & Country Club** is at 24 St. Andrews Drive (off of Linklater Rd.), **www.galianoisland.com/galianogolf/**, 539.5533. For a taxi from the ferry call 539.0202. On Salt Spring Island, **Salt Spring Golf and Country Club** is at 805 Lower Ganges Road (at Vesuvius Bay Road), 250.537.1760, **www.saltspringgolf.com**; and **Blackburn Meadows Golf Club**, is at 269 Blackburn Road, between Fulford and Ganges. 250.537.1707. To ferry to Salt Spring Island, you will need to connect from Fulford Harbour to Swartz Bay in at least one direction.

MINI GOLF
There is no miniature golf on Pender Island. The best in the Victoria area is **Blenkinsop Valley Adventure Golf**, 4239 Blenkinsop, 250.477.4104, *E. See directions to adjacent driving range, above. Smaller courses are at Elk Lake, 250.658.4737, *E, and in Cordova Bay (**Mattick's Farm Mini-Golf**, 5325 Cordova Bay, 250.658.4053).

Golf Resources on the Web
www.bcga.org: British Columbia Golf Association
www.rcga.org: Royal Canadian Golf Association
www.golfmax.ca: See *Where2Play* for scorecard of Pender Island course (no charge). You can also, keep track of your golfing progress on-line (fee).
www.bcgolfguide.com: General information.
www.wanderplanet.com: Click *Activities* on top; then *Golf* then *Victoria* for information on golf courses on the Gulf Islands and Vancouver Island.
Professional Golf: **www.cantour.com**, **www.pga.com**, **www.lpga.com**
Web Tips: **www.golftipsmag.com**: Magazine with free web content;
www.pgaprofessional.com: Comprehensive site with numerous free tips.
SUPPLIES See also *Shopping Guide - Department Stores* and *Sporting Goods* Sections:
Golf Plus, 3400 Douglas, 475.1886
Nevada Bob's, 3088 Blanshard, 475.6177

Disc Golf

Golf Island Disc Park is located on North Pender Island on Galleon Way between Rum Road and Port Road, **www.discgolfisland.com.** The closest disc golf course off-island is Hart Memorial in Ganges on Salt Spring Island. The 18-hole course is in Mouat Park, a short walk from town.

Golf Island Disc Park

Disc golf has a large *cult* following, and one of the best courses in British Columbia (or perhaps anywhere) is located in the Magic Lake Estates neighbourhood of North Pender Island. People of all ages and skill levels play this course, and it is a great way to combine a hike through the forest with a fun and challenging sport. The course, named *Golf Island*, was created in the early 1980's and has the enthusiastic support of the Pender Island community. It contains 27 holes of both the *tone-pole* and

chain basket variety, carved into steep, mixed second growth forest terrain dominated by arbutus, fir and cedar trees. The total course length is 1265 meters, with a par of 84. All holes are par 3 except for holes 14, 24, and 27, which are par 4. A course map is posted at the course entrance and replicated with permission at the end of this chapter.

The course is a public park and is currently free and open to all, but a sign warns that vandalism could potentially change that. Please respect the course and do not litter, cause damage, and smoke only in the shelter. In summer, the Gulf Islands are typically under an extreme wildfire alert. A total smoking ban may be in effect.

Hole 27 is inside an arbutus tree

Course veterans will notice that the course was re-aligned in 2004. Holes 1 through 12 remain the same, holes 13, 14, and 19 through 24 are new, and the rest are renumbered. The old popular hole 13 was removed because of environmental concerns, and the signature hole 18, the one up the cliff with a basket inside of a unique *octopus* arbutus tree, is now hole 27. Watch for loose rocks on this steep and challenging hole. Holes 1 through 9 have remained tone pole holes (a wooden post with a metal covering on the upper portion), whereas holes 10 through 27 have been replaced with chain baskets, with different community sponsors for each one.

Websites: The Golf Island course has a new website which contains a course map, descriptions of each hole with photographs, upcoming tournaments, and a message board, **www.discgolfisland.com**. The site also contains links to maps of other courses and various disc golf organizations such as British Columbia Disc Sports Society, **www.bcdss.bc.ca**. That web site includes information on disc golf tournaments. The Island Disc Golf Society promotes disc golf in Victoria and Vancouver Island, **www.islanddiscgolf.com**.

Tournaments are regularly held at Golf Island. The Pender Classic/bender takes place on the last weekend of May annually. In 2005 the Duck Golf Final occurred in early April and the BC Provincial was held in September.

HOW TO PLAY
Rules for disc golf can be found at the Professional Disc Golf Association (PDGA) web site **www.pdga.com**, and a brief summary is posted at the course. The basic game plan is approached and scored similarly to traditional golf. Start at tee number 1 to the right of the shelter. It is marked by a white plastic bucket (where you can throw your trash) and markings on a rock that contain the hole number, the par (usually 3), the distance to the goal in meters, and an arrow pointing to where the goal is. Stand behind that rock and throw the disc toward the goal, whose number matches the one on the rock. Pick up the disc where it lands and try again. If the lie is difficult, you can take a step with your other leg anchored on the disc landing spot, as long as it is not toward the goal. If the lie is unsafe, you can move it to an immediately adjacent safe location. Do not disturb the vegetation in any case. Continue until you hit the metal part of the *tone pole* (holes 1-9) or land it inside the *chain basket* (holes 10-27). Then, look for the next white bucket, which is probably the location of the next tee. If it is not visible, look for an obvious trail that probably leads to it, and for helpful directional numbers on trees. The course map found in this chapter should help. Check the number on the rock to make sure you found the correct one.

The first nine begins to the right of the shelter. The second nine (holes 10 - 18) begins in front of the shelter, and the third nine (holes 19 -27) begins down a path to the right of and parallel to hole 1. Some of the goals are a straight shot, with trees on both sides of the *fairway*. Others are trickier and require throws that curve around trees. A myriad of situations present themselves along disc golf courses, which is why there are so many types of discs available. There are drivers, chippers and putters, some tending to curve right, or curve left, go a greater distance, and the like. Novices may be better off starting with an all-around disc like the *Shark*.

Golf discs are more compact, heavy, and durable than everyday flying discs such as Frisbees, which tend to get battered and broken as they bash into trees and rocks. On the Pender Islands, golf discs are sold for about $13 - $20 at **Magic Lake Market** (closest to the course) as well as the **Pender Island Pharmacy** and **Driftwood Auto Centre**. Stick to colours that are easier to find (red, white, orange, etc), and write your name and phone number inside them with a permanent marker in case you lose them. Other disc golfers can relate to a lost disc and may actually call you if they find it. Or, they may hang it on a nail inside the shelter. It is good etiquette to help others in your party look for their wayward discs, and to not run ahead of them and get in their way before they throw. Let faster groups play through. Keep score as in regular golf.

Directions: Follow the signs to Magic Lake from the ferry. Once you reach the Driftwood Centre, continue south along Bedwell Harbour Road, which becomes Canal Road. After passing Prior Centennial Campground on the right, bear right onto Aldridge Road when Canal Road veers to the left to South Pender Island. The main road curves sharply to the right and becomes Schooner Way. Continue to a *T* intersection, which is the entrance to Magic Lake Estates. Turn left, continuing on Schooner Way. Make the first right on Privateers Road, then the first right onto Galleon Way. Pass Rum Road, go up a hill, and then look for parking in front of the painted Golf Island sign on the right. If you are hitch hiking, you can ask for a ride to the Magic Lake Fire Hall (#2). A trail to the west of the fire hall (**Map 4B**, Trail **55**) leads through the woods for about 10 minutes to Golf Island. Continue hiking until you reach Galleon Way where the start of the course is located on your left. If you are staying at the Prior Centennial Campground, you can walk to the course on the Heart Trail/Heart Trail Extension, which is about 1.5 km each way (**Map 4B**, Hikes **53** and **54**).

Drinking water, a new outhouse, a new sign with course map, a picnic table, and a shelter are situated at the entrance to the course. Notices of upcoming tournaments are posted.

The Disc Park is operated under the supervision of the Pender Islands Youth Sports Association (PIYSA) as a result of License Agreements between PIYSA and the CRD. Pender Island Parks Commission plays an overall supportive role within the park. Volunteers play an important role in the park's operation and maintenance. Any concerns relating to the park should be expressed to Alex Fraser (course founder) at 629.6494.

The disc must hit the tone pole as shown.

Golf Island Disc Park Map

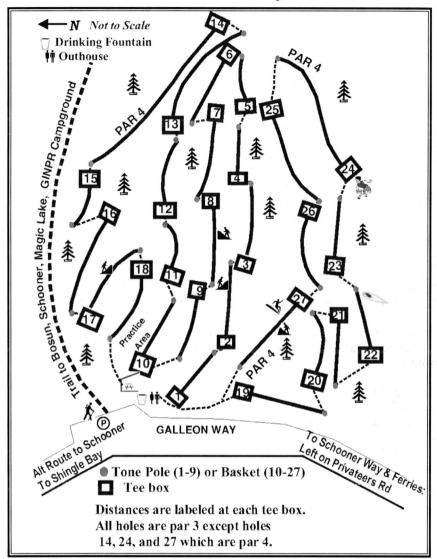

Tone Pole (1-9) or Basket (10-27)

☐ Tee box

Distances are labeled at each tee box.
All holes are par 3 except holes
14, 24, and 27 which are par 4.

Sample Scorecard

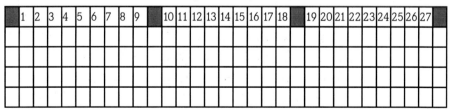

1	2	3	4	5	6	7	8	9		10	11	12	13	14	15	16	17	18		19	20	21	22	23	24	25	26	27	

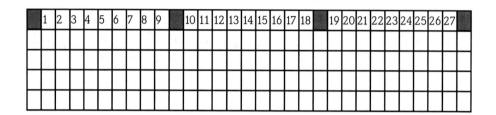

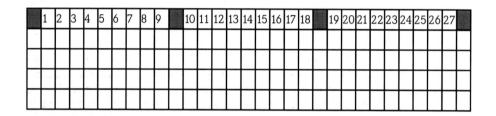

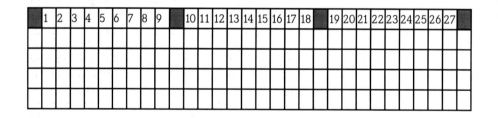

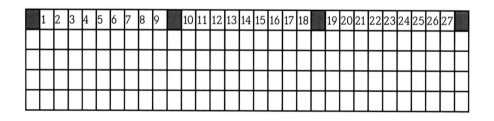

11 COASTAL ACCESS AND HIKING GUIDE - PART ONE

BACKGROUND INFORMATION AND SUMMARIES

Some one hundred trails and ocean accesses are described in this chapter. They are referred to by name and number (i.e. **82**), and are listed by region, from the north end of North Pender Island to the south end of South Pender Island. Features are shown on the *Map Atlas*, and are cross-referenced in this Chapter and the *Table of Contents*.

Overview

The Pender Islands contain a multitude of public lands that have already been designated as parkland or have the potential to be designated as parkland. The process continues to evolve as properties are purchased by various agencies and facilities and/or trails are constructed or improved. The formation of the Gulf Islands National Park Reserve (GINPR) in 2003 was a significant event in the evolution of the Pender Islands, which incorporated existing parkland and added additional land to the bounty. Pender Island Parks Commission (PIPC), under the umbrella of the Capital Regional District (CRD) is working with Parks Canada to link trails all over the Pender Islands creating a cross-island network. Trail routes have already begun to incorporate shore walks, and more ocean accesses are planned. The PIPC will be adding up to 15 additional ocean accesses in the foreseeable future, some sooner than others. Beach walks will be increasingly used as part of the island-wide trail system. Plans continue to connect various trails within the PIPC network, and to connect PIPC trails with GINPR trails. Trail standards will likely follow GINPR standards so that one trail classification system exists throughout the island trail structure. By the time the 2010 Vancouver Olympics take place, the island trail systems could be dramatically different than today. The long-term goal of the CRD/PIPC is to be able to walk from the north end of North Pender Island to the southeast end of South Pender Island through interconnecting trails systems. This description of the Pender Islands' coastal accesses and hikes is taken during a snapshot in time, as the complex of Pender Island parks continue to develop.

Park Agencies

Following is a summary of the various government agencies and their involvement with the Pender Islands' parks. As a hiker, this concerns you if you need to report something you see along the trail, have comments or questions, or are just interested in how the park systems are managed.

Pender Island Parks Commission (PIPC) develops and maintains a myriad of public parks, ocean accesses, and trails throughout the Pender Islands, under authority of CRD Bylaw #2515. Many of PIPC's trails are on Crown Land, typically road rights of way, which are already accessible to the public. PIPC also manages linear parks such as the trail to Gardom Pond. PIPC constructs trails through these areas to provide controlled public access. A side benefit is a kind of *neighbourhood watch* function for locals using the trails that pass by residences. Photographs of some of the PIPC trails and parks appear in their *Park Album* on **www.crd.bc.ca/penderparks**. They will be developing GPS-based trail maps of their trails in the coming years. Some notable PIPC trails on North Pender Island are Found Road Ocean Access, George Hill Park, Oaks Bluff Park, the Heart Trail, and the trails in the Magic Lake Estates area. On South Pender Island, trails include William Walker (connector to Mt. Norman), Castle Road Trail, and Enchanted Forest. Most of the ocean access points are administered by PIPC, except as indicated. Also, North Pender community parks such as the Magic Lake Swimming Hole, Thieves Bay Park, Shingle Bay Park, and South Pender's Lilias Spalding Heritage Park are administered by PIPC. To report a problem on a Pender Parks trail contact the Maintenance Commissioner. Contact their web site and click *Commissioners* for the current parks commissioners and their responsibilities. Golf Island Disc Park and Danny Martin ball field are under the supervision of the Pender Island Youth Sports Association (PIYSA) as a result of License Agreements between PIYSA and CRD. Any concerns relating to these areas should be expressed to the people directly involved: Danny Martin for the Ball Park 629.3739 and Alex Fraser for the Disc Park 629.6494. PIPC plays an overall supportive role within these parks.

Capital Regional District (CRD): The Brooks Point and Gowlland Point reserves on South Pender Island are CRD parks. Mount Norman was once a CRD park, and is now part of GINPR. CRD Parks, 490 Atkins Avenue, Victoria, BC, V9B 2Z8, 250.478.3344, Email: crdparks@crd.bc.ca, **www.crd.bc.ca/parks/**

Islands Trust Fund Reserve: The Islands Trust Fund currently has 50 protected areas established and carefully managed for conservation. Of these, six are located on North Pender Island, and two on South Pender Island. Some of these parcels are parks managed in coordination with other agencies, such as Medicine Beach on North Pender Island and Enchanted Forest and Brooks Point Regional Parks on South Pender Island. Other parcels were acquired only to protect habitat and ecosystems, such as the Sharptailed Snake Covenant, the Cottonwood Creek Covenant and the Dennis and Ledingham Covenant Lands, on North Pender Island. **www.islandstrustfund.bc.ca**; 250.405.5186.

BC Provincial Parks: Prior Centennial Provincial Park/Campground and Beaumont Marine Provincial Park were once BC Provincial parks, and are now both incorporated into the GINPR. Provincial Parks remain on some other islands, such as Salt Spring and Galiano; **www.env.gov.bc.ca/bcparks/**

Parks Canada: The Gulf Islands National Park Reserve (GINPR) was created in May 2003 to preserve a representative portion of the Strait of Georgia Lowlands of British Columbia, a highly urbanized natural region. The park contains various coastal island landscapes on 16 islands, reef areas and numerous small islets throughout the Gulf Islands. Access to the islets in the park system is prohibited to protect the fragile ecosystems. Exceptions are Dock Islet and *Lot 65* next to Samuel Island, which can be used during the day as stopovers for kayakers. On North Pender Island, the principal National Park lands include the Roesland and the Roe Lake areas, Prior Centennial Park and Campground and Mount Menzies. These areas are now Gulf Islands National Park Reserve - North Pender. The only fees charged are for camping, which is allowed at the summer-only campground at Prior Centennial Park. On South Pender Island, the former Mount Norman CRD Park, the contiguous former Beaumont Provincial Marine Park, and the newly acquired Greenburn Lake area are administered by Parks Canada. Blunden Islet off the tip of South Pender Island is also part of GINPR, but access is not allowed. Fees are charged for camping at the primitive Beaumont campground, and for mooring at the marine park in the summer months. These areas are now referred to as Gulf Islands National Park Reserve - South Pender. The various GINPR lands on the Pender Islands are in the process of evaluation for trail development and park management. Local office: 2220 Harbour Road, Sidney, BC, V8L 2P6; 250.654.4000, open weekdays 8-4:30. Email: gulf.islands@pc.gc.ca; Web site: **www.pc.gc.ca/Gulf**. A satellite office is located in the Hope Bay Store on North Pender, with little or no public hours. **Emergency dispatch number for Parks Canada: 1.877.852.3100**

Parking

Use common sense when parking on the Pender Islands. At trailheads where there are no parking lots, park only on safe shoulders and park completely off the pavement along any main roadway, but watch for ditches. There is no designated overnight parking, except for those users of parks and recreational facilities and resorts. The RCMP may tow vehicles that obstruct roadways, especially if it is a main thoroughfare.

Trail Rules, Hazards and Preparedness

RULES
Trail rules may be posted at the trailhead. In general, dogs must be kept under control and may not chase or harm wildlife. Carry a plastic bag to clean up after them. Mountain bikes are not allowed on any island trails or parks to minimize impact to the natural environment. Motorized dirt bikes are especially harmful and riders are subject to a $2,000 fine in the National Park. Respect private property and the boundaries of adjacent property owners. Try to keep noise levels down. There is no need to scare away bears here. Stay on established trails to avoid damaging the natural environment. Do not take any souvenirs, including wildflowers, and leave no trace of your passage. No camping is allowed except at designated campgrounds. Campfires are allowed only at the GINPR campgrounds, and may be banned in summer. The islands are very dry during the summer and fall. All fires are typically banned and smokers should always be very careful with lit cigarettes and matches. Smoking is sometimes banned as well. One careless incident can create an island-wide disaster.

HAZARDS

The large predators (cougars, bears and wolves) were eradicated from the Pender Islands many decades ago. In fact, except on extremely rare occasions when a cougar finds its way here, and with no poisonous snakes, there is not much to worry about in that regard on the Pender Islands. It is always best to hike with a partner, though, since some of the trails are used so infrequently that no one may come along for a long time if you fall and injure yourself. And, most of the trails have slippery spots and tripping hazards like roots and rocks. Occasionally, a park stair will rot out and fail. If you do hike alone in the backcountry, tell someone of your plans, and carry a cell phone (which may not work in all locations) or a two-way radio with someone available at the other end. You may also want to bring a noisemaker, such as a whistle. The hazards that you are most likely to encounter are of the small, pesty variety. See the *Hazards Pests and Emergencies* section in Chapter 18 for information on mosquitoes, wasps, and ticks. Early in the summer, some lesser-used trails may be overgrown which increases the likelihood that a hiker will brush up against a tick. Wasp nests can pop up rather quickly and within inches of a trail. Mosquitoes are plentiful in some areas, mostly the moist ones, and pleasantly absent in others. It is always wise to avoid being bitten by mosquitoes.

BE PREPARED

Consult a local hiking book for a description of all the items that are helpful to carry along on Gulf Islands hikes. Some of the vital safety items are an up to date first aid kit, a compass (directions can get confusing on the Penders), appropriate maps, extra layers of clothing in case you are delayed, waterproof rain gear for unexpected storms, an emergency blanket of some kind, and a flashlight, especially when days are short. Also bring sufficient water (especially on warm summer days) and nutritious snacks.

PAY ATTENTION

Although most of the trails on the Penders are well marked and of fairly short duration, there are areas where you can get lost if you wander off of the main trail, or follow a trail in the wrong direction. This is most likely in GINPR lands, which are large parcels where many trails remain unmarked at time of writing. Old skid roads can confuse matters further. The Roe Lake area is probably the most confusing, since it is crossed by the most old trails and skid roads (**Map 3A**). The trail up from Beaumont Marine Park to the Mt. Norman trail junction (**82**) can also be confusing to follow in places. Greenburn Lake is a new GINPR acquisition, and until official trails are constructed by Parks Canada, the area beyond the main path to the lake will remain an overgrown maze of roads and casual trails. Mt. Menzies can also be confusing in places. Parks Canada discourages bushwacking because the main goal of the National Park is to preserve the Gulf Islands habitat. In the Pender Parks system, most of the trails are marked and easy to follow. The upper portions of the George Hill and Castle Road (Spalding Hill) trails have a few false branches that may confuse some. The Found Road trail also has some confusing off-shoots.

Ocean Accesses, Swimming and Pools

Numerous public ocean access points have been designated throughout the Pender Islands. Some are easily accessed with ample parking. Others require a hike of up to an hour each way. Most of the beaches are rocky, but there are also several wide pebble and sand beaches on the islands. The Pender Parks ocean access points are marked with wooden posts bearing the name of the access. Since many of the beach access points are between private homes, you are reminded here (and by way of signs at most places) to respect private property. The shoreline of Canada is public property between the high and low tide marks. Many of the beaches described here only exist at lower tides; so make sure to become familiar with the current tide table if you plan to do some beach exploring to avoid being stranded. See the *Boating Guide - Tides Currents and Hazards*. In general, the tide changes every six hours, or four times per day. Also described in this Guide are public facilities such as government docks that you can walk out on for a vista, public marinas, lake accesses, and swimming pools.

✿ Indicates a recommended ocean access. ✿ ✿ Are the best.

The three swimming pools open to the public for a fee are at Otter Bay Marina, Port Browning Marina and Poets Cove Marina. At time of writing a new community swimming pool is proposed as well.

Exploring the Shoreline - The Intertidal Zone

Most of the coastal areas around the Pender Islands are sensitive intertidal zones, as described by signs posted at many of the ocean access points. The intertidal zone is the habitat of abundant marine species and is an important indicator of the overall health of the marine environment. The rising and falling tides, which can vary by up to 3 meters in the region, help to create distinct zones of marine life, as species can survive out of the water for various lengths of time.

The Splash Zone is the highest zone, receiving water only from the splashing of waves at higher tides. The black, encrusting Sea Tar Lichen is one of the only organisms able to survive the high salt levels present there, and the periwinkle snail feeds on it. In winter the red alga Red Laver grows in this zone, but is killed off by the hot sun in springtime.

The Upper Intertidal Zone is submerged during high tides, but organisms must be able to survive extended periods exposed to the elements. The upper extent of this zone is marked by the Small Acorn Barnacles that are exposed only during spring tides, and therefore can only feed and breed two times per month. Common Acorn Barnacles are less tolerant to exposure above water, and occur lower in this zone. Both are the white acorn-shaped creatures so commonly seen clinging to rocks (or boats), with snails slowly foraging them.

The Middle Intertidal Zone is submerged about half of the time, allowing more organisms to live there. Here mussels crowd out the barnacles, and Dog Whelks (snails) eat them. This shows how the lower limits of organisms are determined by biological factors such as competition and predation, while the upper limits are determined by physical factors such as desiccation and heat.

The Lower Intertidal Zone is only exposed at low tide, and is the habitat of the Ochre Star, or Purple Star (Photo, right). It is a keystone species, which is one that is vitally important to the health of an ecosystem. This predator lives about twenty years, and can eat eighty California Mussels per year, as well as its share of barnacles. Where Ochre Stars are absent, mussels tend to carpet the lower intertidal zone, eliminating the diversity of the ecosystem. Where they are present, mussels thrive mostly in the middle zone where the Ochre Stars

cannot survive (Cannings, 2004). Recently, a non-native protozoan has been killing the Stars around BC. Besides starfish and snails, the main predators along the rocky shoreline are birds such as the Black Oystercatcher, although they have been on the decline around the Pender Islands because of damage to their nests, which are on the ground. A variety of seaweed and algae are found throughout the lower zones, as well as limpets, bivalves, chitons, sea urchins, anemones, worms and other organisms.

For detailed information on the organisms that flourish along the shoreline, grab a field guide such as *Seashore of British Columbia* by Ian Sheldon and explore. A new local guide is *Get Your Feet Wet* by Julie Johnston and Patricia Haugh of Pender Island, which contains insights regarding the intertidal zone and illustrations by Susan Taylor.

When exploring, be mindful of tides, and be careful when stepping on the slippery seaweed exposed at lower tides. Also, to ensure that the ecosystem remains intact for future generations, it is important to treat it with respect. The Georgia Strait Alliance has prepared some guidelines to minimize impact to these marine communities that are summarized on the following page. Also check **www.georgiastrait.org**.

TAKING CARE OF THE SENSITIVE INTERTIDAL ZONE

* Leave living animals and plants where you found them. Moving species from one portion of the beach to another or removing them from the beach, not only impacts their chance of survival, it can also effect the survival of other organisms, who may depend on the removed species for their survival. Tidepools in different regions of the beach have different salinities, and organisms may die if moved.

* Replace rocks to their original position. If you do turn rocks over, do it gently so as not to crush any animals living underneath. Put rocks back the way you found them, again being careful not to crush the animals underneath. If rocks are not put back the way they were found, the animals that have been displaced may die of exposure to the sun and air.

* If harvesting for clams, oysters, mussels and other shellfish, collect only the number you will eat and stay within the government-set limits. Overharvesting threatens species survival. Contact the local Fisheries and Oceans office to obtain information on the minimum size and maximum number harvestable. Inform yourself about *red tide*, if you plan to harvest shellfish, since paralytic shellfish poisoning can be fatal.

* Avoid walking on animals. At low tide, many animals such as barnacles, mussels, and limpets, close up to protect themselves from drying out. Their protective shell is vital to their survival. Walking on them can damage and crush organisms.

* Fill in any holes. Unnatural piles of sand from excavated holes may kill other animals whose burrows can no longer reach the surface.

* Leave the beach cleaner than you found it. Human garbage such as plastic bags often ends up on the beach. This can kill marine life that either become entangled in it or ingest it. Pick up litter and dispose of it properly.

Hiking Trails - Summary

The relatively small Pender Islands provide a surprising diversity of hiking opportunities, thanks to the plethora of public parks that have been set aside and trails constructed through them. Depending on your length of stay, your athletic ability, and your preferred vistas, you can select from a number of interesting walks and hikes. Each hike will provide you with a unique experience. A stroll to the island shoreline will allow you to interact first hand with the aquatic environment and give you the opportunity to watch for sea mammals or shorebirds. The walks to Roe Islet (**25**) and Brooks Point (**97**) are generally easy and most anyone in your group can participate. Or, you can drive right up to the beautiful Medicine Beach (**42**) or Mortimer Spit (**79**) and explore from there. Beaumont Marine Park (**82**) boasts the only shoreline trail of any length on the Pender Islands, and it is a beautiful one, though it is accessible only by boat or a fairly strenuous hike from land. Hikes along rocky beaches at low tide are possible at several locations, two of which have already been incorporated into trail walks (**10** to **11** and **80** to **81**). Several seaside communities are fun to stroll in as well, including Hope Bay (**Map 1C**), Port Washington (**Map 1B**), and Trincomali (**Map 4D**).

Hikes to panoramic vistas provide awe-inspiring views of the Pender Islands and surrounding areas, including Vancouver and the Coast Range on the lower mainland to the north, Mount Baker and the Washington Cascades to the east, Washington's Olympic Mountains to the southwest, Vancouver Island to the west, with the southern Gulf Islands and Washington's San Juan Islands in between. These hikes require more physical exertion. If you are in reasonably good physical condition, you should be able to handle all of them fairly easily. Otherwise, before hiking up Mount Norman (**82**, **83**, **85**), you may want to try other smaller hills first. Try Oaks Bluff (**70**), then George Hill (**6**) or perhaps Castle Road Trail (**89**), each of which provides its own unique reward.

The Pender Islands also have wonderful inland forest hikes. If you are coming to the Pender Islands from an area resplendent with forest habitat, hiking through these second- growth forests may be a lower priority for you than the coastal or vista hikes. If you live in a city and yearn for a quiet forest escape, or live on the Pender Islands, then by all means try the wonderful forest walks available. The Enchanted Forest on South Pender provides an easy forest stroll complete with interpretive signs (**91**). On North Pender, you can walk the fairly level trails through the peaceful and pretty forest near Golf Island Disc Park (**54 - 57**), or combine your hike with a fun game of disc golf. The area that comes closest to feeling like a mountain wilderness is the Gulf Islands National Park Reserve (GINPR) land around Roe Lake (**29 - 37**). You may get the same feeling in the lush second growth forest as you would in a large park on the mainland, without the worry of encountering a bear or cougar.

Rating the Trails

Trails on the Pender Islands are described in detail in Chapter 12 (*Part Two - North Pender*) and Chapter 13 (*Part Three - South Pender*). They are ranked on a scale of 1 to 10, with 10 being the *Best of Pender*. Ratings are based on the quality of the hiking experience and special features encountered such as vistas or ocean accesses.

10 The best of the Penders.
8 Unique and beautiful, worth a special trip.
6 Very nice, worthwhile if you are in the area.
4 OK for residents of the area, but not worth a special trip.
2 Not the greatest hike, but all preserved areas are worthwhile.

Hikes by Difficulty and Type
Difficulty was geared to the average person in average physical condition. Trails are all relative with regards to the Pender Islands. Some people may find some of the easy trails difficult, while others may find the strenuous trails easy. Trail conditions were taken into account, as some of the trails are not well developed and require some minor

technical maneuvering that may be difficult for some. A few of the more strenuous trails may become moderate if trail conditions are improved with stairs and/or railings.

The types of trails are indicated by *V* for Vista, *C* for Coastal and *F* for Forest. Vista trails all travel through forest. The numbers (i.e. **19**) indicate the hike/trail reference.

EASY HIKES

North Pender Island
• GINPR Roesland/Roe Islet (**25**) C
• GINPR Roe Lake - North Trailhead (**29**) F
• Medicine Beach Loop (**42a**) C
• Hope Bay Area Stroll (**15**) C, F
• Trincomali Area Stroll (**76**) C
• Magic Lake Disc Park Trails (**54-57**) F
• Gardom Pond (**45**) F
• Magic Lake area linker trails F

South Pender Island
• GINPR Beaumont Marine Park Coastal
  (Ocean trailhead - **82**), C, F
• Gowlland Point/Brooks Point (**102**) C
• Enchanted Forest Park (**91**) F

MODERATE HIKES

North Pender Island
• Oaks Bluff Park (**70**) V
• GINPR Mt. Menzies (**19**) V
• Buck Lake Area Tour (**69**) F,C
• Found Road Ocean Access (**11**) F,C
• GINPR Campground to Disc Park (**54**) F
• Mt. Menzies - Pender Parks (**18**) F
• Magic Lake area linker trails

South Pender Island
• GINPR Greenburn Lake (**99**) F
• William Walker Trail (**86**) F

STRENUOUS HIKES

North Pender Island
• GINPR Roe Lake: Cramer Hill (**34**) F
• George Hill Park (**6**) V
• GINPR Roe Lake from South
  Trailhead(33, 37)

South Pender Island
• GINPR Mt. Norman Climbs (**82, 83, 85**) V
• Castle Road Trail to Spalding Hill (**89**)V
• GINPR Beaumont Marine Park from
  Ainslie Pointt Road Trailhead (**84**) F, C

Most Strenuous: The hike over Mt. Norman between Canal Road trailhead and the coast at Beaumont Marine Park is long and strenuous, but is the most rewarding hike on the Penders (**85, 82**) F, V, C

Hiking Club

The Let's Go Walking club has been active on the Pender Islands since 1993. At time of writing the group meets twice weekly, Mondays and Fridays at 9:30 am, at the upper parking area of the St. Peters Anglican Church on North Pender Island. Check the Pender Post for the latest meeting place and times. They walk to a variety of destinations on the Pender Islands as well as occasional excursions to the surrounding islands and beyond. Groups are typically split up based on fitness level.

12   COASTAL ACCESS AND HIKING GUIDE - PART TWO

NORTH PENDER ISLAND

Finding Specific Trails
In each area a Trailhead Reference Point is described, which is typically a main roadway intersection, and is labeled on the corresponding map in the *Map Atlas*. Directions are provided from the ferry terminal to each Trailhead Reference Point, and then further directions are provided under each trail description from the trailhead reference point to that particular trail. ✿ **Indicates a recommended ocean access. ✿ ✿ Are the best.**

Port Washington and Stanley Point Areas

Port Washington was one of the two main centres of population (the other being Hope Bay) when the Pender Islands' European settlement began in the late 1800's. Named for Washington Grimmer, the community developed into a conservative English Anglican rival to the nearby liberal Scottish Presbyterian Hope Bay community. The first government wharf was constructed here in 1891. The community also contained a post office in the Old Orchard Farm house, a general store built in 1910 next to the wharf (vacant at time of writing, photo, above), a community hall at the intersection of Otter Bay Road and Port Washington Road (razed in 1978) and St. Peters Anglican Church (moved in 1997 to the Anglican compound south of the Driftwood Centre). The general store has had many incarnations, the most recent of which is the   W.H.O.L.E women's cooperative that hopes to reopen the general store in the future as part of the Port Washington Historic Trust. The area is mostly residential, with some agricultural activities at nearby farms down Port Washington Road to the east. The government wharf is used as a floatplane and water taxi dock. Several scenic ocean access points are located in the area, as well as a top-notch vista hike up George Hill in the Stanley Point area. It is also a nice area to stroll and take in the history of the area, especially during the colourful spring and fall. Galleries include

Armstrong Studio and the **Renaissance Studio. Maps 1, 1B.**
Trailhead Reference Point
Intersection of Otter Bay Road and Port Washington Road. From the ferry terminal continue to the right on MacKinnon Road to Otter Bay Road. Make a left and follow it past the golf course. Otter Bay Road ends at Port Washington Road. **Maps 1, 1B.**

Washrooms
Facilities are limited in this area. The closest are the Golf Course/Chippers for their customers, or at the Otter Bay Ferry Terminal.

Ocean Accesses

1 PERCIVAL COVE
A signed trail begins on the ocean side of the reference point at Otter Bay and Port Washington Roads. Limited parking is available along the shoulder of Otter Bay Road. A dirt (muddy when wet) trail runs between private homes and is cut between thick blackberry bushes (bountiful in late summer) and native roses. In about 5 minutes one reaches stairs to a sandy/pebbly beach accessible at low tides. Views are to the Port Washington Dock and out Grimmer Bay to Boat Islet, and across Swanson Channel to Prevost and Salt Spring Islands. Armstrong Studio is located near the trailhead.

2 GRIMMER BAY
✿ From the reference point, return back down Otter Bay Road for about 350 metres where the road rounds a bend and nears the shoreline. A wooden *Grimmer Bay* signpost is on the right next to 1211 Otter Bay Road, and limited parking is available along the right shoulder. Steep steps carved into the bank lead down to the picturesque beach, which consists of a small sandy stretch surrounded by flat, rocky fingers that jut into the water, best enjoyed at low tide. The view is to the northwest to a small rocky islet and Boat Islet, Port Washington Dock, and across Grimmer Bay to Prevost and Salt Spring Islands.

3 PORT WASHINGTON GOVERNMENT DOCK
✿ Make a left (west) on Port Washington Road and follow it to the end. Make a left, and descend a short steep hill where there are a few parking spaces. Walk out to the government dock to enjoy a nice view out to Boat Islet and Grimmer Bay. The historic Port Washington General Store near the dock is vacant at time of writing. The water taxi that transports Pender Island students to high school on Salt Spring Island docks here. It is also the main seaplane port for North Pender Island.

4 BRIDGES ROAD

✪Make a left (west) on Port Washington Road and proceed to the end of the road. Make a right, follow Bridges Road up a hill, around a bend to the left where Upper Terrace intersects, and follow Bridges Road straight to the end, where there is limited parking and stairs down to the beach lined with wild roses and sea spray. The beach consists of gravel, sand and shells at times. Otherwise it is rocky, and most fun to explore at low tide, when there are abundant anemone-filled tidepools and a lot of areas to explore. Views are across Swanson Channel to Prevost Island. The beach is a sensitive intertidal area as the sign indicates, and is also a good orca-watching spot.

5 WALDEN ROAD

Make a left (west) on Port Washington Road and proceed to the end. Turn right and follow Bridges Road up a hill, around a bend to the left where Upper Terrace intersects, and follow Bridges Road to a fork. Take the right fork up Stanley Point Road. Make a left on Walden Road. About halfway down the hill is a *Walden Road Beach Access* sign on a post. Find a wide shoulder to park on. The trail, slippery when wet, leads down a moderate grade through a red cedar forest with fern-salal understory, reaching stairs to a rocky beach within 5-10 minutes. After wet periods, the pleasant sound of a stream follows you down the trail, and the stream cascades onto the beach. Views from the beach, which is shared with private residences, are to the northwest up Trincomali Channel between Prevost Island on the left and Galiano Island on the right, with the mountains of Vancouver Island in the distance.

Hiking Trail

6 GEORGE HILL PARK

A moderately steep 20 to 30 minute climb to a spectacular 183-metre high vista point at the northern end of North Pender Island.

Rating: 8 Difficulty/Surface: Moderate to Strenuous. The first half of the dirt trail consists of gradual switchbacks to a viewpoint. Watch for roots, rocks, and slippery areas. Handrails and stairs assist at key points. The second half of the trail to the top of the hill is not well developed and contains a very steep, sometimes slippery stretch. Walking time/distance: About 1.5 km; 30 minutes each way. Allow ample time to enjoy the vista. Elevation gain: Approximately 150 metres. **Map 1B**

Access From the reference point at Otter Bay Road and Port Washington Road, turn left (west) down Port Washington Road to its end. Turn right on Bridges Road that curves to the left at Upper Terrace, then forks in about 300 metres. Take the right fork, which is Stanley Point Road (the left fork leads to the Bridges Road ocean access). In about 500 metres make a left on Walden Road (a sign directs you to George Hill Trail here as well). Go down the hill about 150 metres to Ogden Road. The signed trailhead *George Hill Park* is on your right a few steps up Ogden Road. Park along the shoulder of either road, but watch out for ditches.

The George Hill Hike Proceed south from the trailhead then east through a dark second-growth western red cedar and Douglas fir forest with sword fern understory along a narrow but well-defined path. Follow the railing-lined switchbacks up a moderate grade to the first viewpoint in 10-15 minutes (about 500 metres distance). You will be in open woodland with Douglas fir and some old growth arbutus. In the late spring you may be treated to a brilliant wildflower display. From the bench, the view is partially obscured by Douglas firs. It looks to the south to

View to the northwest up Trincomali Channel with Galiano Island to the right.

Grimmer Bay, Swanson Channel and Portland Island, and to the southwest to Salt Spring Island. Return to the path and turn to the right and into second-growth forest, another meadow where the trail may be obscured at times, and more forest, where the trail is more distinct. The trail curves to the right and down a small, slippery incline, and then emerges onto an exposed grassy hillside with some rock outcroppings. After

View to the south—southwest at Grimmer Bay, Swanson Channel and Salt Spring Island.

a level traverse of the hillside heading northeast, the trail returns to a sparse forest lined with Oregon grape and Scotch broom, and ascends very steeply for about 50 metres. This stretch can be very slippery on the descent. The trail makes a sharp left (to the northwest) and ascends a short distance to a clearing at 1.5 km. This dry hilltop is covered with drought-resistant perennial grasses and seasonal wildflowers, and is surrounded by Douglas fir and Garry oak. Rest on the bench or have a picnic (but beware late summer wasps) and enjoy the sweeping views. To the south are Port Washington, Grimmer Bay, and the rest of North Pender Island. Beyond is Vancouver Island with a backdrop of Washington's Olympic Mountains on a clear day. To the southwest is the large Salt Spring Island. Prevost Island is to the west, and a great view up Trincomali Channel is to the northwest. Watch vessels head toward Active Pass to the north, with the hills of Galiano Island beyond. Further to the north you may be able to see Howe Sound and the Coast Mountains on the mainland north of Vancouver, with ferries passing in front of Bowen Island. From your vantage point, the ferry to Saturna Island seems to hug the North Pender Island coastline far below. Return the same way, using extra caution on the steep and rooted sections.

You can extend this hike to the ocean by walking back up Walden Road for a few minutes and looking for *Walden Road Ocean Access* (5) on the right.

Clam Bay and Hope Bay Areas

The northeast corner of North
Pender Island is peaceful and
scenic. Along with Port
Washington, Hope Bay was one of
the early communities settled on
the Pender Islands in the late
1880's. Hope Bay is named for two
brothers, David Hope, who arrived
in the 1870's, and, along with Noah
Buckley, purchased hundreds of
acres in the area, and Rutherford
Hope, who arrived in 1878. After a
wounded buck killed David Hope,
Rutherford inherited his portion of
the lands, along with their sister,
Helen Auchterlonie. Meanwhile,
Noah Buckley sold his lands in the
Port Washington area in 1882. The

Hope Bay government dock and store, 2005.

Auchterlonie family was the first family to settle on the Pender Islands when they
arrived in 1882. Mt. Elizabeth is named for Helen and Lawrence Auchterlonie's
daughter, Elizabeth. Their land encompassed the valley to the west of Hope Bay. David
Hope built their house at the southwest corner of Bedwell Harbour Road and Port
Washington Road. It remains as the oldest house on the Pender Islands, now the home
of Stribley's pottery gallery. The early settlers of the Hope Bay area were mostly
Scottish and Presbyterian, who tended to be more liberal in philosophy than the
English Anglicans of Port Washington. The Hope Bay community grew to contain an
active wharf built in 1901, a post office, a general store, a community hall and a
church. The store was built by Robert Corbett who arrived in 1902, on his way to
California in search of a better climate for his sensitive health condition. He remained
on the island, purchasing 180 acres from the Menzies Family. His house remains on
Corbett Road, known as *Corbett House,* which is sometimes operated as a B&B (not at
time of writing). The Hope Bay store was built in 1905 and originally contained a post
office. The steamship Iroquois operated between Hope Bay and Sidney on Vancouver
Island, connecting to the Victoria and Sidney Railway. As the population of the area
grew, a new store was built in 1912, and expanded several times since then. The via-
bility of the store diminished with the addition of the front-end loading ferry and dock
at Otter Bay in the 1960's, and the evolution of the Pender Islands into more of a resort
and retirement community. After the Driftwood Centre was established and the Hope
Bay Post Office closed in the late 1970's, the General Store closed down, and reopened
as galleries and crafts shops. It burned down in February 1998, and sat in the limbo of
redevelopment projects until recently, when a group of local investors (Hope Bay
Rising, **www.hopebayrising.com**) re-opened the store in July 2005. It contains the
**Hope Bay Café, Red Tree Artisan Gallery, Sladen's Home Furnishings, Pender
Treasures, The Goldsmith Shop, Dockside Realty**, and various offices. One seaside inn
and a historic B&B that is open periodically are located in this area.

The area contains several beautiful ocean access points, and a featured coastal beach walk. Extended walks include the Found Road hike (**11**) through five ecosystems that ends at the beach, and a stroll on uncrowded roads taking in many of the most interesting sights (**15**). Pender Parks has produced a self-guided nature tour for Welcome Bay (**8**) and Mt. Elizabeth Park (**14**) **Map 1C.**

Trailhead Reference Point

The Hope Bay Store is the reference point, located at the end of Bedwell Harbour Road at Clam Bay Road, and near the east end of Port Washington Road. From the ferry terminal, bear right on McKinnon Road from the ticket kiosk, then bear right on Otter Bay Road and follow it until it ends on Bedwell Harbour Road. Make a left. At the first intersection, carefully make a sharp right around a bend, which keeps you on Bedwell Harbour Road. Follow it until it ends, at the Hope Bay Store, where parking is available in parking lots or along the shoulder of the road. **Map 1C.**

Washrooms

An outhouse is located at Mt. Elizabeth Park. Hope Bay Store has washrooms for its customers.

Ocean Accesses

7 HOPE BAY DOCK AREA

✪ Hope Bay is a scenic and historic area as described above, and a nice place to stroll. In the **Hope Bay Store**, several shops are available to browse, and the **Hope Bay Café** is open most of the day in summer (reduced hours in winter). Fresh fish is sold on the government dock periodically. The rocky outcropping near the parking lot is a nice perch to gaze into the shallow waters of Hope Bay, and with the right lighting, it resembles an aquarium, with small fish darting about amongst the seaweed. Also see *Hope Bay Stroll* (**15**) in the Hiking section for walking options in the area, and the *Birdwatching Guide* in Chapter 17.

Hope Bay is actually a drying inlet.

8 WELCOME BAY

✪Head west on Clam Bay Road for about 650 metres (about 100 m past Mt. Elizabeth Park). A wooden post with *Welcome Bay* painted on it, marks the trail on the right, just past a sign for the Welcome Bay Farm. Limited parking is available along the shoulder of Clam Bay Road. A level trail leads through mixed second growth forest that includes a notable heritage tree. Watch for exposed roots and slippery rocks. After 5-10 minutes walking, stairs lead down to a beach. Welcome Bay is very picturesque, especially since private homes do not surround it. The upland areas beyond the beach are private, including the pretty point with a picnic table to the south, and the lovely arbutus-covered hillside to the north. The beach is pebbly, and has a tendency to collect logs and driftwood. Views are to the east across to small private Fane Island and across Navy Channel and Plumper Sound to the east to Mayne, Samuel and Saturna Islands, with Mount Baker beyond.

9 BRICKY BAY

☼ Head west on Clam Bay Road for about 1 km, and make a right on Coast Shale Road. Follow it for about 150 metres until it ends at Armadale Road. Limited parking is available along Coast Shale Road near (but not in front of) the mailboxes, or around the bend to the left on the right side of Armadale Road. The beach access is to the right about 150 metres down a stretch of Armadale Road where no parking is allowed. Walk along Armadale Road for a couple of minutes, and the signed beach access will appear on the left. A flight of stairs leads to a wide crescent of sand and cobbles. The beach is typically strewn with logs and driftwood, and it is ringed by private homes. The Coast Shale brick factory operated here in the early 20th century, and low tide reveals that the beach is still covered with brick remnants. At low tides, long walks along the shale beach are possible (Study the tide tables before setting out to avoid being stranded). To the west (left facing the water) after a challenge of climbing around boulders at the head of the bay (stay below high tide line; not endorsed by Pender Parks), there is clear sailing for over 2 km. Around the point to the east is a very scenic bay, but a steep rocky slope blocks the route around the next point to Welcome Bay. Views are across Plumper Sound, with Mt. Baker nicely framed between Mayne Island on the left and Saturna Island on the right.

10 TRACY ROAD/CLAM BAY

Head west on Clam Bay Road for about 1 km, and make a right on Coast Shale Road. Follow it for about 150 metres until it ends at Armadale Road. Make a left, and follow Armadale Road past Pearson Road for another 325 metres to Tracy Road. Park along Armadale Road. A rough trail through the forest begins at the intersection on the right side of Tracy Road. It leads to a viewpoint in about 5 minutes between two private homes, and a new (2004) staircase descends to a rocky beach. From there you can walk to the northwest (left) along the beach about 1.5 km to the Found Road ocean access during low tide, a route endorsed by Pender Parks. You may be able to make it to Bricky Bay to the east, although the last bit around the point before Bricky Bay requires boulder climbing, and the portions above the high tide line are on private property. This route is not endorsed by Pender Parks. Make sure to study the daily tide tables before setting out on an extended beach walk, since your route can be blocked by high tides, and remember that walking along these rocky beaches is more difficult than regular trail walking. Watch for slippery seaweed.

11 FOUND ROAD

See the hiking section below for a description of this ocean access to the west of Clam Bay Farm, and for an approximate 4.5 km loop hike (**12**) encompassing the Tracy Road ocean access. Found Road is a moderate to strenuous 25-30 minute hike each way with a steep hill involved, and the beach at the end in Davidson Bay is shared with a private home. From here you can walk about 1.5 km (to the right) to the Tracy Road ocean access at low tide. *Study the tide table before setting out.*

Hiking Trails

11 FOUND ROAD TRAIL - CLAM BAY ROAD TO OCEAN

Interesting trail encompassing five ecological zones through forest and over a ridge to the beach.

Rating: 7 Difficulty: First half easy to moderate. Second half moderate to strenuous, and slippery. Surface: Dirt trail with exposed roots and rocks, boardwalk, stairs. Walking Time/Distance, each way: 25-30 minutes; About 1.1 km; Elevation gain about 60 metres out and 70 m back. **Map 1C.**

Caution: Trail may be hazardous in windy and wet weather. Do not attempt the beach walk if high tide is approaching. Respect private property. Stay on the trail and do not disturb the sensitive ecosystems.

Access

From the Hope Bay reference point, head west on Clam Bay Road about 3 km, past Clam Bay Farm and up a hill. About halfway up the incline, look for the *Found Road Ocean Access* wooden signpost on the right between two private driveways. The trail borders Clam Bay Farm. Limited parking is available along the right shoulder.

The Hike

This trail takes the hiker through a variety of ecosystems and unique features. The first half of the trail meanders through an interestingly diverse forest. The trail is easily navigated, and boardwalks assist through the wetter areas. Highlights include a very lush fern understory to a western red cedar forest with some large old growth trees as well as broadleaf maples. The mix evolves to red alder and grand fir. The cleared area of Clam Bay Farm becomes visible through the forest to the right. Watch for a granite boulder near the trail, referred to as an *erratic*, as it was deposited here from afar by the progression of glaciers during the most recent ice age. Granite is not a part of the Nanaimo Group geologic formation that underlies North Pender Island. Another interesting feature is a large stump that lives through the exchange of nutrients with other trees through its roots. In about 10 minutes the trail begins climbing a moderate grade, and the drier, thinner forest soil supports mostly Douglas firs and western red cedars with a few arbutus and a sparse understory. In another 5 minutes a bench near the top of the hill is reached. This is a good turnaround point for those who desire an easier hike. The trail continues through the forest atop the rocky ridge, about 70 m elevation, guided by surveyors' ribbons. It descends a wooden staircase. The stairs are slippery when wet, and be careful, as I encountered a collapsed stair here once. The trail continues steeply downhill via switchbacks with some slippery areas, and Navy Channel begins to come into view through the trees. Stay on the trail rather than going off on old dirt roads or current private drives that intersect it. Pay attention to your route to ensure you follow the same trail back, as some of the surveyor's ribbons may be related to property boundaries rather than trail markers. A set of stairs at the end of the trail leads to a pebble beach, with a view to the northeast across Navy Channel to Mayne Island. At low tides, you can walk for quite a distance along the beach, sometimes all the way to Bricky Bay to the southeast (right). Pender Parks recommends hiking only to the Tracy Road ocean access. Return the same way. Note that the hike back up from the beach is fairly steep.

12 FOUND ROAD/TRACY ROAD OCEAN LOOP HIKE
At low tides you can hike the shoreline between the Found Road and Tracy Road ocean access points, and complete a hefty loop hike of about 5 km. This loop, endorsed by Pender Parks, involves about 1.2 km on trails, 1.8 km along flat but uneven rocky shoreline, and 2 km on uncrowded roads. Begin with the Found Road hike (**11**). Turn right (east) at the beach and walk beside the short sandstone cliffs. In about 1.8 km a solid new (2004) staircase ascends the cliff just beyond a private home. Follow the trail (**10**) from atop the stairs for about 5 minutes to trails end at Armadale Road. Turn left. Make the first right on Pearson Road, then right on Clam Bay Road. A point of interest, Grover Sergeant Memorial Cairn (**13**) is located along the north side of Clam Bay Road a couple hundred metres west of Pearson Road. See the description below. Continue up the hill along Clam Bay Road past Clam Bay Farm to the **11** trailhead. **Map 1C.**

13 GROVER SERGEANT MEMORIAL CAIRN
On Clam Bay Road, northwest of Pearson Road, past the private homes, a boardwalk leads you on a 3-minute stroll through moist forest to a memorial cairn for the Canadian pilot who crashed his plane at this site while training during World War II.

14 MOUNT ELIZABETH PARK
On Clam Bay Road, about 500 metres west of Hope Bay. Named for Elizabeth Auchterlonie, an early settler of the Hope Bay area who arrived with her family in 1882 at age 13. At time of writing the trail is rough and does not lead to a vista point, but it does provide for a pleasant woodsy stroll with ecological interest. It winds past an impressive swordfern understory through a mixed forest to a moss-covered rock face. Watch for climbing huckleberry, banana slugs, stickweed, and little-cup fungi. Pender Parks has prepared a self-guided nature trail for the park. Near the entrance of the park is a public outhouse.

15 HOPE BAY AREA STROLL

Combine your visit to Hope Bay with strolls on pleasant roadways and trails to ocean access points and forests. Includes Mount Elizabeth Park, Welcome Bay and Bricky Bay ocean accesses, and an option to combine this hike with the 5 km Found Road/Tracy Road Ocean Loop Hike (**12**).

Rating: 7 Difficulty: Easy to Moderate. Surface: Paved roads and optional dirt trails. Walking time/distance: Up to 2 hours and 3.5 km total. Elevation gain: Up to 20 metres. **Map 1C**. *Cautions*: Be careful walking along any roads, no matter how lightly traveled they seem. Walk *defensively* and move to the side when traffic approaches. Plan beach walks for periods of lower tides only.

Access

Park in the vicinity of the trailhead reference point (Hope Bay Store).

The Hike

After exploring the Hope Bay dock and store area, walk northwest up lightly traveled Clam Bay Road, over a moderate hill, enjoying occasional views to Plumper Sound on your right. Mt. Baker may be visible on clear days to the north of Saturna Island. Mt. Elizabeth Park (**14**) appears on the left at 500 metres, where you can explore at your option. An outhouse is situated here.

Across the street is a small Hope Bay Farm stand. In another 100 metres or so, watch for the signed Welcome Bay ocean access point on the right (**8**), just past the Wool Shed (Homespuns and Hand Weaving, hours posted). A 5 to 10-minute trail leads to stairs to a scenic cove ringed by a pebble beach. Return to Clam Bay Road and turn right. Stroll a few minutes to Coast Shale Road, which is about 1 km from your starting point. Turn right, walk about 150 m to the end, then turn right on Armadale Road, to the beach access to Bricky Bay in about 150 m, named for the brick factory at this site in the early 1900's (**9**). Either return to your starting point the same way for a 1-hour hike (plus whatever time you spend at each of the parks), or you can combine this hike with the Found Road/Tracy Road Ocean Loop Hike (**12**). To do this, from the Bricky Bay ocean access, continue northwest on Armadale Road instead of turning left down Coast Shale Road. In a couple of minutes you will reach Pearson Road, which is along the route of loop hike **12**. After considering the tides, decide which direction in which to walk the route. The trailhead to the Tracy Road ocean access appears in another few minutes after the intersection of Armadale and Pearson Roads.

Back at Hope Bay, you can stroll around the inlet of the bay, which dries to mud at low tide. The inlet is a favourite with shorebirds such as Cormorants, Great Blue Herons and Belted Kingfishers, as well as Bald Eagles and wintering ducks. (See the *Birdwatching Guide*). After passing Port Washington Road, look for the Stribley's pottery gallery on the right, that is sometimes open to the public. It is in the oldest existing house on the Pender Islands, known as the Auchterlonie House, built in 1898. At your option, continue exploring along Bedwell Harbour Road or Hooson Road. The walk around the inlet and back using Bedwell Harbour Road, then left on Hooson Road, is about 1 km roundtrip.

Hooson Road Area/Mt. Menzies

Hooson Road begins from the head of Hope Bay and climbs to about 75 metres elevation to provide access to some desirable hiking areas around Mt. Menzies in land managed by GINPR and Pender Parks. Two short trails to ocean vistas are also located along Hooson Road, named after 1880's settlers William Hooson and his sons Evan and John. Mt. Menzies is named for Albert and Henrietta Menzies who arrived on Pender in 1893 and farmed land adjacent to the mountain for 50 years. **Map 2.**

Trailhead Reference Point
Beginning of Hooson Road. From the ferry terminal veer right on McKinnon Road. Continue to the right at Otter Bay Road and follow it until it ends on Bedwell Harbour Road. Make a left, and proceed for about 500 metres to an intersection. Turn carefully and sharply to the right, which continues as Bedwell Harbour Road. In about 300 metres make a right on Hooson Road (about 400 m before the Hope Bay dock). This intersection is the reference point, plotted on **Map 1C**.

Washrooms
No washrooms along Hooson Road. Closest facilities are the outhouse at Mt. Elizabeth Park (500 m west on Clam Bay Road), the Hope Bay Store (for customers), and the Pender Island Community Hall when open.

Hiking Trails

16 WILSON ROAD VIEWPOINT
Wilson Road is about 650 metres east on Hooson Road. Walk down Wilson Road to the signed rough *Loop Trail* on the left that leads in about 5 minutes to a viewpoint above a rocky beach. Views are to the northeast at Plumper Sound, Mayne Island and the islets of the Hope Bay area. Access to the water is possible, but make sure to respect the adjacent private property.

17 SEAWEST VIEWPOINT
About 2 km east on Hooson Road, the signed trailhead is atop a hill on the left after *Lots 11, 12, 13* under a large arbutus tree that leans out over the road. A rough trail leads down and to the left, jogs to the right down a driveway, then back to the left to another rough trail. In about 5 to 10 minutes is a bench with views across Plumper Sound to Saturna, Samuel and Mayne Islands. The elevation of 75 metres enables views to the mainland and the Coast Range behind Vancouver. The view is similar, though not as spectacular as the Mount Menzies vista hike in the GINPR, described below.

MOUNT MENZIES TRAILS

Parkland at the end of Hooson Road consists of two segments managed by Parks Canada as part of the GINPR and one managed by Pender Island Parks Commission in between them. The highlight is an ocean vista trail in the GINPR coastal segment.

Access
From the reference point, follow Hooson Road for about 2.2 km until it ends at a cul de sac. Park here. The Pender Island Parks Commission (PIPC) trailhead is at 2:00 around the cul de sac, marked by a wooden post inscribed with *Mount Menzies Park.* The GINPR coastal segment trailhead is at about 11:00. At time of writing it is not signed, but is an obvious old skid road. The driveway at about 9:00 is private. The legal access to Loretta's Wood Nature Reserve is just north of the PIPC Park, but the access trail has not been constructed through the wetland at time of writing (see below). Plans are underway to construct trails connecting all three contiguous parks.

18 MOUNT MENZIES PARK (PIPC)
Rating: 5. Difficulty: Moderate. Surface: Rough trail with roots, rocks and very slippery sections. Walking Time/Distance: About 25 minutes, 500-metre loop. **Map 2.**
The Hike: The Mount Menzies Park trail meanders up a pretty hillside forest with lush understory along a fairly steep trail through an area that was logged in various stages, and burned over 50 years ago. Along the recovering hillside are bigleaf maples (showy in autumn) and a seasonal wetland at the bottom, followed by western red cedar with fern understory. The trail flattens out for a stretch, then emerges into tall salal (watch for ticks) and open forest dominated by red alder trees, which thrive in a damp recovering environment. The trail forms a loop, with a bench at the top near some lush mossy meadows. It is disappointing though that after the strenuous climb to the top there is no vista. For a good vista, take the GINPR Coastal Trail (**19**).

19 GINPR-NORTH PENDER/MT. MENZIES COASTAL SECTION
Rating: 8. Difficulty: Moderate. Surface: Mostly level and gradual with some roots and rocks along old skid road through thick salal. Walking Time/Distance: About 800 metres/ 25 minutes each way. **Map 2.**
Caution: Viewpoint has steep drop-off and no railings. Ticks may be in salal along trail.

The Hike
The coastal GINPR trail is an unofficial one at time of writing, as Parks Canada has not developed it and it may be re-aligned in the future. It wanders through a 28.6-hectare parcel containing mature Douglas fir/arbutus forest that was last logged in the early 1900's, and features some large grand fir not commonly found in the region. One notable aspect of this trail is that the climb is easier and more gradual than the other Pender Islands vista hikes, making it accessible to more people. Walk up the obvious path that heads gradually uphill to the south along an old skid road lined by western red cedar and bigleaf maple. The trail narrows as it cuts through some thick salal and sword fern (watch for ticks). In 10-15 minutes an obvious trail intersects from the right. Do not take that trail (it leads up to a meadow with no view). Continue on the main trail instead. Proceed down a short, fairly steep hill. In less than a minute, halfway

down the steep part of the hill, look for a trail going off to the left (east) next to a looping cedar tree. This is a connector to a parallel trail to your left. If you miss this connector, there is another one a little further down the hill that cuts back sharply to join the same trail. If you continue too far down the hill and begin to see the Morning Bay Vineyard, you have gone way too far. Avoid the temptation of wandering down the old logging roads onto private land.

Follow the connector trail for about a minute to another obvious trail junction. Make a left (north). The trail loops around to the right (southeast), gradually climbing to a clearing, about 15-20 minutes from the original trailhead. You will emerge to a large blufftop area that is perfect for a picnic (except during wasp season). Look for small Garry oak trees. **Be careful if you have children as there is an unfenced sheer drop-off ahead.** The view from this 139-metre high

View to the southeast at Saturna Island, left, South Pender Island, right, and Orcas Island beyond.

precipice is to the northeast at Mayne Island across Navy Channel, and at Samuel Island, behind which is Point Roberts, Tsawwassen, and Vancouver. Saturna Island is to the east across Plumper Sound, with a great view of Saturna Vineyards. To the southeast is Blunden Islet past the tip of South Pender Island, and Orcas Island (U.S.) across Boundary Pass. Return the same way.

20 LORETTA'S WOOD NATURE RESERVE

This 38.7 ha (96 acre) nature reserve encompassing most of 195-metre Mount Menzies, was transferred to GINPR in 2005 from the Islands Trust Fund. The Loretta's Wood name will live on in the park as the name of a trail through the area that is to be developed at a later date. This name honours the mother of the original donor of the land to the Islands Trust Fund in 2003. Future developed trails will enable an approximate 1 km loop in topography of moderate difficultly, though rough trails already exist. Parks Canada states that the property has high ecological values, featuring four provincially rare or endangered plant communities, one vulnerable plant community, and one Species of Concern as listed by COSEWIC (Committee on the Status of Endangered Wildlife in Canada), the red-legged frog. The property also contains wetland and terrestrial herbaceous ecosystems, both of which have been identified in the joint federal-provincial Sensitive Ecosystem Inventory initiative.

At time of writing, Parks Canada's policy regarding access to this parcel is: "Loretta's Wood is not currently being promoted as a primary visitor use area. In part, this is because there is no suitable public access to the property (the legal access to the property contains a wetland area that precludes access). The informal access that has been used by the public over the years crosses a private driveway. You should ensure you have permission of the neighbouring landowners before accessing the park across private lands. We will be assessing options to ensure suitable public access to the Loretta's Wood property in the future but we will require the public's patience until such time as an appropriate solution is found." The informal access discussed is near the entrance to the Tindalwood development, while the legal access through the wetland is near the end of Hooson Road, to the north of the Pender Park's Mount Menzies Park.

Otter Bay and South Otter Bay Areas

This area stretches from the central coastal section of North Pender Island into the interior agricultural valley near the Pender Island Community Hall. It includes McKinnon Road, the south/east half of Otter Bay Road, and South Otter Bay Road. Highlights of the Otter Bay area include picturesque ocean access points north (**23**) and south (**24**) of the ferry terminal. The South Otter Bay area contains prime GINPR lands including the Roesland coastal park (**25**) that houses

Tip of Roe Islet, GINPR-Roesland.

the Pender Island Museum, as well as the lush forests surrounding Roe Lake, one of the better hiking areas on the Pender Islands (**29-37**). For swimming, you can choose between the pool at Otter Bay Marina (**22**), or perhaps a wilderness experience at Roe Lake (**27**). The popular **Pender Island Golf and Country Club** is about 1 km from the ferry terminal. Accommodations are available at B&B's along MacKinnon Road near the ferry terminal. Restaurants include **Islanders**, **Chippers** at the Golf Course and **The Stand** at the ferry terminal. At the east end of Otter Bay Road, the Pender Island Community Hall grounds host most of the islands' main events, including the Saturday morning farmers markets, the annual Fall Fair and many concerts and plays. The RCMP (police) headquarters, the main fire hall, and the cemetery are also located nearby. **Maps 1, 1A** (Otter Bay); **3 and 3A** (South Otter Bay).

Trailhead Reference Point
The entrance to the Otter Bay Ferry Terminal at MacKinnon Road. **Map 1A**.

Washrooms
Public washrooms at Otter Bay ferry terminal landing (closed overnight), Community Hall (when open), and **Chippers** at the Golf Course (for patrons). Outhouse at GINPR-Roesland near the parking lot.

Ocean Accesses and Swimming

21 OTTER BAY FERRY TERMINAL

You can enjoy the waterfront at the ferry terminal, watching ferries come and go from a picturesque location. Washrooms are open in the waiting room during hours of ferry operation. **The Stand** restaurant has informal outdoor tables next to the ferry berth. A bench is also available across the loading ramp from **The Stand**. No access to the water is available here. Watch for Bald Eagles perched nearby and river otters darting amongst the rocks. **Map 1A.**

22 OTTER BAY MARINA AND POOL

✿ Proceed to the right down MacKinnon Road for about 175 metres to the signed entrance to the marina. The entrance road is down a steep hill. The marina is situated in a beautiful setting, and has two swimming pools (fee), a store, and bicycle, scooter and kayak rentals (certification required except for tours). Walk down the dock to the flag deck that is up the stairs to the right. Flags of the Canadian provinces are displayed here. Picnic tables are available for use of Otter Bay Marina patrons. The new **Currents** vacation home complex surrounds the marina area. **Map 1A.**

23 MACKINNON ROAD

✿ Make a sharp left on MacKinnon Road to a signed beach access on the left in about 1 km, just before the end of the road, and next to the Waterlea property. Along the way you will pass **Islanders** restaurant and the Royal Canadian Legion Hall. Stairs descend to a nice beach comprised of sand and rocks with plenty of room to explore. A sign on the staircase discusses the sensitive intertidal area. Private homes are scattered along the shoreline here, so respect private property. **Map 1A.**

24 NIAGARA ROAD

✿ Go right, down MacKinnon Road, which turns into Otter Bay Road when it intersects from the left in about 500 m. Continue straight ahead on Otter Bay Road and watch for the information kiosk on the left, the recommended place to park for this access. Walk down the road in the same direction for a few hundred metres, and turn right onto the unpaved Niagara Road. The ocean access sign is just past the private home on the right. Parking is very limited here. The

View to Otter Bay with marina and ferry terminal.

5 to 10-minute trail leads down next to a seasonal stream adjacent to private property with constant *Keep Out* reminders. Near the end of the trail the stream plunges down to a lovely sandy beach that looks out to Otter Bay Marina on the right and Roe Islet on the left. Otter Bay Marina guests like to dinghy over to this beach. **Map 1A.**

25 ROESLAND/GULF ISLANDS NATIONAL PARK RESERVE
✪ ✪ See *Hiking Trails* below.

26 IRENE BAY ROAD
✪ Turn right down MacKinnon Road, and straight/right onto Otter Bay Road. Continue for about 1.6 km at which point the main road descends a short steep hill and curves to the left, while South Otter Bay Road intersects at the right, forming a *T* intersection. Carefully turn right on South Otter Bay Road and proceed for about 1.6 km. As the road curves sharply to the left, watch for the *Roesland* sign on the right. Continue past the Roesland access for another 1 km to the intersection with Shingle Bay Road. Continue straight on Irene Bay Road that ends at the beach access in about 300 metres. Limited parking is available near the beach access sign. A short, steep, wide trail leads down to a sandy beach. A small boat such as a kayak can be easily launched by hand from this beach, which is surrounded by two headlands that form Irene Bay. The beach is shared with a private home. **Map 3.**

27 ROE LAKE
✪ See *Hiking Trails* below for directions and a description of Roe Lake. People swim in this peaceful natural lake, but Parks Canada has not conducted water quality studies to determine if there are organisms that may be harmful to swimmers, and emphasizes that people swim at their own risk, with no lifeguards present. Use caution when accessing the water and swimming. There are spots to access the water on both sides of the lake, but no beaches.

Hiking Trails

25 ROESLAND/GULF ISLANDS NATIONAL PARK RESERVE
A delightful coastal stroll through a former cottage resort and along a flat trail across a forested islet with scenic views. The Pender Islands Museum is also on site.

Rating: 9. Difficulty: Easy+ (small hill) Surface: Gravel road, grassy field, dirt trail with roots and rocks. Walking time/distance each way: 10 to 15 minutes, 630 metres from parking lot to end of Roe Islet. Facilities: Outhouse near parking lot. **Map 3.**

Access
From the reference point at the ferry terminal, continue to the right on MacKinnon Road, and right again at Otter Bay Road. Continue for about 1.6 km at which point the main road descends a short steep hill and curves to the left, while South Otter Bay Road intersects at the right, forming a *T* intersection. Carefully turn right on South Otter Bay Road and proceed for another 1.6 km. As the road curves sharply to the left, watch for the *Roesland* sign on the right. An unpaved parking area is visible on the right with a National Park display sign. Park here. Use caution where you park since the lot can become very muddy when wet.

The Hike

Roesland/Roe Islet is part of the new Gulf Islands National Park Reserve, and Parks Canada is in the process of studying existing trails and potential modifications to them. As such, follow Parks Canada trail signs even if they contradict what is printed here. In the future, perhaps Parks Canada will construct a trail through the forest connecting this portion of the park with the Roe Lake area as well as to the other Parks Canada property along the coastline. Currently, you must walk or drive along South Otter Bay Road to the south about 1 km to reach the Roe Lake trailheads from here.

The Roesland property was once a farm that was transformed into a cottage resort beginning in the 1920's with a general store, marine fuel station (on the island to the north) and wharf, and seventeen rental cabins over the following decades. Early brochures from the Roesland Resort provide an idea of the amenities guests may have experienced. They advertised fresh milk from on-site cows, sing-along campfires and glorious sunsets. The Roesland Resort operated until 1991. Most of the property, including several abandoned buildings, was acquired by Parks Canada in 1998, with some buildings set aside as a life tenancy for the owners. The two-storey *Roe House*, the original home of Robert Roe, built in 1908, was renovated by the Pender Islands Museum Society, and opened as the Pender Islands Museum in July 2005. (Open weekends. See the *Historical Guide*).

From the parking lot, a gravel road leads down a gradual hill to the private residences. Blackberry bushes are abundant in this area, as well as several fruit trees that remain from the old orchard. Follow the gravel road, then turn left, following the sign to the Pender Island Museum. Continue to the shoreline of Ella Bay, which is rimmed by a stone wall. Walk parallel to the shoreline to the right. At the wooden bridge to Roe Islet (photo, above) the view is across to Otter Bay Marina. Cross the wooden bridge (a popular birding spot) and follow the trail through the forest along Roe Islet to the end. The islet is populated with large, old arbutus trees and Douglas firs that look windswept from living on this exposed strip of land. The understory is mostly salal, and wildflowers such as chocolate and white fawn lilies, calypso orchids, and stonecrop appear in the spring. Stay on the trail to avoid trampling them. The trail is fairly level but watch out for rocks and tree roots. At the end of the trail are two benches, which look out in different directions. Views are to the northeast to the Otter Bay Ferry Terminal (a great place to photograph the ferries coming), to the northwest to Galiano and Prevost Islands, to the west to Salt Spring Island, and to the southwest looking at the North Pender coastline and down Swanson Channel toward Swartz Bay. This is a fairly good orca-watching point if you have binoculars.

ROE LAKE/GULF ISLANDS NATIONAL PARK RESERVE

Meandering trails through a wilderness of dense mature second-growth forest, around a rare Gulf Islands natural lake, and along a peaceful bay.

Rating: 8. Difficulty: Easy to Strenuous. Surface: Dirt trails are fairly level with roots and rocks. Walking time/Distance: 25 minutes to 2 hours; 600 metres to 4+ km. **Trail Map:** See next page. (Same as **3A**). **Facilities:** Nearest outhouse to north trailhead is at Roesland and to south trailhead is at Shingle Bay Park (planned for 2006).

Two principal trailheads provide access to this portion of GINPR: North **(T1, T2)** and South **(T3)**.
The hikes in the Roe Lake area are listed under their respective trailheads. Each trail segment has been given a unique number that corresponds to the accompanying trail map.

Summary

This jewel of North Pender Island is laced with trails, which at the time of writing are unmarked. Parks Canada is currently studying the trails system, and may rework some of the trails. When they do, follow their signage if it conflicts with what is described here. See the schematic trail map on the following page that shows the current general layout of pre-existing trails. In 2004 Hastings Park was added to the

National Park lands near Driftwood Centre, but no specific plans for visitor access to Hastings Park have been made at time of writing.

SWIMMERS NOTE

Parks Canada advises that if you decide to swim in Roe Lake, you do so at your own risk. Although locals have swum in this lake for years, Parks Canada has not yet done studies on its aquatic organisms and cannot advise on whether or not there may be any that would be harmful to swimmers. There is no lifeguard on duty.

SOME RULES

No fires or camping are allowed in the Roe Lake section of the GINPR. Bicycles are prohibited due to the fragile ecosystem that is being protected with National Park status. Use of motorized dirt bikes in the park is subject to a $2,000 fine.

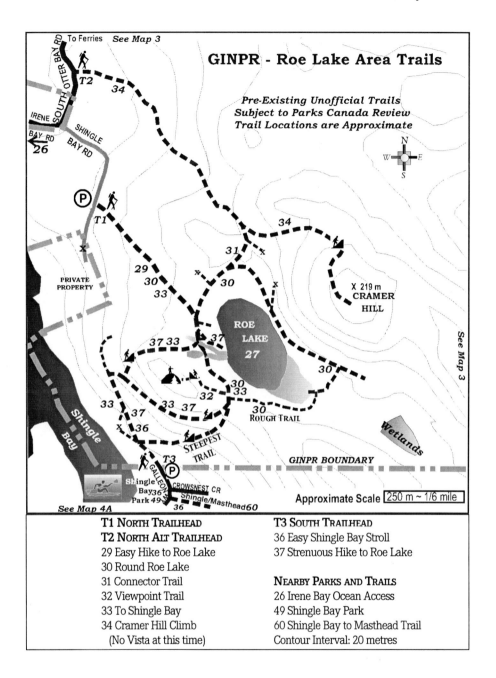

GINPR - Roe Lake Area Trails

*Pre-Existing Unofficial Trails
Subject to Parks Canada Review
Trail Locations are Approximate*

To Ferries   *See Map 3*

SOUTH OTTER BAY RD
T2   34
IRENE
SHINGLE BAY RD
BAY RD
26

T1

X
29
30
33
PRIVATE
PROPERTY

31
30

34

X 219 m
CRAMER
HILL

ROE
LAKE
27

37 33   37

32
30
33

33   37   37
37
X   36

30
ROUGH TRAIL

STEEPEST
TRAIL

30

See Map 3

Wetlands

Shingle
Bay

T3
GALLEON
Shingle
Bay 36
Park 49
CROWSNEST CR
Shingle/Masthead 60
36

GINPR BOUNDARY

See Map 4A

Approximate Scale   250 m ~ 1/6 mile

T1 North Trailhead	T3 South Trailhead
T2 North Alt Trailhead	36 Easy Shingle Bay Stroll
29 Easy Hike to Roe Lake	37 Strenuous Hike to Roe Lake
30 Round Roe Lake	
31 Connector Trail	Nearby Parks and Trails
32 Viewpoint Trail	26 Irene Bay Ocean Access
33 To Shingle Bay	49 Shingle Bay Park
34 Cramer Hill Climb	60 Shingle Bay to Masthead Trail
(No Vista at this time)	Contour Interval: 20 metres

NORTH TRAILHEAD HIKES

T1 NORTH TRAILHEAD

South Otter Bay Road Area: From the ferry terminal, continue to the right on MacKinnon Road, and right again at Otter Bay Road. Continue for about 1.6 km at which point the main road descends a short steep hill and curves to the left, while South Otter Bay Road intersects at the right, forming a *T* intersection. Carefully turn right on South Otter Bay Road and proceed for another 1.6 km. As the road curves sharply to the left, watch for the *Roesland* sign on the right. Continue along South Otter Bay Road another 1 km to Shingle Bay Road. Turn left on Shingle Bay Road, and follow the gravel road for about 325 metres around a bend to the signed trailhead on the left. Parking for several vehicles is found here for the main trailhead to the park.

T2 NORTH ALTERNATE TRAILHEAD

Another trailhead is located prior to reaching the main trailhead described above. From Roesland, Trailhead **T2** appears at 800 m on the left, just before the road curves to the right and leads to Shingle Bay Road (in another 200 metres). The trail proceeds up a gravel road, with an Otter Bay Protected Area sign about 30 metres up on the left. This road actually services the telecommunications tower atop Cramer Hill. Limited parking is available along the shoulder of South Otter Bay Road.

29 EASY HIKE TO LAKE

Easiest Roe Lake Hike, about one-half hour, 1.2 km round trip.

The hike from the north trailhead (**T1**) to Roe Lake is relatively short and easy, taking about 10 to 15 minutes to walk about 600 metres each way. Proceed up the most obvious trail from the main trailhead sign, passing under a canopy of bigleaf maples, progressing to a mix of western red cedar and Douglas fir. Alongside are sword ferns, salal and oceanspray. At the top of the gradual incline you will begin to see Roe Lake. The first junction is a wide trail at a sharp angle to the left, but continue straight ahead. A few steps further along, another trail is visible on the left, which leads to a rocky shore access, though there is no beach area or easy swimming access. A better access is a little further along. Veer to the left at the next fork to find this access. A clearing along the trail to the right looks as if it was used as a campsite, though camping and fires are not allowed here. A marsh is also visible below the embankment to the right. At the end of the trail you will not find a beach or easy access, but with some careful maneuvering on strategically placed flat rocks you can find your way into the water. Or, just pause and watch the dragonflies dart around the water surface. Return the same way.

30 AROUND ROE LAKE

Moderate Difficulty, About 1 hour, 2 km loop around Roe Lake.

A circuit can be made around Roe Lake, although the going is rough along the section above the south shore. Parks Canada is studying visitor safety and environmental impact issues along this stretch before deciding whether to construct a formal trail here. However, a trip halfway around to the east shore is fairly easy and very rewarding. Proceed up the most obvious trail from the main trailhead sign (**T1**).

At the top of the incline you will begin to see Roe Lake (10 minutes). Make a sharp left at the first main trail junction. Stay on the main trail, avoiding minor side trails. At the top of a small hill, a trail veers off to the left (**31**). The paragraph below describes where this diversion leads. Otherwise, skip to the next paragraph.

31 CONNECTOR TRAIL

The trail to the left leads to the Alternate North Trailhead (**T2**) along South Otter Bay Road (and the top of Cramer Hill). To get to Trailhead **T2** from this point, take this trail, make a left when it ends in a few minutes on an old skid road, and continue straight when it joins a service road, reaching South Otter Bay Road in another 10 minutes. Or, make a sharp right on the service road to climb Cramer Hill (Elevation 219 metres) in about 20 minutes (**34**). At time of writing no vista trails exist at the top of Cramer Hill.

Keep right, avoiding side trails even as the main trail narrows. The trail descends to the east shore of Roe Lake. This is probably the most appealing trail section in the park, as the trail hugs the shore of the lake. For a shorter hike, turn around and return the same way. Or, continue on the trail as it veers up hill and away from the lake, looking more and more like an old logging road, which eventually continues into private property. In a few minutes, watch for an obvious trail that descends steeply to the right, marked by a pink surveyor's ribbon at time of writing. After 5 minutes, the trail jogs to the left to cross over a small stream (pretty wetlands are visible to the left) then to the right again. After another 5 minutes, watch for a steep trail up a hill to the left through a rock outcropping, possibly marked with a surveyor's ribbon. This is the trail to continue around the south end of the lake (Otherwise, the main trail that you are on ends at a marsh at the south end of Roe Lake). To continue around the lake, ascend the steep and slippery trail, which levels off and veers to the right. The trail is obvious, but it is not well constructed or maintained and is very rough, requiring climbing over numerous fallen trees, and clinging to hillsides in places like a mountain goat, though there are no sheer cliff drop-offs to worry about. It is a scenic walk with nice views through the trees of Roe Lake. After about 10 minutes walking along this trail, it ends at an obvious trail junction. Go to the right to return to the North Trailhead (**T1**). Almost immediately, watch for a narrow, probably unmarked trail (**32**) on the left. As an option, do the following. Otherwise skip to the next paragraph.

32 VIEWPOINT TRAIL

Follow this steep 250-metre trail up the hill, which leads to a viewpoint in about ten minutes. Views are to the southwest, across Shingle Bay and over North Pender Island to the San Juan Islands, Saanich Peninsula and the Olympic Mountains. Camping and campfires are forbidden here. Carefully return the same way down the very slippery trail to the same trail junction. Make a left on the main trail to reach North Trailhead (**T1**).

Follow the trail down a gradual hill, with views of Roe Lake and adjacent wetlands off to the right. Continue straight at the first trail junction at a marsh with a water depth measuring stick (the trail joining at a sharp angle to the left is another trail to the South Trailhead **T3**). Note that following wet periods when the lake level is high, crossing the marsh over slippery logs may be necessary here. The next two junctions to the right are short trails to access points to the west side of Roe Lake. The first is the most popular. Immediately past the second of these trail junctions is the *Y* junction where you started the route around the lake. Veer to the left to return to the North Trailhead **T1** in about 10 minutes.

33 TO SHINGLE BAY PARK AND RETURN

Strenuous, About 1.5 to 2 hours, 3.2 - 3.7 km round trip;
Elevation gain: About 100 metres on the return from Shingle Bay to Roe Lake.
From the North Trailhead (**T1**), continue straight at the first trail junction (10 minutes). Pass the second junction immediately on the left and keep right at the first fork. The trail drops down between two marshes (when the lake level is high they connect and one needs to cross over logs). Note the water level measuring sticks on both sides of the trail. Immediately after leaving the marsh is a *Y* trail intersection (5 minutes). Both forks lead to Shingle Bay. For now, keep right. You will be returning from the left fork later. Continue on the main trail past a dark and fascinating marsh on your left. A nice viewpoint of Swanson Channel appears in about 10 minutes. Continue down a steep, slippery incline to a fork with a trail that veers off to the left. This is a good return trail back to Roe Lake. For now, go to the right. Continue down the hill until the trail ends at a junction (5 minutes). Turn left (the trail to the right leads to a very primitive trail back to Roe Lake, as well as private property along Shingle Bay), and follow the trail, keeping left when a steep trail/overgrown road veers off to the right down a steep hill. In about 5 minutes, the trail passes the junction with the steepest return trail to Roe Lake on the left, and ends at the South Trailhead. A few minutes along the road is Shingle Bay Park (**49**) with picnic tables and an outhouse (planned for 2006) and a muddy beach access. Return the same way. After re-entering the forest, the first junction on the right is the shortest, steepest route. I recommend continuing straight up the more gradual hill to the second trail junction on the right, found atop an incline after a stretch where the trail is divided by thin trees. Ascend the hill to the first junction, reached in a couple of minutes. Proceed straight on the more level trail when the main trail veers left and up a steep incline. This trail is a nice level walk for about 5-10 minutes, until it ascends to meet another trail. Proceed straight/left as you merge with this trail. A narrow unmarked trail (**32**) to a viewpoint appears shortly on the left, which you can take at your option (See its description in **30** above). Otherwise, to return to your starting point, proceed straight ahead at two trail junctions to remain parallel to the lake. Then veer left at the major *Y* intersection just past the lake, and continue to the North Trailhead (**T1**) in about 10 minutes.

34 ROAD TO RADIO TOWER ATOP CRAMER HILL

Strenuous, 1.1 km, 25-35 minutes, each way. Elevation gain: About 160 metres

Hiking the steep service road to the radio tower atop Cramer Hill (219 metres elevation, highest point on North Pender Island) is a good aerobic workout, but trees obscure the view from the main road at the summit. The service road leads from the North Alternate Trailhead (**T2**), and the walk to the top takes about 25 to 35 minutes.

Another way to get to trail route **34** is from the North Trailhead (**T1**). Make a sharp left at the first trail junction (10 minutes), continue to the top of the hill (10 minutes), make a left at the fork, follow the trail until it ends on an old skid road, make a left, follow it until it joins the service road (5 minutes) and make a hard right to ascend the steep hill to the radio tower (15 minutes).

SOUTH TRAILHEAD HIKES

The South Trailhead to Roe Lake is at the very end of the confusing maze of Magic Lake Estates roads, so visitors may wish to stick with the North Trailheads to Roe Lake, which begin at a higher elevation and are much closer to Roesland and the Otter Bay ferry terminal. If you are in Magic Lake Estates and do not mind the extra climbing, then you may prefer the South Trailhead. See the *Magic Lake Estates Area* for other trails near this trailhead. **Maps 3A, 4A.**

T3 SOUTH TRAILHEAD

From the ferry terminal, find the Magic Lake Reference Point (intersection of Schooner Way and Ketch Road). Turn left (west) on Schooner Way, make the first right on Privateers Road (which eventually turns back into Schooner Way). Make a right to follow Schooner Way at a wide T-intersection at about 1.5 km, rather than continuing straight ahead on Anchor Way. Make the first right on Shoal Road, then the first right on Dory Way. Continue straight along Dory Way (which becomes Galleon Way), around Shingle Bay, to its end, and park in the area provided. The trailhead into the forest straight ahead is obvious. As you cross the threshold of the south trailhead from the Magic Lake Estates neighbourhood, you are treated to an instant feeling of entering into a special wilderness.

36 EASY SHINGLE BAY HIKE

Easy +; 10 - 20 minutes

The easy portion of the trail to Roe Lake is very brief, and does not reach Roe Lake. From the trailhead, mosey up the trail and take in the views of Shingle Bay through the trees. After a few minutes, the grade begins to increase, and can be strenuous for some. Combine the first part of this trail with a stroll around Shingle Bay and perhaps a walk up the trail to Masthead Crescent (**60**), which begins in the forest land just south of Crowsnest Drive. The forest and wetlands are similar to what you would find near Roe Lake.

37 HIKE TO ROE LAKE

Strenuous, 1.8 to 2.3 km loop, 1 to 1.5 hours, Elevation gain: About 100 m to Roe Lake
Soon after entering the forest from the South Trailhead, an obvious trail appears on the right. This is the steepest trail that leads to Roe Lake. Take it if you want the most strenuous climb on the way up, but on the way down it can be very slippery and is not recommended. For a more moderate grade up the hill, continue straight ahead instead. The trail begins to climb steadily. Another trail junction appears to the right after about 10 minutes of hiking from the trailhead. It veers off to the right at the top of this incline, just after the main trail is divided by a thin row of trees. This trail to Roe Lake is also steep, but much more gradual than the first. This is the recommended route. (If you do not veer off onto this trail, but continue straight ahead instead, it leads to a very rough trail to Roe Lake, as well as to private property along Shingle Bay at the end of Shingle Bay Road). So, veer off to the right to follow the trail up the hill.

In a few minutes, the main trail curves uphill to the left, and a level secondary trail continues straight ahead. Either way is a good route, and this hike will be described as a loop using both trails. Continue straight ahead. It follows an enjoyable, level plane for about 10 minutes, then rises uphill to the left. Veer straight/left as the trail merges with another trail, then levels off. In this level area, watch for a trail that cuts through thick salal to the left (**32**). [As an option, take this trail to a nice vista. See Hike **30** for the trail

Natural Roe Lake sits halfway up Cramer Hill.

description. Be careful of steep drop-offs. As you return to the main trail make a left.] Roe Lake will soon appear to the right. Descend to a marshy area If Roe Lake's water level is high, water will cover the trail at this point requiring crossing over slippery logs. After passing another marshy area, watch for a trail that intersects to the right. This leads to a Roe Lake viewpoint, and a possible water access point (use   caution if you swim here). Return to the main trail and turn to the left. (Note: If you turn to the right, you can do optional hikes around Roe Lake and up Cramer Hill - see the North Trailhead hikes). Cross over the first marshy area, then look for a *Y* intersection. You came from the left, but on the return, go to the right. The trail soon passes next to a beautiful wetland area. After a short level stretch, the trail descends a hill and reaches a nice viewpoint to the west over Swanson Channel. Return down the steep hill (slippery, watch your step) to the junction where you originally took the other trail (now to your left). On the return, turn right and descend to the next trail junction. Make a left to return to the Shingle Bay trailhead.

Central Area - Harbour Hill to Medicine Beach

The Central Area of North Pender Island contains the main shopping centre of the islands (Driftwood Centre), the two drive-in campgrounds, several accommodations, restaurants, grocery stores, a pub, and a winery. Refer to the *Accommodations, Dining,* and *Shopping Guides.* **Maps 5, 5a, 5b, 6.**

Several interesting short hikes and strolls are available here, but no extended hikes. For swimming, there is a public swimming pool and two of the best beaches on the Pender Islands, Medicine Beach and Hamilton Beach.

Trailhead Reference Point
Driftwood Centre across from the intersection of Bedwell Harbour Road and Razor Point Road. To get to Driftwood Centre from the ferry terminal, bear right on MacKinnon Road after the ferry kiosk, bear right at Otter Bay Road, and follow it until it ends at Bedwell Harbour Road. Turn right and follow it for about 2 km to Driftwood Centre on the right. **Maps 5, 5B.**

Washrooms and Showers
Public washrooms are located at Driftwood Centre. Pay showers and Laundromats are available at **Driftwood Auto Centre** and **Port Browning Resort**. Outhouses are at Prior Centennial Campground.

Ocean Accesses and Swimming

38 PORT BROWNING GOVERNMENT DOCK
Proceed down Razor Point Road across from Driftwood Centre and continue for 1 km to a small parking area on the right. The long government dock is down a short path, and is a pretty walk above the bay at Port Browning. Hamilton Beach is a better boat launch in the area. **Map 5B.**

39 HAMILTON BEACH
✪✪Leave the Driftwood Centre and turn right (south) down Bedwell Harbour Road. Make the first left onto Hamilton Road. Follow the road past the entrance to **Port Browning Resort**, until the road ends, at the entrance to Hamilton Beach. This is a boat launch area suitable for small trailered boats, with a long sand and gravel beach extending to the left and right, one of the largest on the Pender Islands. Parking is along the road. **Map 5B.**

40 PORT BROWNING RESORT SWIMMING POOL
The resort's swimming pool is available to the public for a fee. From Driftwood Centre, head south (right) on Bedwell Harbour Road to the first left at Hamilton Road. The resort is near the end of the road on the left. **Map 5B.**

41 PENDER CANAL AREA (GINPR)

From the Driftwood Centre, turn right (south) and follow the signs to South Pender Island (follow Canal Road when it turns to the left). Just before crossing the bridge to South Pender Island, two concrete plaques on your left describe the history of this area. The isthmus is referred to by First Nations people as Helisen, or *lying between*, which is how it remained until 1902-1903 when the Pender Canal was dug, separating the Pender Islands into two islands. Excavations conducted here in the 1980's by Simon Fraser University archaeologists revealed evidence of habitation and unearthed thousands of Coast Salish artifacts dating as far back as 5,170 years (See the *Living On Pender* chapter). The area is now part of GINPR, and non-disruptive access is allowed but not encouraged. Tread lightly on this historically significant area. One short unmarked trail leads past the plaques to a picturesque beach with views across to Mortimer Spit. Across Canal Road from the plaques, a 5-minute trail leads out to the spit of land at the south entrance to the Pender Canal, where you can watch boats navigate around a curve and through marker buoys. A sign reminds you that this is a sensitive intertidal area. Closer to the bridge, you can watch the current rush through the bridge pilings when the tide floods and ebbs. **Maps 5, 6.**

42, 43 MEDICINE BEACH

☼ ☼ This natural area is a nice place for a picnic, to enjoy the waterfront and for bird watching in a marsh or offshore. Leave the Driftwood Centre and turn right (south) down Bedwell Harbour Road that becomes Canal Road. Continue straight ahead on Aldridge Road when Canal Road veers off to the left to South Pender. At the point where Aldridge Road curves sharply to the right and becomes Schooner Way, you will see secondary roads straight ahead and to the left. Carefully negotiate crossing Schooner Way to access these roads. The access to the main part of the beach is to the left, and another trail to the beach is off Wallace Road straight ahead. For the first access (recommended), turn left and proceed to the end of the road. An unpaved parking area is provided. To find the second ocean access (**43**), follow Wallace Road for about 500 metres, and after the road curves to the left and then right the ocean access sign is on the left. The short trail winds between two homes and ends on a staircase and ramp. Access is to Medicine Beach except at high tides. To access the stairs from the beach, watch for the sign *Public Access to Road,* which at time of writing is on the third staircase along the cliffs coming from Medicine Beach.

Medicine Beach consists of a scenic pebbly beach, a marsh, and headlands with views to the southeast across Bedwell Harbour. The Pender Islands Conservancy Association and the Islands Trust acquired the 8-hectare property in 1995. The Islands Trust Fund owns the Sanctuary and the Nature Conservancy of Canada and Habitat Acquisition

Trust jointly hold a conservation covenant for long-term protection. The adjacent marsh is protected for its ecological significance but is off limits to humans and their dogs, due to the ground-nesting Virginia Rail. It was used by Coast Salish people over 5,000 years ago, who used plants from the marsh area for medicinal purposes, hence the name. Do not disturb vegetation or remove anything from the preserve.

A steep trail with wood and gravel stairs to assist on most of it ascends from the north side of the parking area to the forested bluff, which provides a panorama of the beach area, complete with a viewing platform and bench. The trail continues along the bluff to a rocky promontory with a bench that faces the outlet to Bedwell Harbour. Do not continue hiking past here. Also, public lands extend from the north side of the Medicine Beach access road back toward the intersection of Aldridge Road and Canal Road. A wide trail (**44**) runs through the lush western red cedar and alder forest to the top of the Aldridge Road hill. See also **42a** *Medicine Beach Walks* below for a description of pleasant walks around the preserve. **Map 5A.**

Hiking Trails

42A, 44 MEDICINE BEACH WALKS
Stroll around this beautiful preserve that encompasses marshland, forest and beachfront.

Rating: 7. Difficulty: Easy to Moderate. Surface: Paved roads (hilly), dirt trails, steep trail to bluff has stairs to assist for most of it, and beach.
Walking Time/Distance: About 25 minutes/700m for loop hike with optional 35-minute extensions. **Map 5A.**   *Note:* Tread lightly in this nature preserve. Stay on established trails. No people or dogs allowed in the marsh.

Access See access to Medicine Beach (**42**) in the Ocean Accesses section, above. An alternate trailhead on Aldridge Road (**44**) is described below.

The Hike
The loop hike combines beachcombing with bird watching near a scenic marsh. From the parking area, turn to the right, and either walk along the beach at low tide, or along the rough trail along the berm. To your right is a productive marsh that may provide for a good birdwatching opportunity, especially in winter. The view to the left is across Bedwell Harbour to Gulf Islands National Park Reserve (Beaumont Marine Park) and Poets Cove Resort on South Pender Island. As you continue past the marsh, cliffs line the shoreline. The beach at the foot of the cliffs may not be accessible at high tides, making a complete loop impossible. After a few minutes, watch for a public access stairway that consists of a wooden ramp and stairs with a sign *Public Access To Road*. At time of writing it is the third set of stairs along the cliffs, when coming from the Preserve. The short trail atop the stairs leads to the Wallace Road Ocean Access (**43**). Turn right and round the bend to the left and down the hill. The marsh is visible on your right. Walk down the quiet road next to the marsh until the road ends at the intersection with Schooner Way. If you like, get a snack at **Magic Lake Market,** which is to the left. Otherwise, turn right and follow the forest-lined road back to the

Medicine Beach parking area. From the parking area look to the left (to the right of the dedication plaque) where a steep trail aided most of the way by gravel and wood stairs leads up to the blufftop. A platform with a bench is available to enjoy a beautiful panorama across Medicine Beach. The trail continues along the bluff and ends at a rocky promontory with a bench where you can sit and gaze out over Bedwell Harbour toward Poets Cove Resort and the mouth of the bay. It is not safe or legal to continue hiking further along the shoreline. Another trail begins at the top of the bluff, to the left of where the stairs emerge onto the blufftop near the platform. It quickly reaches a junction with an old skid road. Turn left, and continue through the lush western red cedar-dominated forest, first downhill then gradually uphill for about 10 minutes, ending at the Aldridge Road trailhead (**44**).

44 ALDRIDGE ROAD TO MEDICINE BEACH

Heading south from Driftwood Centre, after Canal Road curves to the left to South Pender, Aldridge Road is straight ahead. Continue on Aldridge about halfway to Schooner Way, just before the road descends a short, steep hill. A wide dirt turnout is on the left side of the road. A *Nature Preserve* sign marks a trail leading into the woods. You can take this 10-minute trail to Medicine Beach (as described above in reverse). Stay on the trail in this sensitive ecosystem. **Map 5A.**

45 GARDOM POND TRAIL

A short stroll in the Harbour Hill Area through a narrow strip of public access forest and wetland to a viewpoint of a small pond.

Rating: 5. Difficulty: Easy+. Surface: Mostly level dirt trail with numerous roots and a potentially slippery ramp. Walking time each way: 10 - 15 minutes. **Map 5.**

Access

From the Driftwood Centre reference point, turn down Razor Point Road for approximately 2.5 km to Harbour Hill Road. Turn left up the hill for about 650 m to the first road on the right, Gardom Pond Road, which is private. Park along Harbour Hill Road. The trailhead is a few paces up Gardom Pond Road, on the left, and a map of the trail is posted alongside the Gardom Pond Road arch.

The Hike to Gardom Pond

The trail winds through a narrow band of second growth forest surrounded by private properties, but structures are not visible along most of the trail, giving the walk a very peaceful feel. It is quiet with no traffic noise except for whatever activities residents are up to. The trail is level and easy to follow but watch for tripping hazards such as roots and a wooden ramp at the end that can be slippery. The trail leads through the forest and passes a pretty wetland with red alder trees, swamp grasses, ferns and skunk cabbage. It curves around a private maintenance facility, and continues to the small Gardom Pond, at which point a sign reminds you that public access to the pond is forbidden. The last portion of the trail includes a wooden ramp and ends at a bench, where there is a pleasant view of the pond through the trees.

54 HEART TRAIL

Linking Prior Centennial Campground to Magic Lake area and Golf Island Disc Park. See the *Magic Lake Estates Area* for trail description. **Map 4B.**

46 SKEELES ROAD VIEWPOINT

Rating: 2. Difficulty: Easy. Surface: Paved road and dirt trail with roots. Walking time each way: 5 minutes. **Map 5.** Access: Turn down Razor Point Road and drive a little over 2 km to Skeeles Road. Park carefully off Razor Point Road.

The Hike: Walk down Skeeles Road to the signed path that leads to a bench in less than 5 minutes from the start. Trees at the bank obscure the view, which is south across Port Browning to Mortimer Spit.

47 MUMFORD ROAD TRAIL

Rating: 4. Difficulty: Easy+. Surface: Dirt trail with roots and rocks. Walking time each way: 5 to 10 minutes. **Maps 5, 6.** Access: The signed trailhead is along Canal Road on the way to South Pender Island. After passing the school and medical clinic, the road curves sharply to the right, and the signed trail access is on the left.

The Hike: This mediocre trail is steep in places and runs adjacent to private residences before reaching an arbutus-covered point alongside Shark Cove. There is no water access, but you can gaze across to Mortimer Spit and perhaps see river otters frolicking amongst the rocky shoreline below.

Magic Lake Estates Area

Magic Lake Estates, the Pender Islands' *neighbourhood*, had its notorious beginnings in the 1960's, when *Gulf Island Estates* planned a high-density vacation home development on the west shore of North Pender Island. Eventually, about 600 acres of mostly half-acre properties spread out along the waterfront and into the forested hillsides beyond. The subdivision, the largest in Canada at the time, helped inspire creation of the Islands Trust regulatory agency whose mission was to promote more responsible and sustainable development in the Gulf  Islands. Since the properties are amongst the smallest on the Pender Islands, the term *Estates* has become a satirical adjective amongst Penderites. **Maps 4, 4A, 4B.**

In actuality, *The Estates* has become a desirable place to live and offers many amenities to its residents, including two oceanfront parks at Thieves Bay and Shingle Bay, several ocean access points, and two lakes. Magic Lake is open to the public for swimming and rowing, whereas Buck Lake is the main public water supply and is off limits to all except those who reside along its shores. The world-class Golf Island disc golf park is located here. Several trails lead to the disc park and connect to Prior Centennial Campground. A myriad of short hiking trails traverse the Magic Lake area, creating convenient shortcuts and pleasant walks for local residents. The south trailhead to the Roe Lake portion of GINPR begins from the northwest edge of Magic Lake Estates at the end of Galleon Way (See the *Otter Bay Area* section and **Map 3A** for descriptions of the Roe Lake area hiking trails). Best of all, much of the shoreline of the Magic Lake Estates area is frequented by pods of orcas during the summer months.

Trailhead Reference Point
Entrance to Magic Lake Estates. In general, follow the signs to *Magic Lake* from the ferry. Bear right onto MacKinnon Road from the terminal, then bear right again on Otter Bay Road. Follow it until it ends on Bedwell Harbour Road. Turn right and continue to the Driftwood Centre at the corner of Razor Point Road. Continue on Bedwell Harbour Road, which becomes Canal Road. Bear right onto Aldridge Road when Canal Road veers to the left to South Pender Island. Aldridge Road descends a steep hill, curves sharply to the right, and becomes Schooner Way. Follow Schooner Way for about 1.3 km to a *T* intersection, where you will notice a sign describing Magic Lake Estates and its trails straight ahead in front of a Fire Hall. This intersection is the Magic Lake reference point. **Map 4B.**

A Maze of Streets
Navigating around the Magic Lake Estates area can be an interesting experience. The main road, Schooner Way, was at first the only road in the subdivision. Galleon Way was also a principal road. Other roads, such as Privateers, were added later, and proved to provide a more direct route through the area. The best way to navigate is to follow what appears to be the main road, regardless of its name. Most of the time, this will get you to where you are going. Better yet, follow your map carefully.

Washrooms and Services
No public washrooms are located in the area. Outhouses are located at the Disk Park (see **57**), Thieves Bay Park (**51**), Shingle Bay Park (planned for 2006) (**49**), and seasonally at Magic Lake Swimming Hole (**48**) and Danny Martin ball field (See **Map 4B**). The nearest food and drink is available at **Magic Lake Market** near Medicine Beach, 1.3 km from the reference point. Several B&B's are scattered throughout the area.

Lake and Ocean Access

48 MAGIC LAKE
✿ From the reference point, continue left (southwest) on Schooner Way. Magic Lake appears to the left, across from Privateers Road in about 300 m. The lakeside park is nice for picnicking on the two tables along the lake, and hand launching of small non-motorized boats is possible here for a delightful paddle around the lake. The swimming area is at the opposite end of the lake. To find it, continue southwest along Schooner Way to the next intersection, and turn left onto Pirates Road. Follow Pirates Road for 1 km, just past the last of the private homes. After house # 4896, there is a gravel driveway with a *Magic Lake Water Access* wooden signpost on the left. Ample parking

and a seasonal pit toilet are located down the dirt driveway. Follow the trail out toward the lake, to the public swimming area that includes a dock and a swimming float. Wheelchairs may be accessible on the flat, though unpaved walkway to the dock. Water here is warmer than the ocean, and it is a very popular respite on warm summer days. As is the case in most lakes, it is best not to linger in shallow murky lake water where vegetation is growing since it increases the potential of contracting swimmer's itch. The CRD may have information on recent water quality, and they post general information signs regarding swimmers itch around the lake. **Map 4.**

49 SHINGLE BAY PARK

☼ From the reference point, continue to the left (southwest) on Schooner Way and make the first right onto Privateers Road. Continue on Privateers until it rejoins and turns back into Schooner Way. Follow Schooner Way until it turns uphill to the right, while Anchor Way continues straight head (and leads to Thieves Bay Park, described below). Make the first right on Shoal Road, and then the first right on Dory Way. Continue on Dory Way, which turns into Galleon Way, and follow it down the hill and around several bends to the narrow Shingle Bay and Shingle Bay Park on the left. Access to the water is available here at higher tides, as this bay shoals into a muddy bottom at low tide. One can launch a small vessel such as a kayak here at higher tides, and Shingle Bay is fairly protected until it emerges into Swanson Channel. A community park contains picnic tables. An outhouse is planned here for 2006. **Map 4A.** Note that the Roe Lake - South Trailhead (**T3**) of GINPR is near this park at the end of Galleon Way (see the hike description in the *Otter Bay Area* section).

50 HARPOON ROAD/PANDA BAY

Follow the directions to Shingle Bay, but instead of following Galleon Way all the way to the bottom of the hill, make a left on Harpoon Road and proceed to the end of the street. Stairs descend to a pretty, though mostly shady, crescent-shaped rock and sand beach backed by cliffs at Panda Bay, accessible at lower tides. **Map 4A.**

51 THIEVES BAY PARK

☼From the reference point, continue southwest (left) on Schooner Way and make the first right on Privateers Road. Proceed down Privateers Road without making any turns until roads end at Thieves Bay Park and Marina (the road changes names along the way to Schooner Way again and then to Anchor Way). Look for an obvious gravel parking area on the right before the end of the road. The park contains a grassy field, picnic tables, a muddy/sandy beach, an outhouse, and a small boat launching area accessible to small, trailered boats at higher tides due to the muddy bottom. The Magic Lake Property Owners Association (MLPOS) operates the adjacent marina and access to marina facilities is restricted to boat owners and guests (See the *Boating Guide - Marinas*). Parking beyond the marina sign is restricted for use while boat loading, and it is best not to even drive down that road since it is congested, difficult to turn around, and is also used as a sea-ambulance drop-off point.

Instead, enjoy the pleasant stroll from the parking lot to the end of the marina road and breakwater where there is a picnic table and a good view of both serene sunsets and approaching storms. If you are very lucky, a pod of orcas will swim by close to the shoreline, however, this typically occurs a maximum of once on any given day or night in summer, and at no particular time. If you notice a barrage of whale watching boats beyond the breakwater, chances are the orcas are passing by. **Map 4A.**

52 BOAT NOOK

✪ From the reference point, continue southwest (left) down Schooner Way, past Privateers Road and Pirates Road. Schooner Way curves to the right. After Capstan Lane, look for the beach access on the left before Yawl Lane, indicated by a wooden archway engraved with *Boat Nook*. Parking is limited here. A short dirt trail leads between homes to a concrete viewing platform. The remains of an old pier are still present. Wheelchairs may be able to negotiate the trail from the street to the viewing platform. The bay known as Boat Nook is picturesque, though completely lined with homes. At low tide beach access may be available on both sides of the viewing platform by climbing over the rock formation onto rock and sand beaches. Boat Nook is another possible orca-watching spot, though Thieves Bay is better. **Map 4A.**

Hiking Trails

PRIOR CENTENNIAL CAMPGROUND TO DISC PARK AND LINKER TRAILS

A network of hiking trails meander through mixed forest surrounding Golf Island Disc Park. A trail connects Prior Centennial Campground to this area. These trails are of most interest to Prior Centennial campers and nearby residents.

Rating: 6; Difficulty: Moderate (campground to disc park) to Easy (shorter trails near disc park). Surface: Dirt trails with roots and rocks, some stairs and bridges. Walking Time/Distance: About 30-40 minutes each way from campground to disc park, or up to 2-hour circuit depending on trails. About 1.2 km from campground to disc park (Elevation gain: about 40 m). Other distances vary depending on trails taken. **Map 4B.**

Access Five trailheads serve this network of trails. The map below is a replica of **4B**.

T1 Prior Centennial Campground (GINPR): From Driftwood Centre, proceed south on Bedwell Harbour Road about 2 km to the campground on the right. A trail leads to the west from the far end of the camping loop. Parking is at the entrance to the campground. Do not park in designated campsites or block the locked gate when the park is closed.

T2 Magic Lake Fire Hall (Fire Hall #2): The fire hall is just to the west (left) of the Magic Lake Estates Reference Point (Schooner Way and Ketch Road). Just past the fire hall, on the right side of Schooner Way, is a trail entrance with a Fire Hall to Disc Park sign next to a short wooden ramp. Parking is along the shoulder (watch for ditches). This trail leads to Golf Island and merges with a trail that can take you back to **T3** and **T1**.

T3 Ketch Road: At the entrance to Magic Lake Estates, turn to the right onto Ketch Road instead of veering to the left along Schooner Way, as in **T2**. As the road begins to curve to the left, watch for a trailhead sign on the right for Heart Trail. Across the street on the left is another trailhead for Heart Trail Extension that leads to Golf Island Disc Park.

T4 Bosun Way: From **T3**, continue on Ketch Road, and make the first left on Bosun Way. T4 is on the left just after Jolly Roger Crescent.

T5 Galleon Way/Golf Island: From the Magic Lake reference point, continue southwest (left) on Schooner Way, make the first right on Privateers Road, the first right on Galleon Way, and follow Galleon Way up the hill to the obvious parking area and entrance to the disc park on the right. (Or, from **T4**, continue on Bosun Way, and make the second left onto Galleon Way. Follow Galleon Way around the bend to the left to the Golf Island park entrance on the left). An outhouse, water fountain and shelter with picnic table are located at the entrance to the disc park. The signed trailhead is in front of the parking area, just to the left of the disc park entrance.

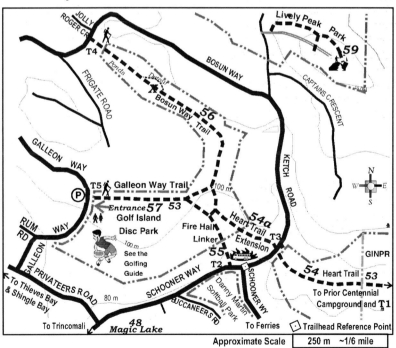

53 PRIOR CENTENNIAL CAMPGROUND TO GOLF ISLAND DISC PARK

From Trailhead **T1**, a 5-minute, level trail begins at the far end of the campground loop and traverses second growth mixed forest within the National Park. A junction near the end of the trail on the right is for the Heart Trail. The trail straight ahead leads to some old stairs up to a hillock, where there may be some sunshine, and a view out over the treetops. Return to the Heart Trail. See description below.

54 HEART TRAIL

The signpost states that volunteers from the Pender Island Parks Commission and the First Open Heart Society of BC constructed this trail. It is a wide trail with some developed portions including stairs and railings, but there are two moderately steep areas, and tripping hazards such as roots are present. The pleasant walk takes 15-20 minutes one way and ends at **T3** at Ketch Road.

54A HEART TRAIL EXTENSION

From **T3**, carefully cross Ketch Road and find the signed connector trail. Continue meandering through the forest up a hill with southern exposure that contains arbutus, Douglas fir and grand fir, then down the other side to a valley with a fern grotto and numerous western red cedar trees. Continue on this trail to the main trail junction near the disc park, which is indicated when the trail squeezes between a large Douglas fir tree and a long fallen Douglas fir log. Note that to your left, at the opposite end of the long log, is the end of the Fire Hall trail (**55**). You can return on that trail to complete a loop. For now, turn to the right, and follow the trail to a fork. At this point the right fork goes to the Bosun Way Trailhead **T4** (See **56**) while the left fork continues to Galleon Way and **T5** along the Galleon Way Linker Trail (**57**). The entrance to the disc park is about 10 minutes away at the end of **57**.

55 FIRE HALL TO DISC PARK TRAIL

Start at Trailhead **T2**. Follow this easy, level trail through the woods and reach the main park trail junction at the long Douglas fir log in about 10 minutes. Signs at the trail junction point toward the Heart Trail, Galleon Way, and the disc park. To get to the disc park entrance, continue straight ahead toward *Galleon Way* from this trail junction, over a small hill, make a quick left at the first junction and walk for about 10 minutes until you reach Galleon Way and the entrance to the disc park on your left.

Also at the fallen tree trail junction, the Heart Trail Extension begins to your right, between the opposite end of the fallen tree and a large standing Douglas fir. You can take that trail back to complete a loop. Or, follow the sign that points to Bosun Way Trailhead **T4** (see description below).

56 BOSUN WAY LINKER TRAIL

To Trailhead **T4**: From the same trail junction at the fallen Douglas fir log (from the end of either the Fire Hall Linker or Heart Trail Extension trails), walk to the right and reach a fork. The right fork follows a pretty forest trail, then crosses a bridge over a stream surrounded by an area resplendent in sword ferns. A huge fallen western red cedar is off to the left. Further along, a trail detour is provided around an ecologically sensitive area. Note the bigleaf maples on the northern slope, amongst the Douglas fir.

After passing a marsh and seasonal pond on the left, the trail ends at Bosun Way in about 15 minutes. Either return the same way, or return via the streets. To get to **T5** (Disc Park) along streets, turn left on Bosun Way, then left on Galleon Way until you reach the disc park. Or, to get back to the campground along streets (and the Heart Trail) from this point, make a right on Bosun Way and a right on Ketch Road until you reach **T3**. Turn left onto the Heart Trail (**54**) to return to the campground.

57 GALLEON WAY LINKER

Begin at Trailhead **T5**. This trail begins to the left of the entrance to Golf Island Disc Park and skirts the perimeter of the park, passing some large western red cedars and reaching a junction with the Bosun Way Linker Trail (**56**), then the Heart Trail Extension (**54a**) and Fire Hall Linker Trail (**55**) in about 5 minutes.

OTHER MAGIC LAKE ESTATES TRAILS

58 CAPSTAN LANE/ROPE ROAD TRAILS

Rating: 6. Difficulty: Easy+. Surface: Dirt with roots, rocks, seasonally muddy areas, bridges, ramps and stairs. Access: Three trailheads are located at the end of Rope Road (off Privateers), the west side of Capstan Lane (north of Bosuns Court), and Capstan Lane near its intersection with Schooner Way. Walking time: About 15 minutes, **Map 4A**. A pleasant trail follows a skunk cabbage-lined seasonal stream through a wetland area. Portions of this trail can be muddy in the winter, which is highlighted by some old growth Douglas fir trees mixed in with the western red cedar, red alder and big leaf maple trees. The trail from the end of Rope Road enables those walking around the central part of Magic Lake Estates a shortcut to the Boat Nook ocean access.

59 LIVELY PEAK PARK

Rating: 6. Difficulty: Moderate. Surface: Dirt with roots and rocks, some stairs and ramps. Walking time each way: 10 to 15 minutes. Elevation gain: About 50 metres. This vista hike is a nice option for locals, but is one of the lower-rated vista hikes available on the Pender Islands. **Map 4B.**

Access: From the Magic Lake reference point, turn right (east) on Ketch Road. The trailhead is located along Ketch Road after the turnoff to Bosun Way, between Captains Crescent and Sailor Road. On the right is a yellow gate for an unpaved service road and *Lively Peak Park* on a wooden post.

The Hike: Walk up the service road about twenty paces and look for a trail sign on the left. The trail is easy to follow but in places is rough and can be slippery at the steep sections. Stairs and railings aid the hiker in places. A sign about halfway up the trail points to two viewpoints. The *left* (east) viewpoint is more rewarding:

Right/west viewpoint: Ascend a steep staircase, cross the gravel road, and walk to a bench with a southwesterly view toward the Olympic Mountains, the Victoria area, Moresby Island, Sidney and the Saanich Peninsula, Portland Island and Salt Spring Island. The view is partially obscured by trees. Return back down the stairs and trail, as the gravel road can be extremely slippery. **Left/east viewpoint:** From the same sign, the trail continues to an area past a water tank and telecommunications equipment. This viewpoint is higher, about 177 m elevation. Two benches are situated here. The first has a lovely view to the east across Bedwell Harbour to Saturna Island and its vineyards, with the Cascade Mountains as a backdrop. The second bench has more of a southwesterly view that is similar to that of the *right viewpoint*. At time of writing the view is not as obscured by trees, but that can change as the trees grow into the viewscape. Return back down the trail the same way.

60 MASTHEAD CRESCENT/SHINGLE BAY LINKER TRAIL

Rating: 7. Difficulty: Easy+. Surface: Wide dirt trail with some roots and muddy areas. Walking time/distance each way: 10 minutes; about 500 metres. Elevation gain: About 50 metres. **Map 4A.**

Access: The east (Buck Lake area) trailhead is on the west side of Masthead Crescent, just off Galleon Way, between the first two homes on the left. Respect the private properties. The west (Shingle Bay area) trailhead is on the east side of Galleon Way, just south of Crowsnest Drive.

The Hike: The trail connects two sections of meandering Galleon Way, providing a shortcut from the north side of Buck Lake to the ocean at Shingle Bay and the south entrance to GINPR - Roe Lake area. From the Shingle Bay trailhead, proceed up the wide, level trail that rises gradually in elevation. A highlight is a grove of red alders growing in a wet draw. The trail continues past large western red cedar and bigleaf maple trees.

61 YARDARM ROAD/SHINGLE BAY LINKER TRAIL

Rating: 2. This steep trail connects Galleon Way, from a point south of the Masthead Crescent/Shingle Bay linker trail, between private homes, to Yardarm Road. This trail is uninteresting and inferior to the Masthead trail. **Map 4A.**

62 BUCK LAKE TRAIL

Rating: 6. Difficulty: Moderate. Surface: Rough trail with roots, rocks and steep hill, aided by stairs and ramps. Walking time/distance each way: About 10 minutes; 275 metres. Elevation change: About 30 metres. **Map 4A.**

Access: This trail connects Spyglass Road (west of Signal Hill Road) with Privateers Road (east of Doubloon Crescent). From Spyglass Road, the trail begins just west of the Buck Lake water treatment facility.

The Hike: From the Spyglass Road trailhead the trail begins on the remnants of a dirt road until a *Trail* sign diverts the hiker onto a narrow path to the left. The trail parallels a seasonal stream of Buck Lake runoff with waterfalls over sandstone formations, and associated wetland vegetation in this draw. The highlights of this trail are about halfway down, where the seasonal stream cascades over a precipice, and a huge old-growth Douglas fir tree stands sentinel. Also along the trail are an interesting old wishbone-shaped western red cedar and a thicket of monkey flower near Privateers Road.

63 SCHOONER-PRIVATEERS TRAIL

Rating: 6. Difficulty: Easy+. Surface: Rough trail with roots, rocks, and hills, aided by stairs and ramps. Walking time/distance each way: About 10 minutes, 250 metres. Elevation change: About 20 metres. **Map 4A**

Access: The two trailheads are on Privateers Road (across from the Buck Lake Trail, east of Doubloon Crescent) and on Schooner Way near Yawl Lane.

The Hike: From Privateers Road, the trail follows the seasonal stream from Buck Lake as it flows over sandstone formations. The draw on your left is carpeted with sword ferns, and supports large western red cedars, Douglas firs and grand firs. About halfway down the trail, stand on the wooden ramp and listen to the rushing stream (in season) that flows through a lush grotto. As you climb away from the valley, you continue to be amongst cedars and firs, then pass through a small wetland dotted with red alders as you emerge onto Schooner Way.

64 ABBOTT HILL PARK

From the intersection of Signal Hill Road and Spyglass Road, Spyglass Road heads west, bends sharply to the left and then right. On your left is Abbott Hill Park, named for Mel Abbott, a surveyor who bought the land that was to comprise Magic Lake Estates. Development began in the early 1960's and was basically completed in 1974, but Mel died in 1970 of a heart attack at age 38. A short but very steep and slippery trail leads from near the park sign to a nice arbutus-covered property. Views are through the trees to the south to Swanson Channel, and to the east to Buck Lake. Future plans include a trail to connect this park with the Buck Lake Trail. **Map 4A.**

65 SANDY SIEVERT PARK

On Spyglass Road, just to the west of Abbott Hill Park, a short, steep trail (aided by stairs and handrails) leads from the north side of the road through Sandy Sievert Park down to Gunwhale Road, making for a pleasant forest diversion during your road walk. **Map 4A.**

66, 67 BUCK LAKE AREA SHORTCUTS

66: The Compass Crescent to Tiller Crescent Linker trail enables residents to walk from the area around Signal Hill Road and the south side of Buck Lake to the north side of Buck Lake and Galleon Way. **Map 4A.**

67: The Starboard Crescent to Compass Crescent Linker trail enables residents in the area of Port Road to walk down to the Buck Lake area and the trails that connect to it. **Map 4A.**

68 SCHOONER WAY TO CHART DRIVE SHORTCUT

This short trail between private homes starts on the right as you round the bend near the end of Schooner Way (be respectful of private property here) and allows residents in this area a shortcut to Shingle Bay Park and the south entrance to GINPR - Roe Lake area. When you reach Chart Drive, there is no public beach access along this road, so turn right, then left on Galleon Way to the end, or stop at the Harpoon Road beach access. **Map 4.**

68A, 68B NEIGHBOURHOOD REST STOPS

68a: A bench is situated in a park at the bottom of Reef Road across Schooner Way. Look southwest through trees to Swanson Channel. **68b:** At the crook of the hairpin turn on Anchor Way is a *rest stop* with benches. **Map 4A.**

69 BUCK LAKE AREA HILLS & SEA TOUR

A combination of strolls along uncrowded streets and wooded linker trails to visit some of the forests, all of the public ocean access points and Magic Lake Estates' reservoir. This hike is probably of most interest to local residents who live near the route, and is just one example of circuits that can be made utilizing the Magic Lake Estates linker trails described in the previous sections.

Rating: 7. Difficulty: Moderate to strenuous (for distance and hills)
Surface: Paved roads and dirt paths varying from smooth to rough.
Walking time and distance: About 2 hours for a complete 6 km circuit plus any extra time spent at viewpoints. **Trail Map:** See the following page for a replica of **Map 4A**.
Facilities: Outhouses at Thieves Bay Park and Shingle Bay Park (planned for 2006).

Access
Pick up this route at any point. It will be described from the trailhead near Shingle Bay Park for the benefit of those combining it with a hike in the Roe Lake section of GINPR (See *Otter Bay Area* 36 - 37). To reach Shingle Bay Park by car, begin at the Magic Lake reference point (Schooner Way and Ketch Road). Continue to the southwest (left), make the first right on Privateers Road and follow Privateers Road without turning. It will turn back into Schooner Way. Follow it to the right as Anchor Way continues straight ahead. Make the first right on Shoal Road and then the first right on Dory Way. Follow Dory Way without turning; it turns into Galleon Way, then winds around to Shingle Bay Park, and ends just past Crowsnest Drive at the south GINPR-Roe Lake trailhead (**T3**). The trailhead for this hike lies at the vacant wooded area just before (south of) Crowsnest Drive, across from Shingle Bay Park. Look for the trailhead sign-post here.

The Hike
This walk encompasses Shingle Bay Park (**49**), the Masthead/Shingle Bay Linker (**60**), a stroll around Buck Lake utilizing the Tiller Crescent/Compass Crescent Linker (**66**), the Buck Lake Trail (**62**), the Schooner/Privateers Trail (**63**), the Boat Nook ocean access (**52**), Thieves Bay Park and ocean access (**51**), and the Harpoon Road ocean access (**50**).

BEGIN FIRST HOUR: 00:00 / 0 METRES
Masthead Crescent/Shingle Bay Linker Trail 49: From the trailhead, proceed up the wide, level trail that makes its way gradually up an incline for its approximately 500 m length. Notice a large grove of red alders growing in a wet draw. The trail continues past large western red cedar and big leaf maple trees and ends after 10 minutes at Masthead Crescent between the first two residences off of Galleon Way.
00:10/ 575 METRES
Turn right onto Masthead Crescent, then a quick left onto Galleon Way. Buck Lake appears on the right beyond the homes. Buck Lake is the Magic Lake Estates water supply and there is no public access except to residents along its shores.
00:20 / 1.1 KM
Make the first right onto Tiller Crescent. At the cul de sac, the Compass Crescent/Tiller Crescent Linker Trail 66 begins at around *11:00*. This 5-minute trail affords nice views of Buck Lake, then turns uphill between homes.

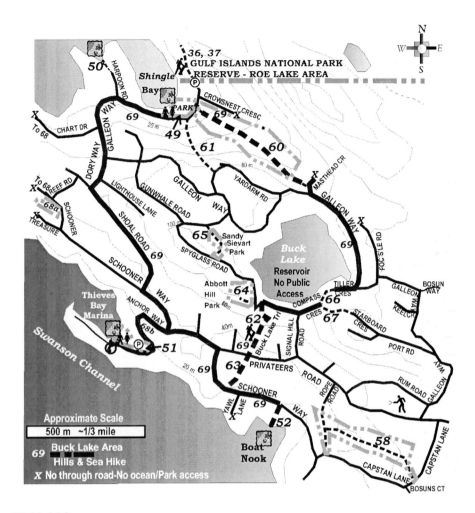

00:30 / 1.3 KM

Make a right onto Compass Crescent, and proceed straight ahead onto Spyglass Road, past Signal Hill Road, with Buck Lake appearing on the right. The *Water Supply* sign is located here, and across the street on the left is the water treatment plant. Just past this facility, Spyglass Road curves sharply to the left. At that point, look for the *Buck Lake Trail* signpost on the left.

00:35 /1.6 KM

Buck Lake Trail **62**: The trail begins on the remnants of a road until a trail sign diverts you onto a narrow path to the left. The trail parallels a seasonal stream of Buck Lake runoff with waterfalls over sandstone formations, and associated wetland vegetation in this draw. The highlights of this 10-minute trail are a huge old-growth Douglas fir tree at its midpoint, and an old *wishbone* shaped western red cedar near Privateers Road.

00:45 / 1.8 KM

Schooner-Privateers Trail **63**: Across Privateers Road from the Buck Lake Trail, this 250 metre trail continues to traverse the seasonal stream with its small waterfalls over sandstone formations. The draw on your left is carpeted with sword ferns, and supports large western red cedars, Douglas firs and grand firs. As you climb away from the valley, you continue to be amongst cedars and firs, then pass through a small wetland dotted with red alders as you emerge onto Schooner Way near Yawl Lane. Turn left, and walk about 200 metres to the signed *Boat Nook* ocean access on your right **52**.

01:00 / 2.2 KM

Walk to the ocean access point, which is between two private homes. A bench is available to enjoy the view of the bay, or explore on the rocks below. If you are very lucky, you may see orcas swimming by in the distance past the small rocky islets.

BEGIN SECOND HOUR 01:00 / 2.4 KM

Return to Schooner Way and turn left, then left again at the intersection with Privateers Road.

01:10 / 2.9 KM

Schooner Way curves to the right at a *T* intersection (at 3.1 km). If you are getting tired, you'd better turn right here to return (right on Shoal Road, right on Dory Way - which becomes Galleon Way - to the end of the road down the hill). Otherwise, continue straight onto Anchor Way. Descend the hill, which leads to Thieves Bay Park **51** (an outhouse is located here). Enjoy the view of the marina from here, or walk to the end of the Thieves Bay Marina access road to the breakwater. This is one of the best places to watch orcas, as they sometimes swim close to shore here, although the chances of them passing by at the moment you arrive are slim. One picnic table is located here, and the view is across Swanson Channel to Salt Spring Island, and also to the southwest toward Vancouver Island. This is a good place to watch storms and sunsets.

01:20 / 3.8 KM

Return the way you came up the hill along Anchor Way, and make the first left onto Schooner Way. Make the first right on Shoal Road, which is a gradual incline, and make the first right on Dory Way atop the hill. Follow Dory Way down the hill; it turns into Galleon Way midway down; continue straight ahead. As an option, turn left on Harpoon Road for a quick walk to the beach access at Panda Bay. Return to Galleon Way and continue (left) down the hill to your starting point at Shingle Bay Park.

END TIME 2:00 / DISTANCE 6 KM　　　　　　　　Below: Thieves Bay Breakwater

Oaks Bluff and Trincomali/Wallace Point

This area southeast of Magic Lake Estates forms the southern end of North Pender Island. It features the dramatic Oaks Bluff area along Swanson Channel on the south shore, and Bedwell Harbour frontage on the north shore, across from South Pender Island. No public ocean access is available until the southern tip of the island, at the Trincomali Neighbourhood. One spectacular view hike is available in the Oaks Bluff area (**70**). Trincomali has three ocean access points, two ocean vista points, and a featured stroll connecting the points of interest (**71-76**). **Maps: North Pender Index, 4C, 4D.**

Washrooms
No public facilities are located in this area. The closest outhouse is at the Magic Lake swimming hole, open seasonally (Down Pirates Road 1 km from Schooner Way, on the left). See the *Magic Lake Estates Area* section (**Map 4**) for information on the Magic Lake swimming hole (**48**), and facilities in that area.

Part One: Oaks Bluff

70 OAKS BLUFF PARK
A climb up a switchback trail to a spectacular 100-metre high lookout across Swanson Channel to the west. A second lookout is to the east toward Poets Cove and Mt. Baker. Great for local residents or visitors who don't have a lot of time but desire an exciting hike.

Rating: 8. Difficulty: Moderate. Surface: Steep dirt trail with boardwalks, aided by stairs and railings in places, but some tricky sections remain.
Elevation gain: Approx: 40 metres. Walking time/distance each way: 15-25 minutes, 500 metres. **Map 4C**. *Warning: Steep drop-off at viewpoint with no railing.*

Access
From the entrance to Magic Lake Estates (Schooner Way and Ketch Road), continue southwest (left), past Magic Lake, to the first left at Pirates Road. Continue on Pirates Road for about 2.5 km and look for an unpaved parking area on the right hand side with a trailhead sign and steps leading up from the left side of the parking lot.

The Hike
The hike through this 5 ha (12 acre) park begins with a gradual climb through a dark forest of Douglas fir, western red cedar, red alder, and various oaks with an understory dominated by oceanspray, sword fern and seasonal wildflowers. The trail steepens as it ascends the bluff through the forest. Listen for evening grosbeaks and robins. The trail varies between smooth and rough, aided in

places by stairs. Watch for roots and other tripping hazards. One area is particularly tricky on the return, requiring maneuvering about 3 metres down a steep incline with protruding roots available to step on. A junction is reached at the summit. To the left is a short stroll to a bench at Viewpoint 1 that looks east over Bedwell Harbour, Poets Cove Resort, and, on a clear day, snow-covered Mt. Baker in the Washington Cascades as a backdrop. Returning to the junction, bear left and head down to Viewpoint 2. A handrail along the trail aids a 3-metre steep, slippery area. In a few minutes the trail emerges at a spectacular vista atop a 120-metre high rocky bluff with no guardrail. Acrophobes may not wish to come here, as the drop-off appears as if it goes on forever, although the embankment actually descends in a series of terraces. Sit on the bench in front of the arbutus trees, and note the trembling aspen

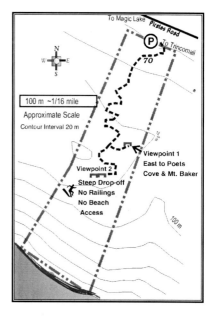

on your right as you look out at the vista down to Swanson Channel below, a popular area for salmon fishing. The view to your left is of Stuart Island (U.S.). The international boundary forms a right angle next to Stuart island: Boundary Pass is in front of it and Haro Strait is to its right. Across Haro Strait to the right are Moresby Island (Canada), Portland Island (now part of Gulf Islands National Park Reserve), and the large Salt Spring Island. Vancouver Island is in the background, with the Victoria area to the left at the southern tip of the large land mass, and the Sooke Hills of Vancouver Island to the southwest. On clear days the Olympic Mountains are visible in the distance beyond Victoria. Enjoy a bird's eye view of soaring raptors (bald eagles, turkey vultures and hawks) and seagulls as they take advantage of the updrafts created by the cliffs. If you are very lucky, a pod of orcas may swim by, looking tiny from your lofty perch. Carefully descend back down the same trail.

Part Two: Trincomali/Wallace Point

Trailhead Reference Point
The very end of Pirates Road at the main Trincomali neighbourhood signboard. From the entrance to Magic Lake Estates (Schooner and Ketch), turn left on Schooner Way, pass Magic Lake, and make the next left onto Pirates Road. Follow it about 3 km, past the *Welcome to Trincomali* sign (where the road changes names to Plumper Way), past the water tanks, to the intersection of Plumper Way and Bedwell Drive. The main signboard and postboxes, as well as a cute fake bus stop sign, are on your left. Park away from the mailboxes along the shoulder on the right. See **Map 4D** which is replicated for Hike **76** in this chapter.

71 STARVATION BAY

☼ From the Trincomali sign-board at Plumper Way and Bedwell Drive, continue to the east (left) down Bedwell Drive, and make the first right on Trincoma Place. The road curves to the left, and then curves to the right where there is a concrete guardrail (no parking here). Behind the guardrail are a bench and an ocean access sign. Search carefully for a wide shoulder in the area to park on, respecting pri-

vate property. Stairs lead down to a picturesque sand and shell crescent beach accessible at lower tides only. Views are across Bedwell Harbour to the Poets Cove Marina.

72 PETER COVE NORTH

☼ Continue past access **71** described above to the cul de sac at the end of the street. A beach access is on the right. Parking is very limited in this area. Stairs lead down to a sandy beach on the north shore of Peter Cove. You can climb over interesting conglomerate outcroppings and watch for marine life in the shallow lagoon.

73 PETER COVE SOUTH

From the signboard, go straight (southeast) down Plumper Way. After the road curves to the left, watch for an obvious beach access trail that leads off from the left. The smooth unpaved trail of moderate grade leads down to the beach in about 3 minutes. Small boats can easily be launched by hand here. The cove is protected and scenic, although it is rimmed by private homes and driftwood.

74 PLUMPER WAY VIEWPOINT

Further along Plumper Way from the above ocean access, the road narrows and ascends a small hill. A signed trail for *Plumper Way Viewpoint* is on the right, and one unpaved parking spot is across the street from it. A short, level, uneven trail leads to a viewpoint with a bench to enjoy the view to the southwest toward Haro Strait (no beach access here). Watch for tricky currents off shore, harbour seals, and if you are very lucky, orcas, porpoises or dolphins.

75 BEDWELL DRIVE

From the signboard, continue to the east (left) down Bedwell Drive, past Trincoma Place. The road curves to the left, and when the road nears the waterfront, a bench for viewing Bedwell Harbour is available on the right. Pender Parks has this spot slated for a future ocean access point.

76 TRINCOMALI NEIGHBOURHOOD STROLL

Trincomali is a quaint seaside neighbourhood at the southwest tip of North Pender Island, with several picturesque ocean access points, described above. For an added treat, do this walk during the Artists of Trincomali show (typically held the day after the Fall Fair in late August), when various neighbourhood artists hold open houses.

Rating: 6. Difficulty: Easy to moderate. Surface: Paved roads, some small hills. Walking Time/Distance: 15 to 60 minutes, 500 metres to 2 km. Map below (**Map 4D).**

The Hike

From the reference point, facing the signboard, walk east (left), down the hill of Bedwell Drive, and make the first right onto Trincoma Place. Walk along the quiet street, and find the *Starvation Bay* ocean access (**71**) behind the concrete barrier as the road curves sharply to the right in about 4 minutes. Explore at your leisure, best at lower tides. Continue to the end of Trincoma Place, and in another 4 minutes, find the ocean access to Peter Cove North at the end of the road on the right (**72**). This scenic area overlooks Wallace Point across the cove to the south. Return the way you came. If you turn right on Bedwell Drive, you can walk along the peaceful street until you reach an ocean view bench and future ocean access point (**75**). Return to the signboard where you started. To extend the walk, turn left down the hill of Plumper Way. After the road curves to

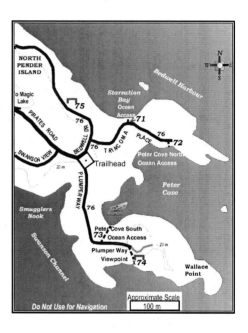

the left, watch for an obvious wide trail on the left, which is slated to have a sign installed as Peter Cove South (**73**). The short, gradual unpaved trail leads to a long crescent beach that is rimmed with logs and private homes. Return to Plumper Way, turn left, then look for the signed *Plumper Way Viewpoint* trail to the right at the end of the paved road (**74**). This leads to an ocean-view bench with views out to the south to Haro Strait and Stuart Island in the U.S. (No ocean access). Return the same way to the starting point. You can extend your hike even further by walking up Plumper Way (to the northwest) to the first left onto Swanson View. At the end of the street, the water-view trail on the left is on private property, but the trail to the right through the woods is a community right-of-way and returns to Plumper Way at the *Welcome to Trincomali* sign. Make a right to return to the starting point, being mindful of vehicular traffic.

13   COASTAL ACCESS AND HIKING GUIDE   -   PART THREE

SOUTH PENDER ISLAND

Finding Specific Trails
Rather than giving directions from the ferry terminal to each trail or ocean access, each area of South Pender Island has a Trailhead Reference Point assigned to it. Directions are given from the ferry terminal to each Trailhead Reference Point, which is also plotted on the appropriate maps. The reference points are usually principal road intersections in the area. Then, directions to each individual feature are described from the nearest Trailhead Reference Point. Some of the maps from the *Map Atlas* are duplicated in this chapter for convenience.
✪Indicates a recommended ocean access. ✪ ✪ Are the best.

Pender Canal Area and Canal Road

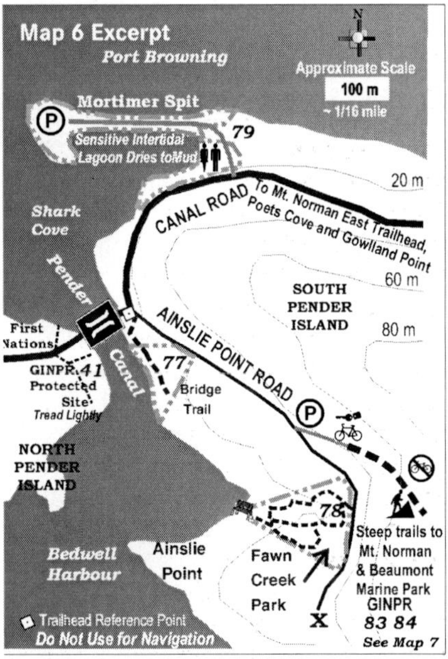

The area on the South Pender side of the Pender Canal contains a high concentration of top-notch hikes and beach accesses (**Map 6,** replicated in inset, right). It includes two short trails to the south of the bridge (**77, 78**), Mortimer Spit beach (**79**), two beach accesses along the north shore of the island (**80, 81 - Map 7A**), and access to GINPR - South Pender, including Mt. Norman and Beaumont Marine Park (**83 to 85 - Maps 6 & 7**). Combined with the Greenburn Lake area, the National Park now occupies 281.4 ha (695 acres), close to one-third of South Pender Island. The canal area was a very active Coast Salish encampment from at least 5,000 years ago.

Map 6 Excerpt

Trailhead Reference Point
The South Pender side of the Pender Canal Bridge. From the ferry terminal, follow signs to South Pender Island: Bear right on MacKinnon Road from the terminal, then right again on Otter Bay Road until it ends at Bedwell Harbour Road. Turn right. After reaching Driftwood Centre, continue on Bedwell Harbour Road to the south, which becomes Canal Road. Bear left to continue on Canal Road to South Pender Island. Use caution crossing the one-lane bridge.

Washrooms and Facilities
Pit toilets are located in the woods next to the Mortimer Spit access road, and along the trails to Mt. Norman from both trailheads. The closest provisions and accommodations are back toward the Driftwood Centre or **Magic Lake Market**, or at **Poets Cove Resort**.

Ocean Accesses and Short Oceanside Hikes

77 BRIDGE TRAIL
Rating: 5. A short trail begins next to the right side of the bridge as you cross onto South Pender Island and turn onto Ainslie Point Road. It takes about 5 minutes to access a viewpoint of the canal and bridge, although there is no water access available here. Use caution near the end of the trail as the bank is eroding. A bench is available to sit and watch the parade of boats navigate the canal during the summer. **Map 6**.

78 FAWN CREEK PARK
Rating: 6. Further along Ainslie Point Road, past the Mount Norman access on the left, look for Fawn Creek Park on the right. The highlight of this park is a riparian ecosystem along a seasonal stream, which supports large red alder, grand fir, western red cedar and Douglas fir trees, with a rich understory dominated by swordfern and salal. The trail descends from the street to a junction with a loop trail depicted on a wooden sign. Go to the right, and follow the trail downhill through the forest. Listen, then watch for the beautiful Pileated Woodpeckers that frequent the old snags present here. Make your way to the bench next to a muddy foreshore where the stream flows into the canal area. Beach access is possible here, but nearby Mortimer Spit is a much better bet. The view is partially obscured by the large cedar trees. Find your way back along the loop trail that follows the stream, or extend the hike by taking the second loop. Total hiking time should be under 15 minutes. **Map 6**.

79 MORTIMER SPIT
✿ ✿ This narrow sand and shell strip of land is perhaps the favourite water access on the Pender Islands. Once across the bridge, proceed down Canal Road to the left, around the bend to the right, and watch for a dirt road on the left that is signed *Mortimer Spit*. A gravel road descends around a bend; a pit toilet is in the woods to the left. The road leads to an ample unpaved parking area that can be very muddy during wet periods. Do not drive down here when high tides combine with stormy

weather, as portions of the spit can become submerged. On a warm summer day the beach is packed with sunbathers, hearty swimmers, and clam diggers. The north side of the spit drops off fairly steeply, while the southern end is shallow, drying to a mud flat (a very sensitive intertidal zone). Hand-carried boats such as kayaks can be launched from the spit. The Pender Canal and bridge are across Shark Cove to the south - be careful of strong currents through the canal. The bay to the north is Port Browning, with Port Browning Marina at its head to the northwest, and the Razor Point area on the opposite shore to the north. Overnight parking is not allowed here. **Map 6**

80 CANAL ROAD OCEAN ACCESS AND BEACH HIKE

✿ From the bridge, turn left and proceed down Canal Road for about 3.5 km. The signed beach access is between property numbers 9858 and 9864 on the left. A wide dirt shoulder is available for parking. A trail leads through the brush to stairs down to the beach. The rocky beach is accessible at lower tides, when it is also possible to walk 1 km to the east (right facing the ocean) along the flat, rocky shore to the Canal Road/ Walker Road beach access (**81**). To find that ocean access from the beach, look for stairs carved into the bank, and the back of a park sign atop the bank. **Map 7A** (below).

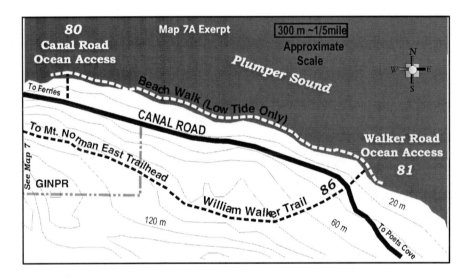

81 WALKER ROAD OCEAN ACCESS AND BEACH HIKE

✿ From the bridge, turn left and proceed down Canal Road for about 4.5 km. The signed beach access is across the street from the William Walker Trail trailhead (**86**). Parking is along the north side of the road. A five-minute developed trail leads down to a rock and sand beach. The beach, accessible at lower tides, is very scenic. The view is down Plumper Sound to the east toward the San Juan Islands. Across the sound to the north is Saturna Island; further to the west are Mayne Island, Galiano Island, and North Pender Island. You can walk 1 km to the west (left) to the Canal Road beach access (**80**) at lower tides (Check the tide tables before proceeding). Walking is mostly along abrasive upturned sandstone beds, so wear appropriate shoes. The sandstone cliffs disappear by the time you reach the other Canal Road beach access, which is obvious. Look for a staircase, a ledge with a rope, and the back of a park sign. See the William Walker Trail description (**86**) in *Hiking Trails* below for a long loop hike.

Hiking Trails

GULF ISLANDS NATIONAL PARK RESERVE - SOUTH PENDER
Formerly Mount Norman Regional Park and Beaumont Provincial Marine Park

Perhaps the best and most rewarding hiking on the Pender Islands is found in the National Park lands that formerly encompassed Mt. Norman Regional (CRD) Park and Beaumont Marine Provincial Park. The area is now managed by Parks Canada, who will gradually evaluate and update the trails. Since these areas have been established parks since the 1980's, however, well-defined trails already exist. The area consists of the shoreline of the popular Beaumont Marine Park, extends to the summit of Mt. Norman, and across to the north side of South Pender Island. In addition to the National Park trails, Pender Parks maintains trails that can be used to extend the hike to other waterfront areas on both sides of South Pender Island. Additional connecting trails are currently on the drawing board. With the exception of the level trails in Beaumont Marine Park accessible by boat, most of the hiking in this area is strenuous. See **Map 7** (replicated below). The other portion of the Gulf Islands National Park Reserve - South Pender is Greenburn Lake, which is described in the *Poets Cove to Gowlland Point* section and shown on **Map 8** in the *Map Atlas*.

Access   Three trailheads serve this section of the National Park. The summit of Mt. Norman can be reached from all three (See **Maps 6 and 7**):

T1 Beaumont Marine Park Campground, accessible by boat.

T2 Ainslie Point Road near the canal bridge (Mt. Norman West Trailhead); and

T3 Canal Road 2.5 km from the bridge (Mt. Norman East Trailhead)

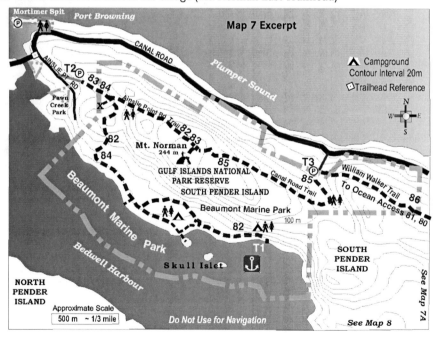

T1 BEAUMONT MARINE PARK TRAILHEAD: BOAT-IN
A staircase leads up from the beach in front of the mooring buoy area of Beaumont Marine Park. This is the eastern extent of the trail system. You can also come ashore at the main campground behind the isthmus to the west.

82 BEAUMONT COASTAL WALK/MT. NORMAN SUMMIT OPTION
Easy stroll through one of the prettiest public waterfront areas on the Pender Islands, with an option for a steep climb to a magnificent vista point atop Mt. Norman.

Rating: 9. Difficulty: Easy+ to Strenuous. **Surface:** Dirt path, some portions level and even, others uneven with ups and downs, roots and rocks. **Map 7.**
Approximate time and distance each way:
Coastal stroll: 35 minutes, 1.5 km;
Climb to the junction with Mt. Norman Trail: Another 25 minutes and 500 metres;
Climb to the Mt. Norman Summit from junction: Another 30 minutes and 1 km;
Total hike: 90 minutes and 3 km. The descent to **T1** takes about 70 minutes;
Elevation Gain: 120 metres to Mt. Norman trail junction; 244 m to Mt. Norman summit.
Facilities: Pit toilets at top of stairs (**T1** trailhead), in the main campground, and at the junction with the Mt. Norman summit trail. **Notes:** The water pump at the campground has been shut down. Also, this area has been used by First Nations people for thousands of years, and continues to hold much significance for them. Please do not disturb or remove any cultural artifacts, and camp only in designated areas.

A 1.5 km trail runs parallel to the shoreline throughout Beaumont Marine Park, up to 30 metres above the water. The trail, one of the prettiest on the Penders, passes through mixed arbutus and fir forest. From the east end of the park, near the stairs to the beach, the trail runs to the west, past two campsites and several benches with nice vantage points of Bedwell Harbour and beyond. (Photo, right). The walk to the main part of the campground takes about 10 minutes. Here the

trail forks; to the left is the campground and access to the shoreline trail, straight-ahead is a loop trail that meanders through the forest. Both trails connect after about 10 minutes. If you take the route through the campground (recommended), it will lead to the highlight of the park. Picnic tables look out over picturesque twin shell beaches and an isthmus. Walk to the end of the isthmus for nice views of the coastline, moored boats, and Skull Islet (a barren rock with a navigational marker). The shoreline trail continues from the west side of the campground (on the left looking from the water). After reaching the junction with the loop trail, it continues parallel to the shoreline. This portion of the trail (Photo, next page) has gentle inclines with a few tricky areas,

such as a detour around a fallen tree, and a short, steep section. Watch for slippery roots and rocks. About 10 minutes from the loop trail junction, a steep offshoot trail descends to the waters edge and two benches are available to sit and admire a pretty cove. Back on the main trail, it continues parallel to the shore for another 5 minutes. Here, a signpost directs hikers to the right and up a steep incline. This marks the end of the easy portion of the trail. If you continue, follow this trail carefully since it can be obscured in places. It climbs up through the forest, up several switchbacks, to the left of a large conglomerate rock outcropping, up through another outcropping, then to the left of the next rock outcropping. In about 20-30 minutes the top of the hill is reached at about 120 m elevation. A small offshoot trail to the right leads to resting spots atop the outcroppings with ocean views through the trees. This is not the summit of Mt. Norman. The main trail cuts through salal down a moderate slope and in about 5-10 minutes reaches the obvious junction with the Mt. Norman summit trail (to the right).

> *Note:* To the left is private property, and straight ahead is a steep gravel road that leads down to Trailhead **T2** near the Pender Canal Bridge in about 5 minutes. Near **T2** are short trails to the Pender Canal and Mortimer Spit (**79**) on South Pender, and the First Nations GINPR lands across the bridge on North Pender (**41**).

As you continue on the trail to the Mt. Norman Summit, in about 25 paces is a sign for an outhouse on the right. The trail then rises steeply for about 1 km from this point to the 244-metre summit. An obvious boardwalk to the right leads to a magnificent viewpoint. For more details on the Mt. Norman climb see hike **83**. A description of the Mt. Norman viewpoint is featured on the following page. Return down the same trail.

MT. NORMAN VIEWPOINT

Below you are a row of now-rare Garry oaks on the warm south-facing slope, then Beaumont Marine Park, Bedwell Harbour, and the south end of North Pender Island. The large cleared parcel with a dock is The Timbers resort. Medicine Beach is at the head of Bedwell Harbour to the right, and Poets Cove Resort is barely visible to the left. Beyond North Pender Island are:

From the Left: Stuart Island of the U.S. San Juan Islands (at 10:00) is just across the border. Between Stuart Island and South Pender Island is Boundary Pass, a major shipping channel. The wide waterway between Stuart Island and Moresby Island (Canada), to its right, (which is at 12:00 in your view), is Haro Strait. The international boundary makes a right angle turn in front of Stuart Island, and continues down Haro Strait and through the Strait of Juan de Fuca to the Pacific Ocean. On a clear day the Hurricane Ridge area of the majestic Olympic Mountains of Washington will be prominent in the background, across the Strait of Juan de Fuca from Victoria. These mountains trap a lot of the moisture that would otherwise make its way to the Pender Islands. The rain shadow effect is most dramatic in Sequim, Washington on the Olympic Peninsula (457 mm/18 inches annual precipitation), and becomes less pronounced as it extends northward toward Pender Island (798 mm/31.4 inches).

In the distance beyond the right side of Stuart Island is the long Sidney Island, in front of which are Rum Island (Isle de Lis Marine Park, GINPR) and Gooch Island. Sidney Island extends to the north (right) of those islands, and you can see the popular Sidney Spit sand bar, also part of the GINPR.

Straight ahead are private Moresby Island (Canada), and Portland Island (Princess Margaret Marine Park/GINPR) to its right. Beyond the north (right) end of Moresby Island in the distance is the Swartz Bay Ferry terminal and the Saanich Peninsula of Vancouver Island. You can watch BC Ferries make their way from Swartz Bay to the Southern Gulf Islands and Vancouver, as they travel on either side of Portland Island. To the right of Portland Island is Salt Spring Island, on which the highest point is Bruce Peak (703 metres). Salt Spring extends beyond North Pender Island through the remainder of your view to the right.

AINSLIE POINT ROAD - TRAILHEAD T2

Turn right after crossing the bridge from North Pender Island, and proceed about 250 metres to the signed trailhead on the left with a short dirt road, a gate, and a bike rack. (No bikes allowed on trails; No overnight parking.)

83 AINSLIE POINT ROAD TO MT. NORMAN SUMMIT

A steep trail to a phenomenal viewpoint. Shorter but not as interesting as the Canal Road approach (85).

Rating: 8. Difficulty: Strenuous. **Surface:** A dirt fire road starts from the trailhead and climbs steeply and steadily to the summit. Wooden elevated boardwalk to the viewpoint at the summit has no railings and several stairs along the way.
Walking time and distance each way: 25-40 minutes, 1.5 km.
Elevation gain: About 220 metres. **Map 7** (Replicated in this section)

The Hike

Start out on a very steep dirt road (slippery on the descent) that leads in about 10 minutes to a junction. A sign indicates that the trail straight ahead leads to Beaumont Marine Park (Hike **84**). To the left, the wide trail (that is also a fire road) continues to the summit of Mt. Norman. To the right is private property. After taking about 25 paces along the Mt. Norman trail, you will see an outhouse in the woods for public use.

Continue on the pleasant trail, which soon begins to climb steadily for the remainder of the hike to the maximum elevation of 244 metres. The trail remains a wide overgrown old skid road for its entire length, with no technical sections. The return down this road can be slippery, especially when wet; try to avoid the wet short grassy growth. The lower portion of the trail climbs through a thick forest of Douglas fir and western red cedar with a salal and Oregon grape understory. Watch for a break in the trees to the left about halfway up the hill for a sweeping vista to the east (on clear days) to Mayne and Galiano Islands, with the Vancouver skyline and surrounding mountains in the distance. The upper portion of the mountain was logged in 1985, so trees in this area are mostly less than 20 years old. Logging ended when Mt. Norman became the first regional park in the Gulf Islands in 1988. At the top of the hill, a boardwalk leads off to your right (Photo, right). The trail straight ahead is Hike **85** from Canal Road/**T3**. The wooden boardwalk is well constructed with a wire mesh surface for traction, but there

are no railings and a few single steps. It leads to your just reward, a viewing platform with railings and two benches. You can enjoy the spectacular vista from the viewpoint (described on the previous page), or wander off to the left or right for more seclusion (be careful of the drop-offs). If you plan to picnic here, you may have plenty of wasps for company in the late summer on this dry south-facing slope. Return the same way, or for a major workout, combine this hike with others such as **85** to Canal Road or **84** to Beaumont Marine Park.

84 AINSLIE POINT ROAD TRAILHEAD TO BEAUMONT MARINE PARK
Climb over a steep hill to one of the most beautiful public shorelines on the Pender Islands.

Rating: 9. Difficulty: Strenuous. **Surface:** Dirt trail with rocks, roots, slippery and very steep sections. Trail is hard to follow in places.
Walking time/distance each way: 60 minutes, 2 km.
Elevation Gain: About 250 metres (125 m each way). **Map 7** (Replicated in this section)

The Hike
Follow the steep dirt road to the top of the hill that you will reach in about 5-10 minutes. The signed trail to Beaumont Marine Park is straight ahead (an outhouse is on the trail to Mt. Norman, about 25 paces to the left). The well maintained though rough trail ascends gradually through salal to the top of a hill with obvious conglomerate rock outcroppings in about 5-10 minutes. Make sure to stay on the main trail, which winds around to the right of the outcroppings, then descends a series of steep grades that can be slippery and requires some simple technical hiking at places. The bottom of the hill is reached after a few switchbacks in about

15-20 minutes. The trail proceeds to the left, in the forest parallel to and about 20 to 30 metres above the shoreline. A bench is available with a nice vista. In about 5 minutes a narrow steep trail leads off from the right and descends to a bench overlooking a scenic cove. The main trail reaches an obvious trail junction in another 5 minutes. The trail to the left loops through the forest and reaches the east side of the Beaumont Campground in about 10 minutes. Follow the more interesting trail to the right that leads through the forest directly to the west side of the campground, where there are outhouses. Walk down past the picnic tables (Photo, above) to the narrow isthmus formed by twin idyllic shell beaches, and onto the isthmus for a view of Bedwell Harbour. A trail continues from the east side of the campground (right side looking from the water). It parallels the shoreline and offers benches with scenic vistas, terminating at pit toilets, campsites #1 and #2, and a staircase to the beach (**T1**). Return the same way. At a trail junction just before the campground, you can take the right fork to use the loop trail through the forest, and bypass the campground if you wish.

CANAL ROAD TRAILHEAD T3
After crossing the bridge from North Pender Island, make a left and proceed about 2.5 km to the park entrance road. Watch for a sign on the right warning of a road intersecting from the right, then look for the gravel entrance road which is marked by a large Parks Canada sign. Proceed up the 200 metre-long hill to a parking area that also has bike racks (No bikes are allowed on trails). *Upon leaving, watch carefully for Canal Road cross traffic that is very difficult to see coming from your left.*

Note that two trails lead from the parking area. The William Walker Trail (**86**) leads from the southeast (left), and the Mt. Norman trail (**85**) from the south (right).

85 CANAL ROAD TO MT. NORMAN SUMMIT
This interesting trail to the summit of Mt. Norman is my pick for the best hiking trail on the Pender Islands. **Map 7**.

Rating: 10. Difficulty: Strenuous. **Surface:** Begins on pleasant unpaved skid road then climbs and becomes a narrow dirt trail with roots and rocks. Wooden boardwalk at summit has several steps and no railings.
Walking time/distance each way: About 30-45 minutes, 1.6 km.
Elevation Gain: About 185 metres.

The Hike
The trail proceeds to the south on a level road through a Red-alder wetland area that can be swampy during rainy periods. The trail is level for the first 5 minutes at which time a public outhouse is visible on the left. By 10 minutes into the hike the degree of grade increases substantially as the trail turns southwest and then west. The trail levels off, then climbs again. About 15-20 minutes into the hike the old skid road narrows into a trail, which becomes rockier. The trail is very scenic as it meanders through the second growth forest dominated by Western red cedar, with Saturna Island becoming visible through the trees. A short (3 metre) semi-technical section (steep with tree roots to use as stairs) is encountered, which should be easy for experienced hikers, though difficult for some others. About 20-30 minutes into the hike the trail becomes steep again. Look back for spectacular views on clear days to the north to Mayne Island, Vancouver and surrounding Coast Mountains, and east to Mt. Baker and the Cascade Range in Washington. (Photo, right). Along the way, listen for grouse and Banded Wood Pigeons. See the *Birdwatching Guide* in Chapter 17. The trail levels off again, but the steepest section of the trail follows, which  should take 5 to 10 minutes to conquer. It levels off on a ridge, then rises one final time to the summit. The wide trail in front of you to the northwest descends to the Ainslie Point Road trailhead (**T2**). The wooden boardwalk to the left leads southwest to the spectacular viewpoint. A description of the Mt. Norman vista is found after the section on Hike **82**.

Options From the Mount Norman Summit

1. Descend the same way to trailhead **T3**. Here you can extend your walk along the William Walker Trail (**86**).

2. Continue down the trail to the west side of Mt. Norman toward the Ainslie Point Road trailhead (**T2**/See hike **83**). After the very steep dirt road levels out near the bottom, you will reach a junction with the trailhead for Beaumont Marine Park, to the left. To the right is the steep descent to **T2**. See **Map 6**. From there you can walk down Ainslie Point Road to the left to Fawn Creek Park (**78**) and access to the water at the Pender Canal. Or, walk to the right until just before the bridge, where Bridge Trail begins on the left (**77**), leading to a canal viewpoint. About 200 metres past the bridge is a dirt road labeled *Mortimer Spit* (**79**) on the left. A pit toilet is available for public use a short distance down the access road on the left. See the *Coastal Access* section, above, for a description of Mortimer Spit, a beautiful and popular place to picnic or take a dip in the cold water. To walk back to **T3** from here is about 2.5 km along Canal Road, which creates an approximate 5.5 km loop.

3. Descend via hike **83** to Trailhead **T2** (described above), but take the trail to Beaumont Marine Park near the bottom (See Hike **84**).

86 WILLIAM WALKER TRAIL
*The trail begins at the Canal Road Mt. Norman trailhead (**T3**), and crosses beautiful forest in the initial GINPR segment, then zigzags through a managed forest (i.e. logging). A circuit incorporating two beach accesses (**80-81**) is possible.*

Rating: 4. **Difficulty:** Moderate to strenuous due to length. Surface: Dirt trail, steep in places, logging roads, some confusing portions, option of rocky beach walk at the end. **Walking time/distance each way:** About 1 hour/1.5 km
Map 7 (west end); **Map 7A** (east end). Both maps are replicated in this chapter.

The Hike
The trail winds its way for 20-30 minutes through the forest, and is steep at times, running parallel to, but about 250 metres away from Canal Road. The first 700 metres or so is within the GINPR and is beautiful and worthwhile. A highlight is an Osprey nest. Once you leave the National Park boundary, however, you are in a logging zone, which can be quite unpleasant, as the trail follows logging roads in places. At the end of the trail, directly across Canal Road is a trail to the Walker Road ocean access (**81**). A sandstone rock beach is reached in about 5 minutes. At lower tides you can walk for about 1 km along the beach to the left (west) to the Canal Road ocean access (**80**). Watch for a steep staircase leading up from the beach and the back of a park sign to signal the appropriate access point. After returning to Canal Road, turn right and walk about 500 metres to the access road to the Mt. Norman trailhead (**T3**) on the left, and another 300 metres up the access road to your car. If you parked at the Ainslie Point trailhead (**T2**), walk an additional 3 km along the road, or up and over Mt. Norman.

Spalding Valley and Boundary Pass Road

The Spalding Valley is a wide agricultural valley at the foot of Spalding Hill along Spalding Road. A scenic vista is available from Spalding Road at the head of the valley, looking east toward Mt. Baker. Boundary Pass Road accesses mostly private property along the north shore of the island, with the exception of two ocean access points (**87, 88, Map 7B**). Hiking opportunities include the flat, peaceful Enchanted Forest (**91**) and the steep Castle Road vista hike up Spalding Hill (**89**). Lilias Spalding Heritage Park (**90**) is a place to reflect on Pender Island history and perhaps bring a picnic (**Map 8**).

Trailhead Reference Point *Intersection of Canal Road, Spalding Road and Boundary Pass Drive* (**Map 7B**). After crossing the bridge onto South Pender Island, turn left to continue on Canal Road and follow it until it ends in about 5 km. Spalding Road is to the right and Boundary Pass Road is to the left.

Washrooms Outhouse at Lilias Spalding Historical Park. Poets Cove Resort has facilities for its customers, as well as the only nearby provisions.

Ocean Accesses

87 ANCIA ROAD/CONNERY CRESCENT

✿From the reference point, head east down Boundary Pass Drive. In about 500 metres is an intersection with Connery Crescent. Turn left. The beach access is around the first bend and is signed Ancia Road. Park on the flat area beside the road just before the sign. Ancia Road is unpaved, flat, and has a gradual grade. A 5-minute walk leads to a nice viewpoint. Fifty-five steps (slippery when wet) descend to a beautiful rocky beach. The bay is rimmed with cliffs and views are to the north to Saturna Island and southeast across Boundary Pass toward mountainous Orcas Island (U.S.). The open

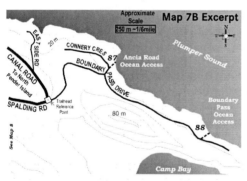

nature of this shoreline makes for good storm watching (from the cliff above the beach). Beach exploring is best at lower tides. **Map 7B** (Replicated, left).

88 BOUNDARY PASS

✿From the reference point, proceed east on Boundary Pass Drive. Continue for about 600 metres (do not turn on Connery Crescent). The access is across from Property #9930. Parking here is limited. A 5-minute trail leads between two homes to a bench and a shoreline that offers a similar view as Access **87**, to Saturna Island and even Mt. Baker on occasion. This spot also has tide pools and a small interesting rocky islet offshore, accessible at low tide. **Map 7B**.

Hiking Trails and Parks

89 CASTLE ROAD TRAIL UP SPALDING HILL
A steep trail, slippery in spots, past interesting rock formations to a spectacular 169-metre viewpoint at Castle Rock.

Rating: 7. **Difficulty:** Moderate to strenuous (due to trail conditions).
Surface: Dirt trail, steep and slippery in places on descent. **Elevation gain:** About 90 m.
Walking time/distance each way: About 20-30 minutes, 1.2 km. **Map 8**

Access
From the reference point, head west on Spalding Road, and then make the first right on Castle Road. Just after the first bend of the road to the left, look for the signed trailhead on the right. Note that Pender Parks advises to park along the shoulder of Spalding Road and walk back up to the trailhead.

The Hike Up Spalding Hill
The trail begins with a series of wooden walks and constructed steps, then meanders in switchbacks through a Douglas fir forest up a steep hill, past some interesting glacially-sculpted conglomerate and sandstone outcroppings, then emerges on a bluff. It continues to the right of a large arbutus tree, down into a ravine, then levels off for a stretch through the forest. It curves around a conglomerate outcropping, then emerges onto another open bluff with a vista to the south. The final ascent is steep and slippery as it climbs through an open grassland with plenty of invasive Scotch broom. Watch for a Bald Eagle that likes to perch in the tallest snag on your right. Atop the conglomerate bluff marked by sev-

eral stately Douglas firs, a trail cuts sharply to the left (south) toward the viewpoint at Castle Rock, which is marked by a bench facing southwest. Watch the turkey vultures soaring above and below you, and possibly Bald Eagles as well. The view encompasses the Spalding agricultural valley below, and the hills of the Greenburn Lake area of the National Park beyond. In the distance (Photo, above) are Orcas and other San Juan Islands. On a clear day the Cascade Range forms the backdrop with Mt. Baker appearing prominently to the east (left), and the Olympic Mountains to the southeast (right). Sidney and Vancouver Island are to the south (far right). Return down the trail the same way, using extra caution not to slip on the pinecones, roots or slippery rocks.

90 LILIAS SPALDING HERITAGE PARK
This 4-hectare homesite has been developed into a historic park.

Access: From the reference point at Canal Road and Spalding Road, head west on Spalding Road, then continue past Castle Road for another 700 metres or so. Look to the right for a two-space parking area off of Spalding Road, just before Spalding makes a sharp turn to the left. Walk up the hill along the paved road to the park. **Map 8**.

The Park contains the homesite of Lilias Mackay and Arthur Spalding, who married in 1889. Lilias Spalding lived in the house, raising four children, until 1938, six years after the death of her husband. Their house was razed in the mid-1950's. Currently, the park consists of the remains of a farm building and an orchard, which is beginning to come back to life after much pruning by volunteers. Also returning are some of the native plantings including rose bushes. An outhouse and picnic tables were installed in 2005. Future plans include a compost installation, a tool shed, and wheelchair access.

91 ENCHANTED FOREST
An easy stroll through a dark forest and marsh area ending at a grotto with a small seasonal waterfall.

Rating: 6. Difficulty: Easy. Surface: Mostly wide, dirt, level trails. Some areas can be muddy. Walking time: About 30-45 minutes to tour the park. **Map 8.**
Access: From the reference point, head west on Spalding Road and follow the road as it curves to the left and to the right. After you round that bend to the right, most of the land to the right is a public park until the road curves again to the left. The obvious signed trailhead is about halfway down this dark stretch of roadway on the right. Park on the grass shoulder, or lock your bike in the rack, as bikes are not allowed on trails.

The Hike: This 3 hectare (7.4 acre) park managed by Pender Parks protects a wet woodland area. A conservation covenant held by the Islands Trust Fund restricts the removal of plant life from the park and requires approval of the Trust Fund Board prior to any development or construction being undertaken. A sign near the trailhead explains that the main trail comes to a junction, where going to the right will lead to a marsh view and going to the left will lead to a seasonal waterfall. Because of the small size of the park, both trails are worthwhile. If time is a factor, choose the left option. Quality interpretive signs along the trail describe the flora of the valley, which is a second growth forest and wetland. The peaceful trail (except for occasional traffic noise since the trail parallels the road) meanders through a beautiful forest, with numerous small wooden boardwalks that cross most of the marshy areas (a short skip over a wet area may be required). Be careful of exposed roots and rocks along the way. Eventually the trail daylights back at Spalding Road to circumvent private property, then continues on the other side of that property's access road. The trail ends at a bench that overlooks a pretty grotto, with the ocean visible through the forest about 200 metres away. Across from the bench is a waterfall, which is typically a trickle, but flows with greater magnitude after a heavy rain, as this stream drains the Spalding Valley area. Return the same way. At the junction of the original trail, you have the option to proceed to the *Marsh View* segment.

Poets Cove Resort to Gowlland Point

Poets Cove Resort is the gateway to the southern end of South Pender Island, a peaceful and beautiful area with a good swimming opportunity at the resort's pool (fee), great beachcombing from several ocean access points, easy strolls in the striking Gowlland Point area, and hiking around the newly acquired Greenburn Lake area of Gulf Islands National Park Reserve. **Maps 8, 9.**

Trailhead Reference Point
Entrance to Poets Cove Resort. From the bridge, turn left and continue down Canal Road until it ends in about 5 km. Make a right on Spalding Road, which twists and turns and ends at the entrance to Poets Cove Resort in about 3 km. The road straight ahead/left is Gowlland Point Road. This intersection is the reference point. **Map 8.**

Washrooms and Facilities
The nearest outhouses to this area are at Lilias Spalding Heritage Park, Mortimer Spit and along the Mt. Norman trails. Poets Cove Resort marina has the only facilities in this sector, with washrooms for its customers and pay showers.

Ocean Accesses and Swimming

92 POETS COVE MARINA AND SWIMMING POOL
✪ The new pool and spa is open to the public for a fee of $5 per adult (free to resort and marina guests). Next to the pool is Moorings Market with a deli and ice cream stand, and an activity centre with various rentals and tours available. The pool tends to be crowded with resort guests. A second adults-only pool is for resort guests. The resort has a marina-side promenade complete with waterfall, a shell beach, and a high-end restaurant and separate lounge. See the *Boating Guide - Marinas*, the *Accommodations Guide* and the *Dining Guide* for further information. **Map 8.**

93 BIDGOOD ROAD
Continue on Gowlland Point Road around a sharp curve to the right past the fire hall. In about 500 metres from the reference point is a concrete barrier on the right that guards a curve. The signed access trail begins behind the barrier. Park on the shoulder past the barrier. The trail has some steps constructed, but it is very steep and precarious in nature. At the bottom is a bench, and a rope handrail is provided to make your way along the rocks to the rocky cove. The view is to the south to the entrance to Bedwell Harbour, across to the Trincomali area of North Pender Island. Also visible is Stuart Island (U.S.) to the southeast, and Sidney Island beyond. The return to the road takes about 10 minutes. **Map 8.**

94 CRADDOCK ROAD/TILLEY POINT
✪ Continue on Gowlland Point Road from the reference point for about 2 km. Look for a *right T* intersection sign, and slow down, since Craddock Road appears suddenly on the right around a bend. The beach access is at the end of Craddock Road in about 500 metres. A well-constructed set of stairs leads to a pebble beach, with a view out to

a small rocky islet, behind which is Boundary Pass and Stuart Island (U.S.). Cliffs rim the shoreline. This is the closest public beach access to Tilley Caves dive spot. **Map 9.**

95 HIGGS ROAD

☼ Continue on Gowlland Point Road from the Poets Cove reference point for about 2.6 km to Higgs Road, and turn right. The ocean access is at the end of the road.

Interesting conglomerate formations jut out into the sea, making for a great perch to observe the marine life. You can also watch shipping traffic passing by in Boundary Pass. Views are to the east to Brooks Point, the southeast across Haro Strait to Orcas and San Juan Islands (U.S.), and to the south to Stuart Island (U.S.). At lower tides you can walk to the left along pebbly crescent beaches to Brooks Point Reserve in about 10 minutes. Note that the legality of accessing this beach walk from Higgs Road is being worked out at time of writing. **Map 9.**

96 GOWLLAND POINT ROAD VIEWPOINT AND ACCESS

☼ Gowlland Point Road ends in about 3.2 km from the reference point, at the Gowlland Point ocean access to Canned Cod Bay. Ample parking is available here, and a flat easy stroll leads to a view deck with a spectacular view out to the east to the Washington Cascades and Mt Baker. Blunden Islet is the small island off the tip of South Pender Island to the northeast, part of GINPR.

MOUNT BAKER
Visible from the east side of North and South Pender Islands on clear days, this heavily glaciated 3,285-metre (10,778-foot) tall mountain in the Washington Cascades is a stratovolcano that could sizzle back to life at any time. The latest activity occurred in the 1970's. The city of Bellingham lies at the shore of Puget Sound about 50 km (30 miles) due west of the volcano.

A large beach is available for exploring below the view deck. You can walk all the way to a CRD-owned parcel (see **98**), which occupies Gowlland Point (with the navigational aid on it). Watch for harbour seals and river otters playing in the water close in, as well as the occasional Dall's porpoise, resembling a mini-Orca further out. Orcas may also pass by in summer. **Map 9.**

97 BROOKS POINT RESERVE

✿✿ To access this beautiful CRD Regional Park nature reserve, you can park at the Gowlland Point parking area and walk back up Gowlland Point Road past Kloshe Road to the trailhead on the left. Parking is also available along the shoulder near the trailhead. This 3.9 ha (9.6 acre) park was acquired by the CRD in 2000 as the result of fund raisers, donations and the efforts of seven groups who worked with the owner, Alan Brooks, to preserve the property. The CRD owns and manages the property as a Regional Park Reserve and the Islands Trust Fund and Nature Conservancy of Canada jointly hold a conservation covenant to ensure the long-term protection of its ecosystem. It has become one of the jewels of the Penders, a great place for a picnic or to watch a winter sunset (the sun sets around the point to the west in summer). The park conserves undeveloped coastal bluff shoreline, Douglas fir forest and grassland. A 10-minute trail leads through the forest, partially along a boardwalk, past blackberry bushes (berries ripen in late summer; forage but watch for wasp nests), to a grassy field with abundant spring wildflowers, and a rocky headland and intertidal area. On clear days, catch spectacular views to the east to the Washington Cascades and Mount Baker, as well as across Boundary Pass to the U.S. San Juan Islands. To the southeast are Orcas Island (with the two *humps*) and private Waldron Island in front of

it. To the south is Stuart Island with San Juan Island beyond. Harbour seals and river otters are commonly seen frolicking in the surrounding waters. Also seen are orcas (mostly during the summer) and Dall's porpoise. On shore you may see a mink or river otter darting amongst the rocky shoreline, or a Bald Eagle perched in a tree. This transitional ecosystem is occasionally a good birding spot, as over 100 bird species have been observed here, including some rare and endangered species. The ocean current off this point can be exceptionally turbulent, and sometimes it sounds like a rushing river. Watch how various smaller boats handle the challenge. At slack tide it is a marvelous place to explore by kayak. At lower tides you can walk to the west (right facing the ocean) to the Higgs Road ocean access (**95**). See **102** in the *Hikes* section for a suggestion of how to extend your walk. **Map 9.**

98 GOWLLAND POINT CRD RESERVE

The CRD acquired the parcel containing Gowlland Point in 2000 with the intention of making it a regional park, a process that is pending at time of writing. Access is allowed, but is discouraged due to sensitive flora, including abundant Chocolate lilies that bloom here in April (Photo, right) as well as Death camus and others. Some refer to this point of land as *Chocolate Lilly Point.* Another highlight is a stately Douglas fir designated as a wildlife tree. A navigational aid marks the tip of the property at the rocky shoreline. The parcel is located at the end of Kloshe Road on the left. Park at the trailheads of **96** or **97** and walk down Kloshe Road. An obvious trail leads from the end of Kloshe Road, to the left of a gate that serves the property to the right. The trail veers to the left. Stay on the trail to avoid damaging the wildflowers. Views are similar as from the Gowlland Point viewpoint (to your left facing the ocean), and at lower

tides you can walk there along the beach in a few minutes. Look for a slippery, precarious trail carved into the bluff to the left of the navigational aid. Do not disturb rare plants growing in the rock faces. Note that private property separates each of the three parks in the Gowlland Point area. See Hike **102** for a suggested area stroll that incorporates this park. **Map 9**.

Hiking Trails

99 GREENBURN LAKE/GULF ISLANDS NATIONAL PARK RESERVE

A walk through the forest up a gravel road to a beautiful lily-filled lake. Trailhead is less than 500 metres from Poets Cove Resort's entrance.

Rating: 8. Difficulty: Moderate due to hill climb. **Surface:** Rutted gravel road and grass paths. **Time/distance each way:** About 15 minutes/800 metres to Greenburn Lake. **Map 8. Elevation gain:** About 60 metres.

Access

From the reference point at Poets Cove Resort continue to the east/straight on Gowlland Point Road. Note the wide shoulder on the right in front of the Church of the Good Shepherd, because you may have to come back and park here. Straight ahead is the South Pender Fire Hall, as Gowlland Point Road curves abruptly to the right. Just before you reach the fire hall, a dirt road rises sharply on your left, marked by a Parks Canada sign. This is the entrance to the park. At time of writing room is available for about two cars to park safely on your left as you face the fire hall, between the fire hall and the Greenburn Lake access road. Make sure to stay off the road, out of the way of the fire hall driveway, and out of the ditch. Otherwise, look for other more appropriate parking places such as back near the church.

The Hike

This new addition to the Pender Islands' public parkland bounty was acquired in 2004 by Parks Canada. A 69-hectare (170.5-acre) property was acquired in April, and includes a depression occupied by Greenburn Lake and its ecologically important wetlands, and hills rising to the north and south. An additional 49.4-hectare (122-acre) parcel (the Reider property) adjacent to the south of the original parcel, containing mostly steep forested hillsides north of Gowlland Point Road, was added later in the year. Hiking opportunities are limited at time of writing, as trails around the lake are either overgrown or non-existent. However, the walk up the road through the forest and the experience of sitting next to this peaceful lake to enjoy the flora and fauna is well worth it. This is one of the jewels of the Pender Islands, and if Parks Canada constructs a trail around the lake it will be a top notch hike. One passable trail already exists that leads to a vista point.

From the gate, walk up the gravel road which rises steeply for the first 5 minutes. The remainder of the road ascends more gently. Along the way some of the trees to watch for are Douglas fir, grand fir, western red cedar, and Garry oak. The understory contains a mixture of salal and various ferns. At the 10- minute mark, an overgrown dirt road intersects on your right. This road currently dead-ends at a small landfill in about 200 metres, but you may want to walk down 10 metres or so to observe a great comparison between a grand fir and Douglas fir, about the same age, on opposite sides of the road. Back on the main road, a large meadow with wetlands is on your right. Watch for Nootka and woodland rose, horsetail, and seasonal wildflowers such as foxglove along the trail here. At 15 minutes Greenburn Lake become visible. If you walk down to the right, you can view the entire lake. Otherwise, continue along the road, which turns into grass past a former homesite. It quickly takes you to a nice clearing with views across the lake. Trails beyond this point are overgrown. You may see Bald Eagles, waterfowl, and songbirds such as Tri-coloured Blackbirds, Song Sparrows, and Evening Grosbeak. Water lilies float peacefully in the lake, while the perimeter is lined with yellow flag (wild iris), cattail, and wild grasses. Parks Canada has not studied the lake's water quality at time of writing, so swim at your own risk.

An unofficial existing trail leads gradually to a vista point (approximately 130 metres elevation) in about ten minutes from the west side fo the lake. Note that Parks Canada has not designated any official trails in this portion of the park at time of writing, and have not checked the trails for safe passage, so proceed at your own risk. It is not as spectacular as the other Pender vista hikes, but worthwhile just the same. Start from the former house site, walk down to the right of the lake and cross over the spillway, and then follow the trail along the earthen dam. The trail curves to the left and follows an overgrown road. In a couple of minutes, look for a prominent trail that cuts sharply back to the right. Follow it until you reach an obvious vista point at a conglomerate outcropping and a stately Garry oak tree. Be careful around the steep cliffs. Please note that the moss on the rocks is sensitive to damage, especially in the dry summer, so please keep off. The vista is to the south to Stuart Island (U.S.) and the Olympic Mountains beyond. When you return to the overgrown road, make a left to return to the main trail. If you go right instead, it follows the overgrown road and leads to the east side of the lake and a sensitive wetland. So, for now, return the same way.

100, 101 CRADDOCK ROAD AREA WALKS
Tilley Road Viewpoint and Craddock-Gowlland Loop.

Rating: 4. **Difficulty:** Easy+. **Surface:** Dirt trails are rough with rocks, roots and over-grown vegetation; roads have sporadic traffic. **Time:** 10 to 30 minutes. **Map 9**.

Access
100: Tilley Road Viewpoint: From the reference point at Poets Cove Resort, continue east/straight on Gowlland Point Road, around a sharp bend to the right. Craddock Road appears suddenly after a short hill and a curve to the right. Make a right, then the first right on Southlands Drive. Go straight into a grassy parking area just after the junction with Tilley Point Road.

101: Craddock-Gowlland Loop: Follow the same instructions as above, but after turning right on Craddock Road and rounding the first bend, look for the first gravel road and trail sign on the left. Park on a shoulder along Craddock Road. The other trail-head is along Gowlland Point Road next to house #9978.

The Hike
The Tilley Road viewpoint is a short (5 minutes) trail that leads through the forest to a mediocre viewpoint of the entrance to Bedwell Harbour, with no water access. The Craddock-Gowlland Loop is a rough trail (10 minutes) through gorse and salal (recently maintained at time of writing) adjacent to private homes that creates a shortcut between Craddock Road and Gowlland Point Road, and avoiding somewhat of a hill. From Craddock Road, walk along the gravel road until it veers off to the left to a pri-vate residence. The trail continues straight ahead. The view over the dry vegetation and the sea beyond is in some ways reminiscent of a Northern California landscape. Actually, it is more enjoyable to walk along Craddock and Gowlland Point Roads than to take this trail. Combine either or both of these trails with a neighbourhood stroll and a visit to a nice beach access at the end of Craddock Road. The annual Art Off the Fence art show is held at Whalepoint Studio at the east end of Southlands Drive (July 22-23, 2006). This is perhaps the most popular art show, due to the oceanfront setting, variety of art, and entertainment. Otherwise, the gallery is open by appointment only.

102 BROOKS POINT RESERVE AND GOWLLAND POINT
An easy stroll through forest to a spectacular coastal stretch and viewpoint, with options to extend your stroll along the beach.

Rating: 9 **Difficulty:** Easy. **Surface:** Level dirt paths with some exposed roots, wooden boardwalk, and rocky shoreline. **Walking time:** 20 - 60 minutes. **Map 9**.

Access
From the reference point at Poets Cove Resort continue east/straight down Gowlland Point Road almost to the end of the road (prior to the Gowlland Point Viewpoint). The trailhead for the park is located on the right, just before the intersection with Jennens Road (left) and Kloshe Road (right). Parking is along the Gowlland Point Road shoulder or at the viewpoint. Respect the private property that surrounds the park.

The Hike
Walk through and between ocean accesses **96** (Gowlland Point) and **97** (Brooks Point) possibly adding **98** (CRD Reserve) and **95** (Higgs Road) as well. Note that private properties separate all of the ocean accesses, so where a low-tide beach walk is not available to connect them, you must return to the public road.

PART I. BROOKS POINT CRD RESERVE (See **97** for details on Brooks Point)
A 10-minute trail leads through the forest, partially along a boardwalk, past blackberry bushes to a grassy field with abundant spring wildflowers, and a rocky headland and wonderful intertidal area (Photo, below). At lower tides, you can walk along a pair of two crescent pebbly beaches to the west (right facing the ocean) to the Higgs Road ocean access in about ten minutes. Either return the same way (recommended) or do a loop back to the Brooks Point trailhead along Higgs and Gowlland Point Roads.

PART II. GOWLLAND POINT ROAD OCEAN ACCESS (See **96**)
From the Brooks Point trailhead, you can continue walking to the end of Gowlland Point Road. Along the way, there are two galleries to the left up Jennens Road that may be open. The rocky beach at Gowlland Point is worth exploring, and at low tides you can hike to the south along the beach up toward the navigation aid on the ecologically sensitive CRD property (See **98**). *Caution: The trail up the bluff is narrow and slippery.*

PART III. GOWLLAND POINT CRD RESERVE (See **98**)
From either the Brooks Point Trailhead or the Gowlland Point Road Ocean Access parking lot, you can walk to the end of Kloshe Road and access the CRD reserve. The unmarked, unofficial trailhead is next to a private property gate, and the trail veers off to the left. Make sure to stay on the trail on this ecologically sensitive property. A slippery trail carved into the bluff at the ocean side of this property allows a low-tide beach walk to the left, back to **96**.

View of Mount Baker from Spalding Road.

Looking out at Bedwell Harbour from
Beaumont Marine Park/GINPR; Trail 82.

Canned Cod Bay at Gowlland
Point (96).

14   BICYCLING GUIDE

CYCLING THE BYWAYS OF PENDER AND BEYOND

Bicycling along the bucolic byways of the Pender Islands can be a challenging but exhilarating experience. Lush interior forests and farmland, ocean vistas and quaint heritage homes await the cyclist along the way. Though the Pender Islands are hilly, there are not as many killer hills as on some of the other Gulf Islands, and most fit cyclists should be able to tackle them. This Guide presents options for several levels of fitness for riding on the Penders, as well as options for some noteworthy cycling nearby off-island.

[handwritten: Otter Bay: bikes $9/hr 60 per day 200 + tax = 5 days   scooters- as listed]

Pender Particulars

RENTALS If you have arrived on foot and wish to rent a bicycle, try **Otter Bay Marina** for bike rentals, 629.3579. Walk up the hill past the ferry ticket kiosk, go to the right on MacKinnon Road, and then walk down the steep hill to the **Otter Bay Marina** on the right. Rates are $12/hour, discounted for extended periods. They also rent scooters for $25/hour or $85/4 hours. Another option is **Poets Cove Resort** on South Pender Island, 629.2100. Rates range from $10/hour to $40/8 hours.

AIR FOR TIRES   Driftwood Auto Centre

REPAIRS   None are known at time of writing, so bring your own repair equipment.

ALSO BRING
* *Plenty of water:* Potable sources are limited along most routes;
* *Plenty of nourishment:* Don't count on any restaurant or stores being open unless you have called in advance to make sure. **Tru Value Foods** at Driftwood Centre is likely to be open, and establishments are open most frequently in the summer; and
* *All safety equipment* that you would use elsewhere.

AND REMEMBER TO Wear your helmet. The local RCMP may ticket you or impound your bicycle if you do not. Use appropriate reflectors and lights if riding at night. Watch for potholes in the road and deer darting out in front of you. The RCMP stresses that all the same rules of the road that apply on the mainland apply on the island, and that you should lock your bicycle when leaving it unattended. The Penders have no bike lanes or shoulders to ride on, so ride defensively. Be careful of golf balls being driven at the golf course.

GUIDES IN THIS BOOK THAT RELATE TO A CYCLING TRIP
Accommodations, Dining, Coastal Access and Hiking.

OFF ROAD RIDING is not permitted on any Pender Island public trail due to the sensitive ecosystems. The nearest public mountain bike trails to Pender Island are on the Saanich Peninsula near Victoria. See the *Off-Island Bicycling Highlights* section.

Road Descriptions

Pavement conditions range from newly-paved, smooth roadways, to pothole-riddled stretches that have not been paved in many years. No bike trails or shoulder bike lanes exist on the Pender Islands, so bicycling involves commingling with automobile traffic. Although most motorists are courteous to bicyclists and the island speed limit is only 50 km/hour (30 mph), there tends to be a lot of 'island style' drivers who weave out of their lanes. So, always ride defensively, ride single file so you do not create a traffic hazard, and wear a helmet. If you are coming from a metropolitan area, or even Salt Spring Island, the roads on the Pender Islands will seem pleasantly uncrowded. However, a few roads can have steady traffic, especially around the time of ferry arrivals and departures.

THE PENDERS' MOST HEAVILY TRAVELED ROADS
The worst road for cycling is *Bedwell Harbour Road/Canal Road/Aldridge Road* between Driftwood Centre and Magic Lake Estates, where most Penderites live. Fairly steady traffic (for the Pender Islands) and about 2 km of steep hills and blind curves to the south of Driftwood Centre create a challenge to many cyclists. Einers Hill, which is the short hill with a hairpin turn along Bedwell Harbour Road just north of Driftwood Centre, is also a potential hazard for cyclists.
Other roads to use extra caution include:
Otter Bay Road and Bedwell Harbour Road from the ferry all the way to Driftwood Centre. You will encounter occasional steady traffic, a few hills and blind curves. However, there are also some nice long, flat stretches past bucolic farmland along Bedwell Harbour Road south of Otter Bay Road.
Canal Road from the South Pender turnoff past the school to the bridge also has fairly consistent traffic and some curves. Use extra caution on the bridge.
In Magic Lake Estates the busiest roads are:
Schooner Way to Pirates Road, and *Privateers Road.* To a lesser extent, *Pirates Road* to the tip of the island at the Trincomali subdivision can have an occasional spurt of fast-moving vehicles.
On the north side of North Pender Island:
Traffic tends to be less, but use extra caution on the main thoroughfares of *Otter Bay Road, Port Washington Road, Corbett Road* and *Bedwell Harbour Road.*
On South Pender Island:
Watch for vehicles rushing to and from Poets Cove Resort along *Canal Road* and *Spalding Road.* Traffic thins out along *Gowlland Point Road.*

Amies Road is one of the least traveled byways, but be careful of potholes and occasional cars due to curves and poor visibility.

PENDER BICYCLE RIDE DESCRIPTIONS

This section describes specific bike rides and routes on the Pender Islands, as follows:

TOUR DE PENDER Explore the entirety of the islands from the ferry terminal with several options to shorten or lengthen the ride.
BEST BICYCLING ROUTES The Three Best and Easiest Bike Rides around the Pender Islands *for the rest of us* are described.

Use the *Pender Islands Map Atlas* in conjunction with this section. Use the *Index Maps* to get a general description of the routes, then refer to the detail maps for topography and features. The *Best Bicycling Routes* are cross-referenced between the maps and the text. See the *Coastal Access and Hiking Guide* for information on numbered features such as hikes and ocean accesses.

TOUR DE PENDER

If you are in great shape and want to see all of the Pender Islands by bike, then this 43 km (26 mile) ride is for you. Or, you can shorten the ride with several options presented. The ride begins at the ferry terminal. Descriptions include points of interest, places to eat, restrooms, and options for various routes. Expect plenty of hills, but nothing too daunting for fit cyclists. Distances are in km. 1 km ~ 0.6 miles. The distance points at which the options are offered are highlighted as in the following example: 3.7

km
0.0   **Maps 1, 1A.** From the ferry kiosk, bear to the right on MacKinnon Rd.
0.7   Left on Otter Bay Road. Follow Otter Bay Road down the hill past the golf course (watch for golfers teeing off from hole numbers 1 and 6!).
1.0   **Chippers Café** at the golf course is frequently open for lunch, and serves beer, wine, and cocktails.
2.0   **Map 1B.** Otter Bay Road skirts a scenic shoreline with a lovely beach access available (Grimmer Bay, **2**).
2.4   Otter Bay Road ends at Port Washington Road. Turn left. Historic Old Orchard Farm is on the right, which may have fruit for sale.
2.7   Follow Port Washington Road to the end. Make a left down the short steep hill to visit the government wharf/seaplane dock (**3**). The small historic store is vacant at time of writing and may reopen in the future as part of a historic trust. Return to Port Washington Road.
3.0   Turn right. Follow Port Washington Road past bucolic farmland to the **Pender Island Home Building Centre** store. **Map 1C.**
4.7   The Home Building Centre store has a cold drink vending machine and sells some snacks. The **Southridge Farms Country Store** across the street features fresh produce, health foods, snacks, cold drinks and a coffee bar.
6.3   After a pleasant, steady descent past farm land the road ends at Bedwell Harbour Road at Hope Bay. Turn left.

6.5   The historic Hope Bay Store at the Government dock (**7**) burned down in 1998, and the new incarnation that opened in July 2005 contains a gallery, shops, and **Hope Bay Café**, a very pleasant place for a biker's meal. Return the way you came, but rather than turning right on Port Washington Road, head south (straight) down Bedwell Harbour Road.

6.9   Bear right at the intersection with Hooson Road.

7.2   **Map 1**. At the next intersection, Bedwell Harbour Road curves sharply upward and back to the left; while Corbett Road is straight ahead.

Shorten your trip: If time or fatigue is a factor, continue straight ahead on Corbett Road. At the next junction (at 7.5 km), Corbett Road turns to the right, but continue straight ahead onto Amies Road. This uncrowded narrow byway ascends a fairly long grade, then leads through a dark forest on a paved but pitted road to Otter Bay Road (at 8.6 km). Ride defensively on this lightly traveled, but dark and narrow road. Make a right onto Otter Bay Road, then follow the signs to the ferry terminal, down MacKinnon Road, to the left (total ride 9.1 km). If you have time left, continue up McKinnon Road where there is a nice beach access (**23**) near the end of the road in 1 km. Or, you can always return to **Chippers** for some refreshment.

7.2   (Continued) Carefully curve around to the left and follow Bedwell Harbour Road up the hill past the library, and in 500 m reach the Community Hall, site of the summer Saturday farmers' markets and a hub of Pender's community activities. Public restrooms are available in the hall when it is open. If you arrive before the market closes (around 1 pm) you may be able to buy various food and drink goodies from the vendors outside, or from inside of the hall.

7.7   Otter Bay Road enters from the right at the Community Hall site.
Note: For another optional route back to the ferry in about 2.5 km, and total ride of about 10.2 km, turn right here.
Map 3. As you continue on Bedwell Harbour Road, note that this is the only route south to the remainder of the Pender Islands. The road is mostly level as it passes bucolic farmland, with a few curves, but then takes a short, steep curvy drop (Einers Hill) as you near Driftwood Centre. Use extreme caution on this road keeping far to the right, as it is at times heavily traveled. You may want to pull over if a line of ferry traffic is passing.

9.8   **Map 5B**. Driftwood Centre is the commercial centre of the island, with the **Tru Value Foods** full service grocery and deli counter, **Pistou Grill** that is frequently open for lunch (with al fresco patio), **Pender Island Bakery**/deli with great lunch items (and outdoor picnic tables), a liquor store, pharmacy, and auto centre with pay showers. The public restroom is in the breezeway in front of the liquor store, past the Bakery. See the *Shopping Guide* and *Dining Guide* for further information on Driftwood Centre.

Optional Sidetrip: If Driftwood Centre is your final destination, you may want to cycle down pleasant Razor Point Road. The first 1.5 km is the most scenic. Port Browning government dock is on the right. The road eventually ends on private property with no beach access, although **Morning Bay Vineyard** is located at the top of Harbour Hill Road, which may be worth the extra effort (**Map 5**).

9.8   (Continued) To continue further, you must traverse the most unpleasant stretch of cycling on the Pender Islands. This is all relative, however; it may seem benign compared to where you are coming from. From Driftwood Centre, turn right on Bedwell Harbour Road. The road curves as it ascends a hill, this is the most heavily traveled stretch of road on the Pender Islands, connecting the main population centres with both the Driftwood Centre and the ferries. Cyclists should stay to the right and ride single file along this stretch, as the curves are blind, and motorists may be approaching from both directions and may also become distracted by deer darting out from the brush.

10.0   The first intersection on the left is Hamilton Road.

Optional Sidetrip: Port Browning Pub and Marina, and Hamilton Beach ocean access (**39**) are 400 m down the hill. You can stop here for a waterfront lunch and brew. They also may have pay showers and primitive camping.

10.0   Continue on Bedwell Harbour Road, which is now named Canal Road.
10.8   **Map 5**. The next intersection is with Scarff Road, followed by St. Peters Anglican Church and the Inn on Pender Island, which features evening public dining hours at Memories restaurant.
11.5   Next on the right is the Prior Centennial Campground of Gulf Islands National Park Reserve, open summer only (see the *Accommodations Guide*). There are pit toilets in the campground. The road descends to an intersection.
11.7   Signs indicate South Pender Island is to the left, which is a continuation of Canal Road (Option 1). Aldridge Road is straight ahead, which leads to the Magic Lake Estates and Trincomali residential areas (Option 2).

OPTION 1: SOUTH PENDER ISLAND: POETS COVE RESORT AND GOWLLAND POINT

11.7   (Continued) Bear left down Canal Road, and ride past the school and medical clinic (open weekdays), around a few curves, steadily downhill to the one-lane wooden bridge that connects to South Pender Island.
12.8   **Map 6.** As you reach the bridge, note the stone plaques on the left side describing the First Nations history of this area. Public access is available here on both sides of the road to the Pender Canal, but tread lightly on these ancient First Nations sites and *do not ride on the trails.* See the *Hiking and Coastal Access Guide* for further information (**41**). Cross the bridge, using caution not to catch your tires in the wooden slats.

12.9   You are now on South Pender Island.

Optional Sidetrip: The road to the right is Ainslie Point Road (a dead end) that leads to a major hiking-only trailhead in about 250 metres on the left. Bike racks are available. Trails ascend steeply to 244-metre Mt. Norman (Hike **83**, the best vista point on the Penders) and up-and down to Beaumont Marine Park (Hike **84**, one of the best shoreline hikes). See the *Coastal Access and Hiking Guide* for information on these, and other shorter trails in the canal area.

12.9   To continue your ride, take the road to the left at the bridge, which is the continuation of Canal Road. The road immediately curves to the right.

13.1   The first signed road on the left leads to the popular Mortimer Spit ocean access (**79**), which has a pit toilet along the access road (the only public-access toilet along the road on South Pender Island).
Maps 7, 7A. From the bridge, Canal Road continues for about 5 km along rolling topography, frequently cooler than other parts of the island due to the shade from the adjacent hillside, with light to moderate traffic. Scenery is forest with glimpses out to Plumper Sound to the north through the private properties.

15.2   Perhaps the best hiking trail on the Pender Islands is to the summit of Mt. Norman from the Canal Road trailhead, located about 2.3 km from the bridge (watch for a Parks Canada sign on the right). A gravel road leads up a 200-metre long hill to the trailhead where bike racks are located (no bikes on trails). An outhouse is found on the left after hiking about 5 minutes along the Mt. Norman trail (Hike **85**).

15.9   Two public ocean accesses are along this stretch of Canal Road:
Canal Road ocean access (**80**) is at about 3 km and,

16.9   *Walker Road* ocean access is at 4 km from the bridge (**81**). At low tide you can walk between these two points along the flat, rocky shore.

18.0   Canal Road ends at the intersection with Spalding Road and Boundary Pass Drive. **Map 7B**. One of the three best bicycling routes begins here. See *Ride **B1*** under *Best Bicycling Routes* for detailed information on the final segment of the Tour de Pender. Following are some of the landmarks along the route:

20.4   **Map 8** Enchanted Forest Park (Hike **91**)

21.1   **Poets Cove Resort** (Ocean access/pool **92**) restaurant, store.

21.4   GINPR - Greenburn Lake trailhead (Hike **99**)

23.9   **Map 9** Brooks Point CRD Reserve trailhead (Ocean access **97**)

24.0   Tip of South Pender Island at Gowlland Point (Ocean access **96**)

Return the same way - except:

40.3   **Map 1** Make a left on Otter Bay Road when you reach the Community Hall along Bedwell Harbour Road.

40.7   Bear right on Otter Bay Road at the junction with South Otter Bay Road.

Optional Sidetrip: Explore South Otter Bay Road (straight ahead). **Map 3.** GINPR-Roesland (**25**) is about 1.5 km from this junction, for an extra 3 km roundtrip along a very pleasant and beautiful stretch of Pender byway.

40.7   Continue on Otter Bay Road toward the ferry terminal.
42.2   **Map 1, 1A.** Bear left at the intersection with McKinnon Road.
42.8   Return to the ferry terminal.

OPTION 2: NORTH PENDER - MAGIC LAKE ESTATES OR TRINCOMALI

11.7   (Continued) **Map 5A:** Proceed straight ahead when Canal Road veers to the left to South Pender Island (Option 1). You are now on Aldridge Road. Carefully descend a hill that ends at an intersection.
12.0   The main road curves sharply to the right and is now Schooner Way. The secondary road to the left is the access to the Medicine Beach Reserve, which is worth a visit (**42**). Be careful at this intersection. Around the bend at Schooner Way, you will notice the Magic Lake Market, which is a good place to stop for refreshments. Continue on Schooner Way, which is relatively flat, but has moderate traffic. The road ends at a *T* intersection, which is the entrance to Magic Lake Estates. **Map 4.**
13.3   In front of you are a fire hall and a sign that depicts the roads and trails of Magic Lake Estates, where the majority of the Pender Islands' residents live. No bikes are allowed on Magic Lake Estates trails.
From here you have the option of exploring the Magic Lakes Estates area, or riding to the tip of North Pender Island and the Trincomali Neighbourhood. See the *Coastal Access and Hiking Guide* for information on these areas.

Magic Lake Estates (and the Disc Golf Course):
Map 4 shows the entire Magic Lake Estates area. **Maps 4B** and **4A** are Detail Maps. From the entrance to Magic Lake Estates (13.3), there are two general routes. The route to the right up Ketch Road is very windy and hilly, but has lighter traffic. Using the maps provided you can navigate around that area of Magic Lake Estates. The route to the left, down Schooner Way is straighter and less hilly. This route is described below:

13.3   (Continued) **Map 4B.** Continue to the left until Privateers Road.
13.7   Turn right on Privateers Road.
13.9   The first street on the right is Galleon Way where you have an option:

Disc Golf Sidetrip: Turn right on Galleon Way, and ride up the hill to Golf Island Disc Park on your right in about 250 m. A water fountain and outhouse are located at the park entrance. See the *Golfing Guide*, Chapter 10 for a map and information.

13.9   Continue on Privateers Road without turning. The road becomes Schooner Way again at 14.9 km. **Map 4A.**

15.6   Schooner Way turns to the right, but continue straight ahead on Anchor Way that descends a short, steep hill down to Thieves Bay Park (**51**). An outhouse, pay phone, picnic tables and private marina are located here.

15.8   The vista point at the end of the short road (bikes/peds only please) is excellent for sunsets and, if you are extremely lucky, orca-watching.

Either return the same way to the ferry (making a left on Otter Bay Road from Bedwell Harbour Road) for an approximate 27 km round trip, or do some additional exploring as follows. You can ride to Shingle Bay and the south entrance to GINPR - Roe Lake:

16.4   Make the first left onto Schooner Way after you leave the marina.

16.6   Make the first right on Shoal Road. Ride up the gradual hill.

17.1   Make the first right on Dory Way.

17.9   Follow Dory Way downhill all the way until it ends (noting that it changes names to Galleon Way halfway down the hill). You can explore the trails into the National Park from here on foot (no bikes allowed). See **Map 3A, 36 - 37**. Shingle Bay Park (**49**) has picnic tables, a muddy beach and an outhouse (expected 2006). Either return the same way, or follow the hillier route by making the first left halfway up the hill, onto Galleon Way, then follow Galleon Way as it curves around, past Buck Lake. Bear left onto Boson Way, right on Ketch, and return to the entrance to Magic Lake Estates where you started. From here, make a left on Schooner Way to head back toward the ferries. Return the same way, except turn left on Otter Bay Road at the Community Hall to cut some distance.

Ride to the Trincomali Neighbourhood/Wallace Point

13.3   (Continued) **Map 4.** Turn left on Schooner Way and pass Magic Lake.

14.0   Make the first left on Pirates Road. From this point on, the ride is the same as featured *Ride B3* in the *Best Bicycling Rides* section. See that section for details on this portion of the ride. Highlights include:

15.0   Magic Lake Swimming Hole (**48**)

16.4   Oaks Bluff Park trail (**70, Map 4C**).

19.0   Entrance to the Trincomali neighbourhood, **Map 4D.**

Return the same way, except make a left at Otter Bay Road to return to the ferry terminal for a total ride of about 33 km.

The Penders' Best Bicycle Rides

This section is for those who wish to ride a shorter distance with fewer hills and can transport their bikes to the starting points by car if necessary. Bike rentals may be available along Ride **B1** and within 2.4 km of Ride **B2**. These segments are presented in order of desirability, and are also incorporated into the *Tour de Pender* ride.

RIDE B1 SOUTH PENDER ISLAND - SPALDING /GOWLLAND PT ROADS

Difficulty: Easy+ (most of Spalding Rd) to Moderate (much of Gowlland Point Road). Watch for potholes, especially toward the eastern end of the island, and traffic, especially on Spalding Road. Ride with traffic, ride single file and keep to the right.
Length and Time: Approximately 1 hour, 12.5 km out and back.
Access by car: From the Driftwood Centre, head south on Bedwell Harbour Road that turns into Canal Road. Follow the signs to South Pender Island where Canal Road turns to the left, rather than staying on the main road that becomes Aldridge Road. Cross over the bridge, stay on Canal Road which veers to the left after the bridge, and follow it about 5 km to where it ends at Boundary Pass Drive to the left and Spalding Road to the right. Park on the right shoulder of Boundary Pass Road. Alternate places to park are found along the route, including Gowlland Point Road just past Poets Cove Resort, or along wide grassy shoulders that can be found at several spots along the route.
Rentals: Poets Cove Resort; 629.2100, 1.888.512.7638.

The Ride is described commencing at the intersection of Canal Road and Spalding Road to correspond with the *Tour de Pender* ride description. **Map 7B.** Another option is to start at sea level at the end of Gowlland Point Road (**Map 9**) and do the ride in reverse so that you get more of the uphill riding out of the way first.

Ride west along Spalding Road on a very gradual uphill slope through a relatively flat bucolic agricultural valley lined with berry bushes. **Map 8**. The road jogs to the left in about 1.4 km, and further down the road one is treated to a spectacular view of snow-covered Mt. Baker on clear days beyond the fields to the east. The road then jogs to the right, and is surrounded by beautiful thick forest. Watch for the sign *Enchanted Forest Park* on the right (**91**). It is a good place for a short stroll through the western portion of the park (no bikes allowed, rack provided). Spalding

Road then jogs to the left, and climbs a small hill of moderate grade. At the top of the hill is a lovely view through trees to **Poets Cove Resort** and Bedwell Harbour beyond. Use caution down the narrow, scenic stretch of road that descends a moderate grade along a ridge with ocean vistas off to the right. (Photo, right). At the bottom of the hill is the turnoff for **Poet's Cove Resort** (**92**) to the right, where a steep hill leads down to the resort. Bypass the resort for now and bear left past the Church of the Good Shepherd. The road jogs to the right just after the Greenburn Lake/GINPR access (**99**) on the left (the South Pender fire hall is straight ahead), then continues with small to moderate rolling hills past large wooded properties to the end of the road at Gowlland Point. **Map 9.** Lock your bikes here and explore either this ocean access (**96**), or the beautiful Brooks Point CRD Reserve (**97**), located a short distance back up the road past Kloshe Road, on the north side of the road (left side looking from Gowlland Point). Return via the same route, with an optional stop at the **Poets Cove Resort** for food or a dip in their nice but frequently crowded pool (fee). Other options along the way include exploration of the beach accesses listed in the *Coastal Access and Hiking Guide* (**93 - 98**).

> **OPTION: POETS COVE BIKE 'N BRUNCH**   Start out at Poets Cove Resort, do either part or all of the bike ride, then return for lunch on the deck of their more casual restaurant, **Syrens**, or a seasonal barbeque at the Moorings Market. The Poets Cove activities department may offer a similar tour.

RIDE B2 NORTH PENDER ISLAND: HOPE BAY - PORT WASHINGTON LOOP

Difficulty: Moderate. **Distance/Time:** 7.6 km loop, About 30 - 40 minutes.
Watch for potholes, especially along Clam Bay Road, and traffic, especially on Port Washington Road. Ride with traffic single file and keep to the right.
Access by Car: From the ferry terminal, bear right at the ferry kiosk, then right at the junction with Otter Bay Road. Continue until the road ends at Bedwell Harbour Road. Make a left, then carefully follow it around to the right when it curves steeply at a junction. Follow Bedwell Harbour Road until it ends at the Hope Bay Store and park in the area. Other parking is in the vicinity of the **Pender Island Home Building Centre** near the Port Washington Road midpoint, and the Port Washington government dock.
Rentals: Otter Bay Marina; 629.3579.

The Ride
Map 1 depicts the entire ride.
For more detail see **Maps 1C, 1B:**
Map 1C: From Hope Bay, ride up the uncrowded Clam Bay Road to the northwest, which begins with a small uphill stretch. Watch for potholes on this road. The route traverses Hope Bay and Welcome Bay then a rural residential area. Mt. Elizabeth Park on the left (**14**) has an outhouse, and Welcome Bay ocean access (**8**) is across the road.

> Optional Sidetrip: Make a right down Coast Shale Road. Turn left on Armandale Road (a diversion to Bricky Bay (**9**) is to the right on Armadale Road), turn left on Pearsons Road and return to Clam Bay Road. Turn right.

The environmental integrity of a scenic portion of the forest along Clam Bay Road has been preserved by an Islands Trust Fund covenant, but other areas are being logged. Continue past Clam Bay Farm, a working farm and resort. A long moderate uphill stretch begins here. Watch your speed on the moderate downhill since the road ends abruptly on Port Washington Road at 2.9 km. Port Washington Road has more traffic than Clam Bay Road, but is still lightly traveled. **Map 1B.** Make a right on Port Washington Road. Ride single file and stay to the right. Small farms along the route sell fresh produce and eggs from roadside stands in season. Continue to the end of Port Washington Road, and make a left to go down the short, steep hill to the Port Washington government dock (**3**) that is the main floatplane port for the island (at 3.9 km). The historic general store is closed at time of writing, but may reopen in the future as part of a historic trust. Return the same way, except instead of turning left on Clam Bay Road, continue straight ahead on Port Washington Road. **Map 1C.** You will pass the **Pender Island Home Building Centre** on the left (soft drink vending machine outside and snacks inside, closed Sunday), and the **Southridge Farms Country Store** on the right that features fresh produce, health foods, cold drinks and a coffee bar. Continue carefully on scenic Port Washington Road down a pleasant gradual grade past farmland and rural residential properties. At the end of the road (at 7.5 km) make a left to return to Hope Bay, for a total ride of about 7.6 km.

> **OPTION: HOPE BAY BIKE N' BRUNCH** Combine a bike ride with a waterfront meal at the **Hope Bay Café**. Check to make sure it will be open before making plans; 629.6668. Another option involves a detour up Otter Bay Road to **Chippers Café** at the golf course; 629.6665. Also, **Southridge Farms** has the occasional summer barbeque; 629.2051.

RIDE B3 NORTH PENDER ISLAND: MAGIC LAKE TO TRINCOMALI

Difficulty: Moderate. **Distance and Time:** 11 km, About 45 minutes roundtrip. Watch for potholes and traffic. Ride with traffic single file and keep to the right.
Access by car: Follow signs to Magic Lake. From Driftwood Centre (best place for provisions), follow the main road to the south as it changes names from Bedwell Harbour Road to Canal Road. Do not make the left turn to South Pender Island. The road then briefly becomes Aldridge Way. When the main road curves sharply to the right, follow it rather than continuing straight on a minor road. You are now on Schooner Way. Pass **Magic Lake Market** (good places for provisions) and follow Schooner Way to a *T* intersection at the entrance to Magic Lake Estates. Make a left, which is still Schooner Way, and pass a fire hall. Just after the intersection with Privateers Road, there is room to park on the left shoulder next to the serene Magic Lake picnic area. Begin your ride here. **Map 4.**

The Ride
Continue southwest on Schooner Way and make the first left on Pirates Road. The signed Magic Lake swimming access appears in about 1 km on the left, after the last private driveway (**48**). An outhouse is open here seasonally, the only one along this route. Continue along Pirates Road, which has some moderate hills, and one long, gradual hill. (See *North Pender Index Map* for a map of this section). The road ends, after changing names to Plumper Way, at about 5 km from the starting point **Map 4D**. You will reach the intersection of Bedwell Drive and Plumper Way, at the entrance to the Trincomali subdivision at the tip of North Pender Island. Turn left onto Bedwell

Drive, and go down the hill, making the first right on Trincoma Place. There are two beach accesses, one on the left behind a concrete guardrail as the road curves to the right (**71**), and the other at the end of the road, on the right (**72**). Return the same way. For a spectacular vista, look for the Oaks Bluff Park (**70, Map 4C**) trailhead, which will be on your left as you return northwestward on Pirates Road, halfway to Schooner Way (in about 2.5 km). Lock your bike at the small, unpaved parking area, and hike to the top for awesome vistas northeast to **Poets Cove Resort** with a Mount Baker backdrop, or a southwest panorama all the way to the Olympic Mountains.

Nearby Off-Island Bicycling Highlights

Some world-class cycling opportunities are available near the Pender Islands, from long tours to shorter trail rides. Several other Gulf Islands beckon the cyclist, and long urban bike trails run through the Victoria and Vancouver areas. Just south of the Pender Islands, Washington's San Juan Islands provide additional challenges.

Saanich Peninsula and Victoria to Sooke

BIKE TRAILS

From the Pender Islands, you can take your bike onto the ferry to Swartz Bay, and ride on the Lochside and Galloping Goose multi-use trails some 80 km all the way to Sooke. The twin trails are part of the Trans-Canada Trail, a national multi-use trail system linking trails from coast to coast. Download the Galloping Goose/Lochside trail map and brochure from **www.crd.bc.ca/parks/brochure.htm**.

The Lochside Regional Trail follows 33 kilometres of former railway line from Swartz Bay/Sidney to Saanich/Victoria. Signs direct the cyclist to the Lochside trailhead, as follows: As you exit the ferry at Swartz Bay, ride in the bike lane past the tollbooths and under the first underpass. Watch for a sign on the right that directs bikers off the highway. Exit here, where a signboard contains a map of area bicycle trails. Head back on the trail toward the same overpass. Make a right to cross the overpass, pass the stoplight, then make the next right (Curteis Road). The Lochside Trail begins at the end of this road past the yacht brokers. Upon returning to the ferry terminal, follow the bike route signs that lead to a break in the fence and a ramp down to the tollbooths. Proceed to the first open tollbooth.

The Lochside trail follows a combination of bike trails, bike lanes, and uncrowded roads that tend to run adjacent to residential areas or highways, but also traverses some scenic agricultural and park lands. After a short trail ride between Highway 17 and the mudflats beyond Cedar Grove Marina, you are dumped onto the shoulder of McDonald Park Drive, which you follow toward Sidney. McDonald Park is an option for camping. Rather than re-joining the off-road trail that parallels the highway in this area, you may want to detour on Resthaven Drive and ride through the peaceful seaside community of Sidney, rejoining the trail near Ocean Avenue and the Washington

Ferry terminal (**Map 10**). Nice diversions along this next stretch of Lochside Drive include the waterfront Tulista Park (6 km from Swartz Bay) and Cy Hampson Park (9 km). At Mt. Newton X Road, the trail parallels the highway again as it passes the Tsawout First Nations Reserve. At Island View Drive (16 km), you will reach Michell Brothers farm stand with fresh produce. Island View Beach Regional Park is located 3 km up over the hill to the left/east where there is a long sandy beach for picnicking, a fragile sand dune area, and a campground. This is a worthwhile side trip or ride destination. Back on the Lochside Trail, a scenic leg is reached further south after Royal Oak Drive, where the trail crosses Blenkinsop Lake on the Blenkinsop Trestle (26 km).

Just south of Swan Lake Nature Sanctuary (33km), the Lochside Trail connects with the Galloping Goose multi-use trail, also a former railway line that moves through urban, rural and wilderness scenery on its 55-kilometre journey from Victoria to Sooke. The southern leg of the Galloping Goose trail heads to the left (south) and leads to downtown Victoria after skirting some commercial and industrial zones. It crosses the Selkirk Trestle over the Gorge Waterway and ends at the Johnson Street Bridge near Victoria Inner Harbour (See **Map 11** and *Road Rides* below). The western leg (to the right) continues through View Royal, Langford and Metchosin to Sooke. In general the scenery becomes wilder as you head west, eventually reaching Sooke Potholes Provincial Park. The trail is mostly paved in the urban areas, but is unpaved in some of the outlying areas.

The CRD recommends several day trips using the Galloping Goose trail. This one is the highlight: Park at Roche Cove Regional Park (on Gillespie Road off Sooke Road), and follow the Galloping Goose Trail to Sooke Potholes Provincial Park (12 km one way). The Sooke Potholes are a series of deep polished rock pools and potholes carved into sandstone by the Sooke River, and makes for a popular summer swimming and picnicking destination. Another suggestion is to park at the Luxton parking area, near the corner of Sooke Road and Glen Lake Road. Follow the Galloping Goose Trail, then Lombard Drive and William Head Road, to Devonian Regional Park (9 km one way).

> Cautions: Vancouver Island is cougar country, and there have been sightings in recent years near various portions of these trails, such as near Blenkinsop Lake. Also, never leave valuables in your vehicle at trailheads, especially at the Sooke area parks that are notorious for break-ins.

VICTORIA ROAD RIDES

Some of the most enjoyable Victoria riding is around Victoria Inner Harbour and the southern coastline. However, it is mostly on-road and best in the off-season due to heavy traffic. You can enter downtown Victoria via the southern leg of the Galloping Goose trail that crosses the Selkirk Trestle and ends at the Johnson Street Bridge (**Map 11**). Use extra caution riding on this bridge, or better yet, walk your bike across in the pedestrian zone. Ride south along Wharf Street and follow Government Street around the Inner Harbour, make a right on Belleville Street past the Parliament buildings, then follow Belleville Street (and Pendray, Kingston and Erie Streets) around the point to

Dallas Road. Walking down the Ogden Point breakwater can be exhilarating, especially if cruise ships are in port. A café is located here. Follow Dallas Road to the east along the shoreline, taking in the spectacular vista of the Olympic Mountains across the Strait of Juan de Fuca to the south. Unfortunately, bikes are now banned from the waterfront walking trails. You have the option of exploring the park drives of Beacon Hill Park or riding along the scenic coastal route to Oak Bay and beyond via Hollywood Crescent, Crescent Road, King George Terrace and Beach Drive. The ultimate bike 'n Sunday Brunch experience involves the Marina Restaurant at Oak Bay Marina (make reservations, see the *Victoria Dining Guide* in Chapter 8), but you will not be able to ride very far afterwards.

> Caution: bike theft is a problem in Victoria. Park your bike in an area with high
> visibility and use a good lock. Or, patronize bike shops that will store your bike by
> the hour, including **Reckless Bike Stores** (see *Rentals*, below) and **Chain Chain
> Chain Bike Check and Cycling Services** (1410 Broad St, 385.1739, $3/day).

MOUNTAIN BIKING

Mountain biking is prohibited on the trails of all the CRD's regional parks with three exceptions: Bikes are allowed on the western portion of the 10 km loop around Elk Lake/Beaver Lake Regional Park, and at designated multi-use trails in Thetis Lake Regional Park. Mountain biking is also allowed on the east slope or Hartland section of Mount Work Regional Park, separate from the main park. Trail difficulty ranges from moderate over rolling hills to difficult steep terrain for advanced mountain bikers. To get to the Hartland entrance, take Highway 17 south from Swartz Bay, cross over to West Saanich Road (17A) and follow it south to Hartland Avenue. Turn right (west) on Hartland Avenue, which leads to the park entrance on the right. For more information on the Mount Work-Hartland mountain biking trails, consult CRD Parks' volunteer partner, the South Island Mountain Bike Society, at **www.simbs.com**. Every Sunday they lead either an introductory ride, a ride for women or youth, or trail cleanup. See also **www.crd.bc.ca/parks/mount_work.htm**.

VICTORIA AREA BICYCLE SALES AND RENTALS

RENTALS ONLY
Sidney: **True Value Hardware**, 2488 Beacon Ave, 656.8611
Victoria
Along the Galloping Goose Trail: **Selkirk Station**, 800 Tyee, 383.1466
Cycle BC Rentals, www.cyclebc.ca, 747 Douglas (behind the Empress), 380.2453.
Cycle Victoria Rentals, www.cyclevictoriarentals.com, 950 Wharf, 1.866.380.2453
Sports Rent, 1950 Government & Chatham, **www.sportsrentbc.com**, 385.7368

RENTALS AND SALES
Victoria
Reckless Bike Stores: **www.reckless.ca**, 1826 Government St, 383.2404
Reno Bikes, 608 Esquimalt, 384.5514
Sooke
Sooke Cycle and Surf: **www.sookebikes.com**: 6707 W. Sooke Rd, 642.3123
SALES ONLY
Sidney: **Russ Hay's The Bicycle Shop**: **www.russhays.com**, 9781A Second St, 656.1512
Fahnini Cycles, 2320 Harbour, 656.3421
Victoria
Fort Street Cycle, 1025 Fort St, 384.6665
Performance Bicycles, 3949 Quadra St, 727.6655
Riders Cycles, **www.riderscycles.com**, 1092 Cloverdale (at Cook & Quadra), 381.1125

See also **www.cyclevancouverisland.ca** for additional listings.

Vancouver

Downtown Vancouver is surrounded by water on three sides, and bike trails traverse seawalls through most of the downtown area. It is one of the most scenic urban bike trail systems in North America. Pleasure boats, freighters, cruise ships and water taxis ply the waterways, while pedestrians stroll, and beachcombers frolic. The Vancouver skyline is ever present from many angles, backed by towering mountains as the bike trails wind around the waterfront and through Stanley Park. You can ride from Canada Place (cruise ship terminal area), along the Coal Harbour Seawalk, 10 km around the entire Stanley Park peninsula along seawalls (one way, counter-clockwise, Photo, above), along the north shores of English Bay and False Creek (choose from several cafés for bike 'n brunch) then around their south shores, past Granville Island, Vanier Park, Kitsilano Park, and connect on trails and uncrowded roads all the way to the University of British Columbia and Point Grays. On a nice day, the Vancouver scenery of mountains, rivers and ocean are spectacular, and the terrain is mostly flat.
Map: **www.englishbay.com/eb/bikemap.htm**.
Rentals: Bayshore Bike: www.bayshorebikerentals.ca, 745 Denman between Robson & Alberni, 604.688.BIKE. Lock your bike securely in Vancouver due to high theft rate.

214   Bicycling Guide

Outer Gulf Islands

The nearby Outer Gulf Islands can be fun to explore on two wheels. Keep in mind that Pender Islands' byways are known to be somewhat less hilly than those on some of the other islands, so if you find Pender riding to be easy, you may enjoy the challenge of the other islands. If you find Pender difficult, you may want to opt for the flat urban bike trails in Victoria or Vancouver. Pick up maps of the islands you wish to explore on the ferries. The maps also contain information on dining, accommodations, camping and points of interest. The ferry schedule from Pender works best to Mayne and Galiano Islands, while sailings are limited to Saturna Island. The ferry trip to Salt Spring Island requires a connection through Swartz Bay in at least one direction. Salt Spring has the most traffic of the islands, with no bike trails or bike lanes. A basic description of the Outer Gulf Islands follow, but you should ask at the local bicycle shops, where applicable, for recommended routes. A local guide is *Bicycle Touring the Southern & Northern Gulf Islands* by Enloe & Richardson (1996).

Galiano Island is very hilly, rated a *3 out of 5* for difficulty. Most of the island's facilities are located at the southern end of the island, near the Sturdies Bay ferry terminal. Highlights along your route are Bellhouse Park, Bluffs Park and Montague Harbour Provincial Marine Park, where you will find the only camping on the island easily accessible by land. Hilly Porlier Pass Road extends to the northern end of the island.
Rentals: Galiano Bicycle, www.galianoisland.com/galianobicycle, 36 Burrill Rd, 539.9906.

Mayne Island is plenty hilly, but does not have as many steep hills as Galiano or Saturna Islands. The ferry terminal is at Village Bay, and most of the activity and facilities are at Miners Bay to the northeast. Ride up the hill into Miners Bay on Village Bay Road, then follow Georgina Point Road to the Georgina Point Lighthouse. From there you can ride out to the Mayne Inn at Bennett Bay, or out Horton Bay Road to the Horton Bay Dock. There are two private campgrounds, at Miners Bay and near Horton Bay. Dinner Bay Park and the Japanese Gardens are about 2 km south of Village Bay.
Rentals: Mayne Island Kayak & Bike Rentals, www.maynekayak.com, Miners Bay, 539.5599.

Saturna Island is the least developed of the Southern Gulf Islands served by BC Ferries. Bicycling is tough due to several steep hills, but is also rewarding. The route is straightforward, just follow East Point Road the entire way, with a worthwhile detour on Winter Cove Road to explore scenic Winter Cove day use area of GINPR. The ride along East Point Road to the East Point Lighthouse affords beautiful vistas of the Georgia Strait and Cabbage and Tumbo Islands. There are no campgrounds on Saturna Island.

San Juan Islands

Cycling on Washington's San Juan Islands is similar to that on the Gulf Islands. Expect hilly terrain with forests, meadows, and rocky coasts. Roads vary in width, availability of shoulders, and traffic. From Pender you can bring your bike onto the ferry to Swartz Bay, ride down the Lochside Trail to the Washington State Ferries terminal in Sidney, and ferry over to San Juan or Orcas Island. An overnight stay will most likely be required. A trip to Lopez Island will require a ferry transfer at San Juan Island. See the *Travel Guide* for details on the ferry service. Or, you can boat over (See the *Boating Guide*). Remember to bring the appropriate documents to cross the U.S. border.

Lopez Island is considered the most bicycle-friendly island in the region. While not flat by any means, it is less hilly than San Juan and Orcas Islands and has wider shoulders. The preferred cycling route is counterclockwise around the island to catch the best ocean views and be able to stock up on supplies near the beginning (Ferry Road to Lopez Road to Lopez Village). Rentals and bike repairs are available at **Lopez Bicycle Works** at Fisherman Bay, 5 miles from the ferry terminal, 360.468.2847. Odlin County Park, located 1 mile from the ferry terminal, has bicycle-friendly campsites. Reservations: 360.378.1842. See *The Best Bike Rides in the Pacific Northwest* by Litman and Kort (1996) for more detailed information.

Orcas Island has perhaps the most exhilarating riding, as you can ride all the way up 734-metre (2,409-foot) Mt. Constitution in Moran State Park, the highest point in the San Juan Islands. This horseshoe-shaped island holds many rewards for cyclists. Rentals are at **Dolphin Bay Bicycles** at the Ferry Terminal, 360.376.4157 and **Wildlife Cycles** in Eastsound, 360.376.4708. See *Short Bike Rides - Western Washington* by Wagonfeld (1997) for ride details for Orcas and San Juan Islands.

San Juan Island is the most populated island, and the main route between Friday Harbor and Roche Harbor gets plenty of bike and vehicular traffic. Hilly West Side Road is a highlight, with Whale Watch Park, popular for spotting orcas. Check the Wagonfeld book for suggested routes, or ask at the local bike shop in Friday Harbor: **Island Bicycles, www.islandbicycles.com**, 380 Argyle Ave, 360.378.4941. The **Pedal Inn** campground caters to cyclists, 360.378.3049.

Plans have been announced to make the three main San Juan Islands more bicycle friendly in the coming years. For example, on San Juan Island, five major walking and bicycling corridors are planned to connect Friday Harbor with Roche Harbor, Limekiln Park/County Park, American Camp/Cattle Point and Turn Point/Jackson Beach. For further information on this project, see the **www.co.san-juan.wa.us/publicworks** site. San Juan Islands web sites include **www.lopezisland.com, www.orcasisland.org, www.portfridayharbor.org** and **www.travelsanjuan.com.**

Bicycling Web Resources
www.gvcc.bc.ca Greater Victoria Cycling Coalition
www.cycling.bc.ca Cycling BC online
www.bccc.bc.ca BC Cyclist Coalition represents interests of BC cyclists
www.victoriacyclingfestival.com Times Colonist family festival in June.
www.canadatrails.ca Biking, hiking and cross-country skiing trails in BC
www.simbs.com South (Vancouver) Island Mountain Biking Society
www.pedaling.com Resources and rides in the U.S. and BC

NORTH PENDER ISLAND

SOUTH PENDER ISLAND

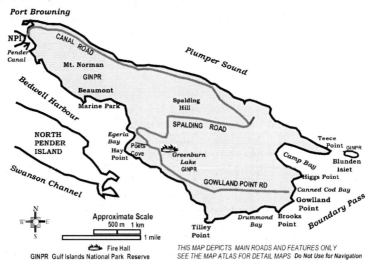

15 BOATING GUIDE

A NARRATIVE GUIDE FOR THE PENDERS AND BEYOND

This narrative guide offers an overview of boating opportunities and services on the Pender Islands and the surrounding area. Included are descriptions of local marinas, anchorages, boat launching spots, boating organizations, kayaking, fishing, SCUBA diving, tides, weather, resources, and a travel guide to nearby boating destinations. The information is not intended for use for navigation. Before setting out, consult the appropriate nautical charts, tide and current tables, weather forecasts, local notices, and various cruising guides. Obtain the relevant certifications, and carry the required safety equipment. See *Boating Resources* at the end of the Boating Guide for additional references for information not covered in the various sections of this chapter.

Orientation and the Basics

The Pender Islands are located in the southern Gulf Islands, just north of Washington State's San Juan Islands, in a region considered one of the premier cruising areas in North America. From the Pender Islands, kayakers explore the coves and bays along its scenic shoreline, or visit other nearby islands. Pender sailors take advantage of blustery days and even winter storms, sailing back and forth in the surrounding waters, or participating in races and regattas to other islands with the informal Pender Island Yacht Club. Penderites with small runabouts use them to go fishing, set crab traps, or to dart to nearby islands. Larger vessels set off on cruises to explore the region and the jewel of the Pacific Northwest, Desolation Sound. Others use their boats to make a living as fishermen, charter operators, or marine mechanics.

Surrounding Waterways

See the *Location Map* and *Index Maps* in the *Map Atlas* for an overview of the waterways surrounding the Pender Islands.

To the west of North Pender Island is Swanson Channel, which extends from Trincomali Channel to the north to Boundary Pass to the south. The channel is a main artery for BC Ferries, whose vessels sail between Vancouver/Tsawwassen, Victoria/Swartz Bay, and the Southern Gulf Islands. Some of these ferries produce formidable wakes, especially the large older vessels like BC Ferries' Motor Vessels (MV) Queen of Saanich and Queen of Nanaimo. The modern super ferries, the Spirit of British Columbia and the Spirit of Vancouver Island, produce large but rolling wakes which tend to be easier to deal with. You can always count on a ferry or two or three passing by, at a fairly quick clip. Occasional freighters, barges, tour boats, and military vessels may be encountered along with pleasure boats and fishing boats of all varieties. Fast moving yachts can create especially scary wakes for small boats. Swanson Channel is also one of main routes of the Southern Resident Pods of orcas, which can be spotted swimming mainly from south to north on many summer days, followed by a barrage of whale watching boats and pleasure craft. Pender Island marine facilities along Swanson Channel, from north to south, are the Port Washington Government Dock (**Map 1B, 3**), BC Ferries' Otter Bay Terminal (**Map 1A, 21**), Otter Bay Marina (**22**), and Thieves Bay Marina (Magic Lake Estates' private marina, not open to the public) (**Map 4A, 51**). Across Swanson Channel to the west are Prevost Island and Salt Spring Island (with the village of Ganges the main destination). Private Moresby Island lies to the south of North Pender Island.

To the east of Swanson Channel around the north end of North Pender Island is the narrow Navy Channel, which separates North Pender and Mayne Islands. Navy Channel connects to the east with Plumper Sound, which forms the eastern shoreline of both North and South Pender Islands. Across Plumper Sound to the east are the southern tip of Mayne Island, private Samuel Island, and Saturna Island. The Hope Bay Government Dock provides access to Plumper Sound and Navy Channel (**Map 1C, 7**). The BC Ferry to Saturna Island uses this route, along with pleasure boats, fishing boats, military vessels, and an occasional freighter that may anchor here while waiting to enter a nearby port. Currents in Navy Channel and Plumper Sound can be quite strong and turbulent at times. Razor Point marks the entrance to Port Browning off of Plumper Sound, and requires a wide berth. Port Browning Marina (with a CANPASS *permit only* customs station) (**40**) and the Port Browning Government Dock (**38**) are at the head of this bay, which is busy with recreational boaters (**Map 5B**). The narrow and historically significant Pender Canal connects Port Browning with Bedwell Harbour to the south, completing the separation of North and South Pender Islands (**Map 6**). Poets Cove Marina (with the only customs port of entry and fuel dock on the Pender Islands) (**Map 8, 92**) and Beaumont Marine Park (GINPR) (**82**) are in Bedwell Harbour off of South Pender Island (**Map 7**). Pender's most popular beaches are in these interior waterways, including Hamilton Beach (**Map 5B, 39**), Mortimer Spit (**Map 6, 79**) and Medicine Beach (**Map 5A, 42**).

To the south of North and South Pender Islands is Boundary Pass, a major shipping route that forms the boundary between Canada and the United States. Freighters, cruise ships, and all kinds of commercial and military vessels share this passage with pleasure craft. Boundary Pass connects to Haro Strait, which follows the international border to the Strait of Juan de Fuca. South of Boundary Pass are Washington State's San Juan Islands.

The waters surrounding the Pender Islands are protected from the large swells of the open ocean for the most part, and do not tend to get as much fog as other coastal areas. During many summer days, the entire Pacific Coast from the west coast of Vancouver Island down to southern California may be socked in with fog, but the Gulf Islands region may remain clear. Although fog can materialize at any time, it tends to be most common in the fall, and more likely toward the southern end of the Pender Islands, which are closest to the Strait of Juan de Fuca where it typically originates. For smaller boats such as kayaks, currents, wind waves and boat wakes can create a hazard, and when storms blow in, all boaters need be aware of small craft or gale warnings. The roughest waters are typically along the south end of the Pender Islands along Boundary Pass, which is closest to open ocean and which also experiences the strongest currents and coastal eddies. However, any of the channels can become rough at any time.

Distances to Nearby Points of Interest

Following are approximate navigable distances in International Nautical Miles (NM) from the four Pender Islands marinas to nearby points of interest. Distances will vary depending on your exact route, and routes that hug the shoreline (mostly applicable to kayakers) will be longer. Distances are rounded to the nearest half nautical mile and may be used for trip planning but not for navigation. The *Location Map* in the *Map Atlas* depicts the places listed. Additional distances are found in the *Kayaking* section, and distances to some regional destinations are found at the end of this chapter.

	PENDER ISLANDS MARINAS			
NEARBY DESTINATIONS	Otter Bay	Thieves Bay	Port Browning	Poets Cove
Otter Bay Marina	–	2	9N 9.5S	11N 7S
Thieves Bay Marina	2	–	7S	12N 5S
Port Browning Marina *	9N 9.5S	7	–	2.5
Poets Cove Marina F C *	11N 7S	12N 5S	2.5	–
Ganges, Salt Spring Island F *	8.5	8.5	15N 16S	14
Fulford Harbour, Salt Spring Island F	7.5	6.5	12.5	10
Lyall Harbour, Saturna Island F	8	9.5	4	5
Saturna Beach/Saturna Vineyards	8	9.5 N, S	3	4
Montague Harbour, Galiano Island F *	8	10	13	14
Miners Bay, Mayne Island F *	6.5	8	12	13
Tsehum Harbour & Sidney Marina F C *	10	8	12.5	10
Brentwood Bay & Butchart Gardens F	17	15	22.5	20
Roche Harbor, San Juan Island (US) F C	13.5	12	12.5	9
Friday Harbor, San Juan Island (US) F C	21	19	18.5	16

- F = Fuel Dock
- C = Customs Port of Entry (U.S. or Canada)
- * = CANPASS Check-in Locations. See *Customs* section for further information.
- N = Northern route option around North Pender Island between points; S=Southern.

Approximate 'Round-Pender Distances
- North and South Pender Islands: 19 NM;
- North Pender Island via Canal: 17 NM;
- South Pender Island via Canal: 9 NM.

Customs

The following customs information is provided as a guideline only since customs procedures tend to change. Contact the appropriate customs agency periodically for the current requirements.

CANADA CUSTOMS

Two types of Canada Customs entry stations are presently in service:
* A designated port of entry is open to all boaters.
* A *permit only* site is open only to those vessels where everyone on board is registered with CANPASS (see the CANPASS section, below).
Note: Upon reaching a customs dock in Canada or the U.S., all must stay aboard while clearing customs, except the skipper or designee.

The Pender Islands have an unmanned port of entry next to Poets Cove Marina at Bedwell Harbour (**Map 8**). Several telephones are available at the customs dock to call in your arrival 24 hours a day from May through September: 1.888.CANPASS (226.7277). Call first to verify allowed check-in hours. During this period, this station is open to both non-CANPASS and to CANPASS boaters.

From October through April, non-CANPASS vessels must check in at a port of entry that is open, such as the Port Sidney Marina. During this period, Poets Cove/Bedwell Harbour is open as a permit-only site, where only CANPASS boaters can check in, during the allowed hours.

Port Browning Marina is a permit-only site year-round, where only CANPASS boaters can check in, during the allowed hours. Boaters can use their cell phone or the phone located at the head of the dock.

The closest Canada Customs port of entry stations beyond the Pender Islands are in the Sidney area, at Canoe Cove Marina, Van Isle Marina and Port Sidney Marina (see the *Nearby Boating Destinations* section). Royal Victoria Yacht Club in Tsehum Harbour also has a reporting station. In Victoria, reporting stations are at Oak Bay Marina, Royal Victoria Yacht Club in Cadboro Bay and Victoria Customs Dock. In Nanaimo, you can check in at the Nanaimo Brechin Point Marina and Nanaimo Port Authority Yacht Basin. In greater Vancouver, reporting stations are at the government docks at White Rock, False Creek and Steveston, as well as Crescent Beach Marina and Coal Harbour/Burrard Inlet.

Boaters arriving from the United States or overseas must check in with Canada customs if they plan to anchor or touch Canadian soil, stop at a dock, or rendezvous with a hovering vessel in Canadian waters. The reverse is true for Canadians entering U.S. waters. A clearance number is provided each time a vessel clears Canada Customs, which should be kept by the boater for future reference.

CANPASS, the Canada Border Service Agency's streamlined reporting procedure that includes private boats, made a comeback in 2003 after being previously curtailed following the 9/11 attacks. The fee is $40 per person for 5 years, with family members under 18 free. Applicants can be citizens or lawful permanent residents of Canada or the United States with no criminal record, customs or immigration violations within the past six years. U.S. citizens must meet normal visitor requirements. The advantage is that you can report to *permit only* sites, including Port Browning (and Bedwell Harbour in winter) on the Pender Islands, as well as Cabbage Island (off Saturna Island), Ganges (Salt Spring Island), Montague Harbour (Galiano Island) and Mayne Island's Horton Bay and Miners Bay. However, there are restrictions. All persons onboard the reporting vessel must be approved CANPASS members. You must telephone in with your estimated arrival time up to 4 hours beforehand by calling 1.888.CANPASS or 250.363.0222, and arrive at that time. You must still have all of your appropriate citizenship and boat registration documentation on board and be subject to inspection upon arrival. For more detailed information on reporting requirements, or to apply online, see **www.cbsa.asfc.gc.ca/travel/canpass**, or call 1.800.461.9999 or 604.535.9346. Note: Although the website states that you can call anytime up to 4 hours before arrival, it is best to give at least 2 hours notice in case they decide to send an inspector to the site so you do not have to wait on board your boat for 2 hours.

U.S. CUSTOMS
In 2005 U.S. Customs revamped its clearance procedures for small craft. The Personal Identification Number (PIN) streamlined clearance system was discontinued due to increased concerns regarding small craft entering the U.S. Replacing it are the I-68 Boating Permit or the NEXUS member proximity card. The I-68 permit must be applied for at a U.S. customs station. It costs $16 per year ($32/family) and allows boaters to stay up to 72 hours in the U.S. Boaters are issued a log number and can then check in by phone using the old PIN phone number, 1.800.562.5943. For information and updates on I-68 see **http://www.cbp.gov/xp/cgov/travel/pleasure_boats/cbbl.xml**. The NEXUS application process is lengthier and costs $50 per person, but lasts five years and allows stays up to six months. For information check the web site **http://cbp.gov/xp/cgov/travel/frequent_traveler/nexus.xml**.

Without pre-clearance, boaters (including kayakers) must check in to a designated port of entry during the allowable hours. Upon reaching a customs dock in the U.S., all must stay aboard until clearing customs, except for the master or designee. If they arrive after hours, all must wait on board until the station re-opens the next morning. A clearance number is provided each time a vessel clears customs, which should be kept by the boater for future reference. Boats 30 feet in length or greater are subject to an annual fee of $25 payable at or before the first arrival of the year. Call the U.S. Customs entry number 1.800.562.5943. Or, try 360.734.5463 if that number does not work. Reporting hours are 0800 to 1700, extended in summer months. Outside of these hours, you must stay aboard your vessel until a report can be made.

The nearest U.S. Port of Entry facility to the Pender Islands is at Roche Harbor, San Juan Island (9 nautical miles from Bedwell Harbour), open 0900 to 1700 June through September, plus possible weekends in May. The best nearby Washington port of entry is at Friday Harbor on San Juan Island, which is open year-round 0800 to 1700. The customs dock is at the entry to the marina. The phone for both offices is 360.378.2080.

Other facilities in Washington include the Port of Anacortes 360.293.2331 (open year round), Port of Bellingham - Squalicum Harbor (open April through September) 360.647.5353, Port of Point Roberts (open 24 hours year round), 360.945.2314 and Port of Sumas, 360.988.2971 (open 24 hours year round). Across the Strait of Juan de Fuca are Port Angeles 360.457.4311 and Port Townsend 360.385.3777. Seattle is open 0800 to 1600 weekdays, requiring 24-hour notice, 206.553.4678.

Fuel Docks

A fuel dock is located at the Poets Cove Marina in Bedwell Harbour (See *Marinas* section). Regular and diesel fuel are available year-round. Call for current hours 629.2111. Penderites with proof of residency have gotten a discount (about 4 cents off per litre) in recent years. Prices on the Gulf Islands tend to be about 20 percent higher than on Vancouver Island. See the *Distances* chart for locations of other nearby fuel docks, and the *Nearby Boating Destinations* section for information on the facilities.

Applicable Recreational Boating Regulations and Certificates

This section should get you started on the basics of recreational boating regulations and certification, and provides links for more in-depth information.

The Office of Boating Safety (now operating under Transport Canada) publishes a free informative *Safe Boating Guide*, which covers the basics of safety equipment, certificate requirements, and navigation. It lists all safety equipment required for each particular type of vessel. Many marine supply, bookshops and public offices may stock these. Read it on line at **www.tc.gc.ca/MarineSafety/TP/TP511/boater.htm**, or call 1.800.267.6687 from Canada or 613.990.5490 in the U.S. Boats are subject to search by both the U.S. and Canadian Coast Guards to check for compliance with safety requirements. Differences in U.S. versus Canadian safety equipment may (or may not depending on the official) be ignored for short visits across either border. The magic number seems to be 45 consecutive days or less in Canada for U.S. boaters for this and other issues.

PLEASURE CRAFT OPERATORS CARD (PCOC)

U.S. residents do not need a PCOC for travel in Canadian waters as long as they stay less than 45 consecutive days. All Canadian boaters will be required to obtain one by September 15, 2009. It is currently required for:
* Those operating a power-driven vessel 4 metres in length or less. This applies to personal watercraft (PWC) as well as dinghies with motors, and
* Those born after 1 April 1983, operating any motor-driven vessel.

The card is awarded following the successful completion of a Canadian Coast Guard accredited test. Also note that those under age 12 must be accompanied by an adult at least 16 years old to operate a vessel with a motor greater than 10hp. For a 40hp motor, those aged 12-16 must also be accompanied by an adult. The minimum age to operate a PWC is 16 years.

The Canadian Power and Sail Squadron (CPS) Boating Course, offered by the Pender Island Squadron, convenes weekly mid-September through early February (with a long break for the holidays in December - January). It is an excellent way to learn the basics of navigation and safety, and to obtain the PCOC. You can meet fellow mariners and take the course in a structured way. Instructors are typically very thorough and enthusiastic. The Pender Island Squadron is part of the Vancouver Island South District. Their website is **www.visd.org,** which contains a link to the Pender Island Squadron's newsletter. On the VISD site, click on *Public Courses* then *Public Course Schedule* on the bottom of the page for the Pender Island course schedule and contact information. Or, call 250.383.6677. Also, look for an ad in the August and/or September Pender Post for the season's course schedule and visit their booth at the Fall Fair. The National CPS number is 1.888.CPS.BOAT and web site is **www.cps-ecp.ca.** Another option is to take the course on your own via the Internet from the CPS Open Learning Centre, **www.cps-ecp.org**. Private providers include **www.boaterexam.com** and others as listed on **www.tc.gc.ca/BoatingSafety/providers/acc.htm**, Transport Canada Office of Boating Safety's web site.

The Pender Island Squadron also teaches Pender Island Grade 8 students the Boat Pro boating safety course, an abbreviated version of the more thorough Boating Course. Students who pass the exam receive the PCOC. Other CPS courses taught on Pender Island during the winter include Fundamentals of Weather and Global Weather, VHF Radio operator's certification and the advanced courses Piloting, Advanced Piloting and Marine Maintenance.

In the U.S., visit **www.usps.org** or call 1.800.336BOAT for information on the U.S. Power Squadrons (USPS). The U.S. and Canada have reciprocal agreements for courses.

NEW RECREATIONAL BOAT LICENSING PROCEDURES
As of April 2006 pleasure boat licenses are no longer issued by the Canada Border Services Agency. Owners of recreational boats 12 metres (15 gross tonnes) or less equipped with a motor of 10 hp (7.5kW) or more are required to have a Pleasure Craft License. These are available at any Service Canada Centre, **www.servicecanada.gc.ca**, 1.800.O.Canada. An individual number is assigned to the vessel, which aids in search and rescue operations. Transport Canada can also answer questions about the licenses and boating safety in general, 1.800.267.6687.

VHF Radio - Use, Channels, Emergencies, Boater Assist

A Restricted Radiotelephone Operator's Certificate - ROC - (Maritime) is required for Canadian boaters who operate VHF radios in Canadian waters. At this time Americans do not need a similar certificate for operating in U.S. waters, but they do need one if operating in Canadian waters. CPS is the sole examiner for the certificate, and the Pender Island squadron conducts the appropriate course, holds exams, and collects the one-time fee. Also offered is a Digital Select Calling (DSC) course, which is an update of Radio Operators Certificate Maritime (ROCM).

As of April 1999, VHF radios on pleasure boats in Canada no longer require a Maritime Mobile Radio Station License, as long as the vessel is not operated in foreign waters, and if the radio operates only on frequencies allocated for maritime mobile communications or marine radionavigation. When Canadian vessels travel into U.S. waters, at present, a marine radio license is required to fully comply with international law, since a treaty between the U.S. and Canada on this issue has not yet been established. The application form is *IC-2378: Application for a Maritime Mobile Marine Radio Station License for a Voluntarily Fitted Ship*, available on the Industry Canada web site **www.strategis.ic.gc.ca** (do a Search for IC-2378).

Following are some VHF Channels applicable to pleasure craft in southern British Columbia and Washington's Puget Sound area. This information is provided as a ready-reference only. For complete descriptions, see other sources such as the most recent *Waggoner's Cruising Guide* and **http://vancouver-webpages.com/peter/marine.txt**.

VHF CHANNELS FOR PLEASURE CRAFT   *(Courtesy of Waggoner's, 2006)*

05A Vessel Traffic System for Northern Puget Sound in WA and Strait of Juan de Fuca west of Victoria in BC. Maintain a listening watch for safety.

06 Intership Safety, for safety communications, and search and rescue (SAR) liason with Coast Guard vessels and aircraft.

09 Intership and Ship to Shore. A working channel for all vessels.

11 Vessel traffic service for Victoria - from Straight of Juan de Fuca east of Victoria, Haro Strait, Boundary Pass and the Gulf Islands.

12 Vessel traffic service for Vancouver and Howe Sound.

13 Vessel bridge to bridge for large vessels in Washington. Low power only.

14 Vessel traffic system - Southern Puget Sound. Maintain listening watch.

16 International distress & calling system. ***All vessels should monitor.*** Do not transmit if a *SEELONCE MAYDAY* is declared. Do not call same station more than once every two minutes. After three attempts, wait 15 minutes. In BC waters, use to contact Coast Guard. In U.S., 09 is an option.

22A Coast Guard liaison. Safety and liaison communications with the Coast Guard. Contact them on 16 first, then they may switch you to this channel.

66A Port Operations: Most marinas in southern BC monitor this station, and Puget Sound marinas are encouraged to as well.

67 Working channel for intership, ship to shore (BC) and intership only (WA).

68,69 Working channels for intership and ship to shore for pleasure vessels.

70 Reserved for digital selective calling devices for distress and calling.

71 Vessel traffic service, Comox (East of Vancouver Island - northern Strait of Georgia to Cape Caution).

72 Working channel for intership for all vessels.

73 Working channel for intership and ship to shore for all vessels (BC).

74 Vessel traffic service for Vancouver - Fraser River and Tofino (West of Vancouver Island).

78a Washington only: Intership/ship to shore for pleasure vessels; secondary channel for marinas.

IN AN EMERGENCY

Practice what to do in case of emergency before setting out. Become familiar with your vessel and the location of all emergency equipment. Follow the procedures set out by the Canadian Coast Guard in publications such as the *Safe Boating Guide*. This section is only a memory aid and does not describe specific emergency procedures:

Using the VHS Radio for a Distress Call

Call out a *MAYDAY* if your or another vessel is threatened by grave and imminent danger and requires immediate assistance. Use VHF Channel 16 (156.8 MHZ) or 2182 kHz to call for assistance. Or, use Channel 70 for VHF DSC (digital only). Victoria Coast Guard responds to calls from the Pender Islands vicinity. If there is no response, try another working frequency. If you have a cellular telephone you can dial 911, or call 1.800.567.5111 (or *16) for Search and Rescue, which is coordinated out of Victoria. Do not use the *MAYDAY* call for non-emergency communications, as it may impede other more life-threatening situations, and you may be subject to a hefty fine.

SAMPLE *MAYDAY* CALL
Assuming your vessel's name is *VESSEL*, (substitute the actual name of your vessel), the emergency procedure is as follows:
1) Operate the radiotelephone alarm signal if you have one for 30 to 60 seconds.
2) Transmit distress signal on VHF Channel 16:
MAYDAY MAYDAY MAYDAY; This is VESSEL VESSEL VESSEL.
3) Then, transmit distress message on VHF Channel 16:
My position is _____. (GPS coordinates are very helpful)
My emergency is _____. *I need* (type of assistance)_____.
My vessel is a _____ *and is* _____ *feet/ metres long. Colour is* _____
I Have _____ (any other important information such as number of people on board), *Over.*

If any boater hears a distress message but the Coast Guard has not acknowledged it, that boater must acknowledge and relay the message to a Coast Guard Radio Station.

Use *PAN PAN* for urgency communications concerning safety of a vessel or person on board or in sight. Call on VHF Channel 16 (156.8 MHz) or 2182 kHz. This is used for information concerning the safety of a ship, such as a powerboat that has damaged a propeller and needs a tow. Transmit: *PAN PAN, PAN PAN, PAN PAN*, then proceed in the same manner as described for *MAYDAY* above.

Use *SECURITE* (pronounced Securitay) to announce a safety of navigation or meteorological hazard that can potentially impact other boaters.

SEELONCE MAYDAY indicates a Mayday is in progress. Do not transmit normal communications. *SEELONCE FEENE* allows resuming of normal communications.

Boater Assist and Towing

In an emergency always call VHF 16 or 911 first. If it is not an emergency you can call VHF 16 and ask for a transfer to a towing company. Look into towing company options at the beginning of each season, rather than waiting until you are stranded at sea. Services and phone numbers have a tendency to change over time. Following are some services active at time of writing:

NON-SUBSCRIPTION:
Classic Yacht Services 250.361.7528.

SUBSCRIPTION (join in advance, like the Auto Club):
Vessel Assist: Charges a nominal annual fee ($30 U.S. with web specials available; CPS member discounts also available) and then offers various levels of service. Call 1.800.367.8222, **www.vesselassist.com**, **www.boatus.com**. For towing, members call 1.800.391.4869.
C-Tow Marine Assistance Network: www.c-tow.ca; 604.574.9074 (office). Approximate rates are $125 for BC coverage only (+$50 per call) or $175 for coverage extending 35 nautical miles into Washington. For towing, members call 1.888.354.5554.

This is only a partial list of towing services. See the *Boaters Blue Pages* (free at marinas, or on line **www.boatersbluepages.com**), or cruising guides such as the latest *Waggoner Cruising Guide* for additional resources.

The Canadian Coast Guard Auxiliary

CCGA has a presence on the Pender Islands, as CCGA-P Unit 20 Salish Sea. With their fast-response rigid hull inflatable vessel, NU-TO-YU-II, they respond to emergency calls around the Pender Islands, Saturna, Mayne, and southeastern Galiano Islands. They now have a floating station, but are still on a fundraising drive to acquire a larger response vessel to enhance their responsiveness. They appreciate donations through the Community Spirit Board at Tru Value Foods.

TIDES, CURRENTS AND HAZARDS

Consult local charts and tables of tides and currents for comprehensive information on the waters around the Pender Islands and the Gulf Islands. Charts include Book 3313 or Charts 3441 and 3442 (1:40,000 scale) which provide the best detail, or you can use Chart 3462 which is 1:80,000 and not as detailed, but it does cover both North and South Pender Islands. Also important is the *Canadian Tide and Current Tables Volume 5* (Juan de Fuca Strait and Strait of Georgia) published annually by Canadian Hydrographic Service. Remember to add 1 hour to the times on the tide charts during daylight savings time (PDT), and be aware that Canadian reference points use different datum than United States reference points. Fulford Harbour is the closest monitoring point to the Pender Islands. For hour-by-hour information on currents, consult the

Current Atlas - Juan de Fuca Strait to Strait of Georgia, also published by the Canadian Hydrographic Service. It consists of a main book that can be used every year by making the appropriate calculations. Or you can use *Murray's Tables* or *Washburnes Tables* published annually to simplify the process. This information is especially valuable to kayakers. Local newspapers such as the *Island Tides* and *Times Colonist* also contain local tide information (already adjusted to PDT as needed).

On the web, local high and low tide information is available from the Canadian Hydrographic Service, Fisheries and Oceans Canada: **www.waterlevels.gc.ca**.
Click on the Gulf Islands region on the map. Hope Bay is the monitoring point for the Pender Islands. Information on predicting currents is not available at time of writing. Washington waters are covered in **www.saltwatertides.com**. For a comprehensive summary of tide and current web sites, see **http://scilib.ucsd.edu/sio/tide**.

Regionally, tides rise from the Strait of Juan de Fuca to the Strait of Georgia. Therefore, high/low water will usually occur in the Strait of Juan de Fuca several hours prior to the high/low water in the Strait of Georgia. Four tides occur within each 24-hour period, and due to a diurnal inequality, the two high tides will vary in height, as will the two low tides. Kayakers and beachcombers should note that many of the beaches around the Pender Islands are submerged during the higher tides.

Check the *Current Atlas* described previously for current directions around the Pender Islands. Very generally, flood current flows clockwise around North Pender Island, while ebb current is counter-clockwise. An exception is the area from around Wallace Point at the south tip of North Pender to Blunden Islet off the south tip of South Pender Island, where flood current is west to east. Current velocity tends to be greater in this area as well. Expect turbulence around the points of South Pender, especially near Blunden Islet. Flood current around the north and east shores of South Pender Island is generally counter-clockwise, and ebb current clockwise. Through Bedwell Harbour and the Pender Canal, flood current is to the north, and ebb current to the south, at about 3 to 4 knots through the canal. The currents tend to be strongest around the bridge pilings. The flood east through Navy Channel meets the flood from Plumper Sound off Hope Bay, causing tide rips. Rough waters from the confluence of the currents can occur anywhere along Navy Channel or Plumper Sound.

In addition to checking the appropriate charts for local hazards, it is helpful to speak to locals regarding trouble spots. For example, make careful note of a submerged rock next to and about halfway down the outside of the Thieves Bay Marina breakwater, and rocks extending from the peninsula at the entrance to Shingle Bay and Port Browning (Razor Point). Rocks can extend outward near the surface from many points of land, so give these a wide berth. Floating logs create a hazard, especially to fast-moving boats. Logs and debris tend to be more abundant in the water after storms and higher high tides. You may see a long line of logs and debris in a zone of tidal interface, but loner logs can be found anywhere. A deadhead, or a log that is mostly submerged, creates the greatest hazard as it is not readily visible. Boaters, especially on fast-moving vessels, should always have someone on watch for logs in these waters. Also, give a wide berth to crab traps or anything having to do with fishing operations, as lines can sometimes extend sideways and nets may be in place. If you see a tug or tow vessel, make sure to check for a barge being towed behind it! And, check your charts for submerged cables before anchoring. Listen for signals from other vessels, especially the urgent 5 short blasts which means either that a signal was not understood, or that another vessel is in danger if they do not change course (most typically sounded by BC Ferries vessels in these waters). Remember that the water in the vicinity of the Pender Islands is COLD (surface temperature is about 10°-12°C/50°-55°F), and is not survivable for very long. For information on other hazards not covered in this section, consult the various resources available, and take the Pender Island Power & Sail Squadron boating course to obtain valuable local knowledge. Being knowledgeable about the hazards to avoid will keep you safer and make your boating experience more pleasurable.

WEATHER FORECASTS

Tune your VHF radio to 21B for West Coast Canadian Coast Guard broadcasts. Forecasts are also available in both English and French on WX Channels 2 (from Salt Spring Island), 4 (from Port Angeles) and 8 (which is the same as 21B, from Mayne Island).

Meteorological Services Canada's (MSC) weather reports by telephone now includes a separate forecast for the Southern Gulf Islands (Saturna Island station), as well as southeastern Vancouver Island and the lower mainland. Marine forecasts are also available. 250.363.6717, 604.664.9010. By radio: 162.4 and 162.55 MHz

On line forecasts can be found at:

www.weatheroffice.ec.gc.ca: Maintained by the MSC, includes weather alerts, marine and aviation forecasts, radar and satellite imagery. Click on British Columbia, then select the new reporting station for Gulf Islands (Southern).

www.theweathernetwork.com: Local weather as monitored from Victoria Airport (Select *Ganges*).

www.weather.com: U.S. Weather site. Enter *Friday Harbor* for nearby San Juan Island weather, which is drier, though fairly representative for the Pender Islands. Check for satellite photos of the area.

www.weatherunderground.com has interesting data including surface water temperature in their marine forecast. Saturna Island is the nearest forecast location.

See the *Natural Environment* chapter (17) for information on the climate of the region.

WATCHING ORCAS AND OTHER MARINE MAMMALS

The Pender Islands are within the area known as the Salish Sea where the southern resident pods of orcas reside during the summer, portions of the spring and fall, and more rarely in winter. See the *Whale Watching Guide* in the *Natural Environment* chapter for further information on these magnificent mammals. Whale watching trips have become immensely popular, and trips leave from Sidney, Oak Bay, and Victoria Inner Harbour. From the Pender Islands, vendors occasionally have offered whale watching excursions. At time of writing, **Sound Passage Adventures** offers Eco Tours but not specific whale watching tours. If you are a visitor with limited

Never approach the orcas or block their path, but if they approach your boat, shut off the engines and enjoy their splendor.

time here and seeing orcas is a priority, you may want to take one of the high-speed whale watching tours, since seeing the orcas from land is hit or miss. The whale watching operators radio each other to discuss sightings, and many travel at high speeds to get to the sighting location. Ask in advance if they have been seeing orcas, and where they have been going to see them. Unfortunately, the proliferation of these loud tour boats may be disturbing to the endangered orcas.

Orcas can appear anywhere around the outer waters of the Pender Islands during May through October, but the most common sightings are of one or several resident pods of orcas traveling from the southeast point of North or South Pender Island, heading northwest along the cliffs at Pender Bluffs, past Thieves Bay Marina, then out toward the centre of Swanson Channel as they make their way through Active Pass. They seldom make the trip in the opposite direction, although sometimes they may turn around at mid-island and head back. They will rarely appear more than once a day or night along the shores of the Pender Islands. Occasionally they will come in closer in the Shingle Bay, Otter Bay, and Grimmer Bay areas. They may be spotted once a day for a week straight, or they may not be sighted for weeks at a time. On rare occasions the orcas have been seen near the Pender Islands in the off-season as well. Resident pods predominantly eat salmon, while transient orcas, which also inhabit these waters, prey on mammals such as seals, dolphins and whales.

Harbour seals can be seen fishing all around the islands, or on several haul out spots on offshore rocks. Dolphins and Dall's Porpoises (which resemble mini-orcas) are sometimes seen offshore, especially at Gowlland Point/Brooks Point. The Pacific white-sided dolphin is the most common dolphin species in British Columbia waters.

Private boaters can also experience the thrill of being amongst the orcas and other sea mammals, as long as special precautions are taken to avoid disturbing or injuring them. The following guidelines have been established for watching marine wildlife. These precautions will not only help prevent damage to these sensitive species, but they will keep you out of trouble as well, as violating these guidelines is illegal and subject to stiff fines. Patrol boats from the RCMP and various orca watchdog organizations are becoming more common. Kayakers and other non-motorized vessels must also follow these rules to avoid disturbing the wildlife.

GUIDELINES FOR WATCHING MARINE MAMMALS AND BIRDS

Cetaceans (Whales, Dolphins and Porpoises, Including Orcas)

Approach areas of known or suspected marine mammal activity with extreme caution. Look in all directions before planning your approach or departure.

Reduce speed to less than 5 knots when within 400 metres/yards of the nearest animal. Avoid making any abrupt changes in speed or course.

Maintain at least 100 metres/yards from the nearest animal.

Always approach and depart animals from the side, moving in a direction parallel to the direction of the animals. Avoid approaching from the front or behind.

Stay on the offshore side of the animals when traveling close to shore. Remain at least 200 metres/yards offshore at all times.

Never position your vessel within the 400- metre/yard area in the path of the animals. Keep the path of the animals clear.

If your vessel is unexpectedly within 100 metres/yards, stop immediately and allow the animals to pass.

Seals, Sea Lions, and Birds , When Animals Are On Land

Maintain at least 100 metres/yards distance from any marine animals or birds.

Slow down and reduce your wake/wash and noise levels.

Pay attention and back away at the first sign of disturbance or agitation. Be cautious and quiet when around haul-outs and bird colonies, especially during breeding, nesting and pupping seasons (generally May through September).

GREEN BOATING

Although currents move the waters around the Gulf Islands and eventually flush pollutants out to sea, it is a slow process. Pollution can linger in certain areas for periods of years, and runoff from urban areas adds to the stress placed on the marine environment. There have already been unusual algal blooms, declining fish populations, and shellfish contamination in the regional waters. Although recreational boaters contribute a small proportion of the pollution in the Strait of Georgia region, it can become concentrated in sensitive foreshore areas and confined bays. Therefore, boaters need to take appropriate measures to minimize their impact to the fragile marine environment. The primary issues involve trying to keep oils and chemicals from getting into the water, and how to dispose of sewage. It has been estimated, for example, that boaters at Montague Marine Park generate more sewage in the summer than the residents of Galiano Island. Boaters there are required to dump in mid Trincomali Channel at a minimum, but are urged to visit a pump out station instead.

The Georgia Strait Alliance, a local conservation group, has developed guidelines in an attempt to mitigate pollution in the local waters.

GREEN BOATING GUIDELINES

Do not pump out sewage at a dock, at anchorages, or near sensitive areas such as shellfish beds. Official no-discharge zones in the vicinity of the Gulf Islands are at Montague Harbour and Victoria Harbour. The United States has more extensive no-discharge areas, including all of Puget Sound.

Install a holding tank or portable toilet. Use shoreside facilities whenever possible. Avoid chemical additives or bleach in your holding tank; instead, use enzyme or bioactive treatments. Read instruction labels carefully. Do not flush any chemicals, detergents, paints, kitchen wastes, or any other foreign objects down your marine head.

Use pump out services whenever possible. The nearest pump out facilities to the Pender Islands are at Ganges Harbour, and in the Sidney area at Van Isle Marina, Port Sidney Marina, and Tsehum Harbour. Roche Harbor and Friday Harbor on San Juan Island also have pump outs.

For further information on Green Boating and other local environmental issues, consult the Georgia Strait website at **www.georgiastrait.org**. Links at that web site can also connect you with other local environmental organizations that deal with the local waters.

Marinas and Government Docks

For boaters visiting the Pender Islands and desiring a slip, one's options are Otter Bay, Port Browning and Poets Cove Marinas. Relatives and guests of Magic Lake Estates residents may be able to arrange for a temporary slip at Thieves Bay Marina. Reservations are recommended at the marinas in summer. All Canadian marinas that monitor VHF radios use Channel 66A. Government docks (no power available) are located at Port Washington, Hope Bay, and Port Browning, although availability is typically very limited. Several good anchorages are located around the islands as well.

For Pender Islands residents, options for year-round boat moorage are as follows:
Magic Lake Estates residents can utilize Thieves Bay Marina, although there may be a long waiting list. Otter Bay Marina offers year-round moorage only if the entire year is paid in advance. Otherwise, it is off-season only. Poets Cove Resort offers monthly moorage in the off-season only. Port Browning Marina has offered year-round moorage,

but on a case-by-case basis due to winter weather patterns. The Government docks at Port Washington, Hope Bay, and Port Browning have very limited capacity for monthly moorage. Some homes have fairly protected docks or mooring buoys, but most are exposed to weather from one direction or another. Dry-docking in winter is available in the Swartz Bay/Sidney area at Canoe Cove Marina and Westport Marina.

Wharfinger contact information for government docks is current as of December 2005. Check the Harbour Talk column in the latest Pender Post for the most recent information. The Southern Gulf Islands Ports Manager is Al Canon, 539.3036.

North Pender Island

OTTER BAY MARINA
48°48'N 123°18'W
Map 1A, 22. Phone: 629.3579
Fax: 629.3589
2311 MacKinnon Road,
Pender Island, BC V0N 2M1
Monitors VHF Channel 66A.
Keep clear and to starboard of green spar U57.
A 10-minute walk (south) from the ferry terminal.

This popular marina is known for being well run and friendly, a regular gathering place for Vancouver boaters. It is set in picturesque Hyashi Cove and features a view deck lined with the Provincial flags. Facilities include slips with 15 or 30-ampere power, and a long outer dock for 70 to 80 foot boats. 2006 rates were not available at time of writing. 2005 rates were $0.99/ft (temporarily reduced due to construction on the premises) plus $3.50 (15 amp) or $5.50 (30 amp) for power. Winter rates are discounted. Monthly-rate moorage has been available November through March. In order to get annual moorage, boaters were required to pay for the entire year in advance. Water is available, but conservation is necessary. Day moorage may be available if the marina is not full ($5 for 4 hours or $10 including shuttle to the golf course. Call first).
A good anchorage is located near the marina (see *Anchorages* section), and a $5 fee (in and out) is charged to dinghy to their facilities. Their boat launch ramp costs $5 (in and out) with a capacity for trailerable boats 26 feet or less.

Ashore facilities include washrooms, showers (fee, open to the public), laundromat, two heated pools (fee for visitors, free for marina guests), a convenience mart/gift shop, a coffee bar, and a barbeque area with large lawn that is popular for Pender Island groups to rent. Bike rentals cost $12 per hour (reduced rates for extended periods). Scooters rent for $25 per hour or $85 for 4 hours (age 19+ with license). Kayak rentals/tours are available from **Kayak Pender Island** (see *Kayaking* section). **Currents** is a new quarter-share ownership condominium cottage complex being built around the marina with the units rentable by the general public from July 2006; 629.2150.

PORT BROWNING MARINA
48°46'N 123°16'W
Map 5B, 40. Phone: 629.3493 Fax: 629.3495. Attn: Kerry.
P.O. Box 126, North Pender Island, BC V0N 2M0
Hamilton Road, off of Bedwell Harbour Road, just south of Driftwood Centre.
www.portbrowning.com, Email: portbrowning@cablelan.net.
Boaters are instructed to enter close to the breakwater.
A CANPASS *permit-only* Canada Customs reporting station is located here.

This Pender Island tradition has offered moorage for boaters for some 40 years, and recently has been an alternative to the nearby higher-end Poets Cove Marina. The facility has 80 berths with 15-ampere service and drinking water available upon request. Transient and annual moorage is available here. Summer (May 20 - September 5) rates are $1.00/foot/day plus $4.00/day for power (plus GST). Off-season rates are $10/day flat rate plus $4/day for shore power. Annual moorage is handled on a case-by-case basis depending on individual boats and how they can be situated to help avoid exposure to winter weather. In general, boats are limited to 35 feet for annual moorage and sailboats are discouraged from winter moorage here. Annual moorage rates are $4/foot/month, plus $35/month for power. *At time of writing the resort is for sale.*

Accommodations on site include a few basic guest rooms and a lawn for dry camping. Facilities include a pub, a café, a licensed liquor store, a Laundromat, showers (coin operated, open to general public), swimming pool, tennis courts an Internet station (fee) and wi-fi hotspot. The Driftwood Centre (The Pender Islands' shopping complex) is a 10-minute walk from the marina. Anchorage is also available outside of the marina near pebbly Hamilton Beach. A public gravel boat launch ramp is located at the end of Hamilton Road. Fishermen sometimes sell their catch on the marina's docks.

Operating at the marina is **Sound Passage Adventures**, which has three vessels available for eco-tours, excursions to neighbouring islands, diving trips and fishing charters. It also operates a dive shop with equipment rentals and air for tanks, holds courses in power and sailing, and operates a water taxi to Sidney and Poets Cove Resort.
www.soundpassageadventures.com, 629.3920.

PORT BROWNING GOVERNMENT DOCK
Map 5B, 38. Located at the head of Port Browning, it can be accessed by land from a small parking area off of Razor Point Road. The dock has 89 feet of space and priority is given to commercial fishing vessels. A boat maintenance grid is available here. For specific information regarding availability of moorage, rates, and use of the grid, contact the wharfinger, Peter Binner, at 629.9990.

THIEVES BAY MARINA
48°46'N 123°19'W

Map 4A, 51. Permanent moorage in this private volunteer-maintained marina is available to Magic Lake Estates Property Owners Association (MLPOS) members only. The marina is located on Anchor Way: From the entrance to Magic Lake Estates, follow Schooner Way to the left, make the first right on Privateers Road, and follow it without turning (the road changes names back to Schooner Way and Anchor Way) until the road ends at the marina. Annual moorage fees are a fraction of what most public marinas charge, although a recent property tax assessment will increase the fees somewhat. The slips have no electrical or water service, and staying on-board overnight is strictly prohibited. Much of the marina is shallow with hazards at low tide that are made known only by word of mouth. A boat maintenance grid with water and elec-

tricity is available for members in the shallow end of the marina. The larger deepwater slips are reserved mostly for sailboats, and the Pender Island Yacht Club is very active all year. The maximum allowed boat length is 40 feet, and the slips for boats over 20 feet typically have a longer waiting list. Upon purchasing a property with a permanent dwelling at Magic Lake Estates, members can join the MLPOS, and put their name on the waiting list. Residents that actually already own their boats are given priority.

MLPOS members may call 629-3686 for further information about the marina and the current status of the waiting list. Occasionally temporary moorage may be available for MLPOS members on the waiting list, but at rates much higher than the regular rate. Slips for visiting relatives or guests of MLPOS members may also be available. The MLPOS member must call the marina to determine availability and to work out the payment. A boat launch ramp next to Thieves Bay Park (**51**) for smaller trailered boats is available to all (no fee), but it is only viable at higher tides because of mud. Four wheel drive is a plus. An outhouse, pay phone and picnic tables are located at the park.

Note that effective April 2006 there is a 72-hour limit for parking boats or boat trailers in the Thieves Bay Park parking lot. Violators may be towed.

HOPE BAY GOVERNMENT DOCK
48°48'N 123°16'W

Map 1C (7). The historic Hope Bay dock is located at the northeast corner of North Pender Island at the east end of Port Washington Road and the north end of Bedwell Harbour Road. The dock was originally constructed in 1901 and was refurbished in 2003. Limited permanent and transient moorage is available. Contact the wharfinger, Peter Binner at 629.9990 for information about availability of dock space and moorage rates. Fishermen sometimes sell their catch from this dock, usually on weekends. The adjacent Hope Bay Store, which burned in 1998, has been re-developed, and this dock provides limited boater's access to the facility, which includes the **Hope Bay Café**. Two mooring buoys are available for Hope Bay Store patrons.

PORT WASHINGTON GOVERNMENT DOCK
48°49'N 123°19'W

Map 1B, (3) Constructed in 1891, the public wharf at Port Washington is located at the northwest corner of North Pender Island at the west end of Port Washington Road near the north end of Otter Bay Road. It is also used as a floatplane port and water taxi stop. Limited space is available here for temporary or permanent moorage. Contact the wharfinger Rod MacLean at 629.6111 for information about availability of dock space and moorage rates. The former Port Washington Store building, vacant at time of writing, may reopen in the future as part of a historic trust.

South Pender Island

POETS COVE MARINA AT BEDWELL HARBOUR
48°45'N 123°14'W
Map 8, (92) Phone: 629.2111, 1.866.888.2683, Fax 629.2110
9801 Spalding Road, RR3, South Pender Island, BC V0N 2M3.
Located at the intersection of Spalding Road and Gowlland Point Road.
www.poetscove.com/marina; Email: marina@poetscove.com
VHF: Monitors 66A; Office hours 8:00 am to 6:00 pm (8:00 pm in July and August).

The Poets Cove Resort and Marina is located on the north side of Bedwell Harbour just southeast of Beaumont Marine Park. Although you cannot walk to Beaumont Marine Park from the marina, you can dinghy there, or take a guided tour from the resort.

Facilities include 110 deep-water slips with 15 or 30 ampere and water service to accommodate boats up to 100 feet long, available for transient moorage. Rates (2006) are $1/foot March 1 - April 30; $1.25/foot May 1 - June 29; $1.40/foot June 30 - September 4; $1.25/foot September 5 - 30; and $0.80/foot October 1 - February 28, 2007. Holiday rates are $1.45/foot and require two-night minimum stay: May 19-21; June 30-July 4; August 4-6; September 2-4, 2006.

Shore power is also charged at $4-$8/night depending on the vessel length. Includes access to pool and hot tub. The floating dock (no utilities) is $1.00/foot per night. Long-term moorage is only available in the off-season only, the cost depending upon length of stay. Winter boat maintenance packages are available as well.

Day Moorage is available on a *first come first served* basis and may not be available during the summer. A $10 fee is collected upon check-in and returned upon presentation of a receipt from the restaurants or spa. Otherwise, they allow day moorage at the outer float (Photo, above), which requires a tender to come ashore, or they can pick you up. An unmanned Canada Customs port of entry is open during the summer, which becomes a CANPASS permit-only site in the winter (see the Customs section). The only fuel dock (gas and diesel) on Pender Island is located here, open year-round. Facilities include a heated view pool and spa ($5 fee /free for overnight guests), a Laundromat, showers, *Moorings Market* that sells various necessities, deli items, ice cream scoops, baked goods and cappuccino. A barbeque is also sometimes fired up for summer lunches.

Kayak Pender Island offers kayak rental, instruction and tours from this location, but their shop is at Otter Bay Marina; **www.kayakpenderisland.com**, 629.6939. Also, Poets Cove Resort has an Activities Department offering kayak, canoe, powerboat, sailing dinghy and bicycle rentals and many *soft adventure* excursions.

Poets Cove Resort has high-end accommodations, two restaurants, and a full-service spa available. See the *Accommodations, Dining*, and *Health Services* Guides.

The former Bedwell Harbour public wharf (fisheries dock) was transformed into a Customs Dock at this location in the mid-1990's. Therefore, there is no longer a public government dock here. The official policy is that boaters can tie up to the dock only while checking into Canada Customs, which can be overflowing in summer.

ANCHORAGES

Much of the Pender Islands are exposed to winds, currents and ferry wakes, but there are several locations that provide desirable anchorages as described below. Depths are reduced to lowest normal tide (zero tide).

This section provides descriptive data only and should not be used for navigation. See the appropriate charts for navigation aids. Thanks to Anne & Laurence Yeadon-Jones, authors of the *Dreamspeaker Cruising Guide* series for permission to use their anchorage depth and substrate data. Their Gulf Islands cruising guide was updated in 2005.

Bedwell Harbour Area

BEAUMONT MARINE PARK
48°45'N 123°14'W

Map 7. The premier destination for mooring and anchoring around the Pender Islands is Beaumont Marine Park, now part of Gulf Islands National Park Reserve - South Pender. The 58-hectare park is located along the scenic north shore of Bedwell Harbour on South Pender Island. The park is centered around an isthmus with idyllic twin shell beaches on either side that makes for a

great place to dinghy ashore (watch for rocks and a reef along the way). Fifteen mooring buoys are available to the east of Skull Islet (the small rocky islet with a navigation aid on it). Note that the single *prime* buoy to the west of the isthmus is now reserved for emergency vessels only. A $10 overnight fee is charged for use of the buoys from May 14 to October 15; no charge the rest of the year. If the buoys are full, as is very common in summer, you can anchor in 6-10 m of water near the buoys in stiff mud with good holding. Be aware that this area is occasionally subject to strong southeasterlies.

A staircase leads up from the beach directly in front of the mooring buoy area. A 1.5 km scenic waterfront trail continues along the bluffs to the west to the isthmus and to the western park boundary. It then connects to a trail to the summit of 244 metre Mt. Norman and a spectacular Gulf Islands vista. See the *Coastal Access and Hiking Guide* for information on Trail **82**.

A primitive campground contains 11 campsites. Campsites 1 and 2 are situated at the east end of the park atop the beach stairs, while the remainder are in the vicinity of the isthmus. Both areas have pit toilets. The water well was shut down by GINPR in

2006. The camping fee is $5/person, free in the off-season. Two information boards contain payment boxes. No campfires are allowed in the park year-round. Once moored at the park, you can dinghy into nearby Poets Cove Resort (**92**) to use their pool or showers (fee charged) and their high-end restaurant or lounge. You can also proceed through the Pender Canal to the Port Browning Marina and pub (**40**), but be very careful of 3 - 4 knot currents and boat traffic through the narrow canal.

MEDICINE BEACH
48°46'N 123°16'W
Map 5A, 42. At the head of Bedwell Harbour, Medicine Beach is a peaceful Pender Island Conservancy area, featuring a shell beach and a saltwater marsh that gets its name from First Nations peoples who used native plants for medicinal purposes. Anchor off the beach in mud and gravel at depths of 4 to 6 metres. Stairs lead to a viewing platform atop the bluff. Walk to Magic Lake Market in 5 minutes.

PETER COVE
48°44'N 123°14'W
Map 4D. Located at the southern tip of North Pender Island, this pretty anchorage is dominated by Trincomali neighbourhood residents who moor their boats here. Additional temporary anchorage may be available for smaller vessels. Check your charts and GPS carefully for a large reef at the cove's entrance.

The Canal Area and Port Browning

THE PENDER CANAL
48°46'N 123°15'W
Map 6. A man-made canal connects Bedwell Harbour to Shark Cove and Port Browning. The centre of the canal has a minimum depth of 2.2 m (7.2 feet). Vertical clearance of the bridge is 8.2 m (27 ft) and 12.2 m (40 feet) between piers. A large tide can create tidal streams of 3 to 4 knots through the canal, so slack tide is preferred. Flood tide is to the north. Boats sometimes announce their approach to the canal on VHF Channel 16, but the local RCMP

states that this is not necessary. Navigate the canal carefully using GPS or other means to avoid hazards. *Important note:* The banks of the canal are being eroded away, causing trees to fall into the canal and historic First Nation sites to be washed away. Obey the 5-knot speed limit through the canal, which is patrolled by the RCMP.

SHARK COVE
48°46'N 123°15'W
Map 6. Shark Cove lies between the bridge and Mortimer Spit. Limited room for small boats is available in this well protected cove. Anchor in mud at 4 metres depth to the west of the main channel, but away from the private floats.

PORT BROWNING
48°46'N 123°16'W
Map 5B. Anchor in mud at 6 - 8 metres off of Hamilton Beach to the southwest, or off of the public wharf on the eastern side. This anchorage is exposed to the southeast. You can dinghy to Port Browning Marina and Resort (**40**), Mortimer Spit (**79**), or through the Pender Canal to Medicine Beach (**42**), Beaumont Marine Park (**82**) or Poets Cove Resort (**92**). You can walk up Hamilton Road from the boat launch ramp or resort, make a right on Bedwell Harbour Road, and reach the Driftwood Centre in about 10 minutes for provisions. A summer shuttle may be available back from the grocery with $25 purchase.

Swanson Channel

HYASHI COVE/OTTER BAY
48°48'N 123°18'W
Map 1A: If Otter Bay Marina (**22**) is full, there is anchorage available to the east of the marina, off of a small beach, where bottom mud is about 4 to 6 m depth. Exposure is to the southwest. Otter Bay Marina charges a nominal fee to dinghy to their facilities.

Boat Launching Sites

The following ocean access sites are available to the general public for launching of boats. See each corresponding number in the *Coastal Access and Hiking Guide* for more detailed descriptions of and directions to the public beach accesses. No fees are being collected for launching at time of writing, except at Otter Bay. Small trailered boats can be launched from Otter Bay Marina (fee), Hamilton Beach, and Thieves Bay Park. Note that the tides can impact the accessibility of most of the launching sites. At low tides, the substrate can be very muddy and slippery. At high tides, beaches may disappear.

North Pender Island, Clockwise from Otter Bay Marina

OTTER BAY MARINA
Map 1A, 22. Off McKinnon Road just east of the BC ferry terminal. This is the closest place to launch a small boat if you have hand-carried it onto the ferry. It requires a very hilly 10-15 minute walk. Launch kayaks or other small boats for a fee of $5 in and out. Kayak rentals and tours available through **Kayak Pender Island**. Also, a boat launch ramp is available for trailered boats up to 26 feet in length for $5 (in and out).

From here kayakers can access Hyashi Cove/Otter Bay and points north and south along Swanson Channel including Roe Islet and the shoreline of GINPR to the south.

MACKINNON ROAD

Map 1A, 23. Turn left from the ferry terminal; in about 1 km, the beach access signpost is next to *Waterlea* near the end of the road. Hand-carry your small craft (kayak, inflatable, etc.) down the stairs to the beach to launch for points north or south along Swanson Channel. This is not the easiest of accesses.

PORT WASHINGTON GOVERNMENT DOCK

Map 1B, 3. At the west end of Port Washington Road: Launch your hand-carried boat off the dock to explore the western shoreline of North Pender Island. At time of writing you can drive onto the wharf. Check signs for current policy. Avoid the floatplane (west) finger.

BRIDGES ROAD

Map 1B, 4. Turn right from the west end of Port Washington Road. Hand-carry your small craft down the short stairs to the beach. From here, access points south on Swanson Channel including Grimmer Bay, and points north around the north side of North Pender Island, as well as Mayne Island and Navy Channel. This is also the closest launch spot to Prevost Island, about 1.3 nautical miles to the west.

HOPE BAY GOVERNMENT DOCK

Map 1C, 7. At the east end of Port Washington Road and north end of Bedwell Harbour Road. Launch your hand-carried boat off the dock to explore the northeast shoreline of North Pender Island along Plumper Sound and Navy Channel. Highlights include Welcome Bay, Bricky Bay and Clam Bay. This is a possible launch spot for Mayne or Saturna Islands. Watch for tide rips here.

PORT BROWNING GOVERNMENT DOCK

Map 5B, 38. Off Razor Point Road. Carry your small boat down this long dock to launch into Port Browning. Hamilton Beach (**39**) is a better bet.

HAMILTON BEACH

Map 5B, 39. At the end of Hamilton Road past the Port Browning Resort turnoff: A gravel boat launch ramp is at the end of the road for smaller trailered boats or hand-carried vessels to access Port Browning. From here you can also explore the Pender Canal area and Bedwell Harbour. Parking is available along the road. Port Browning Pub may be available for an after-paddle libation.

MEDICINE BEACH

Map 5A, 42. Past the east end of Schooner Way, near Magic Lake Market: A parking lot is adjacent to the beach. Hand-carry a small boat across the beach to access Bedwell Harbour, Beaumont Marine Park and the Pender Canal area. Can be exceptionally muddy and slippery at low tide. The adjacent marsh is an ecologically sensitive zone.

PETER COVE

Map 4D. At the southeast tip of the island: The best access is down a wide, gradual trail on the left near the end of Plumper Way, where you can hand-carry or wheel your small craft (**73**). Other accesses are found along Trincoma Place, down stairs at the end of the street (**72**), or at Starvation Bay behind the concrete barrier (**71**). Explore the Wallace Point area at the tip of North Pender Island, as well as the Bedwell Harbour area. Watch for strong currents, coastal eddies, and prevailing southerlies at the tip of North and South Pender Islands.

THIEVES BAY PARK

Map 4A, 51. At the end of Privateers Road and Anchor Way: Launch your small, trailered boat or kayak from the drive-up launching ramp next to the park. The muddy bottom here makes it necessary to wait until higher tides to launch a trailered boat. Traction is sometimes a problem when the ramp is slippery. Orcas may pass close to the breakwater at the entrance to this marina, so if you see a crowd gathered at the breakwater or whale watching vessels hovering nearby, proceed with caution and do not exit the marina if the orcas are passing. More interesting kayaking is to the north (see the accesses below). To the south is the Boat Nook area and the Pender Bluffs (Oaks Bluff) fishing ground, although there is no good place to come ashore between Boat Nook and the southeast tip of North Pender Island. Thieves Bay is the closest launch point for Portland Island (Princess Margaret Marine Park, GINPR) about 3.7 nautical miles to the southwest, and Ruckle Provincial Park on Salt Spring Island (about 2.1 NM to the west). Kayakers bound for Portland Island should minimize time in open water and ferry lanes. It is best to paddle toward Boat Nook (**52**) and Oaks Bluff then make your way across via Reynard Point, Moresby Island. Park in the gravel parking lot of Thieves Bay Park, and not on the narrow marina access road past the marina sign. *Note: Effective April 2006 there is a 72-hour limit for parking boats or boat trailers in the Thieves Bay Park parking lot. Violators may be towed.*

PANDA BAY

Map 4A, 50. At the end of Harpoon Drive off of Galleon Way near Shingle Bay: Hand-carry a small craft down the stairs to the beach. Access Shingle Bay and the coastline of GINPR to the north and Mouat Point to the south. Shingle Bay is an easier launch spot, except at low tide when it becomes muddy.

SHINGLE BAY PARK

Map 4A, 49. At the end of Galleon Way: Hand-carry a small craft from the park down the stairs to the muddy beach, best at high tide. This is a sensitive intertidal zone that shoals to mud at low tide. Access the coastline of the GINPR to the north and Mouat Point to the south.

IRENE BAY
Map 3, 23. At the end of Irene Bay Road, from South Otter Bay Road: Hand-carry your small craft down the short stairs to the beach and a nice launch spot. Access the interesting areas of Ella Bay, Roe Islet and Otter Bay to the north, and the shoreline of the GINPR to the south.

South Pender Island, Clockwise from the Bridge

MORTIMER SPIT
Map 6, 79. Make a left turn just past the bridge to South Pender Island to access this popular launch spot that you can drive to. Hand-carried boats can be launched from here. The parking area becomes very muddy after rainy periods and can be submerged at high tides during storms. Overnight parking is not permitted. Access Port Browning Resort, the bridge/canal area, Poets Cove Resort and Beaumont Marine Park, and Saturna Beach on Saturna Island, about 2.3 nautical miles east across Plumper Sound (check the tide tables and weather conditions carefully before attempting travel through the Pender Canal or across Plumper Sound).

GOWLLAND POINT
Map 9, 96. End of Gowlland Point Road: Hand-carry small craft from the nearby parking area down a short flight of stairs to the beach. To the north are Camp Bay, Teece Point, and Blunden Islet (part of GINPR and a good example of an undisturbed Gulf Island ecosystem - access prohibited). Idyllic at slack tide, but currents can be treacherous at other times, probably the most notorious on the Pender Islands.

CRADDOCK ROAD/TILLY POINT
Map 9, 94. Hand-carry small craft down the short, wide stairs to the beach. Explore the entrance to Bedwell Harbour and the Gowlland Point area. Very strong currents are common here.

POETS COVE RESORT
Map 8, 92. Launch your hand-carried boat from the area of the customs dock. It is a long walk from the limited parking lot, though, and a difficult carry, especially for a double kayak. Sailboat, powerboat, and kayak rentals/tours are available at the marina.

Kayaking

Kayaking the waters around the Pender Islands can be a peaceful and satisfying way to tour its scenic coves and bays. Interesting landscapes, wildlife and the relative protection of the inland sea make kayaking an increasingly popular activity in the region. If you have your own kayak, see the *Boat Launch* section for options of where to set in and areas that can be accessed from each location. Make sure to carry all of the required safety equipment and navigational aids, and be knowledgeable of tides, currents, wind patterns and the weather forecast before planning your route and setting out (See the *Tides Currents and Hazards* section). If you are not familiar with the area, it is always best to tour with a local guide. Kayakers should also be proficient in self and assisted rescues. Be aware that the waters surrounding the Pender Islands are very cold (surface temperature is about 10°-12°C/50°-55°F), and hypothermia can set in relatively quickly. While nothing is certain with the weather, the calmest periods appear to be in the late summer through the early fall if you paddle in the early morning or late afternoon. Kayakers are required to follow the same wildlife-watching rules as other boats, especially with regards to orcas. Kayakers can also be very disruptive to hauled-out seals and sea lions. See the *Watching Orcas and Other Sea Mammals* section, in this chapter.

Rentals, Tours and Lessons

Kayak Pender Island (**KPI**) is located at the Otter Bay Marina, a ten-minute walk from the ferry. They also keep boats at Poets Cove Marina on South Pender Island along Bedwell Harbour. This venerable outfit abounds in local knowledge, and offers kayak rentals, lessons and tours. Tours last for 2 or 3 hours or all day. Renters must have completed instruction from a recognized organization and have knowledge of rescues, navigation, tides and currents. No solo rentals are allowed. However, lessons and beginners' tours are available. Contact **KPI** for information and reservations (recommended) at 1.877.683.1746 (toll-free), 629.6939. Accepts Visa and Mastercard. **www.kayakpenderisland.com**. Also, **Poets Cove Marina** rents sit-on type kayaks.

North Pender Paddling - Swanson Channel

The most popular paddling area of North Pender Island is the 3.5 nautical miles (NM) of Swanson Channel along the west coast between Stanley Point to the north and Mouat Point to the south. If you spend a summer's day paddling this shoreline, you may get to experience the thrill of paddling in the proximity of a pod of orcas, the ultimate kayaking experience. Orcas are commonly seen here during the late spring through early fall, though not every day or at any specific time. Give them a wide berth. You are not allowed to disturb them by law, and you wouldn't want one of these huge creatures bumping into your kayak! Even if the orcas do not appear during your paddle, you will most certainly see playful  harbour seals splashing about as they fish, and Bald Eagles keeping watch from their seaside perches, or even swooping into the ocean to catch fish. As you paddle along Swanson Channel, be prepared for frequent ferry, powerboat and freighter wakes that can be made even trickier by winds and currents. Remember that even on peaceful summer afternoons, winds can whip up suddenly. This is a day trip area only, since no camping is available along this portion of the Pender shoreline. Otter Bay Marina is chosen as the starting point since that is where rentals are available to experienced kayakers, and tours available from **KPI**. A fee is charged to launch your own boat from the marina. See the *Marinas* section for further information.

SOUTH FROM OTTER BAY MARINA

See **Map 1A, 22**. Kayakers typically head south across Otter Bay, around Roe Islet (**Map 3, 25**), across Ella Bay with Roesland, home of the new Pender Island Museum, along its shore. Just to the south is Irene Bay (**26**), a popular launch spot. The rocky, wooded coastline beyond is partly National Park land, and partly private. After reaching a point with exposed rocks that are popular with seals to haul out (do not disturb them), you enter Shingle Bay. The bay narrows beyond the remains of a pier, the site

of a fish reduction plant. From 1926 through 1959 unmarketable fish species were barged over from Fraser River Canneries, and fish oil was extracted here to produce fertilizer. At the head of Shingle Bay, which dries to mud flats at low tide, is Shingle Bay Park (**Maps 4, 4A, 49**), where you will find picnic tables and an outhouse (planned for 2006). A GINPR trailhead starts to the left of the park at the end of Galleon Way and leads to scenic Roe Lake after a 20-25 minute climb (**Map 3A, 36-37**). From Shingle Bay, continue paddling south, past Panda Bay (a public beach access, **50**) toward Mouat Point, where a long-established eagle nest houses a very prolific pair of the large birds (about 1.8 NM from Otter Bay). Beyond Mouat Point, prevailing southerlies may make the going more difficult, but on a calm day, Boat Nook can be an enjoyable destination. Along the way, as you head east around Mouat Point, you will see a break-water, with boats behind it. This is Thieves Bay Marina, a private facility for residents, and behind it is the public Thieves Bay Park (**Map 4A, 51**), where you can easily land (though it is very muddy at low tide) and utilize the picnic tables, lawn, outhouse and pay phone, but no camping is allowed (2.4 NM). Conditions-permitting, continue your paddle around the breakwater and navigational aid, then eastward to Boat Nook (**52**), a public beach access (no facilities, 3.1 NM). Note the concrete remains of a pier, as this was once a small marina and a former contender for the island's ferry landing. Beddis Rock, seaward of Boat Nook is popular as a seal haul-out. Beyond Boat Nook are the foreboding conglomerate cliffs of Oak Bluffs/Pender Bluffs where there is no place to land until the tip of the island, about 3.2 NM from Boat Nook. This stretch with its deep waters is very popular for salmon fishing by humans and orcas alike. Orcas some-times swim close to shore from here, past the Thieves Bay breakwater, and along the southern end of Mouat Point before heading into mid-channel.

NORTH FROM OTTER BAY MARINA

As you paddle west then north from Hyashi Cove in Otter Bay you will encounter a very scenic shoreline. First, be mindful of ferries arriving and departing Otter Bay Terminal. Then, watch for eagles in the tall trees, harbour seals fishing and the possible pod of orcas. The rocky passage encountered as you turn north toward James Point can be navigated at higher tides.

Beyond is a rocky beach, the MacKinnon Road ocean access (**Map 1A, 23**). **Beauty Rest B&B** occupies James Point, beyond which is Grimmer Bay, with Boat Islet in its centre. On the north side of the bay is the Port Washington Government Dock (watch for float planes landing) and the historic General Store, which may re-open in the future as part of a historic trust (**Map 1B, 3**). Two public beach accesses, Grimmer Bay (**2**) and Percival Cove (**1**), are located at the east end of the bay. As you continue northwest past the pier, you will reach the Bridges Road ocean access (**4**) which allows extensive exploration at lower tides. Stanley Point is just beyond, about 2 NM from your starting point. Past Stanley Point is Navy Channel (with Mayne Island beyond) and the North Pender shoreline of Clam Bay (3.2 NM) and the Hope Bay Dock and Store featuring the **Hope Bay Café** (4.8 NM) (**Map 1C, 7**).

North Pender Lake Paddling

For peaceful, fresh-water kayaking, Magic Lake awaits. Launch either at the intersection of Schooner Way and Privateers Road near the entrance to Magic Lake Estates, or at the swimming hole park down Pirates Road (**Map 4, 48**). The two B&B's on the lake, **Betty's B&B** and **Cedar Cottage B&B** also have docks from which their guests can launch kayaks.

Bedwell Harbour and Port Browning

The interior waterways of the Pender Islands are very popular for paddling. The area is more protected than the outer shores and is less subject to the wakes of large passing vessels. However, winds can whip through here, large yachts do go by occassionally, and the water can become fairly rough at times. You will likely see seals and eagles in this area, and perhaps even river otters, but you are much less likely to see orcas than in the surrounding waterways.

BEDWELL HARBOUR LOOP

Mortimer Spit is a good launching spot for this paddle (**Map 6, 79**). You can drive right up to the beach, and there is even a pit toilet on the premises, but no overnight parking is allowed. The cove south of the spit dries to a mudflat at low tide, so most kayakers launch from the west or north. Paddle south through Shark Cove. Note the shell beach straight ahead on the right just before the bridge. This pleasant public beach is the beginning of GINPR lands along the west side of the canal that is a cultural preservation site due to eons of First Nations use mostly as a summer encampment (**Map 6, 41**). Therefore, tread lightly if you go ashore in the canal area. The canal was dug in 1902, and the wooden bridge you see before you was built in 1955. Use extreme caution passing under the bridge and through the canal, which is best done at slack tide. Currents can run 3 to 4 knots through here, and it is a popular short cut for power-boats. The GINPR land on the west (right) side of the canal continues to the sharp bend in the waterway. The east side of the canal is lined with two public parks (Bridge Trail **77** and Fawn Creek Park **78**) and private property. As you round Ainslie Point and paddle on, private homes are replaced by the beautiful shoreline of Beaumont Marine Park, part of the GINPR (**Map 7**). In about 1.2 NM is a popular isthmus with idyllic twin shell beaches. A boat-in campground with picnic tables and pit toilets are located ashore. The water well was shut down in 2006. Some of the best hiking on the Pender Islands is located in this area (See Trail **82**). Beyond the isthmus, watch for rock hazards (consult your charts). A navigation aid is situated on Skull Islet, beyond which is the boat mooring and anchoring area for the marine park. The entrance to **Poets Cove Resort and Marina** is reached at about 1.9 NM (**Map 8, 92**). The dinghy dock is closest to the cliffs on the left. The resort has a pool, spa and showers for a fee, as well as a small store and two restaurants, one of which, **Syrens**, is suitable for a drop-in lunch and libation. The point of land just south of the resort is Hay Point, part of Tsawout First Nations Preserve (2.1 NM). You can continue along this interesting shoreline all the way to Tilley Point (another 1.2 NM), however conditions may roughen in this more exposed area. For a shorter loop in calmer waters, either return the way you came, or cut across Bedwell Harbour to the point of land directly west on North Pender Island (2.4 NM). Continue to the northwest along the shore of North Pender Island until reaching the long, crescent-shaped beach of the Medicine Beach Preserve (3.9 NM). This is a beautiful area to explore, with cliffside trails and a salt marsh (**Map 5A, 42**). You can walk up the access road for about 5 minutes to reach **Magic Lake Market** grocery. Paddle back under the bridge and to your starting point at Mortimer Spit for a total paddle of about 4.7 NM. To avoid the canal you can also launch at Medicine Beach (difficult at low tide), or do a guided tour from **Poets Cove Resort.** To extend your trip, you can paddle from Mortimer Spit northwest to **Port Browning Resort** and visit their pub (about 0.8 NM each way). Camping may also be available here (fee), and the long, pebbly Hamilton Beach (**Map 5B, 39**) is a popular spot. Driftwood Centre, the main shopping centre of the Pender Islands, is a 10-minute walk from there.

ROUND SOUTH PENDER

One of the most beautiful paddles is the 9.5 NM circuit around South Pender Island, however, this is more of an advanced route because of the strong currents and coastal eddies that can be encountered at the tip of South Pender Island, as well as possibly turbulent conditions along Plumper Sound. A local guide would be especially helpful for this paddle. The rewards are many as you tour the coastline of Beaumont Marine Park, the Tilley Point area (a popular diving spot), Brooks Point and Gowlland Point, Camp Bay, and pristine Blunden Islet of the National Park (access prohibited). The eastern shoreline of South Pender Island is also unique and beautiful.

Paddling to Nearby Islands

SATURNA ISLAND
The popular **Saturna Vineyards** are located beyond Croker Point, about 2.3 NM from Mortimer Spit across Plumper Sound. See *Nearby Boating Destinations* for details. The crossing of Plumper Sound can at times be precarious if the winds whistle up from the southeast, which can even occur on a sunny summer afternoon. Currents can be fairly tricky through here as well. One of the classic Gulf Islands kayak routes includes a circuit from Lyall Harbour (the ferry landing at Saturna Island), southwest through Port Browning, the Pender Canal, Bedwell Harbour and around South Pender Island. Less experienced paddlers tend to retrace the route through the Pender Canal rather than risk the rough waters around the tip of South Pender and Blunden Islet. Note that the southeast tip of Saturna Island, East Point, is also known for very treacherous currents.

TO OTHER ISLANDS
Experienced Pender kayakers also paddle to other nearby islands. Remember to use all proper precautions when crossing any channel from the Pender Islands, where you are likely to encounter fast-moving ferries, other shipping and recreational boat traffic, as well as potentially rough waters at any time. See the *Boat Launch* section and the *Nearby Boating Destinations* section for additional information.

> **DISTANCES TO NEARBY ISLANDS FROM NORTH PENDER ISLAND**
> **Prevost Island:** About 1.3 nautical miles (NM) from Bridges Road launch to Richardson Bay GINPR land. Watch for ferries zipping out of Active Pass.
> **Portland Island:** About 3.7 NM from Thieves Bay launch to Portland Island GINPR. Best via Oaks Bluff to Reynard Point, Morseby Island to reduce time in open water and ferry lane. Note that Moresby Island is private.
> **Salt Spring Island:** About 2.1 NM from Thieves Bay Park launch to the closest point, Beaver Point at Ruckle Provincial Park, then 2 NM south to Russell Island Park for hiking and beachcombing but no camping.
> **Mayne Island:** About 1.7 NM from Bridges Road launch to Dinner Bay beach.

Overnight Accommodations and Kayaking Resources
For camping information, see the *Accommodations Guide*. Shorefront camping is available at Beaumont Marine Park on South Pender Island. Another camping option is Prior Centennial Park, but that involves portage of your gear along roadways almost 1 km from Medicine Beach. The advantage of this campground is that it is in walking distance to *civilization* including an adjacent dinner restaurant (**Memories** at the **Inn on Pender**) and nearby stores for provisions. If you want to be in the midst of *civilization*, the **Port Browning Resort** offers camping on a large, busy waterfront lawn and orchard. A few of the campsites are prime, waterfront sites. You can also find an

accommodation that is on the waterfront. See the *Accommodations Guide* for information on lodgings. Some options on North Pender Island are **Port Browning Resort, Oceanside Inn** near Bricky Bay, and **Beauty Rest B&B** and **Arcadia-By-the-Sea** north of Otter Bay. On South Pender Island is the upscale **Poets Cove Resort**. Some of these accommodations may not have boat launching available on site, but may require a short portage of your kayak to a nearby ocean access point. Your best may be to rent one of the many waterfront homes or cottages that have ocean accesses. See the *Accommodations Guide* for agencies that handle these.

Web: **www.paddling.net, www.easykayaker.com, www.wavelengthmagazine.com**. Magazine: *Wavelength* is also available for free in many sporting goods stores. Guidebook: None concentrate on the Pender Islands, but a recent book of local interest is: *Sea Kayak the Gulf Islands* by Mary Ann Snowden (2004).

Fishing

Fishing is an extremely popular pastime for Pender Islanders and visitors alike, as they toil to catch what is left over after commercial fishermen scour the area for the diminishing bounty. Salmon are abundant at certain times of the year, and varieties vary by season. Halibut, rock cod, crab and prawns can be found year round as well. Local waters also yield oysters, mussels and clams that may be harvested at certain times of the year, but check with Fisheries and Oceans first. The premier fishing ground near the Pender Islands is the deep water off of Swanson Channel at the Pender Bluffs/Oaks Bluff area of North Pender Island, but other areas may be lucrative depending on the time of year and type of fish sought after. Nearby, Active Pass funnels salmon through a small area, but it is tricky and potentially dangerous because of strong currents and boat traffic. East Point off Saturna Island is popular, but be mindful of strong currents.

The five main salmon species are managed by Fisheries and Oceans Canada. See the website **http://www-comm.pac.dfo-mpo.gc.ca/english/recreation** for the most current information on fish identification, catch limits, open seasons and closures. Click on *Where Can I Fish, Tidal Waters*. Use the barbless hook and line method for salmon. For open and closed fishing areas, call the 24-hour hotline 1.866.431.FISH.

BC SALMON TYPES WITH BEST FISHING TIMES IN TIDAL WATERS
Open seasons listed below are current as of April 2006 and are subject to change.
Chinook: Black gums and a silver, spotted tail. Largest, most prized game fish. Smaller Chinooks referred to as Springs in BC. Best in Summer. Open all year.
Coho: White gums, black tongues, few spots on upper body. Conservation of species underway due to over-fishing. Hatchery Coho open June - September.
Sockeye: Few teeth, many long gillrakers, prominent glassy eyes, slimmest salmon.
Pink: Smallest salmon has tiny scales, tail heavily marked with large oval spots and no silver. In southern BC waters mostly in odd numbered years. All year.
Chum: Similar to but larger than sockeye. White tip on anal fin. Dog-like teeth. Best in August through October. Open all year.

Fishing Charters

Sound Passage Adventures Inc., located at Port Browning Resort, North Pender Island, picks up at most docks on the Pender Islands, the Southern Gulf Islands and Sidney; **www.soundpassageadventures.com**, 629.3920, 1.877.629.3930. They operate a 26-foot Striper for full and half day fishing charters with an experienced local area guide. They will set crab and prawn traps. Fishing locations depend on where the best fishing is for the species preference. A marine head is available and refreshments are provided.

Razor Point Boat Charters: Mike Burdett is a commercial fisherman and 35-year resident of Pender Island with a bounty of local knowledge. His 22-foot Wellcraft seats four. Hourly rate with a 2-hour minimum; 629.9922, 250.881.5648 (Cell).

Occasionally, other fishing charters may advertise on the community bulletin boards or in the Pender Post. Plenty of charter outfits are based on Vancouver Island, where boats leave from Oak Bay Marina, Victoria Inner Harbour, and Sidney.

Supplies and Licenses

Fishing supplies can be purchased on the Pender Islands at the **Driftwood Auto Centre** store, **Pender Island Home Building Centre**, **Otter Bay Marina** and **Poets Cove Marina**. If you cannot find what you need on the Pender Islands, you can boat to Ganges for the well-stocked **Mouat's Trading Company**, or to **Port Sidney Marina** where several marine supply stores are within walking distance of the marina. See Chapter 6 - *Shopping Guide, Marine Supplies.*

Fishing licenses are sold (cash only) at the **Driftwood Auto Centre** and at **Poets Cove Marina**. On line, try **www.pac.dfo-mpo.gc.ca/recfish** to purchase a license. You will need a connected printer, switched on and loaded with letter-size paper and a valid credit card number for fee payment. Also check that website for a list of vendors that sell fishing licenses. For information call 604.666.0566.

The 2006 licensing requirements and rates for British Columbia tidal waters are:

Adults Aged 16-64: Annual: $22.47 for BC Resident or $108.07 non-BC resident; Five-day: $17.12 (BC), $33.17 (non-BC); Three-day: $11.77 (BC), $20.33 (non-BC); One-day: $5.62 (BC), $7.49 (non-BC) **Juniors under age 16:** Annual Pass is free.

Senior BC Residents: Annual pass is $11.77 (No discount for non-resident seniors).

Salmon conservation stamp: $6.42 annual. Required to retain any species of salmon.

PSP WARNING

Summer is the period most conducive to PSP (paralytic shellfish poisoning) resulting from toxins sometimes found in shellfish, such as clams, mussels, scallops and oysters, and in the liver of crustaceans such as crabs and lobsters. Signs are typically posted or announcements made in the media if an area is closed to harvesting. However, people have been known to contact PSP in open harvesting areas as well. Call 604.666.2828 to find out the current closures in BC, or 1.800.562.5632 in Washington. If your lips become numb or tingly 5 to 30 minutes after eating shellfish, you should immediately seek medical assistance, as the poison can paralyze the respiratory system. See websites such as **www.inspection.gc.ca/english/fssa/concen/cause/pspe.shtml** for information.

Scuba Diving

The nutrient-rich waters of the Gulf Islands contain a vibrant and diverse marine community, making it a premier diving destination. The Southern Gulf Islands offer many unique attractions, such as anemone-encrusted walls, reefs and diver-friendly wrecks. The Pender Islands and surrounding waters boast some of the most amazing dive opportunities, sought after by divers from around the world. Common sea life encountered on dives includes giant Pacific octopus, ling cod, sculpins, sea lions, harbour seals and wolf-eels. The best visibility is typically in the winter months.

On South Pender Island, endless years of erosion have carved out spectacular caves and swim-throughs. Tilley Point caves is one of the highlights, a dive for intermediate to experts. This location can be reached by dive charter (recommended) or from the Craddock Road ocean access. It is best to do this dive at slack tide due to strong currents here, and to weight yourself. The caves are decorated with countless plumose anemones, each competing for the best spot to catch the plankton rich current. When divers turn to look towards the surface the anemones seem to glow on the cave walls.

Drift diving along the walls around the Pender Islands is the best way to see the local wildlife. These wall dives offer incredible drop offs, some dropping straight down to 244 m (800 ft). After establishing neutral buoyancy a diver can drift along the wall passing through schools of shimmering bait fish, while ling cod dart in and out for a snack.

The Pender Islands' dive shop, **Sound Passage Adventures**, is the closest shop to the wrecks of the G.B. Church and the HMCS Mackenzie. The G.B. Church is the first wreck sunk by The Artificial Reef Society of British Columbia. Sunk in 1991 off the southwest shore of Portland Island in 15 fathoms of water, the Church is completely covered by marine life. Trained wreck divers can explore the hallways deep inside the HMCS Mackenzie. At 2,880 tonnes and 111 m (366 ft) long, this former destroyer escort was designed for anti-submarine warfare.

Sound Passage Adventures' dive shop is located at Port Browning Resort on North Pender Island. They operate two 28-foot dive vessels operated by certified skippers. For dive charters, lessons, rentals, information and custom dive packages contact them at 629.3920 or 1.877. 629.3930 (toll free); **www.soundpassageadventures.com**.

If you are not familiar with the local area it is best to dive with a dive charter with local expertise, since they should be aware of local highlights and hazards. Diving fatalities are not uncommon in this region.

Web Resources:
www.ucbc.ca Underwater Council of British Columbia.
www.dive.bc.ca Numerous resources for BC divers.
www.artificialreef.bc.ca Artificial Reef Society of British Columbia.
www.vancouverisland.com/recreation/?id=161 Summary of area diving spots.

Boat Rentals and Sales

RENTALS
Kayak Pender Island rents kayaks to qualified persons from their Otter Bay Marina shop. They also keep boats at Poets Cove Marina (see the *Kayaking* section).
Poets Cove Marina rents 10-foot Walker Bay and 24-foot sailboats (qualifications required), sit-on kayaks (certification not required), paddle boats, and power boats (Boston Whaler and Sea Ray). See the *Marinas* section.

KAYAK SALES
Mouat Point Kayaks (629.6767) sells high-end fiberglass and Kevlar sea kayaks.
Kayak Pender Island sells used kayaks at the end of each season.
Check local bulletin board postings for boats for sale.

YACHT SALES
For a summary of power and sailboats available throughout Canada and the U.S., try **www.yachtworld.com**. Larger stores that sell dinghies and small boats include **West Marine** in Sidney and Victoria, and **Sherwood Marine** in Central Saanich (See the *Shopping Guide - Marine Supplies*). Greg and Rom at **Custom Yacht Sales** at Cedar Grove Marina near the Swartz Bay ferry terminal are very helpful; 250.656.8771.

Nearby Boating Destinations

A plethora of desirable boating destinations are located less than an hour away from the Pender Islands by powerboat; somewhat longer by other boat types. This section presents a sampling of favourite outings of Pender residents and visitors. The region is one of the top cruising areas in the world, and features fabulous destinations further away (not described here) such as Desolation Sound and the Princess Louisa Inlet. Victoria Inner Harbour is another popular destination, which requires a 30 NM journey including a stretch through the sometimes rough Strait of Juan de Fuca to the Harbour entrance. If you venture here, become well aware of traffic pattern requirements since it is also a marine airport, and is patrolled constantly. Vancouver is about 45 NM away. Consult cruising guides that describe these areas in more detail. See the *Map Atlas* for the general locations of the destinations described in this section.

This section is a narrative description of the destinations only, and should not be used for navigation. Information was obtained from personal experience, as well as from the *Dreamspeaker Guide*, *Wagonner* Cruising Guide, the *Boater's Blue Pages Marina Guide* (a free publication of *Pacific Yachting Magazine*), and numerous web sites.

Southern Gulf Islands

The nearby Southern Gulf Islands are each about 30 minutes away by powerboat. Of these destinations, Portland, Prevost, Mayne, Saturna and Salt Spring Islands are also popular with experienced Pender kayakers.

SALT SPRING ISLAND
The largest of the Southern Gulf Islands in both size and population, Salt Spring Island is a popular destination of Pender Island boaters. For comprehensive information on the island, consult **www.saltspringisland.org**.

Ganges (48°51'N, 123°28'W) is a picturesque waterfront village, whose night time lights are visible from the west side of North Pender Island, and Canada Day fireworks can be seen from off shore. Ganges features a bounty of waterfront restaurants, as well as gift shops, **Thrifty** grocery, large **Mouat's Trading Company** store, liquor store, health food store, coffee bars, bookshops, jewelers, and art galleries. Note that the BC Ferry that runs from Otter Bay to Long Harbour on Salt Spring Island docks several kilometres from Ganges. Distances to Ganges are about 8.5 NM from Thieves Bay or Otter Bay and 14 NM from Poets Cove.

The popular Ganges Village Market features crafts, produce, and food on summer Saturdays in Centennial Park, **www.saltspringmarket.com**. Art festivals also are held in Ganges in the summer months. Dock space may be in short supply on summer weekends, especially on Saturdays.

Two marinas service Ganges, both of which monitor VHF 66A:
Ganges Marina is directly adjacent to the downtown area, and has a fuel dock (gas and diesel),**www.gangesmarina.com**. Call 250.537.5242 for reservations for overnight moorage, or to get their opinion on whether non-reservable day moorage will be available. The other marina is **Salt Spring Marina**, requiring a longer walk to town; 250.537.5810. They reserve overnight and possibly day moorage as well. The marinas can be booked solid on summer weekends. For a weekend day excursion, your best bet is a non-holiday Sunday after cast-off time (typically noon). A large government wharf located adjacent to the main village is available for transient moorage, free for up to four hours during the day until 1600 hours. Check posted signs for the current policy. The wharf is typically full most days in the summer, but in the off-season you have a good chance of getting a spot, especially in a smaller vessel. It also has a dinghy dock in case you have to anchor and dinghy in. Floatplanes use the outer finger of this dock. Be careful to avoid their take off and landing area. The other government wharf, around Grace Islet and the breakwater, is typically full with commercial vessels. Anchorage in Ganges Harbour is also available, east of the marinas and *Money Makers Rock*. The substrate is good-holding mud, but conditions can be blustery and choppy in the harbour. A quieter anchorage is in *Madrona Bay* to the east.

Fulford Harbour (48°45'N, 123°26'W) is much smaller scale than Ganges, but does offer a cute village next to the ferry terminal with a coffee shop and small grocery store. BC Ferries' Skeena Queen sails back and forth to Swartz Bay from the ferry terminal all day. The government wharf east of the ferry terminal is usually full with commercial vessels, while the wharf south of the terminal is for short term loading only. **Fulford Marina** is about a 10-minute walk to the village, and also has a fuel dock open seasonally at Roemer's Landing; **www.saltspring.com/fulfordmarina**. For availability of overnight or day moorage call 250.653.4467. **Fulford Inn**, a pub, is a 10-minute walk west from the marina. The harbour is 6.5 NM from Thieves Bay, 10 NM from Poets Cove.

When on Salt Spring Island, taxi or shuttle services may be available. Call in advance to make sure. One service is Ganges Faerie Mini Shuttle, which operates every day except Wednesday; **www.gangesfaerie.com,** 250.537.6758. Pager: 538-9007.

SATURNA ISLAND

Saturna Island is the least populated of the Southern Gulf Islands serviced by BC Ferries, with about 300 inhabitants. Saturna lies to the east across Plumper Sound from the Pender Islands, and is reached most readily from Port Browning. Consult **www.saturnaisland.com** for information on the island.

Saturna Vineyards (48°46'N, 123°12'W) is one of the most popular boating destinations from Pender. The winery has a wine tasting room with a bistro; 1.877.918.3388, 539.5139, **www.saturnavineyards.com**. Access to the vineyard by private boat is from Saturna Beach, located directly across from Port Browning. On a calm day during slack tide, this also makes for a nice 1-hour kayak trip from Mortimer Spit (about 2.3 NM each way, not recommended for novices). At time of writing, vineyard visitors are allowed to use the Saturna Strata dock (the one furthest north) for 2 hours at a time, but there is only room for two to four boats depending on size. If no room is available at the docks, you can anchor in sand or attach to one of four mooring buoys provided, and dinghy to the dock. A public dock is also available, for smaller vessels, adjacent to Thomson Park, although at least half of it dries at low tide. The dock behind the small breakwater to the southwest is private. Thompson Park has a swing and a pit toilet where a set of horseshoes is stored. The winery is about a 15-20 minute walk up a gradual hill. The

Penderites enjoy an excursion to the Saturna Vineyards bistro.

walk is very scenic, especially as you pass the vineyards, and then reach the bistro, which overlooks the vineyards down to Plumper Sound, with the San Juan Islands in the distance. The backdrop is towering Mount Warburton Pike, where you can watch eagles soar above. Call the vineyards the day before your trip to verify the operating hours of the winery and the bistro, which closes earlier. The bistro is occasionally closed for private affairs. Typical open hours for the wine shop and bistro are 11:30 am to 4:30 pm (3:30 pm for the bistro) daily May through September and October weekends. Their fun Harvest Celebration is in September (the 16th in 2006). The vineyard property is for sale at time of writing.

Lyall Harbour (48°48'N, 123°12'W) is the BC Ferries landing for Saturna Island. A government dock is available for limited day or overnight moorage. A fuel dock is also located here with gasoline and diesel. Facilities at Lyall Harbour include a general store (check there if no one is at the fuel dock; 539.2936) and the waterfront Saturna Pub which also serves meals. If you have children with you, you can still be served if you sit outside on the picnic tables, where there is a nice view to the northwest.

Winter Cove Marine Park is accessible between Saturna and Samuel Islands. 48°49'N, 123°12'W. This is a popular anchorage, but it is tricky due to shallow depths in places. Canada Day Lamb Barbeque is held here; **www.saturnalambbarbeque.com**.

Tumbo Island and Cabbage Island (48°48'N, 123°04'W) are beautiful and popular marine parks in the Strait of Georgia off the northeast corner of Saturna Island, and now part of the GINPR. Significant intact Gulf Islands habitat such as wetlands and stands of Garry oak, arbutus and Douglas fir remain on the islands. Cabbage Island is an important nesting site for Black Oystercatchers and Bald Eagles. Primitive camping is allowed on Cabbage Island (fee $5/person). Pit toilets are available, but no water. Tumbo Island is day-use only. Trails around both islands lead to beautiful vistas. Respect remaining private property on Tumbo Island. Mooring buoys are available for $10/night in Reef Harbour, charged after 6:00 pm. Do not use the private dock off of Tumbo Island. Tides, currents, reefs, and northwest exposure make this a tricky area to navigate. Consult the Parks Canada website **www.pc.gc.ca/gulf** for additional further information. Charts: 3442, 18432 (U.S).

MAYNE ISLAND

Mayne Island, located just across Navy Channel to the north of North Pender Island, holds several points of interest for Pender Island boaters. See **www.mayneisland.com** or **www.mayneislandchamber.ca** for information on the island. The BC Ferries terminal is at Village Bay.

Miners Bay (48°51'N, 123°18'W) The hub of Mayne Island, a CRD dock with transient moorage and a marine fuel station with gasoline and diesel is located here. From the dock you can mosey over to the **Springwater Lodge** for waterfront pub fare for breakfast, lunch and dinner (**www.springwaterlodge.com**, 539.5521). Miners Bay is inside of Active Pass, so beware of rough waters from the swift and tricky currents and frequent ferries that traverse the narrow channel. Docking or fueling at the CRD dock can be an interesting endeavour.

Bennett Bay, (48°51'N, 123°15'W) near the southeast corner of Mayne Island, is accessible through scenic Georgeson Passage (east of Lizard Island) between the private Curlew and Samuel Islands. Currents tend to swirl through this narrow passage to the Georgia Strait. The **Mayne Inn** is a good place for a casual family style meal, with views to the east across the Strait of Georgia toward Mt. Baker. A dock is available for a few Mayne Inn patrons, or anchor off the beach and dinghy in. Call 539.3122 for information on open hours, their new expansion project, and condition of the dock; **www.mayneinn.com**.

Dinner Bay (48°50'N, 123°20'W) is at the southwest corner of Mayne Island, directly north of Stanley Point on North Pender, about 3 NM from Otter Bay. Although mostly occupied by private mooring buoys and exposed to ferry wash and the fetch of the Trincomali Channel, it can also be a pleasant place to anchor. At the head of the bay is a beach with stairs leading up to Dinner Bay Community Park, home of the Japanese Gardens, a tribute to the displaced local Japanese people during World War II. A community putting green is also located here. Across Dinner Bay Road from the Japanese Gardens is the splendid **Oceanwood Country Inn and Restaurant,** where you can come for a gourmet fixed 4-course dinner

for around $50; **www.oceanwood.com**. The restaurant owns one mooring buoy that you can reserve along with your dinner or overnight reservation; 539.5074. The buoy is around Dinner Bay Point from Dinner Bay, down Navy Channel in a cove in front of the Inn. The large building with flags and a white buoy in front are obvious. Since there is no dock, you will have to beach your dinghy, which can be tricky depending on the tides and whether a drift log blocks your route. Beaching your small speedboat here is a bad idea. You can also ferry to Village Bay and walk a hilly 2 km to the Inn.

GALIANO ISLAND

The long, narrow and hilly Galiano Island has its own golf course, several restaurants and interesting bluff top parks. See **www.galianoisland.com** for information on the island. The main boating destination is Montague Harbour, where Montague Harbour Marine Park is situated (48°53'N, 123°24'W), on the west side of the island, about 8 NM from Otter Bay and 14 NM from Poets Cove. See Chart 3442 or larger scale 3473. This is a no-discharge zone for sewage, but gray water (shower, dishes, etc.) is OK.

Montague Harbour is home of the friendly **Montague Harbour Marina**, which has facilities for day or overnight moorage, and contains a fuel dock (gas and diesel), and CANPASS-only customs clearance. The facility is open May 1 to September 30, and has 15 and 30 amp service. Water is not potable and is in short supply, so bring your own; **www.montagueharbour.com**. Call for availability, 539.5733. Radio in on VHF 66A upon arrival

for slip assignment. To save the mooring fee, many more people anchor out in the harbour, and all the way over to the marine park, then dinghy in to the public dock. The marina store has a gift shop, some grocery necessities, and moped rentals. Car rentals may also be available. The **Harbour Grill** at the marina serves good food for breakfast (about $10), lunch (sandwiches and interesting salads in the $10+ range) and dinner (seafood, steaks, etc. $15 - $25). A free bus takes patrons to the **Hummingbird Pub** on summer evenings, with an additional stop at the marine park, 539.5472. The **Go-Galiano** shuttle and taxi service (539.0202, **www.gogaliano.com**) runs between various services and points of interest from 9 am to 9 pm including the **Galiano Golf & Country Club** (about $22 per party in 3-person cab roundtrip), 1.877.909.7888. One can walk between the marina and Montague Marine Park on a level, pleasant road, in about 15 minutes. For upscale dining, **La Berengerie** country French restaurant is in a woodsy location with summer outdoor patio about 10 minutes walk from the marina, open Thursdays through Sundays, 539.5392. **Galiano Inn** at Sturdies Bay is home to delicious but pricy **Atrevida** Restaurant, whose curved picture windows overlook the ferry terminal, the entrance to Active Pass, and Mount Baker towering over the Strait of Georgia. A new wine shop offers a unique selection of BC wines. If they agree to pick you up in their van you'll save $25 taxi fare; **www.galianoinn.com, 539.3388.**

Montague Harbour Marine Provincial Park is situated on Gray Peninsula, which is very scenic (as long as you screen out the towering power lines that cross it). Mooring buoys are found to the east of the peninsula ($10 fee charged after 6:00 pm).

A substantial dock is available for dinghies and boats under 11 metres (36 feet). Overnight stays are allowed at the dock, charged at $2 per metre after 6:00 pm. Anchorage is also available there, and along the western side of the peninsula. Trails lead from the dock around the park shoreline, which is dotted with beautiful shell beaches. A primitive campground, also accessible by vehicle, is located here. This park is extremely popular, so expect crowds in the summer  months, and reserve your campsite if staying ashore at: **www.discovercamping.ca**. BC Parks' website is: **www.env.gov.bc.ca/parks/**.

PREVOST ISLAND
The mostly privately-owned Prevost Island is situated between Pender and Salt Spring Islands. Numerous pleasant and protected anchorages make Prevost a popular destination to anchor (Chart 3442).

Along the south side of the island is the popular and fairly well-protected Glenthorne Passage (48°49'N, 123°23'W), located at the southwest corner of the island, surrounded by private property. Ellen and Diver Bays, further to the east, are also picturesque.

Richardson Bay is located at the island's southeast corner, marked by a scenic lighthouse. This small anchorage is fairly exposed to ferry wash, but is a pleasant place to anchor and dinghy ashore to the beach to the east, which is now part of GINPR. A small area of GINPR lands surrounds the Portlock Point light station. No facilities are located here.

Along the west side of Prevost Island is Annette Inlet furthest to the south, which is well protected but shallow. The next inlet northward is Selby Cove, which is also fairly protected. Furthest to the north is James Bay (48°51'N, 123°24'W), which is more exposed (to the northwest) than the other two inlets. The northwest portion of Prevost Island bordering James Bay is part of the GINPR, and the land is accessible to the public. The parkland also extends to the middle portion of Selby Cove. After anchoring in James Bay, you can dinghy ashore to an old orchard at the south head of the bay, accessible from the smaller of two beaches. A pit toilet is situated down a short path. A trail leads from here, around the other beach to the north, then above the cliffs along the northeast shore of James Bay out to Peile Point for a panoramic view to the north up Trincomali Channel.

PRINCESS MARGARET MARINE PARK (PORTLAND ISLAND) GINPR
Portland Island is uninhabited and lies about 3.5 nautical miles southwest of Thieves Bay, North Pender Island. The entire island is Princess Margaret Marine Park, now incorporated into the GINPR. The island has a history of First Nations inhabitation as evidenced by shell middens. Hawaiians settled it in the 1880's who left a legacy of fruit trees, roses and garden plants. It was given to Princess Margaret as a gift in 1958 upon her visit to the area. She donated it to British Columbia for parkland in 1967. Several anchorages can be found around the island, though most are exposed to winds and ferry wash. The main anchorage is along the southwestern side at Princess Bay, also known as Tortoise Bay, which is exposed to the south (4 NM direct from Thieves Bay, 7 NM from Poets Cove, 48°43'N, 123°22'W). A dinghy dock is available here. Stern tie rings are installed along the west shore. Other anchorages include Royal Cove along the north shore next to Chad Island, the area between Brackman Island and Portland Island along the south shore, and a cove north of the Pellow Islets on the eastern shore. Hiking trails circumvent the island, and are accessible from all of the anchorages. The main trailhead is at Tortoise Bay. Hiking is relatively level and easy, with scenic beaches for picnicking and beautiful vistas along the way. This is a popular day trip for groups of Pender boaters. Facilities at the park include primitive campsites at several locations ($5/person fee), pit toilets, and picnic tables. Note that access is prohibited on nearby Brackman Island (to the southwest), also part of the GINPR. Brackman Island contains some old growth forest and a mostly undisturbed natural habitat. See also the Parks Canada website **www.pc.gc.ca/gulf**. Consult Charts 3441 and 3476.

SIDNEY ISLAND - SIDNEY SPIT/GINPR
The northern third of Sidney Island, formerly Sidney Spit Provincial Park, has been incorporated into the GINPR (48°39'N, 123°20'W). Located off Vancouver Island from Sidney, Sidney Island is accessible by private boat or by a 15-minute passenger ferry from Sidney, May through October, that costs about $11 round trip ($9 senior/$8 age 2-12). Call **Alpine Ferry** at 250.474.5145. This service ensures that you will have plenty

of company on warm summer days. The park is known for the longest stretches of sandy beach in the region with water a bit warmer than other beaches in the area. Long, scenic walks along the beach, sunbathing, and wildlife watching in the tidal flats are the main activities here. The island contains the largest Great Blue Heron colony in the southern Gulf Islands, and is a popular stopover for migratory shorebirds in the

spring and fall. Some 35 mooring buoys are available on the western side of the spit, and a $10 fee is charged after 6:00 pm. Anchorage is best off of Paradise Beach. The lagoon beyond the beach is a wildlife reserve, but non-motorized craft are allowed. A substantial public dock is available at the west side of the island next to the main picnic area, open in summer only (8.4 NM from Thieves Bay). Docking during the day is free, and overnight stays are allowed at the dock for $2 per metre boat length, charged after 6:00 pm. The park has picnic tables, primitive camping ($14/party or $7/senior party), pit toilets, and drinking water (warning: high sodium content). From the dock area, a loop trail leads around the forested uplands that you can complete in less than an hour. Displays explain why some of the animals imported to the island by early settlers are different than on other Gulf Islands. Chart: 3441.
See: **www.pc.gc.ca/gulf**.

WALLACE ISLAND MARINE PARK

Wallace Island is located adjacent to the northern tip of Salt Spring Island, west of Galiano Island in the Trincomali Channel. It is about 15 NM from Thieves Bay or Otter Bay Marinas, at 48°56'N, 123°33'W. This BC Provincial Park has two sheltered anchor-ages accessed from Houston Passage. Connover Cove is the most popular anchorage, and a small dock here (Photo, right) is available to boats 36 feet and under. Princess Bay to the north has an octagonal dinghy dock. Both anchorages have stern ties to prevent swinging. Getting into the anchorages can be tricky, so pay close attention to the chart (3442, 3463) and cruising guides for tips. Discharge of sewage and gray water is pro-hibited. Facilities include 18 primitive

campsites at Conover Point, Cabin Bay, and Chivers Bay, pit toilets, water, and picnic tables. Hiking trails run the length of the island. For information, check BC Parks' site:
www.env.gov.bc.ca/parks/.

Southeast Vancouver Island

SIDNEY - SWARTZ BAY AREA

Sidney-by-the-Sea is located a few kilometres south of the Swartz Bay ferry terminal, and about 9 NM from Thieves Bay Marina, the closest marina on the Pender Islands. Sidney is a favourite outing for Pender boaters, who can combine an enjoyable day of strolling and dining with chores such as banking and grocery shopping. Check websites such as **www.sidneybc.com**. Refer to **Map 10** in the *Map Atlas*.

The large, beautiful **Port Sidney Marina**, just two blocks from Beacon Avenue, is one of the most popular in the area, and includes a customs port of entry dock but no fuel dock. Check **www.portsidney.com** or call the office at 250.655.3711 for information. 48°39'N, 123°24'W. The marina is the only option for a visit to downtown Sidney via private boat, so one is subject to their terms, which have changed frequently over the years. Overnight and monthly moorage is available, as well as daily moorage if space is left over. After a 2004 renovation, their day moorage rates jumped to $5 per hour.

Overnight summer rates are $1.35/foot plus power fee and tax. The entrance is between two large rock breakwaters north of the public wharf, which does not have transient moorage available. You can call the **Port Sidney Marina** office before setting out for reservations for overnight moorage, or to see if they have temporary moorage available that day, which they sometimes reserve. They will instruct you to call VHF Channel 66A when you approach for instructions on

where to moor once you arrive. As you enter, the docks are labeled A to H, south to north, with the Customs Dock at Dock F under a large white tent. If you have a problem walking long distances make sure to request a slip close to the marina office, since it can be more than a 10 minute walk from the most remote slips. Check in upstairs at the marina office after docking. The closest fuel docks are in Tsehum Harbour, north of Sidney (see below). From **Port Sidney Marina**, overnight marina guests can take advantage of their free summer shuttle to downtown Victoria or **Butchart Gardens**, or take the public bus service that stops at Beacon and 5th. The #70 Pat Bay bus goes north to the Swartz Bay ferry terminal, and south to downtown Victoria/Inner Harbour. The #75 bus goes to **Butchart Gardens**.

From the marina, a pleasant seaside walkway runs to the north and south. To the south, you will stroll past several waterfront restaurants, the public pier with fish market and café, and eventually reach the Washington State Ferry terminal in about 15 minutes. To the east is a dramatic vista of Mt. Baker rising beyond the Gulf Islands. The main commercial street is Beacon Avenue that ends at the public pier. Most people walk up this street to visit Sidney's restaurants, grocery stores, coffee houses, gift shops, hardware, housewares, and marine supply stores, and a large array of independent book stores. Beacon Avenue is closed on summer Thursdays from 5:00 pm to 9:00 pm for a marvelous outdoor market that features food stands, live entertainment, produce and crafts. Additional information on Sidney is found in the *Shopping Guide*, and in Chapter 8, *Nearby Attractions Off-Island,* which includes a dining guide. Also see the *Bicycling Guide*. Area medical facilities are listed in the *Health Services Guide*.

Tsehum Harbour (48°40'N, 123°24'W) is located north of downtown Sidney just past Armstrong Point. This busy area contains **Van Isle Marina**, beyond the breakwater, which has a customs port of entry dock with a fuel station (gas and diesel, Photo, below), and permanent and transient moorage; **www.vanislemarina.com**, 656.1138. **Dock 503** waterfront café serves excellent food and is popular, so call 656.0828 to reserve, or better yet, call the Van Isle Marina office, which can make reservations and arrange for a free slip to use while dining. Lunches are reasonably priced at this high-end restaurant; **www.dock503.vanislemarina.com**. Also in this area are **The Latch**

restaurant in **Shoal Harbour Inn** (2328 Harbour Road, 656.6622) that has accommodations and a dining room, and **Blue Peter Pub and Restaurant** (2270 Harbour Road, 656.4551) in **Shoal Bay Marina**, which has a dinghy dock. Further into Tsehum Harbour are **North Saanich Marina**, which has a fuel dock (656.5558) and possible moorage, and **Westport Marina** (656.2832), which also may have moorage.

Canoe Cove (48°41'N, 123°24'W) is located further north, along Iroquois Passage, just south of Swartz Bay. Call 656.5566 to see if transient moorage is available; **www.canoecovemarina.com**. The basic **Canoe Cove Coffee Shop** (656.5557) is in the marina, while the beautiful **Stonehouse Pub** that serves good food and brew is just up the street. Swartz Bay Ferry Terminal is about a 15-minute walk from the marina.

LOCALS TIP

To have your boat serviced, try mechanics at Westport Marina or Canoe Cove Marina. You can walk to Swartz Bay Ferry terminal from there to return to the Pender Islands after dropping off your boat. Winter dry docking is also available at these marinas, but reserve your spot well in advance.

SAANICH INLET

The Saanich Inlet is located around the western side of the Saanich Peninsula from the Pender Islands. The scenery becomes more dramatic and fjord-like as you proceed south, past Brentwood Bay.

Brentwood Bay (Chart 3441) is located around the western side of the Saanich Peninsula, about 20 nautical miles (NM) from Bedwell Harbour, or 15 NM from Thieves Bay (48°35'N, 123°28'W). For moorage, try the public wharf, or the completely redone Brentwood Bay Lodge & Spa, which has 65 guest spots, and a new modern pub; 652.3151, **www.brentwoodbaylodge.com**. While the look of the town from the water is degraded by a large, treeless condo complex, there is a nice waterfront walkway, and several restaurants and pubs in town on or near the waterfront, including **Blue's Bayou Café**; 544.1194, which serves Cajun food on a large waterfront deck next to the Government dock.

Butchart Gardens provides five mooring buoys and a dinghy dock to allow visiting the gardens by private boat. The popular buoys are located in the small Butchart Cove, just south of Brentwood Bay at the entrance to Tod Inlet (48°34'N, 123°28'W). Once moored (a stern tie to shore is recommended), you can dinghy to the dock (shared by float planes) and tour the gardens. Admission is sometimes collected at the gate, or you are directed to proceed inside to pay. The upper portions of Butchart's spectacular summer Saturday night fireworks are partially visible across from Butchart Cove if

anchored near the west shore of Brentwood Bay, but expect a crowd for this (and it's not nearly the same as seeing the spectacle from inside; see Chapter 8). The best and most protected anchorage in Tod Inlet is at the lower reaches of the inlet, where most people anchor and dinghy over to the **Butchart Gardens**, or enjoy a peaceful time fishing and sightseeing.

Finlayson Arm South of the Saanich inlet, around Willis Point from Brentwood Bay, is the Squally Reach, (named for occasional southerly squalls). The spectacular fjord-like Finlayson Arm is at the head of the inlet (48°31'N, 123°33'W). The **Goldstream Boathouse** (Chart 3441) may have visitor moorage, as well as a fuel dock with gasoline and diesel (watch for shoal water, call facility for entry advice, 478.4407). Once moored, you can walk to the nearby Goldstream Provincial Park.

Washington's San Juan Islands

The beautiful but heavily-visited San Juan Islands are located just across the U.S. border to the south of the Pender Islands. The nearest customs facilities are at Roche Harbor (seasonal) and Friday Harbor on San Juan Island.

SAN JUAN ISLAND
San Juan Island is the largest and most populous of the San Juan Islands. Consult **www.travelsanjuans.com** for information. The two main destinations are Roche Harbor, which is closest to the Pender Islands, and Friday Harbor. See **www.islandcam.com** for current marine traffic and weather.

Roche Harbor (48°37'N, 123°10'W) is situated at the northwest end of San Juan Island, and is accessible through Mosquito Pass, about 9 nautical miles (NM) from Bedwell Harbour. The large marina has excellent facilities, and a high season U.S. customs check-in facility. See **www.rocheharbor.com** or call the marina at 360.378.2155 or 1.800.451.8910 for information and reservations. The marina monitors VHF Channel 78A. Facilities include a fuel dock, restrooms, showers, Laundromat, groceries, and post office. Also available are waterfront dining, a café, a historic hotel, and gardens. The marina fills up frequently in summer, and for their July 4th celebration they recommend reserving in January.

Friday Harbor (48°32'N, 123°01'W) is located halfway down the eastern side of San Juan Island, but is a straight shot to the southeast from the southern tip of South Pender Island, about 16 NM from Poets Cove/Bedwell Harbour, or 19 NM from Thieves Bay. Currents can be tricky along this route. The expansive **Port of Friday Harbor** has a year-round customs port of entry dock at Breakwater *B* and numerous slips. Contact the port at 360.378.2688 for reservations or consult **www.portfridayharbor.org.** If you do not have reservations, call on VHF Channel 66A when you near the entrance to the marina for instructions, unless you need to check into customs first. In that case, go directly to customs, and contact the marina afterwards. Remember, only the master or designee can leave the boat at the customs dock until you are cleared. The fuel dock sells both gas and diesel. Friday Harbor is a sizable, very scenic town with numerous restaurants, some of which overlook the marina. The main street has shops, galleries, antique shops, a grocery store, liquor store, post office, bike rentals and Laundromat. A nearby 9-hole golf course is reachable by taxi. **Washington State Ferries** stops at Friday Harbor with automobile service to other San Juan Islands, Anacortes and to Sidney, BC on Vancouver Island. **Victoria Express** began summer passenger service from Victoria Inner Harbour in 2004 (see the *Ferries* section in the *Travel Guide*).

ORCAS ISLAND
Orcas Island contains 734- metre (2,409-foot) Mt. Constitution in Moran State Park, the highest point in the San Juan Islands, which is visible from portions of the Pender Islands. A road ascends to the summit, so you can hop on your bike and ride up (see the *Bicycling Guide*). Check **www.orcasisland.org**.

Deer Harbor, (48°37'N, 123°00'W), the closest Orcas Island destination to the Pender Islands, is located at the head of the smallest of Orcas' bays at the western end of the island. The town consists of a small quaint fishing village whose shops are contained in buildings dating back to 1890. The popular **Deer Harbor Marina** has a fuel dock with gas and diesel, a pump out station, showers and restrooms, a dock store that sells beer and wine, a coffee bar, fishing supplies, and a swimming pool. The marina monitors VHF Channel 78A. Call 360.376.3037 or consult **www.deerharbormarina.com**.

Eastsound (48°39'N, 122°53'W) is the largest settlement, located at the head of East Sound. The **Rosario Resort and Spa** at Eastsound is a Rock Resorts upscale resort property that has a 32-slip marina and 23 mooring buoys. They monitor VHF 78A, but advance reservations are recommended at 360.376.2222. Marina guests have access to the resort facilities, including fine dining, swimming pools, tennis, a fitness centre, and spa; **www.rockresorts.com**.

LOPEZ ISLAND
Lopez Island is not as hilly as the other San Juan Islands, and is popular with cyclists. (See the *Bicycling Guide*). Check **www.lopezisland.com** for information on the island. The waters at Spencer Spit Marine State Park at the northeast corner of the island warm up enough to swim in summer. Sixteen mooring buoys are available but fill quickly at this popular park. Two marinas are located in Fisherman Bay on the western side of the island (48°30'N, 122°55'W). **Islands Marine Centre** monitors VHF Channel 69. Call in advance 360.468.3377; **www.islandmarinecenter.com**. **Lopez Islander Resort and Marina** has a fuel dock (gasoline and diesel) and bike rentals; 1.800.736.3434, 360.468.2233, VHF 78A, **www.lopezislander.com**.

OTHER SAN JUAN ISLANDS
See **www.travelsanjuan.com** for information on other San Juan Islands, and consult the various cruising guides available, including the new *Dreamspeaker Volume 4* (2005) by Anne & Laurence Yeadon-Jones.

The west shore of San Juan Island is frequented by orcas.

Distances to Other Destinations

Following are distances (in NM) to and waypoints of locations that may also be of interest to Pender boaters but were not covered in this section. The distances are from Poets Cove/Bedwell Harbour on South Pender Island as presented in Canadian Hydrographic Service's Chart Book 3313 (Gulf Islands). Use the distance table presented earlier in this *Boating Guide* to approximate distances from the other marinas.

FROM BEDWELL HARBOUR TO THE PASSES/POINTS

East Point	9	48°47'N 123°03'W
Active Pass	13	48°52'N 123°19'W
Porlier Pass	25	49°01'N 123°35'W
Gabriola Passage	33	49°08'N 123°42'W

FROM BEDWELL HARBOUR TO VANCOUVER AREA

Via East Point

Point Roberts, WA	20	48°58'N 123°04'W
Blaine, WA	26	49°00'N 122°45'W

Via Active Pass

White Rock	34	49°01'N 122°47'W
English Bay	44	49°18'N 123°11'W

Via Porlier Pass

English Bay	51	49°18'N 123°11'W

FROM BEDWELL HARBOUR TO STRAIT OF JUAN DE FUCA

Victoria Harbour	28	48°25'N 123°23'W
Port Angeles, WA	40	48°08'N 123°26'W
Sooke Harbour	43	48°22'N 123°43'W

FROM BEDWELL HARBOUR TO SOUTHEAST VANCOUVER ISLAND

Cowichan Bay	18	48°45'N 123°37'W
Oak Bay	20	48°26'N 123°18'W
Chemainus	28	48°55'N 123°42'W
Ladysmith	35	49°00'N 123°48'W
Nanaimo	41	49°10'N 123°56'W

Victoria Harbour

Pender Boating Clubs

PENDER ISLAND JUNIOR SAILING ASSOCIATION
Based at the Hamilton Beach ocean access to Port Browning, the name Junior Sailing refers to the small size of the sailboats. The regular sailing season is May and June. Week long *White Sail* sailing classes are offered in July for adults and children, and in August for those over 16 years old only. Check the latest Pender Post or Lions Club phone directory for contact information.

PENDER ISLAND YACHT CLUB (PIYC)
The PIYC was originally formed in the 1970's, and emerged in the 1990's as a large club with sixty boats, three-quarters of which are sailboats. The PIYC has no marina or clubhouse facilities, which makes membership fees inexpensive. The purpose of the club is to promote cruising and racing, good seamanship and sponsorship of junior sailing. PIYC organizes races from October through April on Friday mornings. Cruising excursions take place in the summer, which may last one day, several days, or extended periods to local destinations or even Desolation Sound. Meetings are held the third Monday of every month, October through April. See the Pender Post for the PIYC's latest adventures and contact information. No web site. A member of the Council of BC Yacht Clubs, **www.cbcyachtclubs.ca**.

Boating Resources

CHARTS
The paper charts that cover the Pender Islands include the small scale 3441 and 3442, the larger scale 3477 and Gulf Islands Chart Book 3313. Digital charts from NDI are also available for the area: *Vancouver Island East*, **www.digitalocean.ca**. The CPS store **www.cps-ecp.ca/shipstore** is available to members. Comprehensive global positioning system (GPS) data is also available for sale or download for the region.

CRUISING GUIDES
Check **www.floatplan.com/cruiseguide.htm** for a comprehensive listing. Three examples are:

Dreamspeaker Cruising Guide - Volume 1, Gulf Islands and Vancouver Island by Anne & Laurence Yeadon-Jones (1998; Revised 2005). My personal favourite, this easy and fun to use guide provides detailed drawings, photographs, and data on the most popular nautical destinations in the area. Volume 2 covers Desolation Sound (2000) Volume 3 covers Vancouver to the Sunshine Coast (2003) and Volume 4 covers the San Juan Islands (2005).

Waggoner Cruising Guide by Weatherly: This guide is updated annually and covers from Puget Sound up to the BC Inside Passage and West Coast of Vancouver Island. While not as detailed as *Dreamspeaker* for individual locations, it is a good supplement due to the updated contact data, customs information, and scope of the information covered. **www.waggonerguide.com**.

Wolfersten's Cruising Guide to British Columbia is also a popular guide and includes many beautiful photographs.

ADDITIONAL ON-LINE RESOURCES

www.cbsa-asfc.gc.ca Canada Border Services Agency (CSBA). (CANPASS).

www.ccg-gcc.ca Canadian Coast Guard (CCG).

www.tc.gc.ca/Boating Safety Transport Canada Office of Boating Safety. Includes boating regulations and courses (formerly under the CCG site).

www.marineservices.gc.ca Government regulations, conditions, and links.

www.uscgboating.org US Coast Guard Boating Safety page with helpful links.

http://vancouver-webpages.com/peter/marine.txt Marine VHF channel frequencies.

www.bcfishingreports.com: Information and links regarding local fishing.

www-comm.pac.dfo-mpo.gc.ca/english/recreation/: BC govt sportfishing guide.

www.visd.org: Vancouver Island South District Power and Sail Squadron.

www.waggonerguide.com/juandef.html: Navigation updates for Strait of Juan de Fuca and Strait of Georgia, including the Gulf Islands.

www.georgiastrait.org/greenboating.php: Green boating site of the Georgia Strait Alliance. (Main site **www.georgiastrait.org**).

www.georgiastrait.org/CleanBoating/guidep9.php Map showing pump out stations and no-discharge zones for sewage.

http://boating.ncf.ca Pat's Boating in Canada, a wealth of information.

http://boating.ncf.ca/linksgov.html Pat's government boating links.

www.americanboating.org: American Boating Association, includes miscellaneous information and articles.

www.pacificyachting.com: BC Boating magazine's website contains features including news about boating and facilities in BC.

Thieves Bay Marina

16   THE ARTS AND ISLAND EVENTS

THE ARTS ON PENDER ISLAND

The Gulf Islands attract creative and artistic persons, resulting in a rich culture for its residents and visitors.

Pender Islands Artists

The Pender Islands are resplendent with artists of all types, who work mostly out of home studios. The **Trincomali Community Arts Council** publishes a free brochure each year entitled *Pender Island Artists Guide* which can be found on many BC Ferries serving the Gulf Islands, as well as around the Pender Islands. Note that this association is not affiliated with the Trincomali neighbourhood on North Pender, but is named for Trincomali Channel since it touches most of the Gulf Islands involved in the organization. The brochure lists many practicing Pender Islands Artists, along with their studio location shown on a map, their specialty, and the hours that their studios are open to the public. A list of the annual art shows is also included. Check for it on **http://mayne.gulfislands.com/trincoarts/**. Some of the artists list regular hours, while others are open to the public by appointment only. Using this map, you can plot out your own gallery tour. Many artisans also sell their works at the Saturday morning farmers market, at **Talisman Books & Gallery** in Driftwood Centre, and the **Red Tree Artisan Gallery** at the Hope Bay Store.

The Pender Island Art Society was created in the mid 1960's for Pender Island artists to get together to sketch and paint. The group evolved into a non-profit society in 1990, and continues to participate in activities such as critique sessions and *plein air* outings. Their annual Exhibit and Sale held at St. Peters Anglican Parish Hall is well attended.

The Pender Islands Artisan Cooperative provides a venue for local artisans to market their work. Media includes painting, printmaking, collage, knitwear, hand felting, silk fusion, and photography. Members display their works at the **Red Tree Gallery** located at the Hope Bay Store, and hold art shows during the summer. **www.pendercreatives.com/artco-op/**

Following are descriptions of a few of the art studios of the Pender Islands. These artists all have regular open hours at time of writing and welcome visitors to their studios to view their work. Other artists establish regular gallery hours from time to time, while others simply display an *Open* or *Closed* sign as appropriate. Many other artists welcome visitors, but require an appointment:

NORTH PENDER ISLAND - PORT WASHINGTON AREA
Malcolm Armstrong Studio
1201 Otter Bay Road, near Port Washington Road, 629.6571, **Map 1B.**
Open most days 8:00 am - 6:00 pm. malcolmarmstrong@gulfislands.com
Now in their 19th year of business, Malcolm and Marie's oil paintings and watercolours feature nautical subjects, wildlife and local scenes. They also do hand painted and printed greeting cards.

Renaissance Studio
3302 Port Washington Road, 629.3070, **Map 1.**
Open daily 10:00 am to 5pm or by appointment.
Jan & Milada Huk specialize in restoration and preservation of art works, and sell antiques, objects d'art, paintings, costume jewelery and Persian rugs.

HOPE BAY
Red Tree Artisan Gallery
Downstairs at the Hope Bay Store. Open year round. Hours 10:00 am to 5:00 pm during the summer, reduced hours in winter. 629.6800. **Map 1C**
Works by the Pender Islands Artisan Cooperative, which includes Judith Walker, Mae Moore, Shel Neufeld (see individual listings for web sites), Joy McAughrie (**www.whalepointestudio.com**), Susan Tait (**www.susantait.com**), and others.

CENTRAL AREA
Goose Pond Studio
4715 Scarff Rd off of Canal Rd, south of Driftwood Centre, 629.6432.
Open 11 am to 4 pm most days in spring and summer, or by appointment, goosepond@gulfislands.com; **www.pendercreatives.com/judithwalker/ Map 5.**
Judith Walker's works are displayed in a rustic barn in a lush forest. Her works of real and abstract paintings in oil, acrylic and mixed media radiate unique energy and warmth. Judith also exhibits at **Red Tree Artisan Gallery**.

Wildart Photography Gallery, Shel Neufeld
4543 Bedwell Harbour Rd, north of Driftwood Centre, 1.866.945.3742.
Look for *Open* sign (11 am to 4 pm many days) or call first; **www.shelneufeld.com**.
Shel's nature based colour photography features spectacular images of Pender Island and the BC Coastal wilderness. Buy prints, cards, or gifts at the studio or online.

MAGIC LAKE AREA
The Silk Road Studio and Galleries
Open Sunday Noon - 5:00 pm or by appointment, **Map 4A**:
> **The Three Fates Textile Studio and Gallery** - Joanna Rogers, 3708 Keel Crescent, 629.3550, joannar@gulfislands.com, Original and innovative fibre art exhibited throughout Canada and the U.S; **www.pendercreatives.com/joanna/**.
> **Silly Hill Studio/Gallery** - Jan Ede, 37147 Galleon Way at Keel Crescent, 629.3077, **www.pendercreatives.com/ede/**; Textile and fibre art.
> **Home Studio and Gallery** - June Hayes, 3704 Keel Crescent, 629.8358, 94rex@cablelan.net. Paintings in a variety of media, miniature paintings, fibre art.

Windover Studios
1612 Schooner Way, 629.3863; Saturdays and Sundays 11-4.
April – September. **Map 4**. Fused glass, painting, photography and framing.

SOUTH PENDER ISLAND - GOWLLAND POINT AREA
Blood Star Gallery
9909 Jennens Road, Left near the end of Gowlland Point Road. 629.6661.
Open 11 am - 4 pm most days Easter to Christmas. **www.bloodstargallery.com.**
Displays Susan Taylor's detailed ink and watercolour drawings of marine and island
life, and Frank Ducote's whimsical folk art and eclectic watercolours and acrylics.

BOUNDARY PASS AREA
Naturediver Gallery, Derek Holzapfel
9930 Boundary Pass Road, Open most days 11 am - 4 pm; 629-9983.
www.naturediver.com Beautiful nature/underwater photography, videos and cards.

The Music Scene

Island Musicians

Inspired by the rhythms of nature that surround them, many Pender Islanders excel in
musical expression. Although most restrict their performance to the confines of their
own residences, others share their talents by way of performing in local concerts and
plays or at their church. The depth of local talent is evident in the Pender Island
Choral Society, whose spirited winter and spring concerts are always anticipated and
well attended. Other Pender Island singers and musicians are seen in musical productions and solo concerts, such as classical vocalist Clare Mathias and pop singer/pianist
Zorah Staar. The Pender Highlanders Pipe (bagpipe) Band is an island tradition as they
start off the Fall Fair Parade in August, serenade the Santa Ship at Christmas, or sur-
prise boaters as they march down the docks of the Port Browning Marina.

Pender Island is very fortunate to be treated to frequent concerts by Juno-nominated
recording artist Mae Moore and her husband, Juno-Award winner Lester Quitzau.
(Photo, right, courtesy of Shel Neufeld). Their recent releases have won critical acclaim,

including Mae Moore's adult contem-
porary *It's a Funny World* and Lester
Quitzau's progressive jazz release *A
Big Love*. Lester also tours with the
Juno Award winning roots trio Tri-
Continental, who have produced four
well-received CDs. In 2004 Mae and
Lester collaborated on the wonderful
eclectic folksy effort *Oh My!* and chose
the Pender Island Community Hall for
the CD release concert. It is the perfect
Pender Island album to have playing

in your car as you drive from Gowlland Point to Hope Bay, where you can see Mae Moore's beautiful paintings on display at the new **Red Tree Artisan Gallery**. New for 2006, Mae has organized two four-day songwriter camps on Pender. For information, see **www.redcedarsongwritercamp.ca**. Mae's web site is **www.maemoore.com** and Lester's is **www.lesterq.com**.

Pender Island is also home to Jake (aka John Differ), a talented children's songwriter. His album *Happy All The Time* featured Pender Island children's voices and was nominated for a Juno in 2006.

A 2004 benefit concert teamed Mae Moore with fabulous folkrocker Ferron who boated over from Saturna Island; **www.ferrononline.com**. Another folk icon, Valdy, lives across Swanson Channel on Salt Spring Island. He played Pender Island in 1996 and returned in May 2006 to sing *Songs of the Salish Sea*. His song *Whales* was inspired by the sight of a pod of orcas off the Pender Islands; **www.valdy.com**.

Talisman Books & Gallery tends to stock music CDs by local artists. Their music can frequently be heard on the store's sound system, or you can request a listen. Mae Moore's CDs are also available for sale at the **Red Tree Gallery**.

Venues and Organizations

The Pender Island Community Hall opened in 2000, providing a quality venue for live performance in the upstairs hall. Some of the performers booked at the Hall, in addition to those already mentioned, have included Esquimalt's Marc Atkinson Trio, Ireland's Danu, Martin Josef, Patty Larkin, Gordon Bok, James Keelaghan, Celso Machado, Martha Wainwright, Mae Moore, Lester Quitzau and many others. The Hall's website is **www.penderislands.org**. New for 2006 are movie nights in the hall.

The Gulf Islands Concert Series is presented each year from fall through spring, and subscriptions can be purchased for a discounted price. The lineup for 2006 – 2007 includes Sara Davis Buechner, Piano (October 20), Tillers Folley, Roots Music (November 17), George Zukerman with Art Few, Chamber Music (February 8), and Jane Coop with Andrew Dawes, Piano/Violin (March 30). The school is the typcial venue.

The Pender Island Choral Society was founded in the mid-1970's, and has enjoyed continued participation and community support ever since. Anyone who loves to sing is welcome to join. Besides the winter and spring concerts, they have also performed at various nursing homes in the region. See the Pender Post for contact information.

The Ptarmigan Music and Theatre Society is a registered charity that has been based on Pender Island since 2000. "Its purpose is to provide community programs through music, theatre, dance, and the visual arts. Ptarmigan programs are developed to meet the needs and interests of specific audiences and are created and developed in collaboration with other organizations sharing similar interests. These programs are presented in accessible community venues, and include school touring shows, library programs, Pender Island Community Music School & Children's Band Project, a day-care music program, Artists In The School Project - Pender Island, and a music program for special needs teenagers." Programs are also presented at senior centres in the Greater Victoria region including the Gulf Islands.   Music & Theatre Society, P.O. Box 46, Pender Island, BC V0N 2M0; Phone: 1.866.859-0634; Fax: 629.6419. Check their web site **www.artforchange.ca** for their latest programs; ptarmigan@gulfislands.com

Theatre

Theatre companies on the Pender Islands keep local thespians busy and islanders happily entertained. The community hall is the principal venue, but plays have been performed all over the islands, including various outdoor venues.

The Pender Solstice Theatre Society was formed in 1991 by a small group of Pender actors, and has blossomed into a popular organization that produces several plays each year on Pender Island, and occasionally on neighbouring islands as well. Its plays *Hedda Gabler* (1997) and *The Real Inspector Hound* (1999) were award-winners at the South Island Drama Festival in Victoria. An anticipated production at time of writing is Zorah Staar's island musical *The Goddess Blew a Bubble* for Summer 2006. See the Pender Post for contact information.

Three on the Tree Productions Society is a "Pender Island based arts organization that is committed to bringing the arts to rural and urban communities through original productions, presenting works from across Canada and abroad, workshops, seminar and symposiums, community events, spectacles and special events, working with local schools, touring provincially, nationally and internationally." Past productions have included cabarets and plays, and concerts such as Martin Josef and the Tim Posgate-Horn Band. Three on the Tree is best known as producers of the Magic Lake Lantern Festival held on New Years Eve, with workshops on lantern and mask making and stilt walking leading up to it. See *Annual Events*.
www.pendercreatives.com/threeonthetree/

Writers

The Pender Islands have been known to inspire many a writer, and the results can be seen on the shelves of **Talisman Books & Gallery.** The following is a partial list of published authors with a Pender presence, presented in alphabetical order.

William Deverell is a former Vancouver criminal attorney turned award-winning author who has written thirteen novels in the crime thriller genre and one work of non-fiction, *Life on Trial.* His novels *Trial of Passion* (1997) and *April Fool* (2005) are set on fictional Garibaldi Island, which many have said resembles Pender Island. He also created the Canadian TV show *Street Legal*; **www.deverell.com.**

Mike Harcourt, former BC Premier, has co-written *Plan B: One Man's Journey from Tragedy to Triumph* about his recovery from a near-fatal fall at his Pender Island home in 2002.

Sheila Jordan is a writer, actress, and director who wrote and directed the short film *Kathleen's Closet* that was filmed on Pender Island in 2004.
www.kathleenscloset.ca, **www.pendercreatives.com/seeinghumanpictures/**

Barry Mathias is a writer of historical fantasy novels, plays, and short stories.

Ron Palmer writes mostly about boat building and his own sailing adventures. **www.pendercreatives.com/palmer**

Andrea Spalding's diverse artistic talents are now focused on writing unique children's books such as *Solomon's Tree*. See her website, **www.andreaspalding.com**, for information on all her works including the new picture book *Bottled Sunshine*.

David Spalding writes with a particular interest in the natural sciences and their history, such as in *Whales of the West Coast*. See his website, **www.davidspalding.com**, for information on his other works, many of which involve dinosaurs.

Pender Writer's Circle: Groups and workshops for all levels; 629-2085.

ANNUAL EVENTS AND FESTIVALS

Pender Island organizations put on events that are open to community participation year round. Check each Pender Post for a complete list of monthly events. The Community Hall's website **www.penderislands.org** can also be consulted for events held at that venue. Following are some of the annual highlights that take place on the Pender Islands and some that Penderites tend to participate in on adjacent islands.

JANUARY
* Lions Club New Years Day Polar Bear Swim and bonfire at Hamilton Beach
* Pender Island Golf Club New Years Tournament

EASTER SUNDAY
* Ecumenical Sunrise Service at Mortimer Spit
* South Pender Easter Art Walk
* Port Browning Resort Easter Egg Hunt

APRIL
* Spring Concert by Pender Island Choral Society
* Garden Club's Spring Flower Show and Plant Sale
* Balding For Dollars Benefit for Cancer

MAY
* Health and Wellness Fair at the Community Hall
* Victoria Day Round Salt Spring sailing race, **www.saltspringsailing.ca**
* Pender Classic Disc Golf Tournament at Golf Island (last weekend)

JUNE
* Pender Car Rally, auction & barbeque is a fundraiser for the Pender Island
  School, held on odd years, **www.penderislands.org/carrally**, 629.3377

JULY
* Canada Day Family Events at Driftwood Centre, Danny Martin Ball Park, and
  Community Hall. Evening Legion Hall barbeque
* Canada Day Lamb Barbeque on adjacent Saturna Island (A water taxi is available
  from Pender Islands, see **www.saturnalambbarbeque.com**)
* Pender Islands Artisan Co-Op Spring Show
* Charity Pro-Am Golf Tournament, Pender Island Golf and Country Club
* Art off the Fence Show and Sale at Whalepointe Studio on South Pender
* St. Peter's Church Guild Garden Party with tea service and flea market
* Pender Island Art Society's Annual Show

AUGUST
* Lions Club Dog Show fundraiser.
* Pender Islands Artisan Co-Op Under the Trees Art Show
* Round Pender Yacht Race

PENDER ISLAND FALL FAIR
Pender Island's main event is typically held the last Saturday of
August at the Community Hall
Grounds. Ever since its beginnings
in the Hope Bay Hall in depression-
era 1932, it has been the proud
presentation of the Pender
Farmers Institute, (as well as the
Women's Institute through 1985). It
currently features booths from
local organizations, agricultural
exhibits, sheep sheering demon-

strations, crafts and food booths, various competitions for baked goods and produce, and live entertainment. The small parade that runs from the fire hall
through the fairgrounds still begins with the Pender Highlanders Pipe Band
(Photo, above) at 11:00 am and ends with fire trucks, but in the last few years it
has seen an increase in overall participation. The fair is the main showcase for
many community organizations, and it is worthwhile, especially for locals, to
drop by their booths and chat. Admission is $5. The evening program features a
barbecue (buy the $5 food ticket early in the day), live music, and dancing.
*Artists of Trincomali (Trincomali Neighbourhood) Art Show-Sunday after the Fall Fair.

SEPTEMBER
* Royal Canadian Legion's Labour Day Pig & Lamb Barbeque

OCTOBER
* Thanksgiving Community Potluck dinner at the Community Hall
* Hallowe'en Howl family dance at the Community Hall

NOVEMBER
* Remembrance Day: Lions Club pancake breakfast; Canadian Legion parade
* Pender Island Art Society Winter Art Show
* Christmas Crafts Fair at the Community Hall

DECEMBER
* Pender Island Library's Christmas Book and Bake Sale
* Pender Island Choral Society Christmas Concert
* International Santa Ship arrives at the Hope Bay or Port Washington dock
* Lighted Boat Festival at Poets Cove Resort
* Audubon Christmas Bird Count by Pender Island Field Naturalists

NEW YEARS EVE
* New Years Eve parties at the Community Hall; Legion Hall, and Poets Cove Resort.

MAGIC LAKE LANTERN FESTIVAL

Presented by Three on the Tree Productions, the Lantern Festival is the most unique and ambitious of the Pender Island undertakings. It takes place in the late afternoon in front of Magic Lake at Schooner Way and Privateers Road. Spectators are given sparklers as they line Schooner Way to watch a parade of fire spinners and new age folk characters on stilts, carrying lanterns. It continues with a kayak ballet in the lake performed by lighted kayaks led by a sea serpent.

A staged pageant backed by broadcast new age music depicts the departure of the old year and ringing in the new. The event sometimes culminates with a fireworks display over the lake. Prior to the event, workshops are held to give residents the opportunity to make lanterns for the parade. Lots of volunteers are always needed for this event.

17   THE NATURAL ENVIRONMENT

Both natural and man-made forces have altered the natural environment of the Pender Islands. This chapter discusses its climate, geology, water resources, flora and fauna.

CLIMATE AND WEATHER

Best Climate in Canada

The climate of the Gulf Islands, along with the southeast coast of Vancouver Island from Nanaimo to Victoria, is regarded by many as the best in Canada. Its growing season is over 200 days, the longest in the country, and its average of 2,000 hours of sunshine exceeds even the Okanogan in interior British Columbia. Summers are typically cool and dry, while winters are humid and mild, creating what is referred to as a transitional Mediterranean climate. A typical year on the Pender Islands will consist of a glorious summer with sunny skies and moderate temperatures, and a cool, fairly dreary winter. Spring and fall are much more variable in outlook and are difficult to predict. Each year differs, as there are rainier summers and sunnier winters depending on the many factors that impact regional weather patterns.

Two opposing weather patterns battle for control throughout the year along the southern British Columbia coast. The Aleutian Low Pressure system dominates the climate during October through March, creating a series of storm fronts that swirl in with southwesterly winds, creating rain and gloomy skies. During the summer, the North Pacific High Pressure system moves up from the south and dominates the weather, blocking storms generated by the Aleutian Low Pressure system. This high-pressure system creates the fair weather and prevailing northwesterly winds in the summer (Butler, 2003).

Most of the rainfall generated by the Aleutian Low Pressure system falls on the western slopes of the coastal ranges, creating a rain shadow effect to the east of them. The Pender Islands lie within a rain shadow created by the Olympic Mountains of Washington to the southwest, and the mountains of Vancouver Island to the west. Compared to the 3,200 mm (126 inches) of average annual precipitation near Tofino on the west coast of Vancouver Island, the Pender Islands average only 798 mm (31.4 inches) per year. When rainfall is at or above normal, it is generally sufficient to replenish Pender's water supply as long as reasonable conservation measures are used. However, during drought periods, severe water use restrictions are implemented, as reservoirs are depleted and many wells run dry. The strain on the limited water supply will continue to increase as the population of the Pender Islands grows.

Annual precipitation figures from other area cities, measured at their principal airports are: Vancouver, BC: 1168 mm (46 inches); Victoria/Sidney, BC: 858 mm (34 inches); and Seattle, WA: 944 mm (37 inches). Some of the San Juan Islands in Washington are more impacted by the rain shadow effect than the Gulf Islands. Annual precipitation at Friday Harbor on San Juan Island averages 715 mm (28 inches), while Sequim on the Olympic Peninsula receives only 457 mm (18 inches). Kelowna, in interior BC gets 367 mm (14.5 inches) annually, but temperatures are more extreme as compared to the coastal cities. Victoria/Sidney averages 2082 hours of sunshine per year, versus 1920 hours for Vancouver and 2170 for Seattle. Of these locations, Victoria Airport at Sidney is the closest measuring station to the Pender Islands and is the most representative.

The cool waters surrounding the Pender Islands help maintain moderate temperatures throughout the year. The all time high temperature, set in 2004, was only 34.5°C (94°F) while the all time low was -12.5°C (9.5°F). Although daily low temperatures routinely dip below freezing in the winter months, deep freezes are rare, and it only snows every other year on average. Average annual snowfall is 24.6 cm (9.7 in). Within the Pender Islands themselves, the coastal areas tend to experience more moderate temperatures than the interior sections. Drivers from coastal areas should watch for icy conditions along Bedwell Harbour Road when en route to catch a morning ferry on a winter day.

Winter storms can have a significant impact on the Pender Islands. Although flooding is rare, the strong winds create havoc when they topple tree branches or entire trees onto power lines creating power outages. Wind waves can damage docks and moored boats. The storms most typically blow in from the southwest, but can also come in from other directions as well. One unusual storm on a Summer 2004 afternoon blew in suddenly and fiercely from the east, frightening boaters moored at Beaumont Marine Park.

Summer fog is less common around the Pender Islands compared to most North Pacific coastal areas. Fog that is frequently generated in the Strait of Juan de Fuca typically dissipates by the time it makes its way through Haro Strait to the Pender Islands. Autumn is typically the foggiest period in the Gulf Islands region. Boaters should be aware that fog could materialize locally at any time of year.

Resources and Statistics

Climate Information and Forecasts

www.msc-smc.ec.gc.ca: The Meteorological Service of Canada (MSC) is Canada's source for meteorological information. The Service provides information and conducts research on climate, atmospheric science, air quality, ice and other environmental issues, making it an important source of expertise in these areas.

www.weatheroffice.ec.gc.ca: Maintained by the MSC's national and regional offices, this site is Environment Canada's official online-presence for meteorological information and public forecasts. It includes weather alerts, marine and aviation forecasts, radar and satellite imagery. Click *British Columbia*, then select *Gulf Islands (Southern)*. MSC's weather reports by telephone now include a separate forecast for the Gulf Islands, as well as southeastern Vancouver Island and the lower mainland. Marine forecasts are also available; 250.363.6717, 604.664.9010.

www.theweathernetwork.com: Local weather as monitored from Victoria Airport.

www.weather.com: U.S. Weather site. Enter *Friday Harbor* for nearby San Juan Island weather, which is fairly representative for the Pender Islands. Check for satellite photos of the area.

www.weatherunderground.com: Global site has interesting and helpful data.

Pender Island Statistics

Pender Island artist and amateur meteorologist Malcolm Armstrong has been compiling climatic data from Port Washington since 1989. He presents an insightful article on Pender Island climate monthly in the Pender Post, which provided background information for this chapter. The following table summarizes Pender Island statistics, which Mr. Armstrong has culled from his own data and other statistics. Temperature statistics are since 1971 and precipitation data are since 1925, through the end of 2004. All temperatures are in degrees Celsius and precipitation in millimetres. To convert to Fahrenheit and inches, respectively, see the *Conversions* section in Chapter 1.

PENDER ISLANDS WEATHER STATISTICS

Month	Average Hi Temp	Average Lo Temp	Mean Temp	Extreme High (Year)	Extreme Low (Year)	Total Precip, mm
January	6.9	1.8	4.3	19 (1988)	-9.4 (1972)	120.7
February	8.6	2.5	5.6	16 (1991)	-12.5 (1989)	82.4
March	10.7	3.4	7.5	20.5 (1994, 2004)	-5.0 (1976)	70.0
April	13.8	5.1	9.5	26.5 (1998)	-2.8 (1975)	43.7
May	17.0	7.4	12.2	30.5 (1983)	-2.0 (2002)	34.8
June	19.9	9.7	14.8	32.0 (2003)	2.8 (1975)	32.0
July	22.5	11.2	16.9	34.5 (2004)	4.4 (1977)	20.3
August	22.2	11.4	16.8	32.2 (1997)	3.9 (1970)	26.5
September	19.6	9.9	14.8	31.5 (1988)	1.5 (1984)	35.1
October	14.1	7.0	10.5	26.0 (1987)	-2.2 (1971)	82.5
November	9.5	3.9	6.7	18.5 (1975)	-11.0 (1985)	117.3
December	7.0	1.9	4.5	14.0 (1980)*	-11.5 (1990)	128.4
Avg/Totals	14.3	6.3	10.3	34.5 (2004)	-12.5 (1989)	798.0 Total

Note: A new December record high temperature was set in 2005, at 14.5 degrees C.

FLORA - THE COASTAL DOUGLAS FIR ZONE

The southeastern coast of Vancouver Island and the Gulf Islands are characterized by dry sunny summers that support a coastal Douglas fir ecosystem. Vegetation types around the Pender Islands vary according to soil type, moisture content, and directional exposure.

The Douglas fir (*Pseudotsuga menziesii*, Pine Family: Pinaceae) is the most common tree on the Pender Islands, dominating the hot, dry southwest facing slopes. It is a tall, fast-growing (to over 90 m) conifer with thick, corky and deeply furrowed bark. The grand fir (*Abies grandis*, Pine Family: Pinaceae) and western red cedar (*Thuja plicata,* Cypress family: Cupressaceae) are conifers found in wetter lower slopes and valleys (Henderson, 1997). The grand fir is also a fast growing tree reaching heights of over 90 m, with thin blistery bark on young trees that is roughened into oblong plates divided by shallow fissures on older ones. The western red cedar, BC's provincial tree, is a fast growing tree to over 60 m. The bark is cinnamon red on young trees and grey on mature ones, always shedding vertically. It has bright green scale-like leaves (Varner, 2002).

The wetter northeast-facing slopes are dominated by western red cedar, with occasional Douglas fir, grand fir and western hemlock (*Tsuga heterophylla*, Pine family: Pinaceae) (Henderson, 1997). The western hemlock is the state tree of Washington, and is a fast growing pyramidal conifer that reaches up to 60 m in height. Its bark is reddish brown and becomes thick and deeply furrowed on mature trees (Varner, 2002). The red alder (*Alnus rubra*, Birch family: Betulaceae) grows mostly in wetlands and disturbed areas. Bigleaf maples (*Acer macrophyllum*, Maple family: Aceracea) are also found scattered throughout the Pender forests.

The driest areas of the Pender Islands, including rock outcroppings, are where you are most likely to find the broadleaf trees Garry oak (*Quercus garryana*, Beech family: Fagaceae) and arbutus (*Arbutus menziesii*, Heather family: Ericaceae). These trees populate a very endangered Savanah-like ecosystem. The arbutus is the only naturally occurring broadleaf evergreen tree in Canada. Arbutus-Douglas fir woodlands are common on dry sites such as south-facing slopes with rocky, nutrient poor soils. Examples of these woodlands are found at the summits of the trails at Oaks Bluff and George Hill parks.

The understory of the Pender Islands forests is dominated by the midsized shrub salal (*Gaultheria shallon*). Salal berries are very tasty, and ripen in mid-August to September (Varner, 2002). Other common shrubs are Oregon grape (*Mahonia nervosa*), evergreen huckleberry (*Vaccinium ovatum*) and red huckleberry (*Vaccinium parvifolium*). Salmonberry (*Rubus spectabilis*) is common in moist areas, while swordfern (*Polystichum munitum*), field horsetail (*Equisetum arvense*), skunk cabbage (*Lysichitum americanum*), and vanilla leaf (*Achlys triphylla*) grow in wet areas, such as locations with high water tables, springs and intermittent streams. Introduced species that thrive in disturbed areas, such as those caused by fire or logging, are widespread on the island. These include Scotch broom (*Cytisus scoparius*), American stinging nettle (*Urtica dioica*), and common gorse (*Ulex europaeus*) (Henderson, 1997).

Another prolific invasive shrub on the Pender Islands is Himalayan blackberry (*R. discolor*). Berry pickers dive into the blackberry bushes all over the Pender Islands in late summer to harvest the bountiful fruit. This shrub was introduced from India, and is a very robust, heavily barbed species. Some popular places to pick blackberries are along Bedwell Harbour Road south of the Community Hall, Razor Point Road, and trails to Percival Cove (Ocean Access **1**) and Brooks Point Reserve (**97**). Two other types of blackberries are found in the region. Trailing blackberry (*Rubus ursinus*) is the only native blackberry species. It blooms in April and sets fruit in mid-July. Cutleaf blackberry (*R. laciniatus*), introduced from Europe, is similar to the Himalayan blackberry but less common (Varner, 2002). For a thorough overview of the *Plants of the Gulf and San Juan Islands and Southern Vancouver Island*, including the wildflowers that bloom all over the islands, check out Collin Varner's 2002 guidebook. Some of the more common wildflowers are foxglove, flowering red currant, various roses, daisies and chicory. Chocolate lilies put on an interesting display in locations such as Roe Islet (**25**) and the Gowlland Point CRD Point Reserve (**98**) in the spring.

WILDLIFE

Mammals

Pender Islands wildlife is dominated by the peaceful escapades of the Columbian Black-tailed deer (*Odocoileus hemionus, O.h. columbianus;* Family: Cervidae), considered by many to be a smaller subspecies of the mule deer found in the Rocky Mountain region. Does weigh about 30-66 kg and have their

first offspring at two years of age when food is plentiful. Bucks grow to 57 to 120 kg depending on food supply. Their tyned antlers fork once, with each fork dividing again. Mature males will have five points on each side of their antlers, which grow in summer and are shed in March. Fawns have no scent, and can be left in the underbrush relatively undetected while the parents forage, mostly at dusk, dawn, and overnight (Hill, 1998). Mating occurs primarily in mid-November, and one to three spotted fawns are born the following May or June. These small deer flourish in the absence of natural predators. In fact, unlike most of British Columbia, no bears or cougars are known to exist on the Pender Islands. It is feasible for cougars and bears to swim to the Pender Islands, but that occurrence is extremely rare. The proliferation of the deer is detrimental to the natural environment, as they gobble up the understory and saplings of rare trees such as the Garry oak. As described in the *Gardening Guide* at the end of this chapter, they are a nuisance to many Pender gardeners who need to fence their entire gardens to keep the deer at bay.

No rabbits are known to inhabit Pender Island. Douglas squirrels and Townsends chipmunks inhabit other Gulf Islands, but if they have made their way to Pender they are very rare and live deep in the forest. Plenty of deer mice inhabit the islands, however. Raccoons have lived here in the past, and a few have recently been seen on North Pender Island. Rumours of Norway rats have also surfaced. Beavers have been active near Roe Lake in the past, and some may remain in the area. Beaver ponds are located in GINPR land west of Hastings Airstrip. Mink patrol certain coastal areas (such as Brooks Point), as do river otters. Although sea otters are making a comeback along the west coast of Vancouver Island, they have not made their way to the Gulf Islands.

Birds
Numerous varieties of birds grace the islands throughout the year. See the *Birdwatching Guide* later in this chapter for details.

Sea Mammals
Several types of marine mammals frequent the waters surrounding the Pender Islands, the most notable being the orca, or killer whale. See the *Whale Watching Guide* later in this chapter for details.

The Coastal Environment
The intertidal environment is rich in marine life. See Chapter 11 - *Coastal Access and Hiking Guide* for a description of the ecology of the rocky shoreline.

Reptiles and Amphibians
Several species of garter snakes, including the Striped Garter and the Northwestern Garter (Photo, right), inhabit the islands, as well as the red-listed Sharp-tailed snake. No poisonous snakes are known to live here. Also present are newts, salamanders, Pacific Tree Frogs, and Red-legged Frogs. The Bullfrog is an invasive species that now inhabits the Roe Lake, Greenburn Lake, and Port Washington areas. This frog eats the native frogs, small birds, and snakes, upsetting the local ecology. It is important not to bring these frogs to Pender or transplant materials from the impacted areas to your ponds to help prevent their proliferation.

PROTECTING THE ENVIRONMENT

The natural environment of the Pender Islands has undergone many changes since Europeans first settled here in the late 1800's. Most of the forests were gradually logged, and second growth trees now grow on much of the island. Large portions of the island are protected as parks, but most of the land is still in the control of individual property owners. Property owners are urged to take an environmentally friendly approach when developing or landscaping their properties. Landowners with sensitive or endangered habitat on portions of their properties may consider a conservation covenant through the Islands Trust, to ensure that the ecosystem remains intact for generations to come. Several such covenants have already been established on private property on North Pender Island.

On-line tools are available to evaluate the sensitive ecosystems on the Pender Islands: In 2005, Canadian Parks and Wilderness Society's BC Chapter in cooperation with Parks Canada established The Southern Gulf Islands Atlas, to promote public awareness of the Gulf Islands National Park Reserve, as well as to assist park managers in maintaining the ecological integrity of the parks. The atlas also covers land outside of the GINPR; **www.shim.bc.ca/gulfislands/**. Also, the CRD's Natural Areas Atlas depicts endangered ecosystems and shoreline habitats: **www.crd.bc.ca/es/natatlas/**.

At Risk Species Many wildlife species are threatened or endangered on the Pender Islands or in the surrounding waters. In 2002, the Committee on the Status of Endangered Wildlife in Canada (COSEWIC) listed 487 species throughout the country as either extirpated, endangered, threatened, or of special concern. See **www.speciesatrisk.gc.ca** for the complete list. The Gulf Islands are home to 15 endangered species, 10 threatened species and 13 species of special concern. The magical Southern Resident pods of orcas that are seen from Pender's shores are listed as endangered, while the transients are threatened. Other marine species listed include the humpback whale, which used to feed in the area, as well as the northern abalone, Olympia oyster, Pacific cod, and white sturgeon. Terrestrial species include the Sharp-tailed snake, for which an Islands Trust conservation covenant exists on North Pender Island, Townsend's big-eared bat, and others that range from ferns to butterflies. Birds include the Anatum Peregrine Falcon, Western Meadowlark and the shorebirds Great Blue Heron and Ancient Murrelet. Canada's Species at Risk Act (SARA) (2003) addresses the assessment and recovery of the most at-risk species. Species listed as threatened or endangered (Red-listed) by the BC Conservation Data Centre include Marbled Murrelet, Stellar sea lion and Western Grebe. Harbour porpoises are vulnerable (Blue-listed). Ling cod, many species of rockfish, and Double-crested and Pelagic Cormorants also have experienced steeply declining populations.

THINGS PENDERITES CAN DO TO PROTECT THE ENVIRONMENT
• Use biodegradable chemicals of low-toxicity for cleaning, pest control and landscaping.
• Recycle - Pender Island has a wonderful facility.
• Plant native vegetation and remove exotic invasive plants such as Scotch broom. It is best to clip it at the base each year before it goes to seed, and do not use herbicides.
• Practice green boating (See: *Boating Guide, Chapter 15*).
• Conserve water.
• Respect sensitive intertidal environments. (See: *Chapter 11*).
• Keep your cats indoors so that they do not kill the islands' birds and reptiles.
• Respect the tranquil nature of the islands.

Additional Web Resources - Environmental Organizations
www.landtrustalliance.bc.ca Land Trust Alliance of BC. Maps of lands held in trust.
www.cpawsbc.org Canadian Parks & Wilderness Society - BC Chapter. Conservation org plays key role establishing new protected areas and improves existing parks.
www.georgiastrait.org Conservation org protecting the waters of southern BC.
www.conservationconnection.bc.ca Links to a large number of conservation organizations working in the Capital Regional District.
www.greenpeace.ca The venerable fighters for the environment.
www.sierralegal.org The Sierra Legal Defense Fund.
www.oceansatlas.com A United Nations website to help reverse the decline of the world's oceans and promote sustainable development.
Recommended Reading: *The Jade Coast - Ecology of the North Pacific Ocean* by Robert Butler 2003, Key Porter Books.

WHALE WATCHING GUIDE - ORCAS AND OTHER MARINE MAMMALS

Orcas or Killer Whales

The Pender Islands have the good fortune of being situated in the midst of the Salish Sea, a term used to describe a large inland sea comprised of the waters from Puget Sound and the Northwest Straits of Washington to the Strait of Georgia up to Johnstone Strait. These waters are home to several pods of orcas, or killer whales (*Orcinus orca*), and the frequent summer sightings of these graceful black and white creatures along Pender's shoreline create a flurry of excitement with island residents and visitors.

Orcas are actually large dolphins, or toothed whales (Odontoceti), and are members of the same Delphinid family as dolphins. However, where dolphins average 3 meters (10 ft) in length, male orcas can reach up to 9 m (30 ft) in length, and females to 8 m (26 ft) (Reeves et al, 2002). At birth, orcas are about 2.5 m (7 to 8 ft) long and weigh about 180 kg, with females growing up to about 4 tons, and males up to 6 tons. Females are sexually mature in their teens and give birth to a single calf on average of once every five years, until senescence begins around age 40. Orcas continue to grow until they reach their late twenties.

The Resident Pods of BC and Washington

The orcas found in southern BC and Washington are known as the *Southern Resident Community*, or *J Clan*, which are a separate community than the orcas that live in northern BC waters. The Southern Residents are a large extended family, or clan, comprised of three pods that have been named the J, K, and L pods with 90 members as of July 2005, including three calves born over the previous winter. The *Northern Resident Community* (A, G and R clans), which is usually observed in the Johnstone Strait area and northern British Columbia, is made up of about 16 pods containing 220 whales as of July 2005.

Families within each pod form subpods centred on older females that are usually grandmothers or great-grandmothers. All offspring remain in close association with their mothers for life, which is an extremely rare trait for wild mammals.

From April through September, the Southern Resident pods tend to travel throughout the Salish Sea. From October through June, J pod often continues its activities in the inland estuaries; however, it has not been determined where the K and L pods go. Recently members of the K and L pods were sighted in lower Puget Sound in winter. In winter of 2000, about 50 members of those pods were spotted in Monterey Bay, California feeding on salmon. During winter months Salish Sea orcas are seen along the outer coasts of Washington and Vancouver Island, but it is not known how far into the open ocean they travel. Orcas usually swim from 120 to 160 km every 24 hours, and are capable of swimming at speeds of 50 km/h.

The resident individuals have been identified with a specific alphanumeric designation, such as L3. After surviving their first year, orcas are given more familiar-sounding names, such as *Luna*. The following describes some of the members of the Southern Resident pods, with approximate ages. See **www.whaleresearch.com** (click on *Survey & Research* then click on each pod name) for complete summaries and fin photographs:

THE SOUTHERN RESIDENT PODS
J POD 24 members. Matriarch: J2, early 80's; Mature male: J1, 54 years old.
K POD 21 members. Matriarch: K7, early eighties; Nearly matured male: K21.
L POD 45 members (the largest resident pod); Two mature males: L41 & L58; Five nearly mature males.

An Endangered Species

The Southern Resident pods populations have risen since 1976, when numbers had been drastically reduced by capture attempts for marine parks during 1965 through 1975. At least 13 orcas were killed during captures, and 45 were delivered to marine parks around the world, of which only Lolita remains alive in Miami Seaquarium. Ironically, the performing orcas have captured the hearts of the public, and have helped rally support for the protection of whales. Although orcas were once feared and reviled, there is no record of an attack in the wild on humans, beyond some destruction to their boats. In captivity at least two human deaths and one recent close call were due to orcas dragging people underwater in their tanks, although it is unlikely that the orcas intentionally killed the people (See the story at **www.hsus.org**). Unfortunately, the numbers in the Southern Resident Pods decreased since the early 1990's, and the animals are now listed as endangered by both Canada and, as of 2005, the United States. The decline is blamed on bioaccumulation of contaminants such as PCBs since orcas are at the top of the food chain, declining food supply, and some also speculate that the stress from the abundance of whale watching boats that follow them is taking its toll. Researchers will be watching the seven new additions to the Southern Resident community that have been born since 2003. The Northern resident community is listed as *threatened* at time of writing.

Other Orca Communities

The *Transients* are a completely separate community of orcas from the residents, traveling in groups of one to five individuals. Transients of the Pacific Ocean roam between Mexico and the Bering Sea, and appear only occasionally in the Salish Sea, typically in the spring and fall. Transients tend to stay close to shorelines, often near haulout areas of seals and sea lions, or seal rookeries. Unlike residents that feed on fish (mostly salmon), transients feed mostly on marine mammals, especially seals, sea lions, and porpoises. In October 2003, four transients attacked and killed a minke whale in Ganges Harbour on Salt Spring Island to both the awe and horror of some 200 onlookers. The transients and residents exhibit rare sympatric speciation, which means that they do not compete for food, so that they can inhabit the same waters, even though they speak a different dialect and do not mix or interbreed. About 190 transients have been photo-identified to date, all of which are believed to use similar vocalizations, indicating they are all members of a single, widespread community. While first-born transient males tend to stay with their mothers for life, second-born males will break off contact with their mothers and travel either with other transients or remain solitary, so that the pod sizes remain small enough to pursue marine mammals. Juvenile transient females have also been known to leave their mothers. However, in one documented case, a female returned to her mother after giving birth to her own calf, even though it was several years later and a thousand miles apart, indicating the family's emotional bonds had remained intact.

Yet another Orca community called *Offshores* was discovered in 1991, which are thought to be the ancestral population of the Northern and/or Southern Residents. They are spotted most frequently about 25 to 40 km off the Pacific coast of Vancouver Island and the Queen Charlottes, though members of this community have been seen from the Bering Strait to Southern California.

Orca Behaviour

The J, K, and L pods can go their separate ways for a few days or months, and when they rejoin each other, they typically engage in greeting behaviour. The pods face each other in a ritualized formation for several minutes, then merge into active groups, each consisting of members of all three pods. This is accompanied by spectacular *play* behaviour and underwater vocalizations. Each pod uses a characteristic dialect of calls to communicate, and certain calls are used in common between pods. The calls used by the Southern Residents, which can travel over ten miles underwater, are unique and not used by any other orca community. Their diet, range, social behaviour, kinship system and linguistic system are distinct from other orca populations that occur in the Pacific Northwest. For recordings of various vocalizations visit the Cetacean Research website: **www.cetaceanresearch.com/sounds/index.html**. The most common orca behaviour is feeding, which they do about 75 percent of the time. Orcas also engage in many behaviours just to play, such as kelping when they drag seaweed on a body part. The *Center for Whale Research describes* other observable orca behaviours below:

PORPOISING High speed travel with the majority of their bodies breaking the surface and often creating a *V* of spray alongside their bodies. Can rise up to 2 metres above the water surface and leap 9 to 11 metres horizontally at top speed.

CHASING Makes sudden movements, including lunges and sudden accelerations; especially during hunting.

LUNGE Breaks water with large part of body in a charging mode, possibly with a sideways component especially during a chase.

CIRCLING Circles around, often during a chase.

LOGGING Resting at the surface exposing melon, upper back, and part of dorsal fin for ten seconds or more.

MILLING Surfacing in constantly varying directions while remaining in the same area.

SPYHOP Raises head vertically above water to at least eye level, then slips back under.

AERIAL SCAN Raises head at an angle from the horizontal.

FLUKE LIFT Brings flukes up and down above water in a fluid motion with little force.

FLUKE WAVE Lifts flukes and part of caudal peduncle above water, pauses for at least two seconds, and then bring flukes down gently.

PECTORAL WAVE Lifts pectoral flippers in the air for at least two seconds and brings it down with little force.

ROLLING Rolls halfway or all the way around in the water.

BACKDIVE Leaps out of the water exposing at least two-thirds of body, lands on back.

BELLYFLOP The same as a backdive, but lands on its ventral surface.

BREACH The same as a backdive, but lands on its side.

HALF BREACH Leaps out of water and exposes half of the body, landing on the side.

CARTWHEEL Throws the flukes and rear from side to side in at least a 45-degree arc.

DORSAL FIN SLAP Rolls on the side and slaps dorsal fin to the water forcefully.

PECTORAL SLAP Forcefully lifts and slaps pectoral flipper while lying on the side.

TAILLOB Lifts and slams down tail flukes.

INVERTED PECTORAL SLAP While on its back, raises and slaps down pectoral flippers. Frequently followed by inverted (same behaviour but with flukes).

TAIL TRASHING Violently trashes tail fluke through the surface for hunting.

Orca-Watching From The Penders

Orcas can be seen just about anywhere off the outer shores of the Pender Islands. Most frequently they navigate in Swanson Channel and Boundary Pass, much less frequently in Plumper Sound and Navy Channel, and seldom in Port Browning and Bedwell Harbour. During May through September they are frequently spotted swimming past the Pender Islands, but usually only once per day or night, and at no particular time. Sometimes they will appear every day for a week at a time, and other times no one will report a sighting for a week or more. Winter sightings do occur, but are infrequent. Many of the hosted accommodations (and residents) participate in whale alert telephone trees, and if it works out you may have time to run down to the nearest public park to see them off shore. Otherwise, watch for a barrage of colourful inflatable whale-watching boats, and there is a good chance the whales will be near them. The most common route of the whales is around Gowlland Point and up the entire west coast of North Pender Island, typically traveling northbound toward Active Pass. They may also turn around mid-way up North Pender Island's shoreline.

Public whale watching spots in the Magic Lake Estates area include Thieves Bay Marina (**51**) and the Boat Nook (**52**) and Harpoon Road (**50**) ocean accesses (**Map 4A**). Orcas sometimes swim close to the breakwater at Thieves Bay, making it a favourite outpost. Other times they pass more in mid-channel. Park in the Thieves Bay Park gravel lot, and walk down the marina access road to the end, which only takes a few minutes. From Boat Nook and Harpoon Road, the orcas are always further off shore, so you will want binoculars. You are more likely to see other sea mammals such as harbour seals or river otters, and perhaps a Bald Eagle soaring overhead. If you are lucky, you can see orcas far below from the lookout at Oaks Bluff Park (**70**) off of Pirates Road (**Map 4C**). In Trincomali, the Plumper Way viewpoint (**74**) is an option (**Map 4D**). In the Otter Bay area, the tip of Roe Islet (**25**) is another good place, as it juts out into the sea (**Map 3**). You can also try the McKinnon Road (**23**) (**Map 1A**) and Bridges Road (**4**) (**Map 1B**) ocean accesses, or to a lesser extent the Port Washington Dock (**3**) and Walden Road ocean access (**5**). On South Pender Island, try any of the open-ocean beach accesses such as Gowlland Point (**96, 98**), Brooks Point (**97**), Higgs Road (**95**), or Craddock Road (**94, Map 9**). In general, find out where the whales were sighted, and choose the appropriate beach access point around the islands based on the direction they are traveling.

Boaters are required by law and by conscience to follow guidelines for watching orcas while at sea. See the *Boating Guide's* section on whale watching guidelines.

Whale watching charters are the best way to see whales, as they have a communication network to share information on orcas' whereabouts. Most charters leave from Victoria's Inner Harbour, but some also leave from the new dock in downtown Sidney. Check **www.tourismvictoria.com**, **www.sidneybc.com**, and **www.sidneybc.info** for the latest information and charter contacts. The faster the boat, the more likely you will be taken to where the whales are if they are not close to your port. Some of these charters also provide exciting thrill rides, skimming over the Strait of Juan de Fuca from Victoria. On the negative side, the proliferation of these noisy vessels is suspected to be creating stress on the endangered orcas, which have a very sensitive auditory system.

REPORT YOUR SIGHTING
You can be a part of the BC Cetacean Sightings Network. When you see a whale, dolphin or porpoise log onto the website **www.wildwhales.org** or call their hotline 1.866.I-SAW-ONE. Sponsored by Vancouver Aquarium Marine Science Centre and Fisheries and Oceans Canada.

Photo, Left: Orcas may swim close to shore at locations where there is deep water.

Other Odontocetes, or Toothed Whales

Locals report that dolphin and porpoise sightings from the Pender Islands have diminished over the years, but they are still spotted, most frequently from the Brooks Point and Gowlland Point viewpoints, and occasionally in Navy Channel, Plumper Sound, Swanson Channel, and other locations.

DALL'S PORPOISE (*Phocoena dalli*)
Resembling a mini-orca, Dall's porpoise range from Southern California to Alaska, frequently spotted in the Strait of Juan de Fuca off of Victoria, and less frequently around the Gulf Islands. They are deepwater animals, so will be seen close to shore where there are deep channels or canyons. Dall's porpoises can grow to over 2 metres in length, weigh up to 180 kg, and live to 15 years. Their 55 km/h maximum speed is the fastest of all Cetaceans, and they are known to enjoy bow riding on boat wakes. Dall's porpoise feed on a variety of fish, crustaceans and squid, but are themselves hunted by the transient orcas. They are also hunted by humans for porpoise meat, and frequently become trapped and die in apparatus for catching fish.

HARBOUR PORPOISE (*Phocoena phocoena*)
The harbour porpoise is a more reclusive creature than the Dall's porpoise, and is listed as threatened by the Committee on the Status of Endangered Wildlife in Canada (COSEWIC). They tend to frequent bays and harbours, remaining in coastal waters less than 150 metres deep. It is one of the smallest cetaceans, with an average length of about 1.5 metres, weight of 55 kilograms, and life span 13+ years. They lack the black and white colouring of the other common local porpoises. Their diet consists of squid, capelin, herring and gadoid fishes such as pollack and hake.

PACIFIC WHITE-SIDED DOLPHIN (*Lagenorhynchus obliquidens*)
The fast and powerful Pacific white-sided dolphin enjoys surfing and bow-riding, and can be seen doing leaps and somersaults. At first glance, it may seem like a baby orca with its black and white markings, but its pointed beak differentiates it, as well as its different pattern of markings. Males reach about 2.2 m, females 2.4 m. They weigh up to 140 kg and can live to 30 years. They feed on squid and small fish, mostly in the open ocean, but large groups have been spotted in the interior waterways of BC. Although not endangered at this time, thousands are killed each year by tuna drift nets or by Japanese harvesting.

The Whales: Mysticetes

Baleens refer to the long stiff strips that hang from upper jaws to strain small fish and krill. Baleen whales have no teeth, as opposed to toothed whales such as orcas and dolphins. Baleen whales are seldom seen near the Pender Islands. Gray whales (Eschrichtius robustus) migrate between Alaska and Baja, California each winter, but their route takes them along the west coast of Vancouver Island. Humpback whales (Megaptera novaeangliae) migrate between Alaska and either Hawaii or Baja California (Mexico), but also keep to the open ocean. In the past, Humpbacks frequented the Strait of Georgia in search of herring, but they stopped coming when the herring population dwindled. The herring population has since made somewhat of a comeback, which raises hope that these *singing whales* will return to the area. The minke whale (Balaenoptera acutorostrata) are seen mostly in the summer months off the west coast of Vancouver Island, though one was chased to Ganges Harbour and killed by transient orcas in 2003.

Pinnipeds (Seals)

HARBOUR (COMMON) SEAL (*Phoca vitulina*)
Harbour seals are the sea mammals most frequently spotted off of the Pender Islands' shores. The most common view of these inquisitive creatures is of their head sticking out above the water surface, their big playful eyes probing their surroundings. Then, just before you are able to snap a photo, they silently slip below the surface, where they can remain for some 20-minutes, as their blood pressure lowers and their eyes dilate to adapt for dives of over 500 metres. Seals can also be heard slapping frantically at the water in the middle of an otherwise still night as they hunt for fish. Several haul-out spots are situated  around the islands, where these mottled-looking creatures congregate together on the rocks. They breed locally, and populations have made a dramatic comeback from over-hunting thanks to their protected status.

Harbour seals are the Pinniped species *Phocids*. When on land they undulate on their belly, dragging their hind flippers. They have no ear flaps. Alaskan and western Pacific harbour seals are 1.4 to 1.9 metres in length and weigh 55 to 170 kilograms, while the smaller adult females are 1.2 to 1.7 m in length and weigh 45 to 105 kg. Pups are born 70 to 100 centimetres in length and weigh 8 to 12 kg. Most male Harbour seals reach sexual maturity at age five to six, while females mature earlier, at two to five years. Females live to around 25 to 30 years of age, while males live to about 20 years.

CALIFORNIA SEA LION (*Zalophus californianus*)
California sea lions breed in California estuaries and migrate north in summer, where they are sometimes seen around the Pender Islands. Their range is from Baja, California to Alaska. The sea lion is the Pinniped species *Otariids*, which walk on four flippers. These creatures have ear flaps, and are coloured chocolate brown to tan, but may look black when wet. Their pointed muzzle is reminiscent of a dog, and their playful bark and demeanour solidify their reputation as dogs of the sea. They are highly adaptable and can live in a variety of habitats. When hauled out on rocks they may pile atop each other, and when swimming they tend to raft together. A typical adult male weighs 360 kg, while females average only 115 kg. These fish-eaters use their powerful front flippers to reach speeds of up to 40 km/h.

References and Resources

Information on **orcas** contained in this chapter was referenced with permission from: **www.orcanetwork.org**: Their website contains information on orca whale movement on a daily basis; Includes sighting archives, news, etc; and **www.whaleresearch.com** from Friday Harbor, Washington. This organization presents sightings, programs, and information on the Southern Resident pods; 360.378.5835.

Most of the information on **other marine mammals** was referenced from: Lifeforce Foundation (Brochure), Reeves et al (2002), and **www.tourismvictoria.com**.

Other Orca Web Resources:
www.whalemuseum.org: "Promoting stewardship of whales and the Salish Sea ecosystem through education and research." Located in Friday Harbor, Washington, 360.378.4710, 1.800.946.7227. The museum is open in summer.
www.vanaqua.org: Vancouver Aquarium Marine Science Centre, 604.659.3474.
www.georgiastrait.org/orcapass.php: Proposed *Orca Pass International Stewardship Area* in BC and Washington hopes to establish North America's first transboundary marine protected area. The Pender Islands are in the midst of *Orca Pass*.
www.pugetsound.org: Activists working to restore the waters and shoreline of Puget Sound, including Orca habitat.
www.hsus.org: U.S Humane Society: Articles on marine mammals.

Recommended Reading
Whales of the West Coast by David Spalding (Pender Author), 2001, Harbour Publishing
Killer Whales, by John K.B. Ford et al, 2000, University of Washington Press
Orca-Visions of the Killer Whale, by P. Knudtson, 1996, Sierra Club Books for Children

BIRDWATCHING GUIDE

The Birds of the Pender Islands

The Pender Islands offer wonderful opportunities to admire and identify birds throughout the year. Although the habitat does not generally support large concentrations of birds, a birdwatching outing can be very rewarding just the same. Each season brings a new array of birds that spend a portion of the year here, while others are year-round residents. See the table *Common Birds of the Pender Islands* on the next page.

The most prominent of the birds around the Pender Islands are the Bald Eagles that so elegantly grace many of the shorelines and tops of tall Douglas fir snags. The ultimate opportunists, they scan the water for signs of fish that are close to the surface, then swoop down to pick them up in their talons. They can also pick off small mammals including mice and mink. Although rare, they have been known to get small cats as well. Oftentimes they are hassled by ravens, crows, or osprey as they try to bring their bounty back to their nest or nearby perch. Eagles mate for life and return to the same nest every year. Their nest can become quite immense, since they instinctively add to it all the time. Eventually it can crash to the ground if it gets too big for its supporting tree. The pair will raise one or two chicks every season, which do not develop the characteristic white head and tail feathers for four years. It is fascinating to listen to the parents and the chicks interact, as the chicks first learn to fly, and then are coaxed out of the nest with pieces of food, so they will leave and establish their own territory. While the eagle's chirps sound more like a songbird than a bird of prey, the chick's screams can sound panicky as they make their precarious foray into the world of flight. Once the chicks do move on sometime in late summer, the parents leave their nest to allow it to air out until they return the following winter to begin the process anew, as nesting begins in the spring. When the eagles are gone other birds that may have stayed away from the area, such as gulls, tend to move in to fish the territory.

Other birds create their own excitement around the Pender Islands, such as the return each spring of the Rufous Hummingbird to Pender gardens. Swallows are another welcome visitor in the spring, with the Violet-green Swallows arriving in March and the Tree, Barn and Rough-winged Swallows returning in April. In the forests, the Downy, Hairy and Pileated Woodpeckers are residents and breed here. Two groups of robins spend either summer or winter here, making it seem as if they are year round residents.

COMMON BIRDS OF THE PENDER ISLANDS

YEAR-ROUND RESIDENTS

Sea and Shore Birds

Great Blue Heron*
Canada Goose* **A**
Mallard*
Glaucous-winged Gull*
Marbled Murrelet* **B**
Pigeon Guillemot*
Bald Eagle*
Belted Kingfisher* **C**
Double-crested Cormorant *
Pelagic Cormorant*

Land Birds

Red Tailed Hawk *
Ring-necked Pheasant*
Blue Grouse*
Kildeer*
Northern Flicker* **D**
Song Sparrow*
Northwestern Crow*
Common Raven*
Bushtit*
Chestnut-backed Chickadee*
Pine Siskin*
Red-breasted Nuthatch*
Brown Creeper*
Red Crossbill*
Dark-eyed Junco*
American Robin*
European Starling*
Hutton's Vireo*
Purple Finch*
House Finch *
Spotted Towhee *
Downy Woodpecker *
Hairy Woodpecker*
Pileated Woodpecker*
Barred Owl*
Bewick's Wren*
Winter Wren*
Red-winged Blackbird*
Brewer's Blackbird*
Band-tailed Pigeon*

WINTER RESIDENTS

Sea and Shore Birds

Brandt's Cormorant
Pacific Loon
Common Loon
American Wigeon
Greater Scaup
Lesser Scaup
Bufflehead*
Ring-necked Duck
Harlequin Duck
Black Turnstone
Surf Scoter
White-winged Scoter
Common Murre
Common Goldeneye
Barrow's Goldeneye
Hooded Merganser*
Common Merganser*
Red-breasted Merganser
Pied-billed Grebe
Horned Grebe
Red-necked Grebe
Western Grebe
Mew Gull
Thayers Gull

Land Birds

Varied Thrush*
Sharp shinned Hawk
Coopers Hawk*
Golden-crowned Kinglet*
Ruby-crowned Kinglet
Fox Sparrow
Golden-crowned Sparrow

TRANSIENTS - SPRING AND FALL
Land Bird

Hermit Thrush

* Breeds on Pender Island

SUMMER RESIDENTS

Sea and Shore Birds

Osprey*
Rhinoceros Auklet

Land Birds

Turkey Vulture
Common Nighthawk*
Virginia Rail* **E**
Swainson's Thrush*
Cedar Waxwing*
Warbling Vireo*
Rufous Hummingbird*
Anna's Hummingbird **F**
House Wren*
Wilson Warbler*
American Goldfinch*
Common Yellowthroat *
Northern Rough-Winged
Swallow*
Violet-green Swallow*
Barn Swallow*
Chipping Sparrow*
Savannah Sparrow*
White-crowned Sparrow*
Black-throated Gray Warbler*
Orange-crowned Warbler*
Yellow-rumped Warbler*
Townsend's Warbler*
MacGillivary's Warbler*
Brown-headed Cowbird*
Olive-sided Flycatcher*
Willow Flycatcher*
Western Flycatcher*
Pacific slope Flycatcher*
Tree Swallow*

TRANSIENTS - SPRING AND FALL
Sea and Shore Birds

Bonaparte's Gull
Heerman's Gull
California Gull
Merlin
Water Pipit

A

B

C

D

E

F

Fish-eating Osprey nest on Pender Island in summer, though they winter to the south. They appear to be increasing in numbers, with nests along the William Walker Trail and near Medicine Beach. Peregrine Falcons are also making a comeback here, with new nests appearing along the William Walker Trail, as well as on several private properties. Other bird species have transitioned, such as the Barred Owl (listen for *who cooks for you*), which has completely chased off the once-common Screech Owl. Watch for Owls where forests abut open fields, such as the Found Road Trail and Brooks Point Reserve, as they are sometimes active during the day.

Feral and domestic cats continue to decimate Pender's bird population, especially ground-nesting birds. While the Virginia Rail seems to be holding its own, the Roughed Grouse has been eliminated from the island and the Blue Grouse population has been diminished. The introduced California Quail and Pheasant are also dwindling. Along the shoreline, the ecologically important ground nesting Black Oystercatcher is diminishing due to trampling of its eggs. The appearance of the aggressive Bullfrog also does not bode well for ground nesters.

Pender Island bird feeders attract a variety of birds including Spotted (formerly Rufous-sided) Towhee, Sparrows (Fox, Song, and White-crowned), Dark-eyed Junco, House Finch, American Goldfinch, Red-breasted Nuthatch, Chestnut-backed Chickadee, Northern Flicker, Pine Sisken, Red Crossbill, and Rufous and Anna's Hummingbird.

The Pender Island Field Naturalists have participated in the Annual Audubon Christmas Bird Count since the 1970's and have been active in identifying birds and wildlife around the Pender Islands ever since. The Christmas 2005 count yielded 70 bird species and record sightings of Canada Geese, Mallards, Black Turnstones, Hutton's Vireo's, Hermit Thrushes, Golden-crowned Sparrows, Chestnut-backed Chickadees, Red-breasted Nuthatches, and Winter Wrens. The group needs volunteers for Christmas 2006 to boat beneath Oaks Bluff to look for additional shorebird species, and to watch for owls at night to fill in some gaps in the survey. They also do monthly coastal waterbird surveys on the second Sunday from September through April. The organization's Pender Island presence is substantial considering the relatively small population. For their current activities and contact information, check the latest Pender Post, and see the link in *Resources* below. Membership dues helps to bring interesting lecturers to the Pender Islands, and they typically go on monthly outings to view wildlife. *The Checklist to the Birds of North and South Pender Islands*, compiled by Mary Roddick, is sometimes available for sale at island festivals. The table *Common Birds of the Pender Islands* in this chapter is based on that list. The table includes birds that are either common (seen in large numbers just about every time out) or fairly common (often seen but not every time).

Pender Islands Birding Sites

North Pender Island

HOPE BAY is a drying inlet with an estuary at the end, which attracts a wide array of shorebirds. Year-round residents include Bald Eagles, which have a nest across the bay east of the Store. Great Blue Herons also frequent this area, as well as Belted Kingfishers, and various gulls and cormorants. In the winter, watch for the Bufflehead, American Widgeon, Pacific and Common Loon, as well as Mergansers and Grebes. Low tide is the best viewing time, when the shore birds feed on larvae, worms and crustaceans found in the mud. The Hope Bay dock is a good vantage point. **Map 1C, 7.**

MEDICINE BEACH provides a very good birdwatching opportunity in the winter, when wintering ducks are abundant offshore. The elusive Virginia Rail breeds on the ground in the marsh in summer, and Red-winged Blackbirds, Belted Kingfishers and Great Blue Herons are frequently seen, along with the Osprey fishing offshore. **Map 5A, 42.**

MAGIC LAKE attracts a wide variety of birds, especially in the shallower end along Schooner Way. When lake levels are lower in summer, rocks are exposed less than 100 metres offshore, which is a popular perching spot for Canada Geese and other birds. Besides the numerous accidental spottings of birds that rest at the lake when flying by the area, Coots are seen all year as well as Cormorants and Great Blue Heron. Violet-green Swallows are common in spring and summer. Wintering ducks are plentiful, including Mallards and Ring-neck Ducks, as well as Mergansers and Buffleheads. **Map 4.**

OAKS BLUFF PARK (**Map 4C, 70**) and other blufftop parks are good places to watch raptors soar at eye level as they ride the thermals. Turkey Vultures tend to soar in wide circles, while Bald Eagles and Osprey have more of an agenda as they travel from one location to another, although Eagles also soar with the thermals on occasion. Interactions between various birds of prey can be interesting, such as Bald Eagles with Ravens or Osprey.

PENDER ISLAND GOLF & COUNTRY CLUB may not be the easiest place to score a *birdie*, but chances are you'll see plenty of Canada Geese on the fairways. Once a flock of Trumpeter Swans flew over as we played, so bring your binoculars when dining on the Chippers deck. **Map 1A.**

ROESLAND in the GINPR in South Otter Bay is another good birding location. From the footbridge to Roe Islet, you can see both songbirds flitting about in the nearby brush, and wintering birds on the small island just off shore in Otter Bay to the north. To the south is Ella Bay, which is shallow and attracts wintering shorebirds at lower tides. **Map 3, 25.**

ROE LAKE is a serene place to sit, most likely with no one else around, and watch for a variety of both water and land birds. **Map 3A, 27.**

South Pender Island

MT. NORMAN's forests were logged as recently as 1985, but are now recovering. As you hike up the hill, listen for the *hooting* of the Blue Grouse or the *cooing* of the Band-tailed Pigeon against the mostly quiet forest. Also listen and watch for Crossbills, Kinglets, Warblers, and Pacific-slope and Olive-sided Flycatchers. **Map 7, 82-85.**

FAWN CREEK PARK has old snags that attract the beautiful Pileated Woodpecker. (**Map 6, 78**). Also watch for them on the Beaumont Marine Park trails. **Map 7, 82.**

SPALDING HILL's summit (Castle Road Trail) is another good place to watch for Bald Eagles, which can perch on the tall snags near the summit, and Turkey Vultures soaring at eye level from your vantage point. **Map 8, 89.**

GREENBURN LAKE and the surrounding area of the GINPR contain a variety of habitats. You may see not only waterfowl on the lake, but Bald Eagles overhead and songbirds such as Red-winged Blackbirds, Song Sparrows, and Evening Grosbeak. **Map 8, 99.**

BROOKS POINT RESERVE is not the most prolific of terrestrial birding locations, but is a great place to observe sea and shore birds such as Great Blue Heron (Photo, right), Harlequin Ducks, Mergansers, Scoters, Kildeer, Surfbirds, and Black Oystercatchers. Some rare or endangered species that have been spotted on the property include Peregrine Falcon, Western Grebe, Brandt's Cormorant, Common Murre, Marbled Murrelet, and Northern Goshawk. **Map 9, 97.**

Birding Resources

Birding Guide Recommendations:**www.birding.bc.ca/articles/birding-references.htm** Also check **www.birding.bc.ca** for articles, area checklists, postings, regional hotspots, weather reports, and visiting birder information. The 2000 checklist of Southern Vancouver Island birds is at **www.birding.bc.ca/victoria/victoria-checklist.htm.**
Victoria Rare Bird Alert To report sightings of interest, call 250.592.3381 and leave your name & telephone number plus a brief message describing the birds you have seen. To summon Victoria area birders who can confirm a rare species, call Bryan Gates at 250.598.7789.
www.naturalists.bc.ca Federation of BC Naturalists, includes a description of the Pender Island club and contact info under *List of Clubs - Vancouver Island.*
www.cws-scf.ec.gc.ca/birds/ Environment Canada's migratory birds site.
www.vicnhs.bc.ca Victoria Natural History Society's site includes helpful links.
www.birdzilla.com Comprehensive birding site from the U.S.
www.Audubon.org International birding and conservation organization (U.S.).

GEOLOGY AND WATER RESOURCES

Geology of Pender Island and Southern BC

GEOLOGIC TIMELINE

The process that began the formation of the rocks beneath the Pender Islands started some 360 to 315 million years ago (mya). Metasediments, or sedimentary rock hardened under pressure to metamorphic rock, and volcanic rock created by volcanic eruptions, were formed during the Triassic and Jurassic Periods of the Mesozoic era. Batholithic, or volcanic rocks formed by intrusion into other formations, were created during the Jurassic and Cretaceous Periods. Although these ancient rocks are not exposed on the Pender Islands, except as *erratics*, they can be seen in other locations such as Salt Spring, Portland, Moresby, Sidney and D'Arcy islands (Kenney at al, 1988).

About 150 mya, the Juan de Fuca tectonic plate began to collide with the continental plate that contains the Coast Range in mainland BC. As the approaching plate dove beneath the existing plate, land was scraped off, creating what is now Vancouver Island. This process also created the Georgia Depression within which are the Strait of Georgia and Puget Sound, together known as the Georgia Basin. During the Upper Cretaceous Period of 80 mya, erosion from the Coast Mountains to the east and Vancouver Island to the west created a series of layers of sedimentary rock, the Nanaimo Group, within the Georgia Basin. These layers form the bedrock of the Pender Islands. The Nanaimo Group, described in detail below, contains sandstones, shales and conglomerates, which can be seen in outcroppings all around the Pender Islands. The more resistant rocks such as sandstones and conglomerates tend to be found at higher elevations, while siltstones and fine-grained shales exist mostly in the low lying areas.

About 20 mya (Late Tertiary period), the Strait of Georgia was a wide valley with a river discharging through what is now the Strait of Juan de Fuca into the Pacific Ocean. The Gulf Islands were comparable to the foothills of the adjacent Vancouver Island insular mountains.

The age of the great glaciers began about 2 mya during the Pleistocene Epoch. From about 100,000 to 10,000 years ago, the Pender Islands became covered with ice from the advancing glaciers. Ice flowed generally to the southwest and filled the valley of the Strait of Georgia to up to 1.5 kilometres. About 14,000 years ago, the slow moving river of ice flowed through the Fraser Valley and formed the basin for the Strait of Juan de Fuca. The sea level was about 100 metres lower than it is today. The extreme weight of the ice sheet created a depression in the land by as much as 250 metres. The glaciers eventually melted as the ice surface lowered, releasing huge amounts of water that transported and reformed the glacial debris. One layer was created by the crushing and abrasion of rocks by the ice forming a consistency of concrete, while another layer deposited on top of it was unsorted and unstratified till (Henderson,

1997). Once the ice melted, the ocean invaded the coastal lowlands so that only the highest points of the Gulf Islands were above water. The land responded with isostatic rebound as the sea level was re-established in relation to the land, a process that is ongoing. Scientists believe that the planet is still in a period of recurring glaciation. In fact, the coolest period in the past 10,000 years occurred in the 1800's, as glaciers advanced in the Rocky, Columbia, Coastal and St. Elias Mountians (Cannings, 2004).

In general, the physiography of the Gulf Islands was created by the erosion-resistant formations such as sandstones and conglomerates that formed the promontories, and the softer formations such as shales out of which bays were formed. Glaciers further shaped the rock formations, and even transported some *erratic* rocks to the islands from afar. One example of an erratic can be seen along the Found Road Trail on North Pender Island where a granitic boulder sits.

NANAIMO GROUP - THE ROCKS OF THE PENDER ISLANDS

The stratigraphic units of the Nanaimo Group bedrock were laid down rapidly in a marine environment millions of years before the last ice age, and are visible throughout the Pender coastline and at inland outcroppings. In general, jagged coast-lines are composed of conglomerates, while more linear coastlines are composed of sandstone bedrock. The tip of Roe Islet is a good place to see a contact between conglomerate and sandstone. One is likely to encounter shale at the head of rectangular shaped inlets. Although specific information on Pender is scarce, James Henderson (1997) described the Nanaimo Group rock layers and mapped outcrop locations on the Pender Islands for a Masters thesis. It is presented below for general interest only:

The **Extension Formation** was laid down about 84 mya. It is a conglomerate with minor shale, sandstone and coal, found along the coast of North Pender Island (NPI) from Wallace Point to Thieves Bay, and from Hay Point to Gowlland Point on South Pender Island (SPI).
The **Pender Formation** shale is a mudstone, siltstone and fine-grained sandstone formation. It outcrops at Thieves Bay (NPI), Canned Cod Bay and Egeria Bay (SPI).
The **Protection Formation** is coarse-grained sandstone with fine-grained sand-stone and siltstone, found at Mouat Point, southwest Bedwell Harbour (NPI), Richardson Bluff and Higgs Point (SPI).
The **Cedar District Formation** contains shale, siltstone, and fine-grained sand-stone. It outcrops in Shingle Bay, Hamilton Beach, the Clam Bay shoreline, north-west Bedwell Harbour (NPI) and Camp Bay (SPI).
The **De Courcy Formation** is medium to coarse-grained sandstone with fine-grained sandstone, siltstone and mudstone interbeds, and minor conglomerate and pebbly sandstone. It outcrops from Stanley to Willy Points, Shingle Bay to Ella Bay, Port Browning (NPI), Cove Bay, Bedwell Harbour, Mt. Norman, and Spalding Hill (SPI).
The **Northumberland Formation** consists of grey, silty shales interbedded with thin, very fine- grained sandstone and siltstone, and minor thick bedded, medium to coarse-grained sandstone. It outcrops at Brackett Cove, Grimmer Bay, and the Mt. Menzies coastline (NPI).
The **Galiano Formation** is a thick-bedded, medium to coarse-grained sandstone and pebble to cobble conglomerate, with associated finer grained beds, found on Mt. Menzies, James Point and the eastern shoreline of Otter Bay (NPI).
The **Mayne Formation** is comprised of brownish-grey siltstone and grey mudstone with fine-grained sandstone, outcropping only along the Otter Bay shoreline.

SEISMOLOGY - EARTHQUAKES AND TSUNAMIS

The British Columbia coast is one of the few places in the world where three different types of plate movements take place, resulting in significant earthquake activity. Earthquakes in this region occur along the faults in the offshore region, such as the magnitude 8.1 Queen Charlotte Island earthquake of 1949 (the largest recorded in Canada); within the continental crust, such as the magnitude 7.3 earthquake on central Vancouver Island in 1946; and within the subducting ocean plate, such as the magnitude 6.5 earthquake beneath downtown Seattle in 1965 (and the M=6.8 Nisqually/Seattle quake of 2001). The latter type of earthquake occurred 54 km beneath the Pender Islands in May 1976, registering 5.3 on the Richter scale. No aftershocks followed it. It was felt by most in the region, and some damage such as broken windows were reported in the Lower Mainland and southern Vancouver Island. The other significant recorded earthquakes beneath the Gulf Islands were also within the subducting ocean plate, and occurred in 1864 (M=5.5), 1909 (M=6.0), and 1920 (M=5.5) (Clague, 2002).

The west coast of British Columbia is within the Cascadia Subduction zone, where the Juan de Fuca plate is sliding beneath the North American Plate off the west coast of Vancouver Island, as well as Washington and Oregon. This area has the potential for mega-earthquakes, over 9.0 on the Richter scale. Geological evidence from tsunami deposits in tidal marshes along the Pacific coast from Vancouver Island to northern California indicates that repeated, historically unprecedented great earthquakes have occurred in the *recent* past. These earthquakes may have occurred at least seven times in the last 3,500 years, suggesting a return time of 400 to 600 years. The last known great earthquake in the northwest, the Cascadia Quake, occurred in January, 1700, just over 300 years ago, indicating that a mega quake is possible in the not so distant future. Another possibility is that the 1700 earthquake was the last of an earthquake cluster. Researchers at Pacific Geoscience Centre in Sidney, British Columbia report that the crust is not sliding smoothly beneath Vancouver Island, and it is being strained. Mountains are being pushed closer together and are rising, while the crust beneath the centre of Vancouver Island is being squeezed at different rates (Cannings, 2004). The amount of damage the mega quake causes will depend on the extent of the rupture. If the entire 1,000 km length of the subduction zone ruptures, it will create widespread damage throughout the Pacific Northwest (Clague, 2002). In the meantime, *silent* earthquakes occur at the junction of the tectonic plates every 14 to 15 months, referred to as episodic tremor and slip (ETS). One recent event, detectable only with seismographs, occurred for two weeks in 2003, near San Juan Island and Victoria, which is believed to have released as much energy as the 2001 magnitude 6.7 Nisqually (Seattle) earthquake. These gradual quakes are actually adding a tiny bit of stress to the system rather than reducing stress (AP, 2003). The most recent event was September 2005, where Victoria moved westward about 3 millimetres in two days. Experts believe the possibility of a major subduction earthquake increases 30 fold during these events (Britt, 2005). For information on recent and historic earthquakes, as well as earthquake hazard maps, refer to the Earthquakes Canada website, **www.seismo.nrcan.gc.ca**.

Several faults traverse the Pender Islands, however recent evidence indicates that they are not active (Cassidy, 2005), (Lowe et al, 2001). To evaluate the seismic hazard of a particular property ($60 fee) contact the Pacific Geoscience Centre in Sidney; 250.363.6500, pgcinfo@pgc.nrcan.gc.ca.

The topic of Tsunami hazard in the Gulf Islands region is being debated, with ongoing modelling being conducted in local research institutions such as the Institute of Ocean Sciences in Sidney and Simon Fraser University (SFU) near Vancouver. BC geo-hazards expert John Clague of SFU believes that the Pender Islands are in a low tsunami run-up zone, where a tidal wave is not expected to exceed 1 metre if generated in the open ocean to the west, since it is shielded by Vancouver Island. A strong earthquake in the Strait of Georgia is expected to generate a tidal wave of no more than 2 metres, since the Penders are shielded by other Gulf Islands (Clague, 2000). A submarine landslide in the Strait of Georgia from slippage of the Fraser River delta front has the potential to generate large waves that could impact the eastern shores of Galiano and Mayne Islands. However, experts disagree on the degree of hazard, since no evidence of similar historic events impacting the Gulf Islands has been discovered. For the latest updates, **www-sci.pac.dfo-mpo.gc.ca/osap/projects/tsunami/default_e.htm**, maintained by the Department of Fisheries and Oceans, can be consulted. Also contact your local emergency coordinator.

> Regardless of what shoreline you are on, if the ocean suddenly disappears in front of you, especially after a seismic event, it could mean that a tsunami is imminent, and you should move away from the shore and rush to higher ground.

Groundwater

Groundwater beneath the Pender Islands is found mostly in the fractures of the Nanaimo Group of sedimentary rocks described previously. Groundwater supply is also found in areas where the bedding planes have separated, or at contacts between different formations. Less than 1 percent of the mass of Pender's sedimentary rock formations is capable of transmitting groundwater. Wells used to extract water from bedrock areas tend to be deep, from 15 to 75 metres, the deepest being over 200 metres. The average yield from these wells is reported to be 15 litres/minute. Individual Pender Island households, as well as the community systems of Trincomali and Razor Point on North Pender Island use groundwater from bedrock wells.

Other localized areas have unconsolidated sand and gravel overlying the bedrock, where up to 25 per cent of the formation can contain groundwater, such as in portions of Hope Bay, Port Washington, and Colston Cove. Wells dug in these areas and in areas of wetlands or springs, tend to be shallower and more productive, but can be more affected by drought and water quality issues (British Columbia, 1994).

Studies have shown that upland areas are typically recharge zones, where groundwater is found several metres below the surface. Low-lying regions, such as valleys, ocean waterfront, or toes of slopes, frequently are discharge zones and can have groundwater levels near the ground surface, or perhaps flowing under artesian conditions. Groundwater levels tend to fluctuate during each year in response to the degree of precipitation falling on the islands. The water levels decline during the dry summer and early fall months, reaching a minimum point between October and December (Kohmut, 1993). The fresh water beneath the Pender Islands is underlain by salt water, and there is no connection between the Pender Islands' freshwater supply and any other land. Therefore, rumours that the Pender Islands' water supply comes from Mt. Baker or the Olympic Mountains are untrue (Island Tides, 2003). If it were true, the amount of head (artesian pressure) in Pender Island wells would be monumental.

Groundwater quality varies depending on the location of the well and the water bearing zone it draws from. The areas with the poorest groundwater quality tend to be the discharge zone, which are areas that are the most frequently developed, such as coastal areas and interior valleys. The water quality can be further degraded by groundwater development.

Pender Island wells are usually drilled using the air rotary method, which enables the driller to examine individual water-producing fracture zones for yield and water quality. Wells are typically unlined except for a shallow surface casing that is completed in the overburden materials. Therefore, groundwater flow systems from various depths can become interconnected (Kohmut, 1993).

Surface Water

During the rainy months, small streams flow down hillsides and trickle through wetlands around the Pender Islands. The major drainage systems on North Pender Island are Standen Creek, draining 1.83 sq km of the Hope Bay area; Shingle Creek, with a drainage area of 0.94 sq km between Buck Lake and Shingle Bay; an unnamed creek draining Magic Lake to the south (0.91 sq km), Bryant Creek, draining 0.89 sq km of the central portion of the Pirates Road peninsula to Bedwell Harbour, and an unnamed creek that drains 0.61 sq km of Roe Lake westward to Swanson Channel. The Roe Lake area also drains through a series of marshes to the southeast toward Port Browning. Smaller drainage areas include Gardom Pond south to Port Browning, and Grimmer Bay Creek, draining the golf course area into Grimmer Bay. Other streams are located around Stanley Point and Clam Bay. In Magic Lake Estates, the Buck Lake overflow flows alongside the Buck Lake and Schooner-Privateers hiking trails to the south toward Boat Nook, and drainage through the Disc Park linker trails flows southeast toward Magic Lake. On South Pender Island, Greenburn Creek has the largest drainage area with 0.83 sq km between Greenburn Lake and Egerid Bay. Spalding Valley and surrounding hills drain westward through Enchanted Forest Park (BC Topo, 2004).

The major lakes on the Pender Islands are all available for water supply. On North Pender Island, Roe Lake is Pender's only natural lake, and is a reserve that has not been tapped to date. Buck Lake is the main supply for Magic Lake Estates, and Magic Lake is available as a backup. On South Pender Island, Greenburn Lake is used as a water supply for **Poets Cove Resort** and other users.

GARDENING GUIDE

Gardening on the Pender Islands is a passion for many of its residents, and the Zone-8 sub-Mediterranean climate offers opportunities for a wide variety of cultivation.

The Pender Island Garden Club was created in 1982 as a group of seven lady flower growers, and has emerged into a full fledged organization that hosts flower shows and an annual plant auction, conducts workshops, takes field trips and brings in guest speakers. Their meetings are held monthly except for July and August. See the Pender Post for current contact information.

Island Home Gardens opened in 2005 at the corner of Otter Bay Road and Bedwell Harbour Road across from the entrance to the Community Hall. Operated by the **Pender Island Home Building Centre**, the nursery is open seasonally 10:00 am to 4:00 pm most days, and sells annuals, perennials, trees, containers, soil, pots, baskets, and shrubs. The main store on Port Washington Road sells gardening supplies and plants. Numerous nurseries and garden supply businesses are located on the Saanich Peninsula, and are listed on the following page.

A fence is a much better deterrent for keeping deer out of your garden.

The main obstacle to gardening on the Pender Islands is the abundant black-tailed deer population, which will devour just about any un-fenced garden on the islands. Some plants are deer-resistant, however. In general, look around at what is thriving in unfenced areas. Chances are, those plants are deer-resistant, though as the deer get hungrier, they may eat plants that are lower on their priority list.

Numerous websites contain helpful plant lists and other local gardening tips. Try the following:

www.canadiangardening.com/howto/ideas_deer_proof.shtml
http://wlapwww.gov.bc.ca/kor/wld/garden.htm
www.gardeningbc.com
www.gardenwise.bc.ca (see the next page).

NURSERIES AND LANDSCAPE SUPPLIES - SAANICH PENINSULA
Art Knapp Plantland, Matticks Farm, 5325 Cordova Bay Rd, 658.1013
Big Barn Garden Centre, 1286 McKenzie Ave, 477.4435
Brentwood Bay Nurseries, 1395 Benvenuto, 652.1507
Buckerfield's, 1970 Keating X Rd, 652.9188
Cannor Nursery & Florist, 4660 Elk Lake, 658.5415
Danica Nurseries, 6705 Danica Pl, 652.2718
Dig This, 128-560 Johnson, 385.3212; Broadmead Village, 727.9922;
Do-It Centre, 1720 Cook St, 384.8181
Elk Lake Garden Centre, 5450 Patricia Bay Highway, 658.8812
Four Seasons Nursery, 9100 E Saanich Rd (Sidney), 654.0108
GardenWorks, www.gardenworks.ca, 4290 Blenkinsop, 721.2140;
Home Depot Canada, 2400 Millstream (Langford), 391.6000
Le Coteau Farms, 304 Walton Pl, 658.5888
Little Elf Garden Centre, 1062 Goldstream, 478.4557
Marigold Nursery, 7874 Lochside, 652.2342
Meadow Oak Nursery, 1070 Wain (Sidney), 655.1756
Peninsula Flowers Nursery, 8512 W Saanich Rd (Sidney), 652.9602
Russell Nursery, 1370 Wain (Sidney) 656.0384
Scent-Sational Plants, 830 Sayward Rd, 658.3544
Snapdragon Nurseries, 2360 Beacon (Sidney) 656.5199
Twin Peaks Nursery, 1780 Mills W, 654.0400
Vet's Plant Box, 570 Beaver Lake, 479.2667

Annual Gardening Guide for Coastal British Columbia

A good local website is **www.gardenwise.bc.ca** for information on gardening and suppliers. The following guide is reprinted from that site with their kind permission as a handy reference for Pender gardeners. Make the proper adaptations for Gulf Island living, such as practicing water conservation, using natural fertilizers, and emphasizing native vegetation. Check the BC Native Plant Society's web site: **www.npsbc.org**.

Pender serenity inside a fenced garden.

A greenhouse is a helpful tool for getting your plantings started.

COASTAL BC GARDENING GUIDE

JANUARY

Plan summer gardens and indoor seed planting; order seeds.

Prune grapes, fruit trees, small fruit and late-flowering deciduous shrubs.

Remove heavy snowfall from bushes and evergreens to prevent branch damage.

Water plants under rooflines and close to the house, especially in dry winters.

Spray deciduous trees and shrubs with dormant oil & lime sulphur;Clean up beds.

FEBRUARY

Lift, divide, and replant late-blooming perennials.

Finish pruning ornamental trees and spray with dormant oil; do not prune maples, birch, and walnuts until late July to September.

Most pruning can be done, except spring-flowering shrubs with buds.

Water all plants as appropriate.

Apply dolomite lime to lawn (months end).

Begin weed control in beds.

MARCH

Plant summer-flowering bulbs (or April).

Shop for flowering trees while in bloom.

Spring clean the garden.

Water and fertilize all plant material, including lawns and bulbs.

Plant hardy vegetables and bulbs.

Do most planting of nursery stock.

Start uncovering tender perennials, roses, and the more delicate plant material.

Finish pruning roses and planting bare-root roses.

APRIL

Plant early hardy veggies 'til mid-month.

Prune early-bloom shrubs after flowering.

Aerate the lawn with a core aerator; top dress and fertilize lawns; overseed bare patches.

APRIL (CONTINUED)

Control for dandelions before they flower.

Divide late-blooming perennials.

Fertilize cedar hedges with 30-10-10.

Check lawns for leather-jacket control, if necessary.

Plant all summer-flowering bulbs.

MAY

Buy bedding plants, harden, and plant out after mid-month; plant out dahlia tubers.

Weather permitting, set out all bedding plants (night protection may be required).

Plant patio containers.

Plant new lawns.

Prune back spring-flowering perennials.

Deadhead tulips & daffodils (flowers only) so bulb can produce energy for next year

Thin out annuals.

Remove seed heads from rhododendrons and azaleas.

Fertilize lawn with organic or slow-release fertilizer.

JUNE

Continue watering bulbs until yellowed leaves can be gently pulled off.

Keep newly planted hedges, trees and shrubs well watered.

Plant tomatoes, zucchini and cucumber.

Start roses on a monthly fungicide/insecticide spray schedule, if necessary.

Deadhead roses, annuals and perennials to promote more blooms.

Mulch garden areas to help preserve moisture and keep weeds down.

Plantings more annuals; water well.

Feed all annuals once or twice a month

Continue feeding container plants.

Wisely water lawns & gardens in AM.

JULY

Deadhead roses, annuals and perennials to promote more blooms; water well.

Harvest raspberries & strawberries; remove unwanted strawberry runners and plants that have cropped for three summers.

JULY (CONTINUED)

Cut herbs for freezing and drying.

Keep feeding gardens & container plants.

Water hanging baskets and patio plants at least once a day.

Lift daffodils and tulips for curing; use bulb dust for disease control.

Deadhead roses, annuals and perennials to promote more blooms; Thin grapes.

AUGUST

Continue feeding plants in containers and hanging baskets; water daily..

Prune back wisteria, other vigorous climbers.

Harvest vegetables frequently and keep plants well watered.

Hill potatoes with soil or mulch.

Cut back raspberry canes that fruited this year; Plant peonies; Plant fall rye.

Divide perennials that flowered from spring to early summer.

Fertilize late-flowering plants.

Remove fallen fruit (disease & pests out).

SEPTEMBER

Begin planting spring-flowering bulbs.

Irrigate when needed, but slowly reduce watering so plants get ready for winter.

Plant spring-flowering bulbs; use bulb dust for disease control.

Plant new lawns.

Fertilize all plants (except roses) and lawns with organic or slow-release fertilizer.

Allow lettuce to go to seed and feed the birds this winter.

Apply copper spray to selected fruit trees Check soil and add lime if required.

OCTOBER

Clear beds of annuals by the end of the month and compost.

Put sticky bands of tanglefoot around trees to deter winter moths..

Cultivate in interior regions; enrich in areas you plan to sow in spring.

OCTOBER (CONTINUED)

Plant shrubs, perennials and spring-flowering bulbs.

Dig up tender bulbs for storage; apply bulb dust for disease control.

Dig up carrots, beets and turnips and harvest cabbage for storing.

Don't forget to water plants close to the house or under rooflines.

Bring all tropical patio plants indoors; check them for pests before bringing inside.

NOVEMBER

Ensure plants like dianthus and saxifrage don't get covered in leaves, as they will rot.

Lift, divide and replant spring- and summer-blooming perennials (weather permitting).

Use any clean dead growth from garden beds and containers for the compost.

Protect trees and shrubs from mice, rabbits and deer; do not use plastic to wrap plants.

After first few hard frosts, mound bases of roses and less hardy plants with peat moss or other mulch such as compost.

Water all plants for winter; ensure adequate drainage so roots do not stand in water all winter.

Give roses a final deadheading and a light pruning; apply dolomite lime around established roses.

DECEMBER

Plan to rotate the crops in the vegetable garden next year.

Ventilate cold frames in mild weather.

Clean, sharpen and sterilize all tools.

Shovel clean snow around plants for extra moisture and insulation.

Keep bird feeders filled.

Lightly prune hollies and evergreens; use the clippings for wreaths and seasonal decorations.

**View from George Hill of Swanson Channel
through grasses and wildflowers.**

A deer in Swanson Channel searching for greener pastures.

18   LIVING ON PENDER

This chapter provides a glimpse into Pender's past, and contains helpful reference guides for present day features such as schools, churches, health services, senior citizens services, hazards and emergency preparedness.

New residents of the Pender Islands can join the Newcomers Club, which is comprised of ladies, while their spouses are invited to various functions. See the Pender Post for contact information on this and a plethora of other organizations that welcome new members. Many of the clubs and organizations are described in this book as they relate to the various topics in each chapter. The logistical constraints of island life lead to a high turnover rate of the full time population, about seven years on average. Therefore, new blood is typically welcomed, especially those who contribute to the community through volunteer activities and are good stewards of the environment.

HISTORICAL GUIDE TO THE PENDER ISLANDS

A Pender Timeline

The unique combination of natural forces that created The Pender Islands began over 300 million years ago when volcanic and metamorphic rocks were formed in the region. The collision of tectonic plates led to a sequence of events that created Pender's bedrock, which was later molded by glaciers. As the glaciers melted, the ocean rose and Pender became an island. Coast Salish people inhabited the island thousands of years ago, calling the region *Sqla-lot-sis* that means *homeland*. Explorers from Spain and Great Britain sailed through the area in the 1700's and named some of the nearby islands but did not settle here at first. British surveyors returned in the mid 1800's and named the remainder of the Gulf Islands, including Pender. Since the late 1800's Europeans established permanent Pender settlements as they farmed the land, harvested the timber, and processed the fish. When a canal was dug in 1902, Pender Island was split into North Pender and South Pender, which were joined by a bridge in 1955. The Pender Islands eventually evolved primarily into a recreation destination inhabited by both full-time and part time residents.

Pender Islands' history is described below via a timeline that lays out some of the important events in the history of the Islands, with a few selected historical milestones thrown in to aid in the perspective. Additional historical perspective is found in the *Coastal Access and Hiking Guide* under each area description. Pender Island historical data in this book was compiled mostly from the Pender Island Museum Society's publications *A Self-Guided Historic Tour of the Pender Islands*, *The Lost Heritage of the Penders (2004 Calendar)*, the Society's historical display at their museum, British Columbia Historical Federation books *A Gulf Islands Patchwork*, and *More Tales from the Gulf Islands*, and various articles published in the *Pender Post*.

PENDER ISLANDS TIMELINE

360 TO 315 MILLION YEARS AGO (MYA)
*Volcanic and metasediment rocks are formed which comprise the deep bedrock beneath the Pender Islands.

150 MYA
*Colliding continental plates create the Georgia Depression, within which are the Strait of Georgia and Puget Sound, together known as the Georgia Basin. Sedimentary Rocks of the Nanaimo Group are deposited in a marine environment about 80 mya, forming the bedrock of the Pender Islands.

50,000 - 10,000 YEARS AGO
*First Nations hunters migrate from Asia to North America across the Beringia land bridge of the Pleistocene epoch.

14,000 - 13,000 YEARS AGO
*The glacial retreat causes the Pacific Ocean to enter the Strait of Juan de Fuca, Strait of Georgia, and inlets along the west coast of Vancouver Island, and floods most of the present day lowlands. Vancouver Island has risen hundreds of feet since this time.

5,170 YEARS AGO
*First evidence of Coast Salish people on the Pender Islands according to artifacts found at Pender Canal excavation sites.

985
*Bjarni Herjolfsson, an Icelanic trader, sights North America; The Norse then colonize Newfoundland for a brief period.

1492
*Christopher Columbus lands in the Caribbean.

1534
*Jacques Cartier lands at Gaspe.

1776
*United States declares independence from Great Britain.

1790'S
*Spanish explorers sail through and chart area. Juan Pantoja and JoseMaria Narvaez name Galiano, Saturna, and Valdes Islands.

1790'S CONTINUED
*British explorer Captain George Vancouver names the *Gulf of Georgia* after His Majesty George III. *The Gulf Islands* are also named, although this is a misnomer as the *Gulf* is actually a *Strait*.

1840'S
*Mount Norman named for William Henry Norman, R.N., H.M.S. Ganges.
*Oregon Boundary Treaty with the U.S. sets boundary at 49°N latitude, but leaves Vancouver Island and the Gulf Islands in British hands.

1850'S
*Trincomali Channel named after H.M.S. Trincomalee sailing frigate. Plumper Sound named for H.M.S Plumper (relieved by H.M.S. Hecate).
*First land purchase on Pender Island by a European who remains off-island.
*Fraser River Gold Rush: Miners flood in from California through Victoria.
*Native populations decline sharply from disease brought by the Europeans.

LATE 1850-S THROUGH 1860'S
British Surveyor Captain Richards surveys the area and names various locations for his ship and crew as well as earlier Spanish explorers:
*Pender Island named after hydrographer Daniel Pender, R.N. of H.M.S. Plumper, H.M.S, Hecate and S.S. Beaver.
*Bedwell Harbour named after Edward Parker Bedwell, R.N., Master of H.M.S. Plumper and H.M.S. Hecate.
*Port Browning named after Alexander Browning, R.N., served under Captains Pender and Richards.
*Gowlland Point named for John Thomas Gowlland, R.N. Second Master, H.M.S. Plumper and H.M.S. Hecate.
*Wallace Point and Peter Cove named for Peter William Wallace, M.D., R.N., Assistant Surgeon, H.M.S. Satellite.

1860's
*First European settlers inhabit the Gulf Islands, with seven on Pender Island.
*Dominion of Canada created (1867).
*John MacDonald is first Prime Minister.
1870's
*British Columbia enters Confederation as the sixth province (1871).
*David Hope and Noah Buckley arrive from Scotland and settle the valley near Hope Bay on North Pender Island.
1880's
*The first family to settle on the Pender Islands is the Auchterlonies (David Hope's sister and family).
*Washington and Oliver Grimmer settle the Port Washington area.
*First families on South Pender Island are the Spaldings and the Higgs. Lilias McKay marries Arthur Spalding (homesite is Lilias Spalding Heritage Park).
*Canadian Pacific Railway completed in BC, enabling cross-country travel.
1890's
*The first Port Washington government wharf constructed (1891).
*The Stanley Cup first awarded, to the Montreal AAA hockey team (1893).
*Pender's Farmers Institute created, the first island-wide organization (1899).
1900's
*Hope Bay and Bedwell Harbour government wharves constructed (1901).
*First scheduled ferry service to Pender Island from Vancouver Island twice per week on the private steamship Iroquois. This boosts the Pender Island economy, as produce can be sent to markets, and supplies obtained on a regular basis. The result is an influx of new settlers.
*Pender Island Schoolhouse built, used 1902 - 1977. Now Nu-To-Yu Thrift Shop.
*Pender Island Canal is excavated to facilitate inter-island marine navigation (1902). This enables the Iroquois to travel between the Hope Bay Dock on North Pender Island and Sidney on Vancouver

Island without having to sail around South Pender Island. It also enables private boaters to avoid portage of their boats over the isthmus. Construction of the canal is a controversial issue. The excavation of the canal creates two islands, North and South Pender.
*R.W.S. Corbett opens Hope Bay Store (1903) His house remains and is sometimes operated as Corbett House B&B.
*Pender Island Cemetery created (1904).
*The Roe family purchases 600 acres between Ella Bay and Shingle Bay. (Now mostly part of GINPR).
*First Pender wedding is Clara Menzies and Howard Harris of Hope Bay.
*Presbyterian Church built near Hope Bay (Now United Community Church).
*Hope Bay Community Hall constructed.
1910's
*Port Washington Community Hall constructed at Port Washington and Otter Bay Roads. Spencer Percival builds Port Washington Store (1910).
*Hope Bay and Port Washington have developed into separate and rival communities. Hope Bay has more liberal Scottish Presbyterians, while Port Washington contains more conservative English Anglicans.
*The Coast Shale Company purchases 50 acres on North Pender and constructs a brick factory at Bricky Bay that employs up to 75. Operates for only a few years. Bricks remain imbedded in the beach.
*The Iroquois, overloaded with cargo, lists and then capsizes and sinks in strong winds 15 minutes after leaving the Sidney dock, killing 22, including Pender Island school teacher Fanny Hooson, 38, and her son, Evan, 3 (1911).
*Canadian Northern Pacific railway inaugurates a new Gulf Island ferry service from Sidney, with steamer S.S. Joan (1912).
*Hope Bay Store expands.

•S.S. Queen City takes over ferry service from Sidney. The service is not as regular as the Iroquois had been (1914).

1920's

•The Canadian Pacific Steam Ship (CPSS) line begins regular service to the Gulf Islands, featuring the S.S. Princess Mary.

•Pender Island Fish Products of Victoria begins operation at the entrance to Shingle Bay. Facility extracts fish oil and produces fertilizer and fish meal.

•British Columbia Fish Salteries Ltd., controlled by Japanese interests, begins operations in Hayashi Cove, Otter Bay. Herrings are packed in salt boxes and shipped to the Far East.

•Stock market crash, beginning of the Great Depression (1929).

1930's

•First Pender Island Fall Fair held at the Hope Bay Community Hall (1932).

•CBC founded (1932).

•Canada declares war on Germany (1937).

•Most able-bodied Pender men enlist.

•Church of the Good Shepherd constructed on South Pender (1938).

1940's

•During WWII, the fish saltery plant in Hayashi Cove is confiscated from the Japanese as part of the Japanese relocation to the interior.

•Royal Canadian Legion Branch 239 (Pender Island) receives Dominion Command Charter (1946). Hall is located on MacKinnon Road, west of ferry.

•Earthquake magnitude 7.3 occurs near Courtenay on Vancouver Island (1946).

•Canada's largest quake (M=8.1) hits near Queen Charlotte Islands (1949).

1950's

•South Pender's Andover subdivision constructed in Craddock Rd area.

•Port Browning Government wharf constructed.

•Fish saltery at Hayashi Cove is destroyed by fire (site of Otter Bay Marina).

•CPSS stops ferry service to Pender. Two smaller private companies take over.

•One-lane bridge is built across the Pender Canal to re-join North and South Pender Islands, which have been separate since 1902 (1955).

•Fish Reduction Plant at entrance to Shingle Bay is destroyed by fire (1959). Remnants of dock pilings remain at the site to this day.

1960's

•Canadian Bill of Rights approved (1960).

•BC Toll Authority formed by BC Government to handle BC Ferry service (1960). The name changed later to BC Ferries Corp., a Crown Corporation.

•Magic Lake Estates established, originally called Gulf Garden Estates. Phase 1 consists of 190 lots of eventual 1,200 lots.

•Otter Bay ferry terminal built (1965), stimulating surge of Pender growth.

•Hope Bay Community Hall demolished (1965).

1970's

•Pender Post first published (1971).

•The Islands Trust is created to control development in the Gulf Islands, inspired in part by the large Magic Lake Estates development (1974).

•Driftwood Centre constructed, main shopping centre on the Pender Islands.

•Earthquake M=5.3 occurs at a depth of 54 km beneath the Pender Islands, caused by the subducting ocean plate. No major damage is reported (1976).

•New Pender Islands School is constructed on North Pender Island (1977).

•Port Washington Community Hall is demolished (1977).

1980's

•*O Canada* becomes Canadian National Anthem (1980).

•Pender Island Medical Clinic built (1981).

•Canada Act and Charter of Rights and Freedoms come into effect (1982).

•Hope Bay Store closes as General Store (1984).

1980's CONTINUED
*Logging ceases on Mt. Norman (1985).
*Mt. Norman Regional Park (CRD) created, first on Gulf Islands (1988).

1990's
*Pender Island Public Library built (1990).
*Islands Trust Fund created to protect natural habitat on Gulf Islands (1990).
*Roesland Resort closes; had operated since early 1900's (1991).
*The Newcomers Club is created to acquaint ladies new to the island to elements of island life, and to meet new friends (1994).
*Medicine Beach property acquired by Islands Trust and PICA (1995).
*Current Pender Island Community Hall is constructed.
*Hope Bay Store burns, most recently used as Arts & Crafts Centre (1998).
*Parks Canada buys Pacific Marine Legacy Lands (1998; Roesland/Roe Lake).
*Full service Tru Value Foods store moves in to Driftwood Centre.

2000
*Brooks Point on South Pender acquired by CRD as a conservation area.
*Gowlland Point Parcel purchased by CRD for future Regional Park.

2001
*9/11 terrorist attacks in the U.S. Border security begins to tighten.

2002
*Bedwell Harbour Resort on South Pender Island is closed and demolished.
*Poets Cove Resort begins construction in its place.

2003
*Gulf Islands National Park Reserve (GINPR), Canada's 40th National Park, is created which includes Mt. Norman (formerly CRD park), Beaumont Marine Park and Prior Centennial Campground (formerly BC Parks), Pacific Marine Legacy Lands at Roe Lake and Roesland, and a portion of Mt. Menzies.
*Hope Bay Store reconstruction begins.
*Same-sex marriage legalized in BC (Legalized federally in July 2005).

2004
*Poets Cove Resort Opens.
*Greenburn Lake and adjacent properties on South Pender acquired for GINPR.

2005
*Loretta's Wood parcel joins GINPR.
*Hope Bay Store re-opens with restaurant, shops, gallery and offices.
*Pender Island Museum opens at site of old Roe House in Roesland, GINPR.
*Morning Bay Vineyard opens as the Penders' first winery.

2006
*Currents, a vacation home development is completed at Otter Bay Marina.

Schoolhouse to NuToU

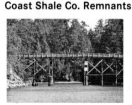

Coast Shale Co. Remnants

Driftwood Centre

United Commun. Church

The Bridge

Poets Cove Resort

The Coast Salish People

The Coast Salish people lived in the Gulf Islands region after the glaciers retreated. They called it *Sqla-lot-sis* [phonetic pronunciation], which means *homeland*. The *Salt Water People*, as they called themselves, relied mostly on seafood for sustenance, and travelled extensively by water. Pender Island was a favourite fishing location because of the salmon migrating to the Fraser or Columbia River. Bedwell Harbour (called *Ste'yus*, or *Wind Drying* in the Hul'qumi'num language) was one of the best places to harvest shellfish. Shell middens, consisting of empty shells deposited by humans over the millennia, were left around Bedwell Harbour and the Pender Canal area.

Much of what is known about the Coast Salish people that inhabited the Pender Islands is a result of excavations conducted in the region, including the site of the Pender Canal. This area was known as *Tl'e'ulthw*, or *Permanent Houses* in Hul'qumi'num. During the summers of 1984 and 1985 Simon Fraser University archaeologists coordinated the efforts that included clearing the underbrush on the Crown Land, constructing two-metre grids, and carefully sifting through 10-cm segments for artifacts. A plethora of artifacts were unearthed and catalogued. Most of the artifacts dated back 2,500 to 4,000 years, but the oldest items were 5,170 years old. Artifacts included bone awls, antler wedges, slate knives, and basalt abraders, among others. A slate box probably used for storage was discovered. Burial sites were unearthed that revealed findings ranging from entire intact skeletons to bone fragments.

The Pender Island Museum Society (see description below) erected a descriptive plaque along Canal Road on the North Pender side of the bridge in 1993. It states: "First Nation peoples lived here from 6000 to 2000 years ago. They call it Xelisen (Helisen) meaning *Lying Between* for the isthmus that connected North and South Pender Islands. It was an encampment used for harvesting the food resources of nearby waters and beaches. Archaeologists have recorded information from sites on both sides of the isthmus. It is a provincial heritage site."

The native peoples made good use of the indigenous plants and trees on the Pender Islands. The Douglas fir was used for teepee poles, smoking racks, spear shafts, fishhooks and firewood. The grand fir was used to make canoes, fishhooks, hand tools and firewood. Natives used the wood of the western red cedar to make dugout canoes, fishing floats, bowls, masks, totem poles, ornamental boxes and spear and arrow shafts. The bark was used for clothing, diapers, mats, blankets, baskets and medicine. The wood of the western hemlock may have been used for spear shafts, spoons, dishes, roasting spits and ridgepoles, while the bark was boiled to extract red dye for basket and wool material (Varner, 2002).

A Tsawout First Nation Reserve currently exists south of Poets Cove Resort (**Map 8**). There are no permanent dwellings on the land.

The Pender Islands Museum

The Pender Islands Museum Society was created in 1986 with the goal of establishing a museum to house artifacts relevant to the community of the Pender Islands. By 1994, their goals expanded to acquire photographs, media, and documents that illustrate Pender's history and heritage. The Society created a permanent display in the Pender Island Library foyer containing First Nations artifacts recovered from the archaeological excavation at the Pender Canal in the mid-1980's, and erected a cairn with a descriptive plaque at the canal describing the site. The Society also presents a regular column in the Pender Post entitled *Memories*, which draws from its archives to purvey a story of historical interest. On July 16, 2005, the goal of the Society was realized with the opening of the Pender Islands Museum in the old Roe House at the Roesland site of the Gulf Islands National Park Reserve. The Society received a long-term lease on the house in exchange for rescuing and restoring it. The museum features rotating exhibits and contains various archived materials. A display formerly housed at the Pender Island Library containing documents and photographs relevant to the history of the Pender Islands has been moved to the museum. Admission to the library is by donation, and various publications and postcards are for sale. Initially, the museum is open Saturdays and Sundays from 11:00 am to 4:00 pm. **Map 3 (25)**.

Directions: From the ferry terminal, bear right on MacKinnon Road, and again at Otter Bay Road. Continue for about 1.6 km at which point the main road descends a short steep hill and curves to the left, while South Otter Bay Road intersects at the right, forming a *T* intersection, where a directional sign to the museum is posted. Carefully turn right on South Otter Bay Road and proceed for another 1.6 km. As the road curves sharply to the left, watch for the *Roesland* sign on the right. An unpaved parking area is visible on the right with a National Park display sign. Park here. Use caution since the lot can become muddy when wet. An outhouse is located beyond the park sign. Walk about 3 to 5 minutes down the gravel driveway (a gentle hill) and follow the signs to the museum, avoiding the private residence at the end of the road.

Historic Buildings and Monuments on the Pender Islands

Although many of the early buildings constructed on the Pender Islands were demolished as a practical matter, several buildings of historical interest do remain, and are listed below. History buffs should purchase the Museum Society's pamphlet *A Self-Guided Historic Tour of the Pender Islands*, at the museum or **Talisman Books & Gallery**, which contains detailed information on these structures, as well as the history of the various areas of the Pender Islands. Most of the buildings are private residences and public entry is prohibited. Refer to the *Pender Islands Map Atlas* in this book for location of the numbered items, i.e. (**3**). These features are also described in the *Coastal Access and Hiking Guide.*

North Pender Island

PORT WASHINGTON AREA - Map 1B
The Port Washington government wharf, the first on the Penders, was built in 1891. Prior to this structure, all deliveries were done on beaches. Spencer Percival built the General Store in 1910 (**3**).

HOPE BAY/CLAM BAY AREA Map 1C.
Hope Bay Store (1902) and Dock (1901): The new Hope Bay Store is built at the site of the original Hope Bay Store, which burned down in 1998 (**7**).

Port Washington Road and Bedwell Harbour Road, southwest corner:
The Auchterlonie House, built by David Hope in 1878, is the oldest remaining house on the Penders. It is now occupied by Stribley's Pottery.

Corbett Road, between Port Washington Road and Amies Road:
Corbett House, built in 1902 by R.S.W. Corbett, founder of original Hope Bay Store, is sometimes used as a B&B (but not a time of writing).

Clam Bay Road, West of Pearson Road
Grover Sergeant Memorial Cairn: A monument to a Canadian flyer who crashed here during WWII (**13**).

OTTER BAY AREA
Grimmer Valley: Otter Bay Road and Grimmer Road near the golf course:
The bronze sculpture is of Washington Grimmer who originally farmed this valley (Photo, right). By the late Ralph Sketch, a noted equestrian sculptor. **Maps 1, 1A.**

OTTER BAY AREA continued

MacKinnon Road: Near the end of the road on the left: Waterlea (1910), second home of John MacKinnon, whose first home was at the site of the ferry parking lot. The current owners maintain a rare Canadian olive grove. **Map 1A**.

Roesland, South Otter Bay Road: The Roe House (1908) has been preserved as the Pender Island Museum. Other former resort buildings remain on site. **Map 3 (25)**.

COMMUNITY HALL AREA

Bedwell Harbour Road, west side, between its intersections with Corbett Road to the north and Otter Bay Road to the south, as shown on **Map 1**:
* United Community Church (1907) was originally the Presbyterian Church.
* Nu-To-Yu thrift shop occupies the former schoolhouse (1902-1977).
* John MacDonald House (1895). Early settler who mostly worked off-island.

Bedwell Harbour Road, south of Otter Bay Road, west side, as shown on **Map 3**:
Pender Island Cemetery, on land donated by Rutherford Hope in 1904.

CENTRAL/DRIFTWOOD CENTRE AREA

Canal Road, south of Scarff Road (**Map 5**):
St. Peter's Anglican Church built in Port Washington in 1916, moved here in 1997.

CANAL AREA

Canal Road, north side near bridge: Plaques commemorate the Coast Salish encampment dating back over 5,000 years. **Map 6 (41)**.

SOUTH PENDER ISLAND

Canal Area - Canal Road, left side past the bridge:
Log cabin built by the Walker Brothers (1909). **Map 6**.

Spalding Valley - Between Spalding and Castle Roads:
Lilias Spalding Heritage Park at her early 1900's homesite. **Map 8 (90)**.

Poets Cove Area - Gowlland Point Road
The Church of the Good Shepherd was built in 1937. **Map 8**.

HEALTH SERVICES GUIDE

The Pender Islands are fortunate to have dedicated and highly qualified health care professionals. Services are available on-island up to a point, and then patients are referred to facilities in larger metropolitan areas. The need of more frequent and advanced medical treatments is one of the primary reasons why people leave Pender, or other small rural communities. The information provided in this guide is current as of Fall 2005, with the Pender Islands data updated as of Spring 2006. Most of the Pender Islands information can be found in the latest Pender Post, which should always contain the most up to date listings. In addition to Pender Islands health care services, this chapter also contains Pender veterinary services and massage/fitness, as well as helpful information for travel to nearby medical facilities, and lists of those facilities in the Gulf Islands and Sidney-Victoria areas.

The Pender Islands Health Centre

The Pender Islands Medical Clinic is located at 5715 Canal Road. From the Driftwood Centre, turn right (south) on Bedwell Harbour Road, which turns into Canal Road. Follow the signs to South Pender Island, making a left at the continuation of Canal Road, and look for the Medical Clinic on the right hand side, across from the school. The clinic is open Monday to Friday 9:00 am to 12:30 pm and 2:00 pm to 5:00 pm. **Maps 5, 5A.**

The clinic was constructed in 1981 from a combination of government funds and a strong community effort led by the Lions Club. It is operated by the Pender Islands Health Care Society (PIHCS). Recent renovations to the facility have included upgrading and expanding of the emergency treatment and examination rooms, and acquisition of a new defibrillator and other vital equipment.

Medical
The Pender Post frequently contains letters of appreciation to the dedicated Pender Island health care professionals. Two doctors are on staff at the clinic (Dr. Gerald Moore and Dr. Mike Hudson). To phone their office during regular office hours, call 629.3233. For serious medical problems that occur after office hours, do not call them at home, but do call 1.800.866.5602 and ask for Pager 5214. The on-duty doctor should return your call. Call 911 for a medical emergency. At time of writing the two doctors are accepting new regular patients off of a waiting list only, which at time of writing is about 200, equivalent to two or three years. PIHCS plans to request a third doctor from the Vancouver Island Health Authority. Most patients on the waiting list travel to the Victoria area for routine treatment.

Two or three community nurses are available 10:00 am - 5:00 pm, with before/after hours and weekend appointments possible; 629.3242. A public health nurse is available at 250.544.2400 or toll free 539.3099. For other services not offered on the Pender Islands, patients are typically sent to the Victoria area clinics and hospitals, or even Vancouver if appropriate.

For emergency care, there is one ambulance on the island, which transports patients to the Medical Clinic, or to Thieves Bay Marina for transport by boat to Sidney. Acute emergency cases are airlifted by helicopter from the helipad at Hastings Airstrip, located just north of the Driftwood Centre.

If you are not a member of the BC Health system or Canadian provinces or territories with reciprocal agreements with BC, you will probably be required to pay for your services up front and then apply for reimbursement from your health care provider. The exception is the ambulance, which will send you a bill. At time of writing, Quebec does not have a reciprocal agreement with BC.

Dental
One dentist, Dr. Brian Nord, practices at the Medical Clinic typically Tuesdays, Wednesdays and Thursdays. 629.6815. He has a good reputation on Pender. Dentists are private practitioners and not a part of the BC Health system.

Other Services Provided at the Medical Clinic
Optometrist: Dr. David Schaafsma, 629.3322
Acupuncture: Trevor Erikson, 629.3322
Jin Shin Do Acupressure: Nicole Povey, 629.6916
Physiotherapy: Kim Reschke, Shirley LePers & Michele Cook 629.3322
Psychiatrist: Dr. Jaime Smith, 250.656.4403
Crisis Counselling: Rob Willingham, 629.6700
Lab Services: Sonya Fulawka, 629.3233
Registered Massage Therapist: Karen Mani Lang, 629.6639

Outside Pender's Health Centre

Licensed Health Professionals Regulated by the BC Ministry of Health
Chiropractor: Mark Wensley, 629.9918
Licensed Practical Nurse: Virginia Mundy, 629.6730
Pharmacist, Christine Swan: 629.6555 (See the *Shopping Guide - Pharmacies)*
Psychologist: Jean Richardson, 629.6000
Registered Physiotherapist: Mieke Truijen, 629.9910

Veterinary
Drs. Maureen Stone and Gordon Oudman operate a veterinary clinic in Magic Lake Estates at 4847 Cutlass Court (**Map 4**, *D*). Take Schooner Way past Pirates Road, then left on Cutlass Court to the end of the street. These popular, community-minded vets are open Monday to Friday 10:00-4:00, and offer 24-hour emergency service. 629.9909.

TRAVEL ASSISTANCE PROGRAM
The Travel Assistance Program (TAP) offers travel discounts to eligible BC residents who must travel within the province for non-emergency medical services not available in their own community, and whose travel expenses are not covered by third-party insurance or other government programs. A physician referral is required, and the TAP form must be provided by that physician's office. TAP is a private and public sector corporate partnership program, which is coordinated by the Ministry of Health Services. The Ministry does not provide direct financial assistance with travel costs; rather, it is the transportation partners who agree to waive or discount their regular fees. No compensation is provided for meals, accommodations, fuel, and local transportation. Benefits include free travel on BC Ferries for the patient and vehicle (and escort, if authorized by the physician) and discounts off of fares on Harbour Air, Central Mountain Air, Air Canada, Air Canada Jazz, BC Rail, VIA Rail, and Pacific Coach Lines. Angels Flight provides free air transport to ambulatory people, whose medical conditions make it difficult or impossible for them to travel by conventional means, to and from hospitals, clinics, doctor's offices and other medical facilities on the lower mainland and points on Vancouver Island. Call 250.818.0288 for more information and to arrange flights via Angels Flight. For more details on the information described above, see **www.hlth.gov.bc.ca/rural/tap_patient.html** or call 1.800.661.2668.

Spa, Massage & Fitness

Poets Cove Resort operates **Susurrus Spa** that features a Sandstone Steam Lodge and rock grotto. The spa offers a wide range of treatments. Examples are Hot Stone Massage ($125/hour), Sports/Deep Tissue Massage ($105/hour), Swedish Massage ($95/hour), Aromatic Sea Clay Massage ($125/hour), Water Lilly Wrap ($125/hour), and Hydro Tub ($50/half-hour). They also offer a full line of aesthetics treatment including an organic facial ($100), waxing ($15 - $70), manicures ($55), and pedicure ($65). For appointments, log onto **www.poetscove.com** or call 1.866.604.5561 or 629.2113.

Revolution Fitness and Dance at the Driftwood Centre has four cardio machines, fixed resistance machines, free weights, and studio space with mats, abs balls and sport tubing. Classes include yoga and dance. No locker facilities. Check for open days and hours, 2006 rates (+gst): $7 drop in; Monthly $50, annual $550. Family rates, personal trainers and individual instruction are also available, 629.3122

Check the latest *Pender Post* for ads for massage therapists. As of April 2006 they are:
Ahh Spa, Massage, salt glow body polish, facials, energy work, intuitive counselling, 629.6259 and 629.3750. Located next to Magic Lake Market.
Carol Hoffman, Reflexology and Chakra Balancing, 629-6810.
Shelley Easthope, BA, RST, Reiki & Shiatsu Treatment, 629-3036, **www.shelleyeasthope.com**.
Wayne McNab, Reiki Master, Treatment, Workshops, 629.6804, wmcnab@gulfislands.com.
Celeste Varley, Reiki treatment , Heartsong Studio, 629.6326, **www.pendercreatives.com**
The Spa at Driftwood Centre, Massage, tanning, aesthetics, 629.9969.

NEARBY OFF-ISLAND MEDICAL FACILITIES (Area code 250):
Salt Spring Island
Lady Minto Gulf Islands Hospital, 135 Crofton, 538.4800
Galiano Island
Lady Minto Gulf Islands Hospital, 539.2026 (local call)
Victoria - Sidney Area
Hospitals:
Royal Jubilee Hospital, 370.8000, 1900 Fort Street, Victoria
Saanich Peninsula Hospital, 652.3911, 2166 Mt Newton X Road, Saanichton
Victoria General Hospital, 727.4212, 1 Hospital Way (Canada 1 at Helmcken)
Walk-In Clinics and Treatment Centres:
Admirals Health Centre, 380.9002, 105-1505 Admirals Road
Bevan Avenue Walk in Clinic, 656.4177, 2-2379 Bevan Avenue, Sidney
Broadmead Medical Clinic, 727.9970, 140-777 Royal Oak Ave
Colwood Medical Treatment Centre, 478.8833, 102-1910 Sooke Road
Cook & Quadra Medical Clinic, 386.6161, 3461 Cook Street
Esquimalt Treatment Centre, 382.4296, 918 Esquimalt Road
Fairfield Medical Treatment Centre, 592.3496, 1594 Fairfield Road
Gordon Head Treatment Centre, 477.4777, 103-1595 McKenzie
James Bay Medical Treatment Centre, 388.9934, 100-230 Menzies
Lansdowne Medical Treatment Centre, 592.4212, 120-1641 Hillside
Mayfair Medical Treatment Centre, 383.9898, 210-3147 Douglas Street
Oak Bay Medical Clinic, 598.6744, 101-1640 Oak Bay Avenue
Saanich Plaza Medical Clinic, 475.1101, 3944 Blanshard Ave
St Anthony's Medical Centre, 478.6242, 582 Goldstream Road
Shelbourne Medical Treatment Centre, 598.3200, 3200 Shelbourne
Tillicum Mall Medical Clinic, 381.8112, 3170 Tillicum Road

VICTORIA LODGING DISCOUNTS
Reduced lodging rates are available to those visiting the Victoria area for
medical reasons. The hospital's social worker can assist you, but following is a
list compiled by the respective hospitals:
ROYAL JUBILEE OR VICTORIA GENERAL
Dominion Hotel, 759 Yates, 384.4136
Accent Inns, 3233 Maple, 475.7500
Traveller's Inn, 2828 Rock Bay Ave, 385.1000 and 3025 Douglas, 978.1000
Travelodge, 229 Gorge East, 388.6611
Comfort Inn, 101 Island Hwy, 388.7861 (Best bet for Vic General)
Kelly's Place B&B, 4168 Carey, 727.2777
Also near **Royal Jubilee** are these health care-related accommodations:
Canadian Cancer Vancouver Island Lodge, 2202 Richmond, 592.2662
Easter Seal House, 2095 Granite, 595.6060
Heart House, 1580 Pembroke, 595.1931
SAANICH PENINSULA HOSPITAL
Quality Inn - Waddling Dog, 2476 Mt. Newton X Rd, 1.800.567.8466
Super 8 Motel, 2477 Mt. Newton X Rd, 1.800.800.8000
Western 66 Motel, 2401 Mt. Newton X Rd, 1.800.463.4464

Health Care Resources

BC Health Website: www.gov.bc.ca/health The Province of British Columbia's Ministry of Health Services. Also surgical wait times and helpful links.
Health Files: www.bchealthguide.org/healthfiles/index.stm A series of fact sheets about a wide range of public and environmental health and safety issues.
General information Line: 1.800.465.4911, Victoria 250.952.1742: For Ministry of Health's programs, services and initiatives including. cardiac care services, cancer diagnostic and treatment services, organ transplant programs, hospital funding, and other related health care initiatives, 8:30 a.m. - 4:30 p.m., Monday to Friday.
BC Healthguide Nurseline (24 hours) 1.866.215.4700; TTY: 1.866.TTY.4700
Puts you in touch with a Registered Nurse who will answer your questions about symptoms, health concerns, recommended course of action, when to see a health professional and further health resources.
Vital Statistics Hotline: 1.800.663.8328. Registration of births, deaths and marriages, changes of names, Adoption Reunion Registry, Wills Registry, genealogical and biostatistical information, and access to services such as marriage commissioners, marriage licenses and burial permits. 8:30 a.m. to 4:30 p.m., Monday to Friday.
Medical Services Plan Subscriber Information 1.800.663.7100
Pharmanet 1.800.554.0250; **Fair Pharmacare** 1.800.387.4977
Ambulance Bill Service 1.800.665.7199
The Vancouver Island Health Authority (VIHA) is one of six health authorities in British Columbia. VIHA provides a full range of health care services including hospital, community, and home care, as well as environmental and public health services, which include education and prevention. The Pender Islands are within the southern, or Capital Region within the VIHA. Their headquarters is at 1952 Bay Street, Victoria BC V8R 1J8, **www.viha.ca** Phone 250.370.8699.
Health Canada (Federal) web site: **www.hc-sc.gc.ca** Ottawa 613.957.2991;
TTY: 1.800.267.1245; Vancouver Regional Office, 757 West Hastings Street, Suite 405, Vancouver 604.666.2083.

Alcohol & Drug Substance Abuse Info & Referral: 663.1441;
Arthritis: 321.1433; **Diabetes:** 286.4656;
Dial-A-Dietician, free nutrition line: 667.3438;
Kidney Foundation: 361.7494; **Mental Health Information:** 661.2121;
Multiple Sclerosis Society: 268.7582; **Poison Control Centre:** 567.8911;
Mammography Screen: 663.9203;
STDs and AIDS: 661.4337 (24 hours);
British Columbia Transplant Society: 1.800 663.6189 **www.transplant.bc.ca**;
Cancer Info: 1.888.939.3333; **Heart & Stroke Foundation:** 1.888.473.4636
Gulf Islands 24 Hour Crisis Line: 1.877.435.7544.

SCHOOL AND CHURCH GUIDE

Schools

The Pender Islands are within the Gulf Islands School District 64 (SD 64) that includes the five major Southern Gulf Islands (Pender, Salt Spring, Galiano, Mayne and Saturna). SD 64 is the second largest employer on the Gulf Islands (after BC Ferries), with 15 principals or vice principals, 113 teachers and 89 support staff. The Board of School Trustees includes a Chair, a Vice Chair, and five trustees. In 2005-2006, SD 64 initiated a 4-day school week to help bridge a budget shortfall, as a result of decreasing enrolment in recent years on all the islands except for the Pender Islands. SD 64's headquarters is at 112 Rainbow Road, Salt Spring Island, BC, V8K 2K3. Phone: 539.5023 (local call from Pender) or 250.537.5548; Fax: 250.537.4200. Web Site: **www.sd64.bc.ca**.

The Pender Island Elementary Secondary School was constructed in 1977 after having operated in the building now occupied by the Nu-To-Yu thrift shop since 1902. It is located on Canal Road on North Pender Island, across from the Medical Clinic (**Maps 5, 5A**). Phone: 629-3711. In 2003, an expansion was completed that added to the existing seven classrooms, library, computer lab, and gym. It created a foods room, an electronics shop, a science lab, a new classroom, more kindergarten space, a multi-purpose/stage area, as well as more space for administration and health, counselling, general storage and a media and high tech computer centre. The staff consists of a teaching principal, seven teachers, two special education assistants, one part-time counsellor, a school secretary, two custodians, and a bus driver. Limited assistance is also available to Pender students in the areas of English as a second language, occupational therapy and speech therapy. Enrolment is around 150 students from North and South Pender Islands in grades K through 12. About two-thirds are in K-8, which consists of an independent kindergarten, and split grades for 1-2, 2-3, 4-5-6 and 7-8. Upon completing Grade 8, most students transfer to Salt Spring, Gulf Islands Secondary School, or complete schooling on the Pender Islands according to the Distributed Education Programme with the assistance of the school's Student Learning Centre. Those who attend school on Salt Spring Island ride the school bus every morning to the Port Washington dock, where a water taxi arrives after having already picked up students from other Gulf Islands. They trek across the Swanson Channel in all but the most severe weather, reaching Ganges on Salt Spring Island in about 40 minutes, where the secondary school is located. Many students arrange for places to board on Salt Spring Island, which limits the amount of time they spend commuting to school.

The school has an active Parent Advisory Council (PAC) that provides advice, organizes fundraisers and hosts musical and other artistic productions in order to benefit the school. School spirit tends to be high, and the community is very supportive of the school and its activities. A roller-hockey rink on campus is popular with students and local clubs.

For pre-school, accredited Montessori Educator Anne Davis operates the licensed Port Washington Montessori Children's House for children aged 18 months to 6 years. 629.6111. The Dragonfly Daycare Centre, attached to the Pender Island School, also provides excellent pre-school programmes for local children.

The Pender Island Playgroup provides a place for young babies to begin interactions with other small children, while parents socialize and share information about parenting. Grandparents, children and caregivers also participate. Membership is $10 per month per family ($15 for summer only membership) and $3 for drop-in. Located next to the Nu-To-Yu thrift shop near the library (**Map 1,** *B*). See the Pender Post or Lions Club phone book (under *Youth Associations*) for contact information.

Summer Story Time for kids features various presenters at the Pender Island Public Library on summer Thursdays. See the Pender Post for schedules.

Churches

Three churches serve the Pender Islands' Christian community. The latest information on church services and phone contacts is always found in the Church Bulletin of the monthly Pender Post. The Anglican Church is the largest church, with four congregations, three on the Pender Islands and one on Saturna Island. The United Community Church has one church building north of the Community Hall on North Pender Island, and the Roman Catholic Church operates out of a small building on North Pender Island as well. All three churches get together for an Ecumenical Easter sunrise service at Mortimer Spit, followed by breakfast at the Anglican Parish Hall. An Ecumenical dinner is also held at the Parish Hall in January.

The Parish of Pender and Saturna Islands, Anglican Church of Canada holds services on Sundays. A traditional Holy Eucharist morning service is held at St. Peters, which is at the congregation's main complex on Canal Road, south of the Driftwood Centre past Scarff Road (**Map 5**). This church was built in 1915 in the Port Washington area and relocated to this 10-acre site in 1996. The Parish Hall was built at this site in 1996. A Contemporary Eucharist service (the Circle Service, featuring contemporary music) is held in the hall on Sunday mornings. A Holy Eucharist service is also held on Sunday afternoons at the Church of the Good Shepherd on South Pender Island (built in 1937) next to Poets Cove Resort on Gowlland Point Road (**Map 8**). The Anglican Church is active with a food bank, wheels to meals for seniors, and a Kids Club after school program. The Parish Hall is also used by the community for meetings, performances, art shows, and as a designated disaster centre. 4703 Canal Road, RR1, North Pender Island, V0N 2M1; Church Office: 629.3634; Anglican Hall Bookings: 629.3816. No web site; See the Diocese of British Columbia, Saanich Deanery site **www.bc.anglican.ca/saanich.htm** and for general information on church see **www.anglicansonline.org/Canada**.

Chapel of Saint-Teresa - Roman Catholic Mass: Roman Catholics began conducting their own services on the Pender Islands at the United Community Church in the late 1980's, but later moved into a permanent location on the shore of Magic Lake (**Map 4,** *K*). Services are held on Sunday mornings. If a priest is available to visit from offisland, then Mass is held. Otherwise, a communion service is conducted; 4705 Buccaneers Road, Pender Island BC V0N 2M2; 629.3141; National Site: **www.cccb.ca**.

The Pender Island United Community Church is located on Bedwell Harbour Road to the north of the Pender Island Library (**Map 1,** *A*, Photo, below). Built in 1907, this church once was the meeting place for the Presbyterian community. It eventually became part of the United Church of Canada, but closed its doors in the 1960s due to lack of attendance. In the 1970's it became an interdenominational church, and has emerged into a locally autonomous congregation with its own bylaws and governing body. Sunday morning services feature rotating ministers and a variety of soloists and musical talent. The church has an open door policy and is welcoming to all Penderites, as they seek to be a people desiring to make Christ relevantly alive in today's society. Programs include Sunday school for children and bible study for adults and children. 4405 Bedwell Harbour Road, Pender Island, BC V0N 2M1; 629.3822; No web site.

SENIOR CITIZEN GUIDE

The Pender Islands are a favourite location for Canadians to retire. The senior citizens of Pender tend to be active volunteers in various organizations and enhance the Pender Island community and its amenities. A top-notch medical clinic provides health care services up to an extent, but many services are available only off-island. Eventually, many older Penderites decide to move off-island to be closer to other family members or more comprehensive medical facilities.

Island Services

Dedicated volunteer organizations assist with the needs of the Pender Islands' elderly through the Community Volunteer Program and Community Support Services. Volunteer services include visiting, driving, respite care support, adult day care, meal delivery, and home repairs. Programs include Hospice/Palliative Care Outreach Program, Senior's Group, Meals on Wheels, plus support and volunteer resources to other community organizations. Located at the Medical Clinic, 5715 Canal Road, RR1, Pender Island, BC V0N 2M1. For information call 629.3346. Fax: 629.3314, Email: picvp@yahoo.com. For updates on this organization, see the latest Pender Post. See also the Vancouver Island Health Authority Website's community services directory at **www.viha.ca/finding_care/community_services_directory/**

Meals on Wheels: Provides and delivers nourishing meals to seniors at low cost. Meals are delivered several days a week by volunteers and Home Support Workers to residents needing support with meal preparation. Participants require a medical referral, and availability is for residents eligible for Long Term Care. Contact the Community Nurses at 629.3242. Volunteer drivers are always needed.

Wheels to Meals: A family-style lunch is served every Friday for seniors and people with disabilities living in the community. Transportation is provided. Located at the Anglican Parish Hall, 4703 Canal Road. $5.00/person. 629.3634. Wheelchair accessible.

Seniors Group: A support group and social organization meets generally the second Tuesday of the month (except July and August) in the lounge of the Community Hall. Wheelchair accessible.

Telephone Tree: A daily point of contact through a telephone tree is available for residents who live alone. 629.3446.

Volunteer Drivers: Transportation is provided for seniors or people with disabilities who are unable to drive themselves to medical appointments on and off Pender Island, shopping, the library, bank, hairdresser and essential services. The service is free but donations for gasoline are welcome. Call 629.3346 with as much notice as possible. For rides to medical appointments on the Saanich Peninsula or in Victoria, Peninsula Community Services can be contacted at 1.800.655.4402.

Pender Centre for Adult Day Care: Located at Plum Tree Court, 5719 Canal Road on North Pender Island (near the Medical Clinic). A full program is offered that includes gentle exercise, word games, art and music therapy, and socialization. Lunch and refreshments are provided. Wednesdays 9:00 am - 4:00 pm, $5 fee. Wheelchair accessible. Phone 629.3731 on Wednesdays.

Subsidized seniors housing on the Pender Islands is available through the Capitol Regional District (CRD): Plum Tree Court, built in 1988, contains 6 one-bedroom bungalows, located at 5719 Canal Road, North Pender Island, BC V0N 2M1, near the School and Medical Clinic. The cost is based on an individual's income. Contact the Pender Island Seniors Housing Society at 629.3731. Eligibility requirements and applications are available from the CRD at **www.crd.bc.ca/housing**.

Resources and Senior Discounts

WEB SITES

www.seniors.gc.ca: The government site Seniors Canada On-line provides access to Web based information and services that are relevant to those 55 and over, their families, caregivers and supporting service organizations. For help using the site, click on *Contact Us* for a telephone number. Or, call 1.800.622.6232 from Canada or the U.S., Monday through Friday 5:00 am to 5:00 pm for information on Canadian programs.

www.CanadaBenefits.gc.ca. This site contains information for all Canadians. Of interest to seniors in particular are Old Age Security, Guaranteed Income Supplements, Seniors Supplemental Allowance, Home Adaptations for Seniors Independence, Shelter Aid for the Elderly, Renters Property Tax Deferment Program, Independent Living BC, Provincial Housing Program, bus pass discounts, Discount Allowance for the Survivor, International Pension Benefits, and Adult Care.

www.viha.ca: The Vancouver Island Health Authority (VIHA) is one of six health authorities in British Columbia, and is the one in which the Pender Islands fall. The Pender Islands are considered to be in the South Island area, which is the Capital Region. Search for Community Services on this site. The services related to senior citizens on the Pender Islands were described in this section of the guidebook. The South Island headquarters are at 1952 Bay Street, Victoria, BC V8R 1J8; Phone 250.370.8699, Toll Free 1.877.370.8699.

www.canadianelderlaw.ca: This website is dedicated to social and legal issues affecting seniors in Canada. The purpose of the site is provide information and raise awareness of key issues to help advance their rights as full citizens in Canadian society.

www.seniorhousing.bc.ca: For those needing to move off-island, the Seniors Housing Information Program (SHIP) is a non-profit organization that provides information on housing and services for seniors living in or wishing to live in Vancouver and the Lower Mainland of British Columbia.

www.independent-living.ca: BC Living Independent Services (BCLIS) provides housing and associated home care and attendant care services to physically disabled individuals who wish to live independently in apartments in Vancouver and Victoria.

SENIOR DISCOUNTS

The BC Ministry of Health Services issues the **BC Gold Care Card** to seniors a few weeks before turning age 65. This card is helpful in proving age of 65 and over and BC Residency. Many senior benefits and discounts are available only to seniors who are BC residents.

Fishing licenses: Senior BC Residents can get an annual pass for $11.77, but there is no discount for non-resident seniors. Discounted hunting licenses are also available.

BC Ferries (See the **www.bcferries.com** site under *Fares* for current status): BC Seniors travel free Monday through Thursday except on holidays. This applies only to the passenger fare, and not the vehicle. Must show BC Gold Care Card. Note that free BC Ferries travel is available (at time of writing) to those travelling for non-emergency medical services not available on the Pender Islands, with the appropriate documentation from the patient's physician through BC's Travel Assistance Program (TAP). Other transportation companies offer discounts, including several airlines, rail and bus. See the *Health Services Guide* for details.

JEAN ROGERS, PENDER'S SUPER SENIOR

Her Excellency the Right Honourable Adrienne Clarkson, former Governor General of Canada, and His Excellency John Ralston Saul, visited British Columbia in November 1999 and presented the Governor General's Caring Canadian Award to Pender Island's Jean B. Rogers, considered to be the island's guardian angel for thirty years. Some of her accomplishments included co-founding the local palliative care society and Canadian Cancer Society, running a visitor program and support group, organizing a group of volunteers to drive Island residents to medical appointments and establishing the Pender Island Care Bears to visit and assist people who are elderly, sick, isolated or lonely. She also helped found an adult day care and a social awareness council, was active in her church, volunteered at the Nu-To-Yu thrift shop, and belonged to a variety of other local organizations. *GranJean* was a favourite storyteller at Summer Story Time at the library, where she also volunteered. Ms. Rogers continued to be active in numerous volunteer pursuits until she left Pender Island in 2006. She leaves very big shoes to fill.

GOVERNMENT GUIDE

This Guide summarizes the levels of government under which the Pender Islands fall. Included are relevant agencies and contact information for them.

THE MONARCHY
Her Royal Highness is the Queen of Canada. Official web site of the British Monarchy: **www.royal.gov.uk** Foreign & Commonwealth Office: **www.fco.gov.uk** The Governor General is the Queen's representative and the Head of State, and opens parliament for elections: **www.gg.ca/governor_general/role_e.asp**.

FEDERAL
Canada's Parliamentary government is led by a Prime Minister, based in Ottawa. One Member of Parliament (MP) represents the north Saanich area and the Gulf Islands.

General Info
www.canada.gc.ca: The main Federal Government web site. Find contact information including the Member of Parliament (MP) for this region (Gulf Islands/ Saanich). **www.pm.gc.ca**: Office of the Prime Minister of Canada.

The Parks Canada federal ministry is responsible for the Gulf Islands National Park Reserve onPender Island; **www.pc.gc.ca**; See the *Coastal Access and Hiking Guide*. Gulf Islands National Park: **www.pc.gc.ca/gulfislands**; 250.654.4000.

Taxes
www.cra-arc.gc.ca: **Canada Revenue Agency** (CRA) was formerly a part of the Canada Customs and Revenue Agency (CCRA). The CRA administers "tax laws for the Government of Canada and for most provinces and territories; and various social and economic benefit and incentive programs delivered through the tax system." Contact phone numbers: Individual Income tax: 1.800.959.8281; Business Enquiries and registrations: 1.800.959.5525; Forms and publications: 1.800.959.2221 (also download on line); Individual non-resident and international enquiries: 1.800.267.5177. See the web site for additional phone numbers including TTY (teletype) numbers.

Customs
www.cbsa-asfc.gc.ca: Canada Border Services Agency (CSBA) was created on December 12, 2003. It is part of the new portfolio of Public Safety and Emergency Preparedness, which includes emergency preparedness, crisis management, national security, corrections, policing, oversight, crime prevention, as well as border services. The CBSA reports to the Deputy Prime Minister and Minister of Public Safety and Emergency Preparedness. From this website you can link to border wait times, cross-border currency reporting, information for Canadian residents travelling abroad, the NEXUS and CANPASS programs, Canadians moving back to Canada, etc. To locate a customs office or for enquiries, see the web site, or call: From Canada: 1.800.461.9999; Outside Canada: 204.983.3500, 506.636.5064 (long-distance). Agents available 8-4 nationwide.

Immigration

www.cic.gc.ca: **The Citizenship and Immigration Canada** (CIC) web site. "The Department admits immigrants, foreign students, visitors and temporary workers who enhance Canada's social and economic growth; resettles, protects and provides a safe haven for refugees; helps newcomers adapt to Canadian society and become Canadian citizens; and manages access to Canada to protect the security and health of Canadians and the integrity of Canadian laws." You can download and print application kits or obtain other services. Information phone numbers, from Canada only are: Citizenship and Immigration: 1.888.242.2100; Permanent Resident (PR) Card: 1.800.255.4541. Service agents, and the TTY number 1.888.576.8502 are available 8:00 am to 4:00 pm (all Canadian time zones). Outside of Canada, contact the Canadian embassy, high commission or consulate responsible for your region.

For Non-Canadians: www.canadainternational.gc.ca: Canadian government web site with links to services, information and resources, for citizens of other countries.

PROVINCE OF BRITISH COLUMBIA

Victoria is the British Columbia (BC) Provincial Capital, led by a Premier. One Member of the Legislative Assembly (MLA) represents the Gulf Islands.

www.gov.bc.ca: Main **BC Government Website**. Send comments to the Premier, or contact your MLA. Look up any Provincial government ministry.

Enquiry BC: Call centre provides services to all British Columbia residents, on behalf of provincial government ministries, Crown corporations and public agencies.
Victoria: 250.387.6121; Vancouver: 604.660.2421; rest of BC: 1.800.663.7867;
Outside BC: 604.660.2421; Telephone service for the deaf: 604.775.0303;
From Vancouver, or elsewhere in BC: 1.800.661.8773; EnquiryBC@gems3.gov.bc.ca.

www.bcstats.gov.bc.ca: Various government statistics including population.

www.gov.bc.ca/healthservices: **BC Health Services** web site, includes link to surgical wait times. See also the *Health Services Guide*.

REGIONAL: CAPITAL REGIONAL DISTRICT (CRD)

The CRD, based in Victoria, is the regional governing body. The CRD includes the areas between Sooke, Victoria and the Saanich Peninsula on Vancouver Island, as well as the Southern Gulf Islands. A CRD building inspection office is located at the Driftwood Centre, open Monday, Wednesday, and Friday, 629.3424.

The Pender Island Parks Commission (PIPC) receives authorization from the CRD. The CRD manages Brooks Point Regional Park, and the new Gowlland Point land purchase and future Regional Park. The PIPC manages numerous public parks and ocean accesses around the Pender Islands; **www.crd.bc.ca**.
Main reception, Victoria: 250.360.3000.

LOCAL: THE ISLANDS TRUST

The Islands Trust is a "unique federation of local island governments with a mandate from the Islands Trust Act to make land use decisions that will preserve and protect British Columbia's Gulf Islands. The Trust Area covers the islands and water between the British Columbia mainland and Vancouver Island, including Howe Sound and as far north as Comox." Local trustees are elected every three years. There are two trustees for each of North and South Pender Islands, which are Trust Areas 1 and 2, respectively. The Islands Trust was established in part due to the creation of Magic Lake Estates on North Pender Island, which, in the 1960's, was the most extensive planned community in Canada at the time. The agency was created to help establish a more moderate rate of development for the Gulf Islands. The Islands Trust Fund currently oversees 50 protected areas established and carefully managed for conservation. Of these, six are located on North Pender Island, and two are on South Pender Island. Some of these parcels are parks managed in coordination with other agencies, such as Medicine Beach on North Pender Island and Enchanted Forest and Brooks Point Regional Parks on South Pender Island. Other parcels were acquired only to protect habitat and ecosystems, such as the Sharp-tailed Snake Covenant, the Cottonwood Creek Covenant and the Dennis and Ledingham Covenant Lands, all on North Pender Island. A small office is located in Pender's Driftwood Centre, with limited hours. Victoria Office: Suite 200, 1627 Fort Street, Victoria, BC, V8R 1H8; 250.405.5151, Fax: 250.405.5155; Open weekdays 8:30 - 4:30.
www.islandstrust.bc.ca; Information@islandstrust.bc.ca.

Tip of GINPR - Roe Islet with Queen of Cumberland leaving Otter Bay Terminal beyond.

HAZARDS, PESTS AND EMERGENCIES

Hazards and Pests

Peaceful Pender Island is a relatively safe place. However, a few hazards do exist here, some of which are described below. This is not a complete account of hazards. Other hazards may exist that are not included in this section.

Biological Hazards

Mammals
In contrast to mainland BC and Vancouver Island, the Pender Islands do not have any large predatory mammals such as cougars or bears. So, unless one decides to take a very long swim the chances are remote that they will be encountered here. However, watch for numerous deer along the roadways at all times, but especially at night. They can jump out unexpectedly causing injury to motorists and cyclists. Gardeners should keep this in mind with regard to fencing and deer-resistant plantings. River otters like to crawl up onto docks, open boats, or beneath unsecured waterfront home crawl-spaces to regurgitate fish bits that can create quite a stink. River otters and mink have infectious bites that can prove fatal to domestic pets. Feral cats that roam the island also can have nasty bites. Raccoons have inhabited the islands in the past, and a few sightings have been reported on North Pender of late. Raccoons can be a nuisance to unsecured trash cans, and as cute as they are, should not be approached. Visitors and residents should not introduce exotic animals to the island, including rabbits, squirrels, exotic turtles, or even goldfish, as it could create an environmental nightmare.

Deer mice can be plentiful and tend to move into houses in the winter. Mice are a concern because they can carry diseases such as Hantavirus, although no known case of Hantavirus has been reported on Pender. See the BC Centre for Disease Control BC health alert **www.bccdc.org**. Do not breath airborne particles when cleaning up mouse droppings. Spray the material first with water and wear a mask and gloves.

Birds
Although very uncommon, Bald Eagles can potentially grab a small cat or dog.

Reptiles
No poisonous snakes have been reported on the Pender Islands. The common small snakes found throughout the islands are of the garter variety.

Insects and Spiders
Yellow jackets (wasps) are abundant on the island, especially in August, so be careful not to rummage in unfamiliar brush, old tree stumps, or other areas where a nest may exist. If you are allergic, carry the proper medication. The Pender Pharmacy may or may not carry it when you need it, and is closed on Sundays. As with many locales, an outdoor picnic can be ruined by the onslaught of these pests. The severity varies year

to year and from location to location. Pest control experts recommend setting wasp traps in the spring so that you can catch queens before they establish their nests. Wasps can still swarm out of the their nest after dark if it is disturbed, so it is best to consult an expert before removing a nest.

Mosquitoes can be plentiful at dusk, mostly earlier in the summer and near damp areas. Avoid keeping stagnant water where they breed. West Nile virus is expected to reach British Columbia by 2006. See the latest press release at **www.bccdc.org**.

Ticks are most prevalent from May to November, frequently lurking on wide-leafed shrubs such as salal, though they can be on just about any vegetation, especially 3 feet or less from the ground. Certain varieties of ticks found on the Pender Islands can carry Lyme disease, a bacterial infection, although the occurrence of cases in the entire province has been sporadic to date. Some preventative measures include: Walk on cleared trails; wear a hat, long sleeves and pants and light-coloured clothing; tuck pant legs into socks or boots; use an insect repellent containing DEET on clothing and exposed skin. After being in an area where ticks may live, it is important to inspect your clothes for ticks and then wash them. See the complete April 2005 (or later) BCCDC press release on this topic at **www.bccdc.org**.

Poisonous spiders are uncommon on the Pender Islands, but like most locations, black widows and brown recluse spiders live here. Be careful when handling woodpiles or in dry, dark areas such as basements and crawlspaces where these spiders tend to lurk.

Tent Caterpillar blooms occur in multi-year cycles, which peak about every 7 to 10 years. They tend to attack fruit and alder trees. Small tents can be pruned off and burned or drowned in soapy water.

Other Pests that attack homes on the Pender Islands include carpenter ants, fungal woodrot, powder postbeetles, and termites. Homes should be inspected periodically.

Lake Parasites
See the notices posted at Magic Lake for information on Swimmer's Itch. Different Penderites have different opinions on lake swimming here; some swim all the time and swear by it, while others stay away for fear of leeches or parasitic infection. Parks Canada has not yet tested Roe or Greenburn Lake for lake parasites at time of writing.

Natural Disasters

Fire
As precipitation diminishes in the summer and fall, vegetation on the island becomes dry and the fire hazard increases. Signs posted around the island display the current fire hazard. All fires (including incinerators) are typically banned in July, August, and September. When the hazard gets most extreme, many hiking trails are closed. Although there is less lightning in this area (the Pender Islands receive an average of two thunderstorms per year) as compared to other areas like interior BC, wildfires can

easily start as a result of human carelessness. Homeowners should take precautions to clear flammable vegetation away from their homes, and choose a fire-resistant roof. Smokers should never throw lit cigarettes on the ground.

Earthquake and Tsunami
The Pender Islands are within a zone of high earthquake hazard. See the *Geology and Water Resources* section in the *Natural Environment* chapter for a description of local seismology. The CRD office at Driftwood Centre has brochures on earthquake preparedness. Also be prepared to take care of your pet. See *Emergencies* below. The Pender Islands are not believed to be in an area of significant tsunami hazard since Vancouver Island acts as a shield from ocean waves to the west, and other Gulf Islands protect from a Strait of Georgia seismic event. However, additional study is ongoing, and the results are pending. If you are on the beach and the tide is suddenly sucked out in front of you, especially after a seismic event, a tsunami may be imminent, and you should seek higher ground. For updates on tsunami research, see the Fisheries and Oceans site **www-sci.pac.dfo-mpo.gc.ca/osap/projects/tsunami/default_e.htm**.

Wind
Wind gales can wreak havoc in the Gulf Islands, occasionally cancelling ferries, knocking boats from their moorings, toppling trees, and creating power outages. Certain areas of the Pender Islands are more susceptible to wind damage than others. The most frequent winds on Pender are southwesterlies and southeasterlies, but there are also occasional strong winds from other directions. Homeowners may wish to have their trees evaluated by an arborist for potential falling hazard.

Crime and the RCMP

Crime levels in the Outer Gulf Islands (OGI) are proportionate to the size of the community, which is comparable to other communities of similar size. The OGI has a high number of seasonal residents and rental properties. Owners are encouraged to have their property checked frequently during periods of vacancy to decrease the chances of vandalism or break-ins.

The Royal Canadian Mounted Police (RCMP) has one main Detachment near the intersection of Otter Bay Road and Bedwell Harbour Road on Pender Island, and two satellite detachments on Galiano and Mayne, respectively. Pender Island is staffed with two Regular Uniformed Members, one Corporal and one Constable, as well as one Auxiliary Constable, two part-time Victim Services positions and one full time Office Manager. Galiano and Mayne each have one Regular Uniformed Member.

RCMP have full jurisdiction on all the OG I, including surrounding waters and both Provincial and Federal Parks, under the National Parks and Wildlife Acts and the Capital Regional District By-Laws. They are assisted by Parks Canada Park Wardens and By-Law Enforcement Officers. RCMP also have authority at the designated Customs checkpoint at Bedwell Harbour, under the Customs Act, and often assist the seasonal Customs Officers. RCMP will also assist and board BC Ferries should they have a need for police assistance.

Visitors and Residents should note that all the same rules apply to the OGI as they do elsewhere in British Columbia, including the Motor Vehicle Act, Fire Prevention Act and Controlled Drugs and Substances Act. There is an enforced 24/7 Noise By-Law on Mayne and Pender Islands, preventing any excessive noise.

In addition to traditional police response, the Outer Gulf Islands RCMP also provides a wide range of community based services. There are volunteers working in several different programs at the Detachment where they are supported by the efforts of the Restorative Justice, Block Watch, Marina Watch, Coastal Watch, Police Advisory Committee, DARE/Drug Awareness and School Liaison to name a few. Volunteers offer an invaluable service to the community and to the Detachment.

Emergencies

Medical Emergency

Medical emergency: Dial **911**. An ambulance carries patients to the medical clinic and/or waiting boat or helicopter for transport to hospital. Non-urgent medical problems will be asked to take the next ferry to a hospital in the greater Victoria area. After hours (but not an emergency): 1.800.866.5602, ask for pager 5214. For non-emergency information see the *Health Services Guide*.

Community-Wide Emergency

The disasters that the Pender Islands are most susceptible to are wildfires and earthquakes. The tsunami hazard on the Penders is likely low, as it appears the Pender Islands may be shielded from severe Tsunami damage. Studies are continuing in this area (see the *Geology and Water Resources* section).

Residents should visit the local CRD office or their Neighbourhood Contact to pick up brochures that explain how to prepare themselves and their pets in advance and what to do in case of an emergency. Everyone should register with their local Neighbourhood Contact, attend periodic meetings, and become familiar with their neighbourhood assembly and first aid points. The Neighbourhood Contact establishes a Telephone Tree, and keeps notes about each household such as number of people and whether there are persons that would need special assistance. Services and equipment you are willing to volunteer during an emergency is also noted. The information is shared with the RCMP, fire department and emergency services personnel. The telephone tree is used for vital announcements, such as a *water boiling* order for those on community water systems or a warning that evacuation may be required due to fire.
In the event of a major fire, emergency sirens in Magic Lake Estates should sound con-

tinuously. *Note:* there will be shorter tests of the siren as well on the first Thursday of summer months. When you hear the siren, you will probably be instructed to get ready to evacuate. Listen for instructions from emergency personnel in your area, which may be the RCMP, Fire Department, or your Emergency Program Neighbourhood Contact. Turn the TV to Cable Channel 3 and radio to CFAX 1070 AM; refrain from using the telephone if possible in case the Neighbourhood Contact is trying to call with critical instructions. Use common sense; if danger is imminent, flee to safety. In an earthquake: *Drop, Cover and Hold.* Take cover under a sturdy table. Find a safe place and stay there. Keep away from windows. If you are inside stay there. If you are outside do not go back in until you are sure that it is safe. Once you leave your home during a disaster, leave a status note in front of your home since volunteers will be checking each home. Either leave your emergency placard displayed with *OK* or *Need Help*, or leave a note explaining the condition and whereabouts of the inhabitants.

FOR VISITORS
If you are on island visiting for the day and hear an emergency siren or feel a major earthquake, tune your car radio to CFAX 1070 AM and listen for instructions. If you are not sure what to do, go to one of the reception centres, if safe. (See below).

RECEPTION CENTRES
Anglican Parish Hall, located on Canal Road, south of the Driftwood Centre just past Scarff Road, and north of the turnoff to South Pender Island (**Map 5**), and
The Royal Canadian Legion Hall, on MacKinnon Road, to the north (left) from the Otter Bay Ferry Terminal, on the right (**Map 1A**).

These facilities have emergency generators and kitchen facilities. If it is not safe to get to these facilities (i.e. a fire on mid-island) alternate centres may be established. These could be fire halls or water evacuation sites like Thieves Bay Marina (with perhaps a ferry waiting offshore). Trained volunteers from Emergency Social Services (ESS) will staff the reception centres, and will try to accommodate you with lodging, food and clothing when necessary. A field hospital may be established at the Pender School (**Map 5**).

In case of fire, communications will likely be via telephone, and the neighbourhood telephone tree will operate. In case of major earthquake, all utilities may be out. Neighbourhood Contacts have radios to coordinate with emergency personnel, but each neighbourhood needs to be self-sufficient until outside help can arrive. Testing of the radios has found good coverage throughout most of North Pender.

In case of a regional disaster such as **major earthquake**, it may take several days for emergency personnel from Vancouver Island to reach here. It is important for anyone with first aid or medical skills to register with the neighbourhood contact and to help stabilize patients during the interim period or help in the Field Hospital if needed.

EMERGENCY PHONE NUMBERS
See the *Pender Islands Map Atlas* for emergency phone numbers.

REFERENCES

Associated Press (AP), March 26, 2003, *Experts: Northwest Quake Underway,* http://sfgate.com/cgi-bin/article.cgi?f=/news/archive/2003/03/26/state1636EST7193.DTL

British Columbia Historical Federation, Gulf Islands Branch, 1999, *A Gulf Islands Patchwork,* Pender Island, BC

British Columbia Historical Federation, Gulf Islands Branch, 1994, *More Tales from the Outer Gulf Islands,* Pender Island, BC

British Columbia Ministry of Environment, Lands and Parks, 1994, *The Pender Islands Groundwater Pilot Project Final Report*

Britt, Robert, 2005, *Slow Seismic Slip Event Underway,* **www.livescience.com**

Butler, Robert, 2003, *The Jade Coast - The Ecology of the North Pacific Ocean,* Key Porter Books, Toronto, ON.

Cannings, Richard and Sydney Cannings, 2004, *British Columbia - A Natural History,* Greystone Books, Vancouver, BC

Capital Regional District, 2005, *Natural Areas Atlas,* **www.crd.bc.ca/es/natatlas/**

Carlson, Roy, 1996, *The Late Prehistory of British Columbia,* UBC Press,Vancouver,BC

Cassidy, John, 2005, *Personal Communication,* Pacific Geoscience Centre, Sidney, BC

Clague, J.J, Bobrowsky, P.T. and Hutchinson, I, 2000. *A review of geological records of large tsunamis at Vancouver Island, British Columbia, and implications for hazard.* Quaternary Science Reviews 19, 849-863,

Clague, John J, 2002. *The Earthquake Threat in Southwestern British Columbia,* Simon Fraser University and Geological Society of Canada, **http://collection.nlc-bnc.ca/100/200/301/ocipep-bpiepc/earthquake-e/clague.pdf**

Hale, Robert, 2005, *Waggoner Cruising Guide 2006 Edition,* Weatherly Press

Hanson, Diane K, 1995, *Subsistence During the Late Prehistoric Occupation of Pender Canal, British Columbia,* in Canadian Journal of Archaeology, vol 19, pp 29-48

Henderson, James D, 1997, *An Ecosystem Approach to Groundwater Management in the Gulf Islands,* A Masters Thesis, University of Calgary

Hill, Donna, 1978, *The Columbian Black-Tailed Deer*, **www.naturepark.com**.

Kenney, E.A., L.JP van Vliet and A.J. Green, 1988, *Soils of the Gulf Islands of British Columbia*, Volume 2, Report No. 43, British Columbia Soil Survey, Vancouver, BC

Kohut, A.P., J. Foweraker and W. Hodge, 1993, *Groundwater Resources of British Columbia*, 9.1.3 Gulf Islands,
http://wlapwww.gov.bc.ca/wat/gws/gwbc/C0913_Gulf_Islands.html

Leon, Vicki, 1989, *A Pod of Killer Whales*, Blake Publishing, San Luis Obispo, CA

Littman, Todd and Kort, S, 1996, *Best Bike Rides in the Pacific Northwest,* Globe Pequot

Lowe, C., Baker, J and Journeay, J.M. 2001, *Ground-Magnetic Investigations of Cenozoic structures in the northern Cascadia forearc, British Columbia*, Geological Survey of Canada, Current Research 2001-A12, 16 p

National Audubon Society, 2000, *Field Guide to Birds, Western Region*, Alfred A. Knopf

Neering, Rosemary, 2003, *Eating Up Vancouver Island*, Whitecap Books

Pender Island Parks Commission, 2002, *Community Parks Guide*

Pender Post Society, *Pender Post*, August 2002 through April 2006, Pender Island, BC

Pender Post Society, *Pender Post Millennium Edition*, 2000, Pender Island, BC

Reeves, Randall R., Stewart, Brent S., Clapham, Philip J, and Powell, James A, 2002, *National Audubon Society Guide to Marine Mammals of the World*, Alfred A. Knopf, New York

Sheldon, Ian, 1998, *Seashore of British Columbia*, Lone Star Publishing, Vancouver, BC

Varner, Collin, 2002, *Plants of the Gulf & San Juan Islands and Southern Vancouver Island*, Raincoast Pocket Guides, Vancouver, BC

Wagonfeld, Judy, 1997, *Short Bike Rides Western Washington*, Globe Pequot Press

Yeadon-Jones, Anne and Laurence, 1998, *Gulf Islands & Vancouver Island, A Dreamspeaker Cruising Guide*, Raincoast Books, Vancouver, BC

Yorath, C.J. & H.W. Nasmith, 1995, *The Geology of Southern Vancouver Island, A Field Guide,* 1995, Orca Book Publishers

Additional website references are listed in the appropriate chapters.

PENDER ISLANDS MAP ATLAS

The Map Atlas contains a series of maps depicting the Pender Islands (plus Sidney and Victoria). The basemaps for roads, topography, shorelines and park boundaries are referenced from *CRD National Areas Atlas* (2005). Hiking trails are plotted from field observation. The locations of all features should be considered as approximate.

LOCATION MAP
The Pender Islands are shown in relation to the area between the Tsawwassen ferry terminal on the mainland and Swartz Bay ferry terminal on Vancouver Island. Other regional points of interest described in this book are also shown.

INDEX MAPS
North and South Pender Island are shown in their entirety with major roads, surrounding waterways and geographic highlights, to provide a general orientation to the islands. The index maps depict the extent of the area maps and detail maps.

AREA MAPS
From the north end of North Pender Island to the south end of South Pender Island, most areas are covered and include most roads, accommodations, dining establishments, stores, marinas, public agencies, and points of interest. All known public trails, parks and ocean accesses are shown, with topographic contours (20 metre intervals) to depict elevation changes. Trails and ocean accesses are numbered to correspond with their numerical designations used in the *Coastal Access and Hiking Guide chapters*.

DETAIL MAPS
Areas with a high concentration of features are shown in a larger scale, and these maps are labelled with letters, such as *5A* or *5B*. The exception is the Canal Area, which is *Map 6*, as it spans both North and South Pender Islands. Several of the maps are duplicated in the *Coastal Access and Hiking Guide* for easy reference.

LIST OF MAPS

Pender Islands Location Map
North Pender Island Index Map
South Pender Island Index Map
North Pender Island
Map 1 North End North Pender Island
Map 1A Otter Bay Area
Map 1B Port Washington/Stanley Pt
Map 1C Clam Bay/Hope Bay Area
Map 2 Hooson Rd/Mt. Menzies Trails
Map 3 South Otter Bay/Central Valley
Map 3A GINPR/Roe Lake Trails
Map 4 Magic Lake Estates
Map 4A Buck Lake Area
  (West Magic Lake Estates area)
Map 4B Disc Park Area
  (East Magic Lake Estates)

Map 4C Oaks Bluff Park
Map 4D Trincomali
Map 5 Central Area
Map 5A Medicine Beach Arera
Map 5B Driftwood Centre Area
South Pender Island
Map 6 Canal Area
Map 7 GINPR-Mt. Norman/Beaumont
Map 7A Canal Road Ocean Access
Map 7B Boundary Pass Rd Ocean Access
Map 8 Spalding Valley, Poets Cove
  and Greenburn Lake
Map 9 Tilley Point to Brooks Point
Off Island Excursion Maps
Map 10 Sidney and Vicinity
Map 11 Downtown Victoria

FEATURED LOCATIONS
AND PHONE NUMBERS

Phone numbers are all 250.629.xxxx
or as indicated.

N = North Pender
S = South Pender;
Followed by the map number(s).

TRANSPORTATION
Otter Bay Ferry Terminal N 1, 1A
Floatplanes - Poets Cove S 8
Port Washington N1, 1B
PUBLIC FACILITIES
RCMP (Police) 6171: N 3
Fire Hall #1 (Main; permits) 3321: N 3
Fire Hall #2 (Magic Lake) 3325: N 4, 4A
Fire Hall #3 (South Pender) 3400: S 8
Elementary/Secondary School 3711: N 5, 5A
Public Library 3722: N 1
HALLS
Community Hall/Fairgrounds 3669: N1, 3
Anglican Parish Hall 3816: N 5
Royal Canadian Legion Hall 3441: N 1A
PLACES OF INTEREST
Golf Course 6659: N1,1A
Disc Golf Course N 4, 4B
Nu-To-Yu Thrift Shop 2070: N 1
Pender Island Museum N 3
Morning Bay Vineyard 8351: N 5
SHOPPING CENTRES
Driftwood Centre N 3, 5, 5B
Hope Bay Store N 1, 1C
Hardware 3455/Southridge 2051: N 1, 1C
Magic Lake Market 6892: N 5A
RESORTS AND MARINAS
Otter Bay Marina 3579: N 1, 1A
Pt Browning Resort/Marina 3493: N 5, 5B
Thieves Bay Marina (Private) N 4, 4A
Poets Cove Resort & Marina 2100: S 8
MAIN BEACH AREAS
Hamilton Beach N 5, 5B
Medicine Beach N 5, 5A
Mortimer Spit S 6, 7
Gowlland/Brooks Pt S 9

GINPR (NATIONAL PARK) SECTIONS
Roesland N 3; Roe Lake N 3, 3A
Mt. Menzies N 2
Prior Centennial Campg N 5,5A
Mt. Norman S 6, 7, 7A
Beaumont Marine Park S 7
Greenburn Lake S 8
RESTAURANTS
Islanders 3929: N 1, 1A
Hope Bay Café 6668: N 1, 1C
The Stand 3292: N 1, 1A
Pistou Grill 3131: N 5B
Chippers Café 6665: N 1, 1A
Pender Isl Bakery Cafe 6453:N5B
Memories at the Inn 3353: N 5
Port Browning Pub & Cafe 3493: N 5, 5B
Aurora at Poets Cove 2115: S 8
Syrens at Poets Cove 2114: S 8
MEDICAL AND VET
Medical Clinic 3233: N 5, 5A
Veterinarian Drs.Oudman/Stone 9909: N4

OTHER PHONE NUMBERS
Pharmacy: 6555
Dentist: 6815
Ambulance, Office: 6344
Bookings:1.800.461.9911
Towing: 6692
ICBC: 1.800.663.3051
Local road conditions: 3431
CRD - Driftwood Centre: 3424
BC Hydro: 1.888.POWER.ON
BC Ferries: 1.888.BCFerry
Oil Spill: 1.800.663.3456
Magic Lake: Water/sewer problems: 6611
Animals lost/found etc: 3398
Animal Control: 1.800.665.7899
EMERGENCY PHONE NUMBERS:
Ambulence/Police Fire Emergency: **911** Clinic
after hours: 1.800.866.5602; Pager 5214
Poison Control Center 1.800.567.8911
Emergency Operation Centre: 6194
Land Search/Rescue: 3113
Coast Guard Emergency - Marine and
Aircraft Distress 1.800.855.6655
If at sea with VHF radio: Channel 16
BC Coastal Watch 1.888.855.6655

STREETS OF THE PENDER ISLANDS

Ainslie Pt Rd   S 6, 7
Aldridge Rd   N 5, 5A
Amies Road N 1
Anchor Way   N 4, 4A
Andrew Rd   N 1B
Armadale Rd   N 1, 1C
Bedwell Dr   N 4D
Bedwell Harbour Rd   N 1, 1C, 3, 3B, 5
Bosun Way   N 4, 4A, 4B
Bosuns Ct   N 4, 4A
Boundary Pass Rd   S 7B
Bridges Rd   N 1, 1B
Brigadoon Cres   N 4, 4A
Buccaneers Rd   N 4, 4B
Canal Rd   N 5, 5A, 5B S 6, 7, 7A, 7B
Cannon Cres   N 4
Capstan Ln   N 4, 4A
Captains Cr   N 4, 4B
Castle Rd   S 8
Chart Dr   N 4, 4A
Clam Bay Rd   N 1, 1B, 1C
Coast Shale Rd   N 1, 1C
Corbett Rd N 1, 1C
Compass Cr   N 4, 4A
Conery Cr   S 7B
Craddock Rd   S 9
Crowsnest Dr   N 4, 4A
Cutlass Ct   N 4
Dory Way   N 4, 4A
Doubloon Cres   N 4, 4A
E Bedwell Harbour Rd   N 5B
East Side Rd   S 7B
Foc's'le Rd   N 4, 4A
Frigate Rd   N 4, 4B
Galleon Way   N 4, 4A
Galley Cr   N 4, 4A
Gowlland Point Rd   S 8, 9
Grimmer Rd   N 1
Gunwhale Rd   N 4, 4A
Hamilton Rd   N 5, 5B
Harbour Hill Rd   N 5
Harpoon Rd   N 4, 4A
Higgs Rd   S 9
Hooson Rd   N 2
Irene Bay Rd   N 3
Jennens Rd   S 9
Jolly Roger Cr   N 4, 4A, 4B
Keel Cr   N 4, 4A
Ketch Rd   N 4, 4B
Kloshe Rd   S 9

Lagoon Cr   N 4, 4A
Liberto Rd   N 3
Lighthouse Ln   N 4, 4A
Lookout Cr   N 4B
Lupin Rd   N 5
MacKinnon Rd   N 1, 1A
Masthead Cr   N 4, 4A
Mate Rd   N 4
Niagra Rd   N 1, 1A
Ogden Rd   N 1B
Otter Bay Rd   N 1, 1A, 1B, 3
Paisley Rd   N 1B
Pearson Rd   N 1, 1C
Pirates Rd   N 4, 4C, 4D
Plumper Way   N 4D
Port Rd   N 4, 4A
Port Washington Rd   N 1, 1B, 1C
Razor Point Rd   N 5, 5B
Reef Rd   N 4, 4A
Rope Rd   N 4, 4A
Rum Rd   N 4, 4A, 4B
South Otter Bay Rd   N 1, 3, 3A
Sailor Rd   N 4
Scarff Rd   N 5 S 9
Schooner Way   N 5, 5A, 4, 4A, 4B
Sextant Cr   N 4, 4A
Shingle Bay Rd   N 3, 3A
Shoal Rd   N 4, 4B
Doubloon Cres   N 4, 4A
Short Rd   N 3
Signal Hill Rd   N 4, 4A
Southlands Dr   S 9
Spalding Rd   S 7B, 8
Spyglass Rd   N 4, 4A
Starboard Cr   N 4, 4A
Storm Cr   N 4, 4A
Sunrise Dr   N 2
Susan Point Rd   N 1B
Swanson View   N 4D
Tiller Cr   N 4, 4A
Treasure Cr   N 4, 4A
Trincoma Pl   N 4D
Upper Ter   N 1B
Walden Rd   N 1B
Wallace Rd   N 5, 5A
Westwind Rd N 1B
Wilson Rd   N 2
Yardarm Rd   N 4, 4A
Yawl Ln   N 4, 4A
N= North Pender **S**=South Pender

LOCATION MAP

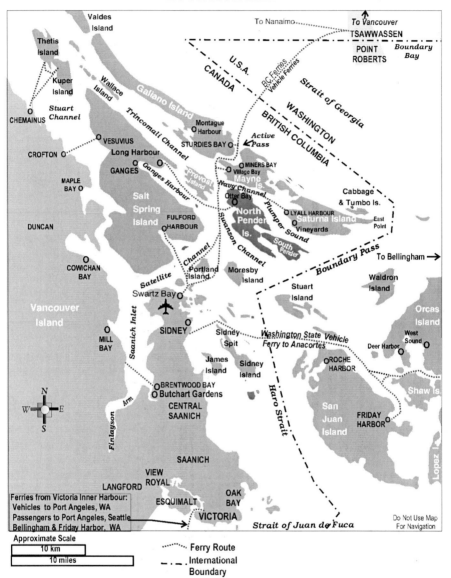

Valdes
Island

To Nanaimo....
To Vancouver
TSAWWASSEN

Thetis
Island

POINT
ROBERTS

*Boundary
Bay*

U.S.A.
CANADA

Strait of Georgia

Kuper
Island

*Wallace
Island*

Galiano Island

WASHINGTON
BRITISH COLUMBIA

BC Ferries
Vehicle Ferries

Stuart
CHEMAINUS   *Channel*

Trincomali Channel

Montague
Harbour
STURDIES BAY

*Active
Pass*

VESUVIUS

CROFTON

Long Harbour

Ganges Harbour
GANGES

MINERS BAY
Village Bay

MAPLE
BAY

Salt
Spring
Island

FULFORD
HARBOUR

Navg Channel
Otter Bay

*Prevost
Island*

*Mayne
Is.*

Cabbage
& Tumbo Is.

DUNCAN

North
Pender
Is.

LYALL HARBOUR
Vineyards

Saturna Island

East
Point

Plumper Sound

South
Pender

COWICHAN
BAY

Channel

Portland
Island

Moresby
Island

Swanson Channel

Satellite

Swartz Bay

Stuart
Island

Boundary Pass

To Bellingham →

Waldron
Island

*Vancouver
Island*

Saanich Inlet

SIDNEY

Sidney
Spit

*Washington State Vehicle
Ferry to Anacortes*

*Orcas
Island*

West
Sound

Deer Harbor

MILL
BAY

James
Island

Sidney
Island

ROCHE
HARBOR

Shaw Is.

Finlayson Arm

BRENTWOOD BAY
Butchart Gardens

CENTRAL
SAANICH

Haro Strait

*San
Juan
Island*

FRIDAY
HARBOR

Lopez I.

SAANICH

VIEW
LANGFORD   ROYAL

ESQUIMALT

OAK
BAY

Ferries from Victoria Inner Harbour:
Vehicles to Port Angeles, WA
Passengers to Port Angeles, Seattle
Bellingham & Friday Harbor, WA

VICTORIA

Strait of Juan de Fuca

Do Not Use Map
For Navigation

Approximate Scale

| 10 km |
| 10 miles |

N
W   E
S

········· Ferry Route

─ · ─ · International
Boundary

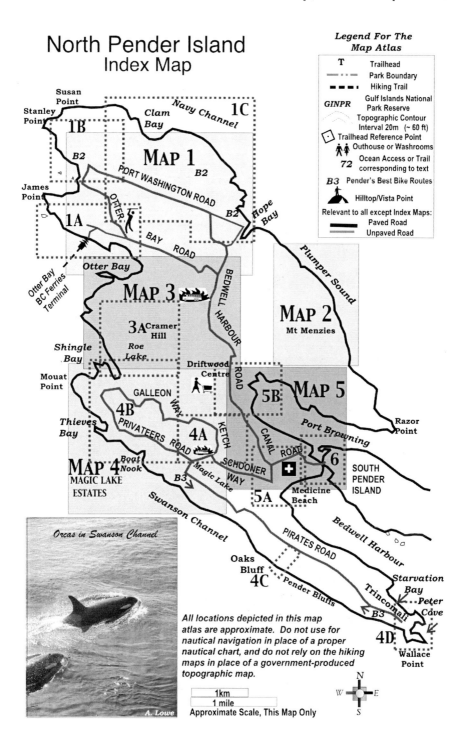

North Pender Island
Index Map

Susan Point
Stanley Point
Clam Bay
Navy Channel
1C
1B
B2
MAP 1
B2
B2
James Point
PORT WASHINGTON ROAD
OTTER
Hope Bay
1A
BAY ROAD
Otter Bay BC Ferries Terminal
Otter Bay
MAP 3
BEDWELL HARBOUR
Plumper Sound
3A Cramer Hill
Roe Lake
MAP 2
Mt Menzies
Shingle Bay
Driftwood Centre
Mouat Point
GALLEON
WAY
5B
MAP 5
4B
PRIVATEERS ROAD
4A
KETCH
ROAD
CANAL
Port Browning
Razor Point
Thieves Bay
SCHOONER WAY
6
SOUTH PENDER ISLAND
MAP 4
Boat Nook
Magic Lake
B3
✚
MAGIC LAKE ESTATES
5A
Medicine Beach
Orcas in Swanson Channel
Swanson Channel
PIRATES ROAD
Bedwell Harbour
Oaks Bluff
4C
Pender Bluffs
Starvation Bay
Trincomali
B3
Peter Cove
4D
Wallace Point

All locations depicted in this map atlas are approximate. Do not use for nautical navigation in place of a proper nautical chart, and do not rely on the hiking maps in place of a government-produced topographic map.

A. Lowe

1km
1 mile
Approximate Scale, This Map Only

N
W — E
S

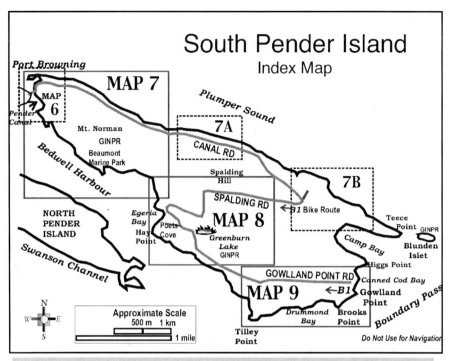

South Pender Island
Index Map

Port Browning

MAP 7

MAP 6

Pender Canal

Plumper Sound

7A

CANAL RD

Mt. Norman
GINPR
Beaumont
Marine Park

Bedwell Harbour

Spalding
Hill

7B

SPALDING RD

B1 Bike Route

NORTH
PENDER
ISLAND

Egeria
Bay

Poets
Cove

Hay
Point

MAP 8

Greenburn
Lake
GINPR

Teece
Point GINPR

Camp Bay

Blunden
Islet

Swanson Channel

Higgs Point

GOWLLAND POINT RD

Canned Cod Bay

MAP 9

B1

Gowlland
Point

Drummond
Bay

Brooks
Point

Boundary Pass

N
W E
S

Approximate Scale
500 m   1 km

1 mile

Tilley
Point

Do Not Use for Navigation

Vistas like this one of Mt. Baker make the Gowlland Point area a Pender highlight.

MAP 1   North End of North Pender Island

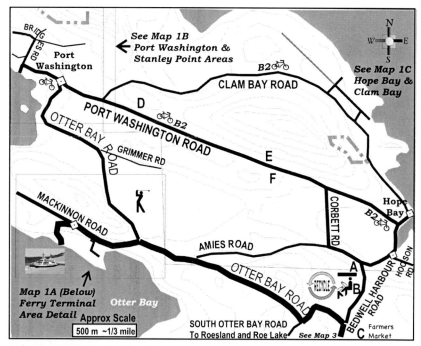

A: United Community Church **B:** Pender Island Library; Nu-To-Yu Thrift Shop; Playgroup **C:** Community Hall
D: Renaissance Studio **E:** Pender Island Home Building Centre **F:** Southridge Farms Country Store 🚲 Bike Route

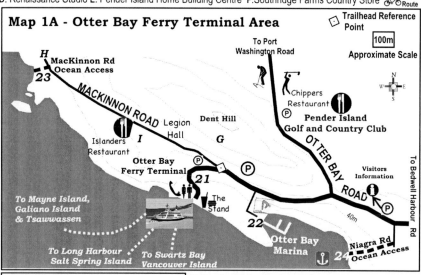

Accommodations: G: Sunraven Wellness Retreat | **22** Otter Bay Marina: Heated pool, boat ramp, kayak rentals/tours,
H: Beauty Rest By-the-Sea B&B   **I:** Arcadia B&B | showers, laundry, store, coffee bar, bike & scooter rentals

Ocean View: 21 Otter Bay Ferry Terminal; **Ocean Access: 23** MacKinnon Road; **24** Niagra Road

Map 1B   Port Washington & Stanley Point

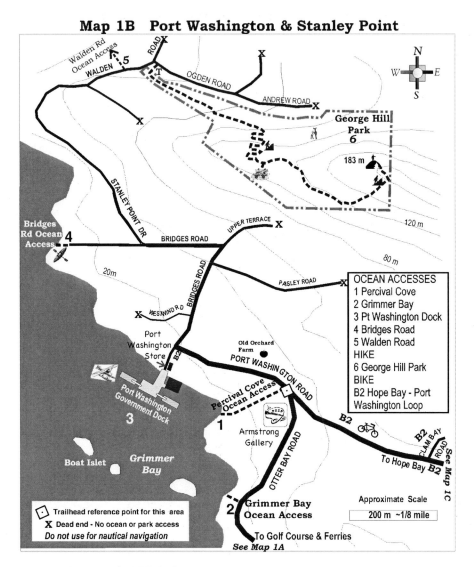

OCEAN ACCESSES
1 Percival Cove
2 Grimmer Bay
3 Pt Washington Dock
4 Bridges Road
5 Walden Road
HIKE
6 George Hill Park
BIKE
B2 Hope Bay - Port
Washington Loop

Trailhead reference point for this area
X   Dead end - No ocean or park access
Do not use for nautical navigation

Approximate Scale
200 m ~1/8 mile

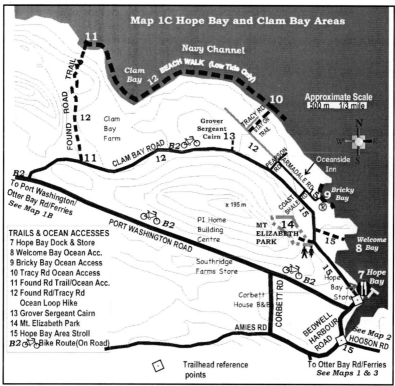

Map 1C Hope Bay and Clam Bay Areas

Navy Channel

Clam Bay

BEACH WALK (Low Tide Only)

FOUND ROAD TRAIL

11

12

12

Clam Bay Farm

10

Approximate Scale
500 m   1/3 mile

N
W   E
S

TRACY RD
STATION TRAIL

Grover Sergeant Cairn 13

B2

CLAM BAY ROAD

12

PEARSON RD

ARMADALE RD

Oceanside Inn

B2

To Port Washington/
Otter Bay Rd/Ferries
See Map 1B

PORT WASHINGTON ROAD

B2

x 195 m

PI Home Building Centre

Bricky Bay 9

COAST SHALE RD

MT ELIZABETH PARK 14

15

TRAILS & OCEAN ACCESSES
7 Hope Bay Dock & Store
8 Welcome Bay Ocean Acc.
9 Bricky Bay Ocean Access
10 Tracy Rd Ocean Access
11 Found Rd Trail/Ocean Acc.
12 Found Rd/Tracy Rd
   Ocean Loop Hike
13 Grover Sergeant Cairn
14 Mt. Elizabeth Park
15 Hope Bay Area Stroll
B2 🚲 Bike Route(On Road)

Southridge Farms Store

Welcome 8 Bay

B2

15

Hope Bay Store

7 Hope Bay

Corbett House B&B

CORBETT RD

AMIES RD

BEDWELL HARBOUR ROAD

See Map 2

15

HOOSON RD

To Otter Bay Rd/Ferries
See Maps 1 & 3

◻ Trailhead reference
   points

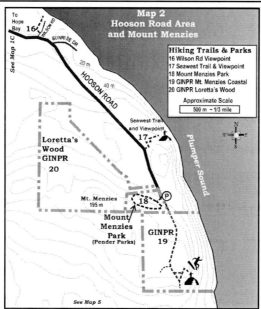

To Hope Bay 16

WILSON RD

SUNRISE DR

**Map 2
Hooson Road Area
and Mount Menzies**

See Map 1C

20 m

HOOSON ROAD

40 m

Hiking Trails & Parks
16 Wilson Rd Viewpoint
17 Seawest Trail & Viewpoint
18 Mount Menzies Park
19 GINPR Mt. Menzies Coastal
20 GINPR Loretta's Wood

Approximate Scale
500 m ~ 1/3 mile

N
W   E
S

Loretta's Wood GINPR 20

Seawest Trail and Viewpoint 17

Plumper Sound

P

Mt. Menzies 195 m 18

Mount Menzies Park
(Pender Parks)

GINPR 19

See Map 5

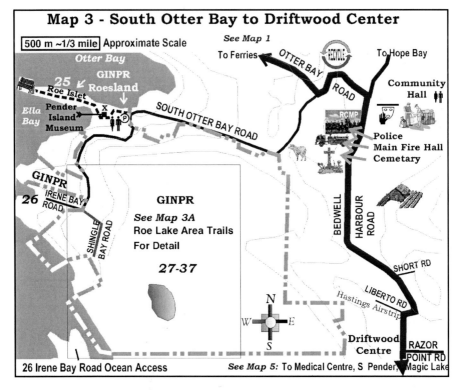

Map 3 - South Otter Bay to Driftwood Center

| 500 m ~1/3 mile | Approximate Scale

See Map 1

To Ferries
OTTER BAY
RECYCLE
To Hope Bay

OTTER BAY ROAD

Otter Bay

GINPR
Roesland

25
Roe Islet

Community
Hall

Ella
Bay

Pender
Island
Museum

RCMP

Police
Main Fire Hall
Cemetary

SOUTH OTTER BAY ROAD

GINPR

26
IRENE BAY
ROAD

GINPR

See Map 3A
Roe Lake Area Trails
For Detail

27-37

SHINGLE BAY ROAD

BEDWELL HARBOUR ROAD

SHORT RD

LIBERTO RD
Hastings Airstrip

N
W   E
S

Driftwood
Centre
RAZOR
POINT RD

26 Irene Bay Road Ocean Access

See Map 5: To Medical Centre, S Pender, Magic Lake

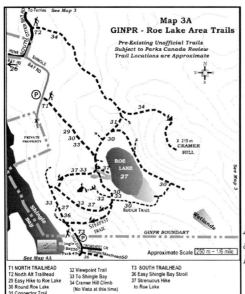

To Ferries *See Map 3*

Map 3A
GINPR - Roe Lake Area Trails

*Pre-Existing Unofficial Trails
Subject to Parks Canada Review
Trail Locations are Approximate*

SOUTH OTTER BAY RD

T2   34

IRENE BAY RD
26
SHINGLE BAY RD

P
T1

34

31

29
30
33   30

X 219 m
CRAMER
HILL

PRIVATE
PROPERTY

ROE
LAKE
27

37 33   37

30

30
33
32
37   33   37   30
ROUGH TRAIL

33
37
36

See Map 3

Wetlands

STEEPEST TRAIL

P
T3

GINPR BOUNDARY

Shingle
Bay36
Park 49
PROSPECT CR
Shingle/Masthead 60

Approximate Scale | 250 m ~ 1/6 mile

See Map 4A

T1 NORTH TRAILHEAD	32 Viewpoint Trail	T3 SOUTH TRAILHEAD
T2 North Alt Trailhead	33 To Shingle Bay	36 Easy Shingle Bay Stroll
29 Easy Hike to Roe Lake	34 Cramer Hill Climb	37 Strenuous Hike
30 Round Roe Lake	(No Vista at this time)	to Roe Lake
31 Connector Trail		

A larger scale version of this map appears in the Coastal Access and Hiking Guide in the Otter Bay Section.

Map 4 - Magic Lake Estates

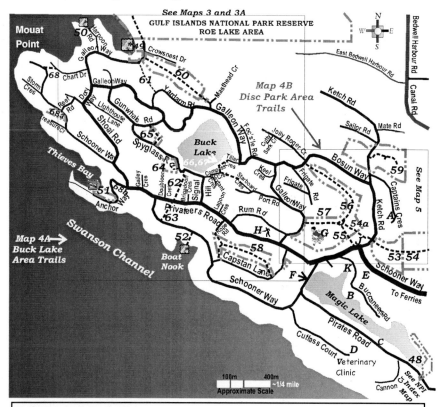

48 Magic Lake Swimming Hole
49 Shingle Bay Park/Ocean Access
50 Harpoon Road Ocean Access
51 Thieves Bay Park/Ocean Access/Marina
52 Boat Nook Ocean Access
53 Prior Centennial Campground
    to Golf Island Disc Park Trails
    54 Heart Trail   54a Heart Trail Extension
    55 Fire Hall Linker 56 Bosun Way Linker
57 Galleon Way Linker Trail

58 Capstan Lane/Rope Road Trails
59 Lively Peak Park Trail
60 Masthead Crescent/Shingle Bay Linker Trail
61 Yardarm Road/Shingle Bay Linker Trail
62 Buck Lake Trail   63 Schooner-Privateers Trail
64 Abbott Hill Park   65 Sandy Sievert Park
66 Compass Crescent to Tiller Crescent Linker
67 Starboard Crescent to Compass Crescent Linker
68 Schooner Way to Chart DriveLinker
68a Reef/Schooner Bench   68b Anchor Way Bench

B&B's: A: Sunshine Hills; B: Betty's
C: Cedar Cottage D: Gnomes Hollow
Ferndale on Pender: *See Map 4A*
Recreation: E: Danny Martin Ball Field
F: Picnic Area/Lantern Festival Site
G: Golf Island Disc Park (See Detail Maps)
H: Magic Lake Tennis Courts & Playground
Other: V: Veterinary Clinic
J: Fire Hall #2   K: Catholic Church

Thieves Bay Marina

Map 4A - Buck Lake Area Trails

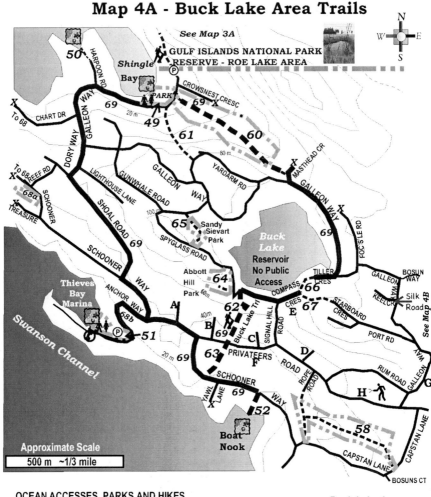

OCEAN ACCESSES, PARKS AND HIKES
49 Shingle Bay Park/Ocean Access
50 Harpoon Road Ocean Access
51 Thieves Bay Park: Ocean Access/Boat Ramp/
   Playfield/Picnic Tables/Outhouse/Phone/ Marina
52 Boat Nook Ocean Access
58 Capstan Lane/Rope Road Trails
60 Masthead Crescent/Shingle Bay Linker
61 Yardarm Road/Shingle Bay Linker
62 Buck Lake Trail
63 Schooner-Privateers Trail
64 Abbott Hill Park   65 Sandy Sievert Park
66 Compass Crescent - Tiller Crescent Linker
67 Starboard Crescent - Compass Crescent Linker
68 Chart Dr Schooner Way Shortcut
68a Reef/Schooner Bench   68b Anchor Way Bench

Buck Lake Area
69 ■ ■ ■ Hills & Sea Hike

OTHER SUGGESTED WALKS USING
TRAILS & ROADS: Round Buck Lake: 66,65
Capstan/Buck Lake: 58, 52, 63, 62

ADDITIONAL STREETS : A Galley Crescent
B Doubloon Crescent C Brigadoon Cresc
D Lagoon Crescent E Sextant Crescent
OTHER FEATURES
F Ferndale on Pender B&B
G Golf Island Disc Park (SeeMap 4B & Text)
H Magic Lake Estates Tennis Courts (fee)
 & Playground

X No through road-No ocean/Park access

Map 4B - Disc Park Area Trails

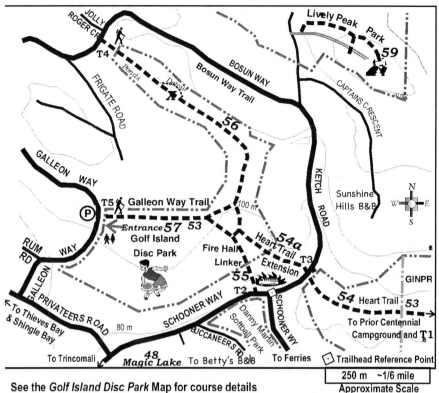

See the *Golf Island Disc Park* Map for course details
TRAILHEADS: T1 - West end of Prior Centennial Campground Loop
T2 - Fire Hall Linker Trail west of Fire Hall #2 T3 - Ketch Road/Heart Trail
T4 - Bosun Way T5 - Galleon Way at Disc Park Entrance
TRAILS: 53 Prior Centennial Campground to Golf Island Disc Park
54 Heart Trail 54a Heart Trail Extension 55 Fire Hall to Disc Park
56 Bosun Way Trail 57 Galleon Way Trail 59 Lively Peak Park

Map 4C - Oaks Bluff Park

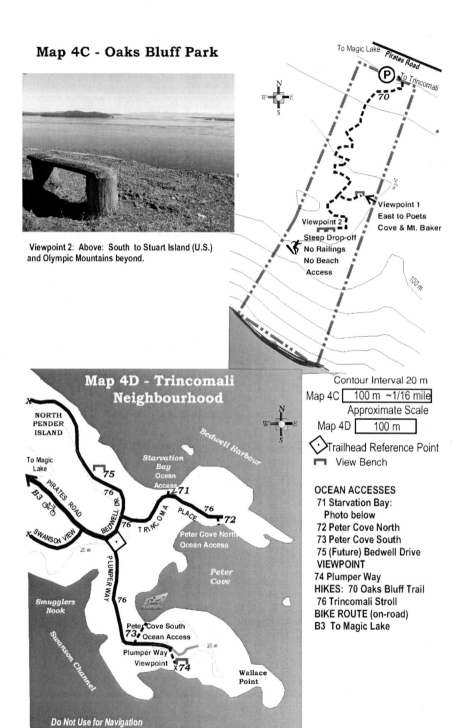

Viewpoint 2: Above: South to Stuart Island (U.S.) and Olympic Mountains beyond.

To Magic Lake   Pirates Road
To Trincomali
70

Viewpoint 1
East to Poets
Cove & Mt. Baker

Viewpoint 2

Steep Drop-off
No Railings
No Beach
Access

100 m

Map 4D - Trincomali Neighbourhood

NORTH
PENDER
ISLAND

To Magic
Lake

B3

PIRATES ROAD

SWANSON VIEW

75

76

BEDWELL DR.

76

TRINCOMALI PLACE

Starvation
Bay
Ocean
Access

71

76

72

Peter Cove North
Ocean Access

Bedwell Harbour

Peter
Cove

20 m

PLUMPER WAY

Smugglers
Nook

Swanson Channel

76

Peter Cove South
Ocean Access

73

Plumper Way
Viewpoint

74

20 m

Wallace
Point

Do Not Use for Navigation

Contour Interval 20 m
Map 4C   100 m ~1/16 mile
Approximate Scale
Map 4D   100 m

◇ Trailhead Reference Point
⌐ View Bench

OCEAN ACCESSES
71 Starvation Bay:
   Photo below
72 Peter Cove North
73 Peter Cove South
75 (Future) Bedwell Drive
VIEWPOINT
74 Plumper Way
HIKES: 70 Oaks Bluff Trail
76 Trincomali Stroll
BIKE ROUTE (on-road)
B3 To Magic Lake

Map 5 - Central Area

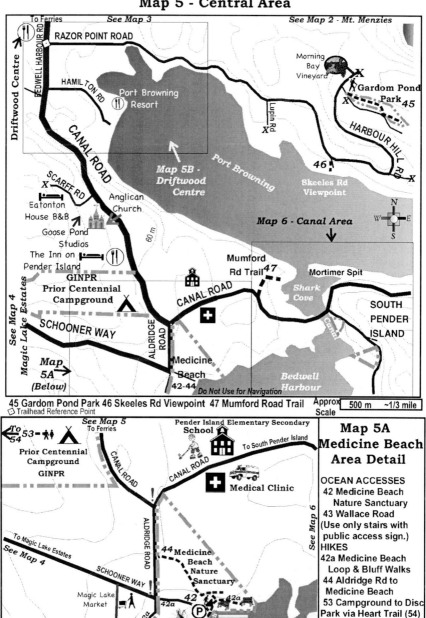

45 Gardom Pond Park 46 Skeeles Rd Viewpoint 47 Mumford Road Trail
◌ Trailhead Reference Point

Map 5A
Medicine Beach
Area Detail

OCEAN ACCESSES
42 Medicine Beach
   Nature Sanctuary
43 Wallace Road
(Use only stairs with
public access sign.)
HIKES
42a Medicine Beach
   Loop & Bluff Walks
44 Aldridge Rd to
   Medicine Beach
53 Campground to Disc
Park via Heart Trail (54)
(*See Maps 4 & 4B*)
*Medicine Beach Nature
Sanctuary is a fragile area.
Stay on trails. No dogs in
marsh due to ground
nesting Virginia Rail.*

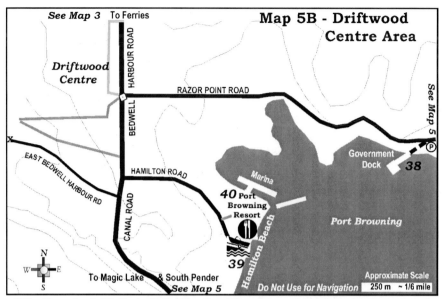

38 Port Browning Public Dock 39 Hamilton Beach/Boat Ramp 40 Port Browning Resort & Marina: Pool, tennis, motel, café, pub, camping, liquor store, showers, laundry, charters.

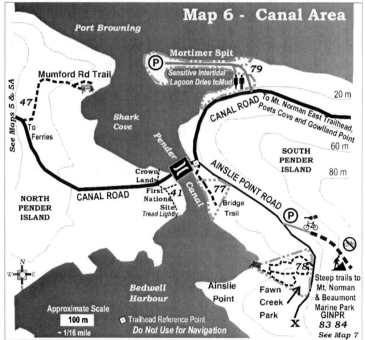

47 Mumford Rd Trail *77* Bridge Trail *78* Fawn Creek Park *79* Mortimer Spit Beach; GINPR: *82* Beaumont to Mt. Norman; *83* Ainslie Pt Rd to: Mt. Norman; *84* to Beaumont; *85* Canal Rd to Mt. Norman; *86* Wm Walker Trl

Map 7 - GINPR Mt. Norman and Beaumont Marine Park

Mortimer Spit
Port Browning
CANAL ROAD
AINSLIE PT. RD
Plumper Sound
Fawn Creek Park
83 84
Ainslie Point Rd Trail 8283
82
84
Map 6 Canal Area
Mt. Norman
244 m
85
GULF ISLANDS NATIONAL PARK RESERVE SOUTH PENDER ISLAND
85
Canal Road Trail
William Walker Trail
To Ocean Access 81, 80
86
N
W
E
S
Beaumont Marine Park
82
100 m
Beaumont Marine Park
Bedwell Harbour
Skull Islet
Mooring Buoys
SOUTH PENDER ISLAND
NORTH PENDER ISLAND
Approximate Scale
500 m ~1/3 mile
Do Not Use for Navigation
See Map 8
See Map 7A

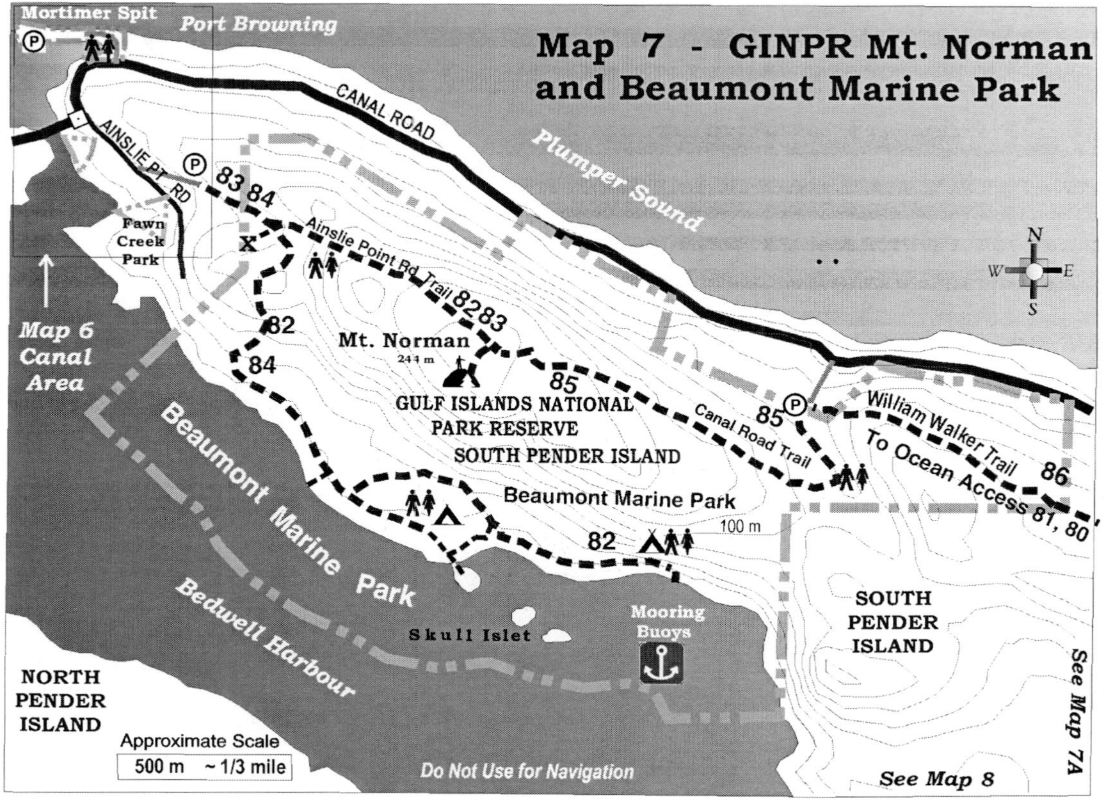

GINPR:

82 Beaumont Marine Park to Mt. Norman
83 Ainslie Point Road to Mt. Norman
84 Ainslie Point Road to Beaumont Marine Park
85 Canal Road to Mt. Norman
86 William Walker Trail

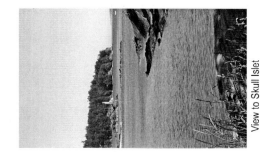

View to Skull Islet

Map 7A - North Shore Detail

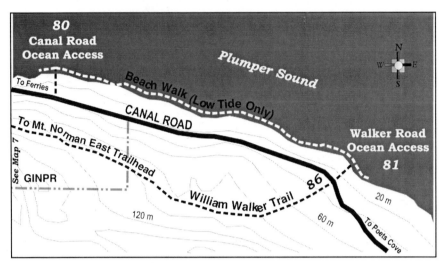

Map 7A	OCEAN ACCESSES: Above: 80 Canal Road 81 Walker Road
300 m ~1/5mile	Below: 87 Ancia Road 88 Boundary Pass
Approximate	TRAIL AND WALKS: Above; 80-81 Beach Walk at Low Tide
Scale	86 William Walker Trail to Mt. Norman East/Canal Road Trailhead
Map 7B	BIKE ROUTE: B1 TO Gowlland Point
250 m ~1/6mile	*Do Not Use These Maps For Nautical Navigation*

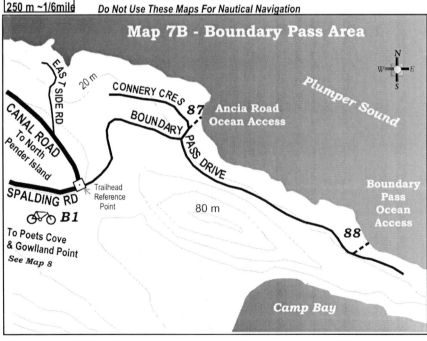

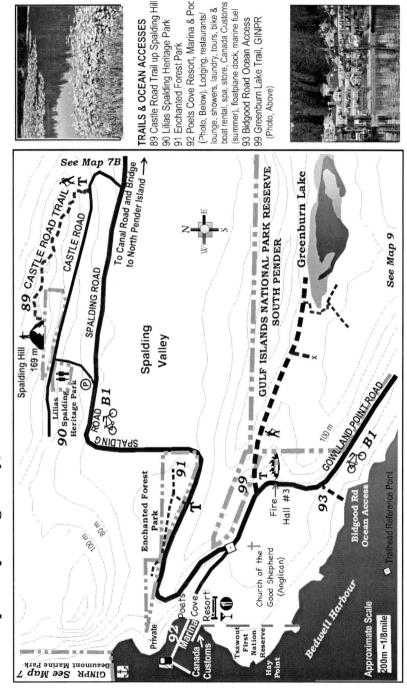

Map 8   Spalding Valley, Poets Cove & Greenburn Lake

TRAILS & OCEAN ACCESSES
89 Castle Road Trail up Spalding Hill
90 Lilias Spalding Heritage Park
91 Enchanted Forest Park
92 Poets Cove Resort, Marina & Poc
(Photo, Below). Lodging, restaurants/
lounge, showers, laundry, tours, bike &
boat rental, spa, store, Canada Customs
(summer), floatplane dock, marine fuel
93 Bidgood Road Ocean Access
99 Greenburn Lake Trail, GINPR
(Photo, Above)

See Map 7B

CASTLE ROAD TRAIL
CASTLE ROAD
SPALDING ROAD
To Canal Road and Bridge
to North Pender Island

89

Spalding Hill
169 m

Lilias
Spalding
Heritage Park

90

SPALDING ROAD

B1

Spalding
Valley

N E S W

Enchanted Forest
Park

91

100 m
80 m

GULF ISLANDS NATIONAL PARK RESERVE
SOUTH PENDER

Greenburn Lake

See Map 9

99

Fire
Hall #3

GOWLLAND POINT ROAD

93

B1

100 m

x

Private

92

Poets
Cove
Marina
Resort

Canada
Customs

Tsawout
First
Nation
Reserve

Hay
Point

Church of the
Good Shepherd
(Anglican)

GINPR See Map 7
Beaumont Marine Park

Bedwell Harbour

Bidgood Rd
Ocean Access

Trailhead Reference Point

Approximate Scale
200m ~1/8mile

Map 9 - Tilley Point to Gowlland Point

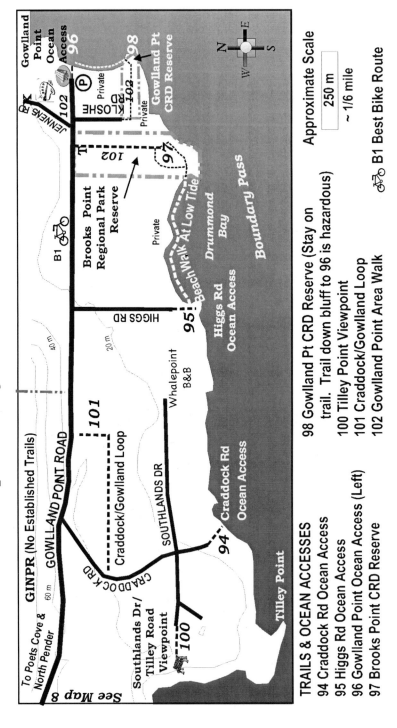

TRAILS & OCEAN ACCESSES
94 Craddock Rd Ocean Access
95 Higgs Rd Ocean Access
96 Gowlland Point Ocean Access (Left)
97 Brooks Point CRD Reserve

98 Gowlland Pt CRD Reserve (Stay on
  trail. Trail down bluff to 96 is hazardous)
100 Tilley Point Viewpoint
101 Craddock/Gowlland Loop
102 Gowlland Point Area Walk

Approximate Scale
250 m
~ 1/6 mile

B1 Best Bike Route

Map 10 Sidney Area

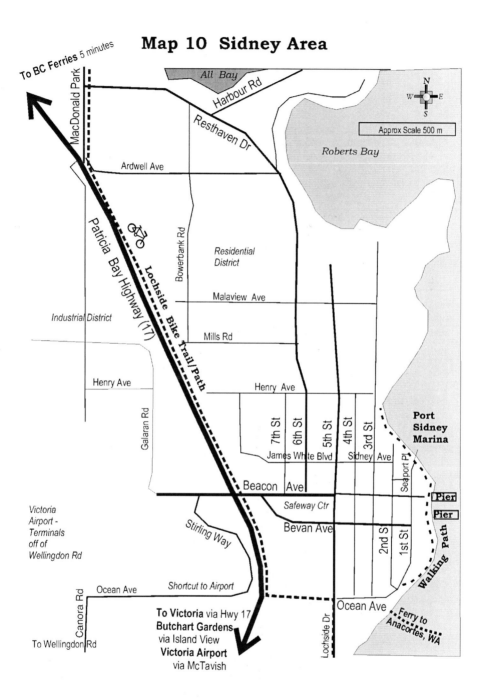

Map 11 Downtown Victoria

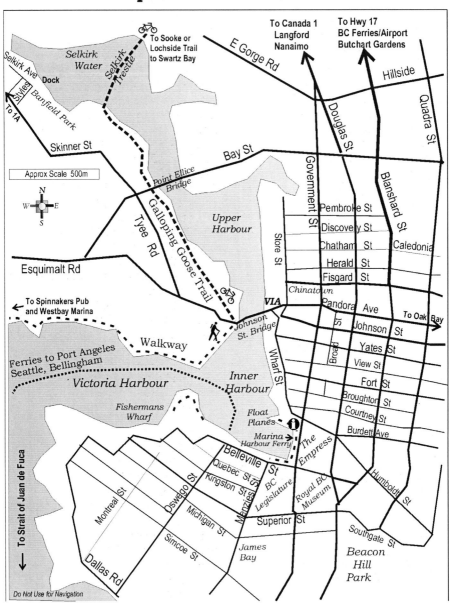